Age and the Rate of Foreign Language Learning

SECOND LANGUAGE ACQUISITION
Series Editor: Professor David Singleton, *Trinity College, Dublin, Ireland*

This series brings together titles dealing with a variety of aspects of language acquisition and processing in situations where a language or languages other than the native language is involved. Second language is thus interpreted in its broadest possible sense. The volumes included in the series all offer in their different ways, on the one hand, exposition and discussion of empirical findings and, on the other, some degree of theoretical reflection. In this latter connection, no particular theoretical stance is privileged in the series; nor is any relevant perspective – sociolinguistic, psycholinguistic, neurolinguistic, etc. – deemed out of place. The intended readership of the series includes final-year undergraduates working on second language acquisition projects, postgraduate students involved in second language acquisition research, and researchers and teachers in general whose interests include a second language acquisition component.

Other Books in the Series
Effects of Second Language on the First
    Vivian Cook (ed.)
Age and the Acquisition of English as a Foreign Language
    María del Pilar García Mayo and Maria Luisa García Lecumberri (eds)
Fossilization in Adult Second Language Acquisition
    ZhaoHong Han
Silence in Second Language Learning: A Psychoanalytic Reading
    Colette A. Granger
Age, Accent and Experience in Second Language Acquisition
    Alene Moyer
Studying Speaking to Inform Second Language Learning
    Diana Boxer and Andrew D. Cohen (eds)
Language Acquisition: The Age Factor (2nd edn)
    David Singleton and Lisa Ryan
Focus on French as a Foreign Language: Multidisciplinary Approaches
    Jean-Marc Dewaele (ed.)
Second Language Writing Systems
    Vivian Cook and Benedetta Bassetti (eds)
Third Language Learners: Pragmatic Production and Awareness
    Maria Pilar Safont Jordà
Artificial Intelligence in Second Language Learning: Raising Error Awareness
    Marina Dodigovic
Studies of Fossilization in Second Language Acquisition
    ZhaoHong Han and Terence Odlin (eds)
Language Learners in Study Abroad Contexts
    Margaret A. DuFon and Eton Churchill (eds)
Early Trilingualism: A Focus on Questions
    Julia D. Barnes
Cross-linguistic Influences in the Second Language Lexicon
    Janusz Arabski (ed.)
Motivation, Language Attitudes and Globalisation: A Hungarian Perspective
    Zoltán Dörnyei, Kata Csizér and Nóra Németh

For more details of these or any other of our publications, please contact:
**Multilingual Matters, Frankfurt Lodge, Clevedon Hall,
Victoria Road, Clevedon, BS21 7HH, England**
http://www.multilingual-matters.com

SECOND LANGUAGE ACQUISITION 19
Series Editor: David Singleton, *Trinity College, Dublin, Ireland*

Age and the Rate of Foreign Language Learning

Edited by
Carmen Muñoz

MULTILINGUAL MATTERS LTD
Clevedon • Buffalo • Toronto

Library of Congress Cataloging in Publication Data
Age and the Rate of Foreign Language Learning / Edited by Carmen Muñoz.
Second Language Acquisition: 19)
1. Language acquisition–Age factors. 2. Language and languages–Study and teaching.
I. Muñoz, Carmen. II. Second Language Acquisition (Clevedon, England): 19.
P118.65.A373 2006
418–dc22   2006003667

British Library Cataloguing in Publication Data
A catalogue entry for this book is available from the British Library.

ISBN 1-85359-892-5/ EAN 978-1-85359-892-0 (hbk)
ISBN 1-85359-891-7/ EAN 978-1-85359-891-3 (pbk)

Multilingual Matters Ltd
UK: Frankfurt Lodge, Clevedon Hall, Victoria Road, Clevedon BS21 7HH.
USA: UTP, 2250 Military Road, Tonawanda, NY 14150, USA.
Canada: UTP, 5201 Dufferin Street, North York, Ontario M3H 5T8, Canada.

Copyright © 2006 Carmen Muñoz and the authors of individual chapters.

All rights reserved. No part of this work may be reproduced in any form or by any means without permission in writing from the publisher.

Typeset by Saxon Graphics.
Printed and bound in Great Britain by the Cromwell Press Ltd.

Contents

Acknowledgements vi

Introduction
Carmen Muñoz vii

1 The Effects of Age on Foreign Language Learning: The BAF Project
   Carmen Muñoz 1

2 The Development of English (FL) Perception and Production Skills: Starting Age and Exposure Effects
   Natalia Fullana 41

3 Age Effects on Oral Fluency Development
   Joan C. Mora 65

4 Age and Vocabulary Acquisition in English as a Foreign Language (EFL)
   Immaculada Miralpeix 89

5 Accuracy Orders, Rate of Learning and Age in Morphological Acquisition
   Carmen Muñoz 107

6 Rate and Route of Acquisition in EFL Narrative Development at Different Ages
   Esther Álvarez 127

7 Age and IL Development in Writing
   M. Rosa Torras, Teresa Navés, M. Luz Celaya and Carmen Pérez-Vidal .. 156

8 Age, Proficiency Level and Interactional Skills: Evidence from Breakdowns in Production
   Gisela Grañena 183

9 Reported Strategy Use and Age
   Elsa Tragant and Mia Victori 208

10 Language Learning Motivation and Age
    Elsa Tragant 237

General Appendices 269

Index 277

Acknowledgements

This book would not have been possible without the support of many colleagues and friends over the years and in many different parts of the world. J.D. Brown, Michael Long and Craig Chaudron set us on the right track for conducting the research, and we have benefited from Craig Chaudron's valuable insights along the years. Maribel Peró and Antoni Sans assisted with the statistics on many occasions. David Singleton offered his unfailing encouragement all through the long process of writing the book. Most sincere thanks are due to all of them, but for the weaknesses of the final result we alone are responsible.

Many people have helped with data collection for over a decade. I offer my sincere gratitude to the teachers, principals and heads of study who allowed us to go into their schools and interrupt their classes, and to all the students who wrote for us and talked to us.

I wish also to express my appreciation for the financial support provided for the research by the Spanish Ministry of Education through grants PB94-0944, PB97-0901, and BFF2001-3384, and by the 2002 Joan Morley (TIRF) grant. Essential human support was provided by the University of Barcelona and the DURSI of the Generalitat de Catalunya through grants awarded to the research assistants for work on the project. Special thanks are due to Màrius Rubiralta of the University of Barcelona for affording the help to get us started.

For their essential collaboration on the research, I would like to thank all the research assistants who have worked with us, collecting, transcribing and managing the data. In order of appearance they are: Natalia Fullana, Marilisa Birello, Josep M. Armengol, Immaculada Miralpeix, Gisela Grañena, Laura Sánchez and M. del Mar Suárez. Meritxell Figueras and Beatriz Santiago generously provided their help too.

Finally, heartfelt thanks are due to our families for their encouragement throughout, and in particular to our children, who have grown up multilingual while we were studying how this is made possible.

Introduction

The widespread belief that *the younger the better* in second language acquisition is partly grounded in informal observations of immigrants in natural settings, as well as in evidence from majority language children in school immersion settings from Canada to Catalonia. Certainly, empirical research in those contexts has shown that individuals who begin to learn a second language very early in life generally attain higher levels of proficiency than those who start at a later stage. However, an inferential leap is made in the assumption that learning age will have the same effect on students of a foreign language, when they are exposed to only one speaker of that language (the teacher, who is not usually a native speaker) in only one setting (the classroom) and only during very limited amounts of time. The neglect of environmental factors characteristic of nature-oriented perspectives has, no doubt, contributed to the playing down of differences between natural and formal language learning settings.

For those of us interested in second language acquisition in the classroom, such an inferential leap is a matter of concern, particularly when it exerts an influence on language-in-education planning policies. From this concern sprang the motivation to embark on a nine-year research project focused on the process of acquisition of a foreign language by learners with different starting ages. The necessary conditions for the research appeared naturally when a change in the school curriculum brought forward the introduction of foreign language instruction, and the old and the new curricula in fact coexisted over a number of years. These circumstances provided the impetus for the BAF (Barcelona Age Factor) Project, which has been the framework for multiple research directions on the various ways in which age affects the process and the product of second language learning in a school setting. Like other age-oriented studies, the BAF Project has examined the effects of the initial age of learning but, in contrast with the majority of studies, this project has also analysed the effects of age across the spectrum of the learning process. Because of its focus on the process of foreign language learning during a limited length of time, the BAF Project has been more concerned with the rate of learning than with ultimate attainment. Equally, due to its formal learning setting, the project has focused on the optimal levels that are realistically attainable through school education, rather than on unattainable native-likeness.

The chapters in this volume present selected results from the BAF Project. A number of them examine the evidence drawn from formal language learning, in areas such as pronunciation or morphology, for confirmation of previous age-related findings in naturalistic language acquisition. Others explore aspects that have seldom been studied in relation to age differences, such as oral fluency, vocabulary, interactional skills or learning strategies. All of them have the twofold aim of contributing to the study of age-related effects in language learning, while at the same time contributing, empirically and sometimes also methodologically, to the study of a particular area of second language acquisition. Further distinguishing characteristics of these studies are their concern with research of low-proficiency learners in a foreign language setting and the learners' bilingual condition, which makes the findings relevant for the emerging area of third language acquisition.

In Chapter 1, "The Effects of Age on Foreign Language Learning: The BAF Project", Carmen Muñoz presents the project: its setting, research design and the materials used to elicit the samples of learner language and the learners' responses that are anaysed in the following chapters. The chapter then provides an overview of the results, which includes a comparison of the performance on a series of tests of two groups of subjects who were followed longitudinally, as well as a general comparison of all of the groups with a different initial age of learning. The discussion of the findings challenges the inferential leap mentioned above arguing that age intervenes in the process of second language learning in school settings in ways that differ from those observed in natural settings, in terms of both rate and of long-term attainment.

In the next chapter, "The Development of English (FL) Perception and Production Skills: Starting Age and Exposure Effects", Natalia Fullana analyses the influence of age of onset of foreign language learning and exposure on the acquisition of a foreign language phonology and argues that these factors are not conclusive determinants for perceiving and producing English sounds in a native-like manner in a formal language learning context. Late starting age tends to result in a somewhat better perception of English segments in the short and mid terms, but not in the long term, and the differences in production are never significant. The author suggests that the lack of any definite effects of starting age and exposure may be due to the limitations in quantity and quality of the input delivered in this type of formal language learning setting.

In Chapter 3, "Age Effects on Oral Fluency Development", Joan Carles Mora investigates age effects on the oral fluency of two groups of English as a foreign language (EFL) learners matched with respect to amount of second language exposure but differing in onset age of learning. The picture-elicited narratives produced by the two learner groups were analysed and evaluated according to a number of well-established quantitative oral fluency measures. In relation to these, the paper suggests that in the analysis of highly dysfluent non-native speech, speech rate may be a more reliable oral fluency measure than pause frequency. The results of the comparison of the two learner groups reveal that late starters outperform early starters on most of the oral fluency measures used and support the view that an early start does not necessarily imply an advantage in the acquisition of a second language in the formal learning context.

In Chapter 4, "Age and Vocabulary Acquisition in EFL", Immaculada Miralpeix uses data from a variety of tasks to analyse vocabulary development in two groups of learners, one that started foreign language learning at 8 and the other that started at 11, when both learner groups had received 726 hours of instruction in English. The chapter provides findings in the area of lexical acquisition, which has not attracted much attention in age-related studies, and explores new ways to analyse lexical data from low-level students (e.g. the D measure). The results generally show differences in free and controlled productive vocabulary in favour of the late starting pupils. Other significant findings are of a methodological kind, including task effects and the relative advantages of different lexical measures in the study of second language lexical acquisition.

Chapter 5, "Accuracy Orders, Rate of Learning and Age in Morphological Acquisition" by Carmen Muñoz, analyses the use of a set of English morphological functors by children and adult learners of different proficiency levels. The study provides evidence against the existence of a qualitative difference in the way different-aged students progress in learning to use these forms accurately. It also reveals a superior rate of learning in older than in younger learners, particularly in the initial stages of language acquisition. The role of proficiency level and learning setting are discussed in relation to the comparison of the accuracy orders observed in this study with the average order of those functors shown by previous studies.

In her contribution, "Rate and Route of Acquisition in EFL Narrative Development at Different Ages", Esther Álvarez focuses on the narratives produced by children, adolescents and adults with the aim of outlining the order in which learners of different ages proceed in the use of a variety of linguistic elements in discourse. The author identifies nine developmental stages, in which the morphosyntactic and discourse components interact. A comparison of the learner groups in terms of their assignment to those stages reveals a rate advantage for older learners, which begins to fade when age differences diminish and with longer exposure to the target language.

Chapter 7, "Age and IL Development in Writing", by María Rosa Torras, Teresa Navés, María Luz Celaya and Carmen Pérez-Vidal, considers the issue of the development of EFL written competence as an effect of the interaction between age and instructional time: that is, whether and how the number of hours of instruction affects both the rate of acquisition and the pattern of development at different ages. Results show that an early start at 8 years of age does not involve higher levels of attainment at 16, after 726 hours of instruction. The authors suggest that the amount of exposure to the target language after the age of 12 may be crucial in explaining the results obtained. The analysis of the profiles of development of both groups indicates that neither the domains analysed nor the variables included in them develop in tandem and that their rate of development seems to be affected by age.

The following three chapters deal with age-related differences that may impinge on the process of learning a foreign language. In Chapter 8, "Age, Proficiency Level and Interactional Skills: Evidence from Breakdowns in Production", Gisela Grañena focuses on learners' appeals for assistance during the completion of a picture-elicited narrative task. The aim of the study is threefold: to explore how learners of different ages and proficiency levels demonstrate a gap in their interlanguage when faced with a production breakdown during task-based interaction; to examine the type of input provided by the learners' interlocutor; and finally to investigate the occurrence of uptake as an indication of potential acquisition. Results suggest that older and more proficient learners elicit help in a more explicit manner and that the degree of explicitness of the learners' signal has an effect on their interlocutor's response. Age may also be an explaining factor of differences in the level of uptake among the more proficient learners.

In Chapter 9, "Reported Strategy Use and Age", Elsa Tragant and Mia Victori examine the use of language learning strategies by different groups of learners on the basis of their answers to a series of questions in a written questionnaire. The authors find significant variation in learners' use of strategies within and across three different data collection times. The study also follows a group of learners over an extended period of time and finds that learners tend to undergo developmental changes in strategy use as they increase in age, regardless of their level of proficiency or learning stage, although the changes are not always systematic. It is also suggested by the findings that students' reported use of strategies varies depending on the skill under investigation, which may indicate that their domains of perceived strategic knowledge may not develop homogeneously for all skills.

Finally in Chapter 10, "Language Learning Motivation and Age", Elsa Tragant reports on a study of the levels and types of motivation expressed by different-aged learners in their answers to a series of questions included in the students' written questionnaire. Motivation seems to be stronger among older students than among younger students, which may be due, according to the author, to the greater awareness of the role of English worldwide at more advanced ages. The finding that having students start learning English earlier does not significantly alter the level of motivation in students makes the author hypothesise that more drastic changes may be needed in the educational system to raise motivational levels. The types of orientations identified in the study vary with learners' age: older students mention extrinsic types of orientation while students in primary school make more references to attitudes towards the learning situation, which may also explain the lower levels of motivation these students show.

The book is addressed to professionals and graduate students interested in the field of second language acquisition. It will also be of interest to language teachers, language planners and all of those aiming to improve the learning of foreign languages. The book will, hopefully, show them that introducing a foreign language earlier in the school does not automatically result in general higher levels of proficiency and that the conditions of the learning environment cannot be ignored.

Chapter 1
The Effects of Age on Foreign Language Learning: The BAF Project

CARMEN MUÑOZ

The idea that there is a critical age for language learning that finishes before puberty was popularised by the Canadian brain surgeons W. Penfield and L. Roberts in their book *Speech and Brain Mechanisms* (1959). Penfield enthusiastically defended an early start for second language learning, basing his ideas on his studies on brain damage and his experience with his own children. According to Penfield, the time to begin schooling in second languages was between the ages of 4 and 10. Theoretical support came soon from E. Lenneberg who, in his *Biological Foundations of Language* (1967), noted that the rapid growth of nerve connections, which ceases at puberty, coincides with the child's acquisition of language. Lenneberg supported his neurological account of the Critical Period Hypothesis (henceforth CPH) with evidence from aphasic patients, who showed a more rapid recovery if the damage had taken place before puberty, and with feral children, children who had suffered social isolation and had not learnt language before puberty. Their inability to learn language after that time, Lenneberg argued, constituted evidence that language acquisition was impossible after the critical period.

However, the extant evidence of language learning by feral children is so scarce that it cannot be used to provide strong support for either this or opposing views. The case of Genie, a girl who had lived in social isolation until the age of 13;7, proved that language acquisition was not impossible after puberty, though it seemed to be incomplete (see Curtiss, 1977). Linguistic evidence from the Genie case is still in need of clarification (Jones, 1995), and the regression she suffered after several traumatic events underlines the fact that the social and psychological circumstances of feral children cannot constitute valid evidence for a firm conclusion regarding the critical period for language acquisition. Likewise, the pathological kind of evidence provided by aphasic patients needs to be treated with caution. More relevant evidence has recently come from the field of the acquisition of sign language, which suggests that morphology and syntax may be affected by late acquisition in the case of deaf persons who are not exposed to their first language (sign language) until later childhood or adulthood (Newport, 1990).

From a theoretical point of view, the idea of a critical period sprang from an innatist conception of language, which the prevalence of Chomsky's proposals in the field of linguistics in the second half of the 20th century strongly reinforced. A biologically determined period for language acquisition fitted perfectly well in a theory that concedes a crucial role to biology in human linguistic competence. Recently, however, the field of child language acquisition seems to be drifting away from formal linguistics proposals, disappointed by their failure to explain how human children become skilled users of a natural language. Tomasello (2003) argues that one of the reasons for this failure lies in the continuity hypothesis, which attempts to explain children's language in terms of the structures and rules used to account for adult language. The best known theoretical alternatives to generative grammar at the moment, the connectionist accounts (e.g. Elman, 2001) and the construction-based (usage-based) accounts (see Tomasello, 2003), are both data based. In the latter perspective, one of the reasons underlying children's observed advantage in second language acquisition may be the fact that they are more flexible learners than adults in skilled activities.

The CPH and Second Language Acquisition

The study of second language acquisition originated from the field of first language acquisition, and has since been fed by hypotheses and theories first developed in the parent field. Among these, the hypothesis of the existence of a critical period for (first and second) language acquisition soon motivated a wealth of empirical studies in the 1970s. The work of that decade was summarised in the following three generalisations:

(1) Adults proceed through early stages of syntactic and morphological development faster than children (where time and exposure are held constant).

(2) Older children acquire faster than younger children (again, in early stages of syntactic and morphological development where time and exposure are held constant).

(3) Acquirers who begin natural exposure to second language during childhood generally achieve higher second language proficiency than those beginning as adults. (Krashen *et al.*, 1979/1982, reprint: 161)

These generalisations led Krashen *et al.* (1979) to make a very important distinction between *ultimate attainment* and *rate*. Older learners have a superior learning rate, particularly in the first stages of the acquisition of morphosyntactic aspects, while younger learners are slower at first, but eventually show a higher level of ultimate attainment. The latter was held to constitute evidence for the existence of a critical period, beyond which second language acquisition cannot reach native-like levels of proficiency.

Since then, a large number of studies have compared native-likeness among younger and older starters. The most robust evidence for the existence of maturational constraints in second language acquisition seemed to be provided by the study by Johnson and Newport (1989) of Korean and Chinese learners of English using grammaticality judgement tests (Long, 1990). Many other studies have also focused on the acquisition of second language (L2) morphosyntax (e.g. Coppieters, 1987; DeKeyser, 2000; Johnson & Newport, 1991; Patkowski, 1980; Schachter, 1996).

However, agreement is far from complete. Johnson and Newport's findings have been questioned on both methodological and empirical grounds (but see a recent confirmatory study in DeKeyser, 2000). Methodological criticisms can be found in Bialystok (1997), and Bialystok and Hakuta (1999). Replications of Johnson and Newport's (1989) seminal study have cast some doubt on the neurobiologically-based explanation of the younger learners' advantage. For example, replications have found evidence of native language effects (Birdsong & Molis, 2001; van Wuijtswinkel, 1994, cited in Kellerman, 1995) and of post-maturational age-related effects (Birdsong & Molis, 2001), which are held to constitute grounds for refutation of the CPH (Pulvermüller & Schumann, 1994).

Other studies have also found evidence of native-likeness among post-puberty starters, which appears to disprove the CPH in relation to L2 acquisition. Examples are, in the area of Universal Grammar principles, the work by Birdsong (1992; Birdsong & Molis, 2001), and White and Genesee (1996); in the areas of perceptual abilities, production skills and underlying linguistic competence, the report by Ioup *et al.* (1994); and in the area of pronunciation, Bongaerts *et al.* (1997), and Bongaerts (1999), among others.

On the other hand, evidence has accumulated that an early start does not always guarantee native-like achievement (see Harley & Wang, 1997). Hyltenstam and Abrahamsson (2000, 2003) claim that native-like proficiency in a second language is unattainable even for very early starters due to the strong influence that maturation has on second language outcomes. Further, these authors maintain that previous research has failed to find non-native features because they may be imperceptible except in detailed and systematic linguistic analyses, that is, the sort of analyses that should be undertaken with apparently exceptional late learners.

In sum, although an early starters' long-term advantage (for ultimate attainment) is recognised, the CPH itself does not seem to have unanimous support at present (see Birdsong (1999) for a review of the two positions). On the other hand, late starters' short-term advantage for learning rate was firmly established by Snow and Hoefnagel-Höhle's findings (1978). These researchers conducted a large study in a natural setting involving close to 100 subjects, English learners of Dutch in The Netherlands, ranging in age from 3 years to adult. Subjects were tested three times (some four) for a period of approximately one year: 6 weeks, 4–5 months, and 9–10 months after the first exposure to Dutch. Results from the first testing time showed that the teenagers did better than the two younger groups, suggesting an older learners' superior rate of learning. However, they also did better than the adult group in most measures, probably due, in the authors' view, to motivational and environmental factors. With longer residence in The Netherlands, the teenagers' advantage over the younger groups diminished, and by the third time the scores of the 6–7-year-old learners were approaching those of the 12–15-year-old learners. The older learners were observed to be especially good at syntactic and morphological rule acquisition, and also at metalinguistic ability and vocabulary. The authors noted that the non-conversational nature of the tasks used was clearly cognitively demanding and context-reduced, which may have favoured the older learners (1978: 1123). Differences were smaller and less persistent in listening comprehension and storytelling, and the older subjects were only better at pronunciation in the first test session. Interestingly, a 12–15-year-old native Dutch-speaking group did better on the morphology- and vocabulary-related tasks than a 6–7-year-old native-speaking group, supporting the interpretation that older L2 learners have a maturational advantage over younger L2 learners in academic tasks of this kind, in accordance with their superior cognitive development.

The issue of time, and not just the initial moment of learning (age of onset), has proved to be crucial in age-related studies. As seen above, in a naturalistic learning situation with unlimited exposure to the target language, the advantage of older learners begins to disappear after one year (Snow & Hoefnagel-Höhle, 1978). Snow (1983) points out that data for studies in which adults show superior results were collected during the first two years of residence or social immersion. This observation may be extended to younger and older children, since as Slavoff and Johnson's (1995) study reported, no difference was found between a group of learners who arrived in the United States between the ages of 7–9 and a group whose age at arrival was between 10–12, after only three years of residence. This is why it has been suggested that a minimum of five years of residence (Snow, 1983) and, more recently, ten years (DeKeyser, 2000) may be necessary in CPH studies in order to ensure methodologically that it is ultimate attainment, and not rate, that is being measured.

Theoretical Explanations of the CPH

The theoretical explanations of the CPH are many and varied (see Singleton & Ryan, 2004, for a recent complete review), but the most influential proposals have been of two types: neurological and developmental-cognitive. Neurological explanations were popularised by Penfield (Penfield & Roberts, 1959), who appealed to the loss of brain plasticity with maturation, and by Lenneberg (1967), who elaborated a proposal based on the process of lateralisation of language functions in the left hemisphere (see for related proposals Diller, 1981; Molfese, 1977; and Seliger, 1978). Later, the reduction of plasticity in the language areas of the brain more or less until puberty has been seen as an effect of the process of myelination affecting neurons with maturation (Long, 1990; Pulvermüller & Schumann, 1994). More recently, attention has been paid to the spatial representation in the brain of early and late L2 acquisition (Abutalebi *et al.*, 2001; Kim *et al.*, 1997; Perani *et al.*, 1998; Wattendorf *et al.*, 2001). The available evidence now supports a dynamic view in which brain structure and organisation may be as much the consequence as the cause of L2 learning (Abutalebi *et al.*, 2001; Perani & Abutalebi, 2005; Perani *et al.*, 2003; Perani *et al.*, 1998), a view shared by a number of cognitive psychologists (see Bialystok & Hakuta, 1999).

Maturational explanations have come from theorists working within a nativist framework, in which Lenneberg's proposals have been fully compatible with Chomsky's linguistic theories. One of these explanations is the Competition Hypothesis proposed by Felix (1985): although postpubertal learners still have access to the innate acquisition system, this system competes with the more general problem-solving cognitive system which develops beyond the Piagetian stage of formal operations. In contrast, the Fundamental Difference Hypothesis, proposed by Bley-Vroman (1989), denies adults direct access to Universal Grammar. According to this hypothesis, the inborn mechanism that children have is no longer operative in adulthood and adults must rely on general problem-solving procedures instead. The lack of access to Universal Grammar explains the fact that second language acquisition is not as successful in adults as in children.

DeKeyser's (2000) interpretation of the Fundamental Difference Hypothesis attempts to explain not just the young learners' long-term superiority but also older learners' short-term superiority. According to DeKeyser, 'somewhere between the ages of 6–7 and 16–17, everybody loses the mental equipment required for the implicit induction of the abstract patterns underlying a human language' (2000: 518). Hence, it is the younger learners' use of implicit learning mechanisms that explains their advantage over older learners. This formulation agrees with Lenneberg's characterisation of the critical period: '... the incidence of 'language-learning-blocks' rapidly increases after puberty. Also *automatic acquisition from mere exposure* to a given language seems to disappear after this age, and foreign languages have to be taught and learned through a conscious and labored effort' (1967: 176, my emphasis). The superiority of implicit mechanisms explains the younger learners' advantage in a natural setting: children do better in terms of ultimate attainment because many elements of language are hard to learn explicitly, especially for those adults who have limited verbal ability.

In contrast, older learners learn faster because their capacities for explicit learning let them take short cuts (De Keyser, 2003: 335), an ability that explains their advantage in the initial stages. That is, adult second language acquisition (SLA) is mainly explicit, and adults rely on analytical thinking to acquire their second language. It is important to note that DeKeyser argues in favour of the existence of a critical period for language acquisition, provided that the CPH is understood as applying only to implicit learning of abstract structures.

Relevance of the CPH for Foreign Language Learning

With very few exceptions, such as DeKeyser and Larson-Hall (2005), the L2 learning context has not been included as an important factor in the discussion of the CPH, and findings from second language learning in naturalistic contexts have been generalised to foreign language learning in instructed contexts. Therefore, a critical examination of the CPH with the foreign language learning situation in mind may be in order here. Colombo (1982) outlined five aspects in the analysis of a critical period: onset; offset; an intrinsic maturational component; an external component; and a system that is affected. The first two components, determining the relevant age limits, and the last one, determining the aspects of language involved, appear as most relevant for foreign language learning.

The age limits of a privileged period for learning languages may constitute essential information to take into account when deciding not only when to begin the teaching of a foreign language at school, but also the period in which instruction is to take place, and probably the intensity required at different moments of the process as well. Unfortunately, and surprisingly in view of the widely held idea that *the younger the better*, the age limits of the critical period are not clear. Lenneberg (1967) suggests that the lower bound of the critical period is situated at age 2 because this is the moment at which the first two-word combinations appear: it is these combinations, according to Lenneberg, that mark the onset of syntax. The higher bound of the critical period for Lenneberg is situated at puberty and caused by hemispheric lateralisation. Seliger (1978), also on the basis of studies showing different types of aphasia in different age groups, argues in favour of different timetables for different language abilities. This is the view held by Long (1990), who suggests different offset points for different language aspects: age 6 for phonology and 17 for morphosyntax. More recent evidence, however, has shown that speech perception abilities develop in the first months of life, and may wane as early as 6–9 months of age or, more specifically, become attuned to the native language (see Doughty, 2003, for a review).

The most widely held view of the CPH emphasises the need to begin L2 acquisition before the end of the critical period. For example, Long (1990: 252f) in his formulation of the maturational state hypothesis characterises successful learners as '... those learning (or *at least beginning to learn*) an SL during the sensitive period...' (my emphasis). This raises a very important question for foreign language learning, in which exposure to the target language and possibilities for learning are very limited: what if the process of learning a second language begins during the critical period but learners are still in the initial stages by the time of offset? That is to say, how much of the language is to be learnt before the end of the critical period in order to benefit from the advantage of an early learning onset? Arguably, in a situation of foreign language learning with limited language exposure, the actual *period* in which second language learning takes place may be more relevant to the learning process than age of onset. A related point is made by Patkowski (2003: 183), who referring to the methodological requirements for studies designed to test the CPH, claims that 'early' acquisition should consist of subjects who clearly have had the opportunity not only to begin but also to complete their second language acquisition during childhood. Patkowski goes on to argue that the CPH specifically applies to language acquisition under sustained conditions of naturalistic or informal exposure thereby excluding its generalisation to situations of instructed foreign language learning.

The second aspect of Colombo's analysis of the critical period that appears particularly relevant to foreign language learning is the system that is affected, that is, the aspects of language that are subject to maturational constraints (in a strong maturational position), or by age effects (in a more recent perspective, see Birdsong, 2005). Again, no consensus has been reached to date. Lenneberg (1967) emphasised the effects on morphosyntax and phonology. Scovel (1988) argued that phonology was the only aspect affected by age constraints because of its neuromotor etiology. In contrast, Long (1990) held that all aspects of language are affected including lexis. As will be seen below, some empirical evidence of differential age effects has been found.

Empirical Evidence from School Settings

As stated previously, the findings concerning the long-term advantage of younger starters come from studies of naturalistic second language acquisition, that is, contexts of full immersion in the language community. Two other learning settings are examined below: school immersion and foreign language learning.

Studies conducted in Canada show that in general early immersion students obtain better results than late immersion students, but naturally the amount of exposure is also higher (see, e.g. Swain, 1984). Even so, several researchers have reported findings from comparisons between early immersion and late immersion students, in which no linear relationship has been found between time and proficiency (e.g. Cummins, 1983; Harley, 1986; Swain, 1981). For example, a study contrasting performance in French of early immersion students, who had accumulated over 4000 hours starting at age 5, with late immersion students, who had accumulated 1400 hours of French starting at age 12, found the former group to outperform the latter solely on listening comprehension, while the late immersion group performed better on reading comprehension, and there were no differences between the groups on a cloze test. For the authors, these results suggested the interdependence of academic skills across languages, that is, older learners come to the acquisition task equipped with L1 reading and writing skills, lexical and grammatical knowledge (Lapkin *et al.*, 1980: 124–125). In fact, Cummins (1980, 1981) and Cummins and Swain (1986) have argued that older learners show higher mastery of L2 syntax, morphology and other literacy-related skills such as vocabulary and reading comprehension, due to their greater cognitive maturity (see also Harley, 1986; Snow & Hoefnagel-Höhle, 1978). However, they do not show an advantage in the areas of pronunciation and oral fluency because these appear to be among the least cognitively demanding aspects of both L1 and L2 proficiency. That is, measures of basic interpersonal communicative skills may be less sensitive to individual cognitive differences and to academic development.

Several Scandinavian studies provide support for Cummins' proposition that older learners have an advantage on context-reduced, cognitively demanding tasks. For example, Ekstrand (1976) analysed the proficiency in Swedish (L2) of over 2000 learners aged 8–17 years who had been in Sweden for an average of 10.5 months. A positive correlation was found between age and performance on all tasks, except on a test of free oral production in which students described the contents of pictures. On that test, which may be regarded as a relatively context-embedded, natural communicative task, performance showed the strongest relation with length of residence or time, and not with age.

Similar results were found in a study that compared early immersion, middle immersion and late immersion students with comparable amounts of instructional time (Turnbull *et al.*, 1998). The early immersion students clearly outperformed students from middle and late immersion programmes on speaking ability, but did not do better on a multiple-choice test of listening comprehension or on any measures of French literacy. According to the authors, these findings support the theory that in school settings older learners accomplish some aspects of L2 learning more efficiently, but they make the proviso that older students may have higher aptitude and stronger motivation (i.e. they self-select more than the other groups).

In contrast to the wealth of research studies on the effects of age on naturalistic second language acquisition, very few studies have investigated these effects in formal learning situations, in which the amount of exposure to the target language is very limited. After short periods of instruction (e.g. 25 minutes (Asher & Price, 1967), 18 weeks (Ekstrand, 1976), 1 year (Grinder *et al.*, 1962)), older children show a faster learning rate, confirming the rate advantage of older children in the initial learning stages in an instructed situation as well.

After longer periods of time, younger starters do not outperform later starters either. In the EPAL experiment in Sweden (Holmstrand, 1982), with the same total amount of lessons, no differences were found in Grade 6 between a group with initial instruction in English in Grade 1 and a group who began in Grade 3.

In other school situation studies, earlier and later starters have typically had dissimilar amounts of exposure. In such cases, older children, with shorter exposure due to a later start, have been found to catch up with younger children, who had had a longer exposure due to an earlier start. For example, in an experiment in a school in Japan with pupils that began in primary school and pupils who began in secondary school, Oller and Nagato (1974) found that by Grade 11 the early starters did not retain their superiority, in spite of the additional six years of English study they had had in primary school.

Special mention should made of the *Pilot Scheme* in Britain, which began in the early 1960s and involved the teaching of French to British pupils in primary education from the age of 8. The NFER (National Foundation for Educational Research in England and Wales) evaluation of the *Pilot Scheme* compared pupils who had begun at age 8 and pupils who had begun at age 11 and found no substantial gain in mastery; listening comprehension was the only skill on which the early starters outperformed the late starters after a few years (at the age of 16) (Burstall, 1975). However, certain methodological flaws of the study cast doubt on the generalisability of the results. For example, as was also the case in the study by Oller and Nagato (1974), early starters were at some point mixed in with late starters in the same class, a situation that may have had a levelling effect. The fact remains, however, that the early starters retained a certain level of superiority only in the area of listening comprehension. Furthermore, when the two groups were matched for instruction hours the older pupils' performance was consistently superior to that of their younger counterparts who had started earlier.

Cenoz (2002) reports the results of a comparison of two groups of Basque-Spanish bilingual pupils after six years and a total of 564 instruction hours in English. The younger starters had an average age of 13 (Grade 8 at testing; starting age 8) and the older starters were 16 (Grade 11 at testing; starting age 11). Grammatical development was measured through a specific grammar test and also on a scale (out of five) with which oral proficiency was measured. In both cases the results indicated that the difference in favour of the older starters was significant (2002: 134–136). This was also the case in all the measures (cloze test, written composition and oral narration) except for pronunciation, in which the younger group obtained significantly higher scores than the older group, and in listening comprehension, in which differences were only marginally significant.

As part of the same research project, Lázaro (2002) investigated the effects of age on the acquisition of morphosyntactic aspects (the verb *to be*, subject pronouns and inflections) by three learner groups, with starting ages 4, 8 and 11, at two different times: the first group at age 7 and 9, the second group at age 11 and 13, and the third group at age 14 and 16. They had had a similar number of instructional hours at comparison times. The comparison of the results shows that the late starters achieved higher levels than the early starters after similar amounts of instructional hours. The findings also show very different paces of learning among different-aged learners.

To date, few other studies have been carried out on the effects of age on second language acquisition in an institutional setting. The aim of the research project presented in this book was to focus specifically on this situation.

The Older Learners' Rate Advantage

The review of research on the age factor shows that while most of the studies have been mainly concerned with the CPH and its implications for ultimate attainment in a second language, an advantage of older learners over younger learners has persistently emerged. This advantage appears, however, to be limited both in time and in scope.

Snow and Hoefnagel-Höhle (1978) provide empirical evidence that the older learners' lead in a naturalistic situation may be short-lived. Specifically, they report that after 12 months older children were approaching the teenagers' scores. Unfortunately, the study was not long enough to observe whether the younger children later caught up with older learners and eventually surpassed them. In addition, Snow and Hoefnagel-Höhle observed that adults improved relatively slowly between the first and the third measurement times (which were approximately 8 months apart), though their acquisition prior to the first measurement (after 6 weeks of arrival) had been comparatively very fast (Snow, 1983: 143). Krashen *et al.* (1979) conclude from their review of studies of age effects that the older learners' advantage is seen only in the initial stages of second language acquisition and that in the long term younger learners achieve higher second language proficiency than older starters. An explanation of the older learners' advantage is provided by DeKeyser and Larson-Hall (2005), who argue that it is due to their using faster, explicit, learning mechanisms. The younger learners' use of implicit mechanisms instead explains why their learning proceeds at a slower pace.

On the basis of the evidence gathered in naturalistic learning situations, Singleton (1995) predicts that younger starters in an instructed foreign language situation will also catch up with and eventually surpass older starters, if given enough time and exposure. Clearly the way in which the temporal dimension of the older learners' advantage is manifested in an instructed foreign language learning situation with limited exposure to the target language is spanning longer periods of time than those conducted until now.

The older learners' advantage may also be limited in scope, that is, it may apply to some language aspects but not to all. It has been seen above that in their generalisation of research findings Krashen *et al.* (1979) limited the older learners' rate superiority in the initial stages of second language acquisition to morphological and syntactic aspects. Snow and Hoefnagel-Höhle (1978) found that the advantage of the older learners over the younger learners was especially high for the aspects of second language skill that strongly depended on rule acquisition – the tests of syntax, morphology and metalinguistic ability – and for vocabulary. On the other hand, the tests of communicative skill, such as story comprehension and storytelling, showed smaller and less persistent age differences. The shortest-lived advantage of older learners was found in pronunciation, which disappeared after the first test administration (after the first 6 weeks of exposure to the second language). Snow (1983: 142) sees these findings as supporting the existence of different age effects for different components of L2 skill.

As seen above, Cummins and Swain (1986: 88; Cummins, 1980: 180) argue that older learners acquire cognitive/academic L2 skills more rapidly than younger learners because these are related to the development of literacy skills in L1 and L2. In particular, older learners show higher mastery of L2 syntax, morphology and other literacy-related skills, such as vocabulary and reading comprehension. However, this is not necessarily the case for those aspects of L2 proficiency that are unrelated to the cognitive/academic dimension, such as oral fluency and accent. Interestingly, Cummins (1980) observes that the composition of a cognitive/academic dimension in an L2 context may be influenced by factors related to the language learning situation. For example, pronunciation ability or syntactic development may load on that factor when the L2 is taught as a subject in a formal classroom setting, but not when it is being acquired through interaction with native speakers in the environment (1980: 178–179).

The difference in outcomes in different aspects of L2 proficiency is ultimately related to the older learners' greater cognitive maturity, which allows them to better handle cognitive-demanding tasks which are also context-reduced (Cummins, 1982).

From a cognitivist approach, Bialystok also proposes a model of the underlying system that may be seen as parallel and complementary to Cummins's educational approach. Bialystok (1994: 554) proposes a model in which language is represented in (at least) two different ways. One form of linguistic representation is universal and biologically specified in humans; it is built up early, before 5 years of age, and is most clearly revealed in situations in which language is used orally and aurally. A second form of linguistic representation contains language-specific details (LSD); it includes the arbitrary aspects of language, such as vocabulary and parts of morphosyntactic structure and allows learners to solve more formal problems with language. According to Bialystok, formal tests such as grammar tests, which are solved by consulting knowledge explicitly represented in the LSD are often handled better by older learners. In contrast, younger learners usually show an advantage on oral comprehension and pronunciation tests.

Research Questions and Predictions for Foreign Language Learning: Rate of Learning and Differential Achievement in Different Language Subcomponents

Both the early review by Krashen *et al.* (1979) and the more recent assessment by Singleton and Ryan (2004) coincide in pointing out that older learners are faster and more efficient learners than younger learners, at least in the first stages of second language acquisition. These authors also conclude that in the long term those who have an earlier exposure to the second language reach a higher ultimate attainment than those with a later exposure. Singleton (1995) predicts that also in a formal language learning setting younger learners will catch up with and surpass older learners in the long term.

On the basis of findings from previous research on the influence of age on second language acquisition, two general research questions related to learning rate are posed. The first one sets the focus of the study: will there be an age-related difference in the rate of foreign language learning? Previous research results lead to the prediction that older foreign language learners will show a faster rate of acquisition than younger learners in the first stages of foreign language acquisition. If that hypothesis is confirmed, a second research question follows: will younger foreign language learners eventually surpass older learners in the same way as naturalistic second language learners are generally observed to do?

With regard to age-related differences in achievement in the various language subcomponents, the revision of research evidence led Krashen *et al.* (1979) to note that the older learners' advantage was most remarkable in aspects of morphosyntactic development. The study by Snow and Hoefnagel-Höhle (1978), as well as evidence from research in immersion situations seen above, has highlighted different age effects for different language aspects. The work by Cummins (e.g. 1980) has selectively connected the older learners' advantage to those measures of language proficiency that draw on a cognitive/academic dimension of language proficiency. Bialystok's (1994) theoretical proposal also distinguishes between two ways of linguistic representation that are tapped by different language tests. In sum, findings from educational and second language acquisition research, as well as theoretically motivated proposals, suggest that age may affect the different aspects of language in different ways, which raises the third research question: in which ways does age affect different language subcomponents in foreign language acquisition?

The Barcelona Age Factor (BAF) Project

Presentation

The BAF Project began in 1995 at a moment when the changes in the timing of foreign language instruction brought about by a new Education Law were being progressively implemented in both primary and secondary schools around Spain, entailing an earlier introduction of the foreign language in primary education from Grade 6 (11 years) to Grade 3 (8 years).

The replacement of the previous curriculum by the new curriculum took eight years, during which time it was possible to find pupils who had begun English instruction at the age of 11, under the previous curriculum, and pupils who had begun English instruction at the age of 8, under the new curriculum. Data collection began in 1996, when it was already possible to find pupils from the two curricula who had had the same amount of instructional hours in English. In addition, the students from the new curriculum were not the first cohort of the new system, a factor that would have introduced an unwanted effect in the study. Due to the (partly) longitudinal nature of the study, data collection extended up until 2002, when the third comparison between early starters and late starters with the same number of hours of instruction could be made. In addition to these central groups, other age groups were also included in the design of the study, as described below.

Languages used in the state school system

The research on age effects on the learning of English as a foreign language was conducted with students from state schools in Catalonia (Spain). Catalonia is a bilingual community with a majority language, Spanish, known by practically the totality of the population, and a minority language, Catalan, which is the community language. Catalan and Spanish originated from Latin and have been in close contact in the territory of Catalonia, when not in conflict, since the 9th century.

Catalan is the language of instruction in the state school system in Catalonia. Infant education begins in state schools at age 3 and it constitutes an immersion period for children from Spanish-speaking families. In primary education, Spanish is introduced in Grade 1 as a subject, and

Catalan is the main language of communication in the classroom. In secondary education, although Catalan is the official language of instruction, in practice it is much less used than in primary education. The use of Catalan as the language of instruction and communication in general, and in secondary education in particular, varies according to the individual teacher and school, and environment demographic factors. The competence in both Catalan and Spanish of school students is very high and most students can be considered balanced bilinguals (see Muñoz, 2005 for a recent account).

English is the first foreign language in most schools and hence it is the third language of school pupils. The recent earlier introduction of the foreign language entailed a decrease in intensity. Whereas English had been taught for 3 hours per week under the former curriculum (beginning in Grade 6), at the time of data collection in the new curriculum it was taught for 2.5 hours per week on average from Grade 3 to Grade 10, and for 2 hours per week in Grades 11 and 12. The total number of English hours was of around 750 under the former curriculum, distributed over seven years; and of approximately 800 hours, distributed over ten years, under the new one.

The interest that parents have in promoting their children's learning of English is reflected in the number of children and adolescents that attend additional English courses either outside the school, mainly in privately-run non-official language schools, or inside the school, as an extracurricular activity at the end of the school day. In many cases extracurricular tuition in English precedes the regular introduction of instruction in school at age 8 (see Torras *et al.*, 1997). Specifically, more than one-third (35.6%) of the subjects for which data were collected for the BAF Project had had some sort of extracurricular tuition in English (see Muñoz, 2005), and for that reason they could not be included in the main study.

Subjects and design

The two central groups of subjects began English instruction at the age of 8, and 11, respectively. Three other groups were also included in the study, although with fewer subjects: a group of 17 very young learners with age of onset (AO) between 2 and 6; a group of 51 pupils with AO = 14; a group of 135 adults, who began instruction in English at the age of 18 or older.

The youngest learner group consisted of children in infant and primary education schools and the analysis of their performance in English constituted a separate sub-study. The learners who began English instruction at 14 were pupils belonging to one of the following two groups. A first group was formed by pupils who in the previous curriculum had studied French as the first foreign language in Grades 6 through 8, and who in Grade 9 at entering non-compulsory secondary education switched to English, and then they were mixed up with mainstream students who had studied English in the previous three years. A second group was formed by pupils who in the new curriculum took English as the second (optional) foreign language also at the age of 14, and were studying French simultaneously as their first foreign language. The adult group consisted of learners who had begun instruction in English at the age of 18 or older; they had all studied a different foreign language (usually French) in secondary school.

With the exception of the youngest learners (AO = 2–6), subjects were pupils in schools in the state system. They were drawn from 30 different state schools, although 10 of those provided most of the subjects. Schools were located in three central districts in Barcelona, with a mixed population that included low-middle class, mid-middle class and professionals. One school was located in a population near the French border where comparatively more students had taken French as their first foreign language, and hence it was easier to find students who had begun English at the age of 14 (as the second foreign language). Adults were drawn from four different adult schools, either in the public system or attached to a university.

Data were collected at three times: after 200 hours of instruction, 416 hours and 726 hours (Times 1, 2 and 3, respectively). There were 1928 subjects in total, but a number of them had had more hours of instruction, either because of extracurricular exposure or because of repetition of a course grade. Pupils with only school exposure (OSE) fulfilled the conditions for comparison. Table 1.1 indicates the number of subjects in each group, the age at which they began instruction in English and the age each group had at the different data collection times. The youngest learner group is not included in the table because the sub-study extended along a shorter period of time and, due to the gross differences with the other older groups, comparisons were only possible between the sub-groups: AO = 2, 3, 4, or 5[1] (Gálvez & Hernández, 1998; Muñoz, 1998).

Table 1.1 Main subject groups

	Group A AO = 8		Group AO = 11		Group C AO = 14		Group D AO = 18+	
Time 1 200 h	A1	AT = 10;9 N = 284 OSE = 164	B1	AT = 12;9 N = 286 OSE = 107	C1	AT= 15,9 N = 40 OSE = 21	D1	AT = 28;9 N = 91 OSE = 67
Time 2 416 h	A2	AT = 12;9 N = 278 OSE = 140	B2	AT = 14;9 N = 240 OSE = 105	C2	AT= 19,1 N = 11 OSE = 5	D2	AT = 31;4 N = 44 OSE = 21
Time 3 726 h	A3	AT = 16;9 N = 338 OSE = 71	B3	AT = 17;9 N = 296 OSE = 58	–		–	

AO = age of onset; AT = age at testing; N = number of subjects; OSE = only school exposure

Materials: Tests and questionnaires

In view of the fact that there may be different age effects for different components of second language skill, the BAF Project used an extensive test battery (as in Snow & Hoefnagel-Höhle, 1978). The isolation of the different language components is also necessary in an ultimate attainment study in order to address the hypothesis of the existence of several sensitive periods for the different language subcomponents (Long, 1990; Seliger, 1978).

Tests and testing procedures

Testees were asked to listen to oral data and to speak, write and read in English with the aim of assessing the four macroskills: speaking, listening, writing and reading. In addition, testees were given two tests in each of their two first languages (or first and second language, in other cases), and were asked to complete a questionnaire written in Catalan, the school language. Instructions were given in Catalan and/or Spanish by the test administrators, who were members of the research group. The class teacher was not usually present in the classroom during the two sessions in which the tests were administered. The order in which the tests were administered varied so as to control for possible tiredness and lack of attention problems. The following tests were used in the BAF Project:[2]

- Dictation (in English, Catalan and Spanish)
- Cloze (in English, Catalan and Spanish)
- Listening comprehension
- Grammar
- Written composition
- Oral narrative
- Oral interview
- Phonetic imitation
- Phonetic discrimination
- Role-play

Several of the tests involve two macroskills, although the involvement of the two is sometimes unequal (e.g. cloze test, where the writing activity is limited to inserting individual words in the gaps), or arises from the nature of the testing situation rather than from the requirements of the test itself (as when help is needed from the interviewer in order to complete the narrative task and hence comprehension skills are also engaged).

The tests used in this study can also be classified in terms of whether their component items focus on a single point of knowledge – that is, *discrete point* tests – or whether the tests integrate knowledge of various components of language systems and an ability to produce and interpret language appropriately in context – that is, *integrative* tests (Oller, 1979).

Three of the tests in the present study are discrete point tests: the phonetic discrimination test, the phonetic imitation test and the grammar test. The remaining tests are all integrative. In addition, the oral interview and the role-play could be considered *communicative* because they pay attention to the social roles that testees are likely to assume in real-world settings (McNamara, 2000). Both integrative and communicative language tests meet the condition of being performance tests that require the learner to be engaged in an extended act of communication, either receptive or productive, or both (see Savignon, 1997). Finally, from a task-based perspective, some of the language tests in this battery can be considered communication tasks because (1) meaning is primary; (2) there is a communication problem to solve; and (3) there is some sort of relationship to comparable real-world activities (see Chaudron, 2003: 778; Skehan, 1998: 95).

The tests were trialled with different learner groups of the same age as those targeted in the research design. However, the fact that for the sake of comparability it had been decided to use the same tests for all the groups – the school groups ranging between 10 and 18 years of age and the adult groups – inevitably meant that not all the tests were equally suitable for all the groups. On the basis of test piloting, certain modifications were made to the initial tests in order to grade their difficulty and thus improve their face validity.

Test validity and reliability

The battery of tests used in the present research is assumed to be valid because it measured the knowledge learners had gained through the English lessons. This knowledge was, to a large extent, declarative, for example, vocabulary items (often forms equivalent to words in their native language(s)) or morphosyntactic rules (for example, involving verbal inflections and agreement). The battery also included tests that measured procedural knowledge acquired through practice in productive and receptive language skills, for example tests involving word recognition and oral fluency. Taken as a whole, the tests used seem to guarantee the requirements of validity in this type of study.

The quality of the tests was assessed by estimating their internal consistency. An item analysis was performed of the following tests: the three cloze tests (in English, Catalan and Spanish), the three dictations (one in each language), the listening comprehension test, and the grammar test. The following statistics were used: item difficulty; item discrimination; and analysis of response options (or analysis of distractors, which was performed only in the listening comprehension test since distractors in the grammar test had already been submitted to reliability procedures; see below). The global measure of reliability used was Cronbach's alpha.

For the item analysis 10 subjects per item in each test were selected, resulting in 250 subjects in some tests and 300 subjects in others, except in the case of the dictation where a maximum of 300 subjects was set a priori. In order to avoid a ceiling effect, the group with the highest proficiency level was chosen as the target group. Consequently, half of the subjects in each analysis were randomly chosen from groups in Time 1 and Time 2, and as many as half of the subjects were drawn from the most proficient groups: subjects from Time 3, as well as native speaker subjects (48 native speakers were included in the case of the cloze test, and 25 in the analysis of the dictation). The native speakers' mean age was 15, the mid-point in the age range of the subjects. The subjects were chosen randomly from the different schools so that all the schools were represented in the sample.

The item difficulty analysis distributed items per each group in five categories: 'very easy' (74% or above), 'easy' (between 55% and 74%), 'moderate' (between 45% and 54%), 'difficult' (between 25% and 44%), and 'very difficult' (25% or below). The results of the analysis were satisfactory in that the difficulty indices increased with proficiency level in all tests, meaning that more subjects were able to answer more items correctly. The discrimination analysis distributed items per each group into four categories: 'very good' (0.40 or above), 'good' (between 0.30 and 0.39), 'fair' (between 0.20 and 0.29), and 'poor' (0.19 or below). Cronbach's alpha indices were satisfactory, in that the marginal means for all the tests were higher at intermediate levels than at elementary or advanced levels, as had been expected. No differences were found between their average values for groups when the groups were separated by starting age. The Cronbach's alpha of each test is included in the following description of the tests submitted to item analysis.

To ensure the reliability of the scoring of most oral tests, two and sometimes three raters were required. Reliability was estimated on the basis of an inter-rater reliability coefficient. This was the case of the different measures in the interview, the narrative and the role-play (see the description of each below). In the phonetic imitation test, however, several judges were required to score subjects accentedness, and a sample of responses to the test by native speakers was produced to form the corpus/input that the native judges used to make their ratings.

Test description

In this section a description is provided first of those tests which were given to whole classes and which required a written response (ranging from a tick in the case of the listening comprehension test to a full text in the case of the composition), and of oral tests that were administered only to a sub-sample of learners selected randomly from those who had had no extracurricular exposure. The Catalan and Spanish tests that were given to the learners in whole classes are presented, followed at the end by a description of the written questionnaire.

The cloze test – an integrative test with a constructed test format – consisted of a text with 30 gaps, approximately 1 every 10 words (see Appendix 1). Readers were required to use pragmatic knowledge as well as grammatical, lexical and contextual knowledge, to supply the appropriate missing words. This was a cognitively demanding test for the less proficient learners, requiring understanding of a text that they found difficult. In order to lessen cognitive demands, the text was a simplified version of a well-known fairy tale (*Little Red Riding Hood*). It was visually divided into three parts in increasing order of difficulty, and only the more advanced learners were instructed to complete the whole text. The contextually appropriate scoring method was followed (Oller, 1972), after piloting the test with five native speakers of English. Agreement between scorers on what constituted an acceptable answer was achieved in the process of scoring and a record was kept for scoring tests from later administrations. The Cronbach's alpha for this test was 0.88 (the mean of the values for each group).

The dictation test also fulfilled the condition of pragmatic naturalness, that is, that the language user's grammar be engaged in contextual production or interpretation of language under the normal constraints of communication (including real-time processing), as characterised by Oller (1983) (see MacNamara, 2000: 135). Like the cloze test it was expected to predict overall ability, with the advantage of involving listening ability (Hughes, 1989: 72). It contained a 50-word text that had been audio-recorded by a British native speaker, since it was considered that this accent was closest to the model these learners had had in class or in teaching materials. The text was an adaptation of a literary text prepared for classroom use with school students. It was divided into ten segments and students were helped to progress by means of a pre-prepared sheet with ten lines, one for each segment. Students were instructed to write down all the words they recognised and were given one point for each word up to a maximum of 50. The Cronbach's alpha of this test was 0.88 (mean of the values for each group).

The grammar test was a standardised test (EPT)[3] with two different levels and two parallel forms for each one. It was presented in multiple choice format with three alternatives for each item. At the first administration time, after 200 instructional hours, half of the 50 items were omitted and were re-introduced at the second administration time, after 416 instructional hours. This modification was deemed necessary in order to improve the face validity of the test for the younger and less proficient learners. At the third (and fourth) administration time, the two different forms for more advanced students were used, with also 50 items. The reliability coefficients of the lower level parallel forms were 0.91 for one, and 0.92 for the other, and form correlation was 0.93. The reliability coefficients of the higher level parallel forms were 0.88 and 0.89, respectively, and form correlation was 0.86. Because this test had originally been standardised with a population of second language learners in the USA, and the lower level forms had been shortened for the first administration of the test, it was decided also to analyse its fit to the population in this study. The Cronbach's alpha obtained when this test was administered to our learners was 0.75.

The written composition dealt with a familiar topic (the students' own life); the specific title was 'Introduce yourself'. It was written in a set time (15 minutes), the same for everybody. Younger and less proficient learners did not use up all the time they were given because of their language limitations. Compositions were scored initially for 14 different measures grouped under 3 categories: accuracy, complexity and fluency, although in subsequent analyses more measures were added to the original set (see Celaya *et al.*, 2001; Torras *et al.*, this volume).

The listening comprehension test was a picture selection task in which subjects were required to match the word or utterance they heard to one of three pictures presented (see Appendix 2). The language used in the stimuli was simple and referred to topics common in the school activities and daily lives of the subjects. It consisted of 30 items in increasing order of difficulty. The first 3 items, which together constituted a warming-up phase, were vocabulary recognition items. The remaining 27 items consisted of full sentences, simple at the beginning and complex at the end. Subjects were given one point for each correct answer. The Cronbach's alpha for this test was 0.68.

An interview was the first of the tasks that were orally performed in a face-to-face situation with a researcher. It was a semi-guided interview that began with a series of questions about the subject's family, daily life and hobbies; these questions were considered not to be cognitively demanding for learners of any age. This constituted a warming-up phase which helped students feel more at ease, since for many of them, especially the younger and less proficient learners, this may have been the first time they had been asked to use the target language productively and 'spontaneously' for longer than a controlled response in a typical teaching exchange. In general, interviewers attempted to elicit as many responses as possible from the learners, and accepted learner-initiated topics in order to create as natural and interactive a situation as possible. At the same time, the questions previously established were for the most part all posed by the interviewers to guarantee the comparability of interviews across learners and groups (see Appendix 3).

Learners' performance on the interview was assessed by means of two separate scales, one for productive skills and one for receptive skills. The same procedures were followed in the construction, piloting and assessing phases. The scales were piloted with three different raters until the level of inter-rater agreement was found to be satisfactory. In the end, a seven-level scale satisfied accuracy and reliability requirements for both production and reception skills. The final evaluation was conducted by four raters, and each interview was independently assessed for production and reception by two of them. The Pearson product-moment correlation coefficient between the judgements of the pairs of raters for oral production was very high: 0.91 ($p = 0.000$) on average for the different groups (range 0.85–0.96), and it was also high for reception skills measurements: 0.80 ($p = 0.000$) on average (range 0.83–0.75).

The picture-elicited narrative, or story re-telling with a picture mode (see Chaudron 2003: 779), was elicited from a series of six pictures (from Heaton, 1966) that the subjects could look at freely before and while they were telling the story in the presence of the researcher. In the story there are two main protagonists, a boy and a girl, who are getting ready for a picnic; a secondary character, their mother; and a character that disappears and later reappears, a dog that gets into the food basket and eats the children's sandwiches. The subjects were scored on three measures: vocabulary, textual cohesion and narrative development. The vocabulary measure used in this study was the verb/noun ratio, which is supposed to be a good measure of lexical richness at beginner levels, as in our case (Broeder et al., 1993). The textual cohesion and the narrative development scores were calculated on the basis of an assessment instrument that allowed the subjects' productions to be classified in one of five bands, and be given a score (on a ten-point scale, distributed equally among the five bands) (see Álvarez & Muñoz, 2003; Muñoz, 2001a). Four raters assessed the narratives from the different groups, and each narrative was independently assessed by two of them. The Pearson product-moment correlation coefficient between the judgements of the two raters for textual cohesion was 0.78 ($p = 0.000$) and for plot development was 0.79 ($p = 0.000$). A sub-set of these picture-elicited narratives was also analysed with the aim of setting up stages on the learners' development (see Álvarez, this volume).

The phonetic discrimination test was an experimental task which testees usually completed after the storytelling task. It was a discrete point test, with 14 minimal pairs and 6 distractors. Testees were asked to decide whether the two words of each pair were the same or different after listening to each pair. Item selection was based on an analysis of the features that are difficult or problematic for Catalan and Spanish learners of English (see Fullana, this volume). The phonetic imitation test was given after the discrimination test. It consisted of a list of 34 words that the testees had to repeat after listening to the recorded stimulus. The words contained vocalic and consonant sounds known to be difficult for Catalan-Spanish learners of English (see Fullana, this volume).

The role-play task was performed in randomly chosen pairs. In the role-play one of the students was given the role of the mother/father while the second student was given the role of the son/daughter. The latter had to ask permission to have a party at home and both students were asked to negotiate setting, time, activities (music, eating, drinking), etc. The researcher gave the initial instructions and when needed also elicited talk by reminding learners of topics for discussion or led the task to its completion by asking about the outcome of the negotiation. Role-plays were assessed for communicative effectiveness (of the pair of students) and for linguistic performance (of each testee). Agreement percentage between two raters reached 89.28% in both measures.

A dictation and a cloze test in Catalan and in Spanish were given to the testees. These were chosen because they are integrative tests and provide good measures of overall ability in the language. Besides, the dictation involves listening skills, while the cloze test measures reading skills as well. The Cronbach's alpha for the Catalan cloze test was 0.71 (the mean of the values for each group). For the Spanish cloze it was 0.73. The Cronbach's alpha for the Catalan dictation was 0.72, and for the Spanish dictation 0.78 (the mean of all the values).

The questionnaire was written in Catalan, the school language, and contained three types of questions (see Appendix 4). The first type elicited factual data concerning the learners' language learning history (e.g. age of initial instruction in English), amount of time spent in an English-speaking country, or any exposure to the English language outside the regular school periods. A second group of questions elicited behavioural information, such as how many graded readers learners had read, and what strategy learners followed to learn new words or to learn how to pronounce English words (see Tragant & Victori, this volume). The questionnaire also included attitudinal questions concerned with the study of English (see Tragant, this volume). Questions were for the most part closed-ended, and the few open-ended questions that were included were very specific, meaning that answers were usually not longer than a clause (see Dörnyei, 2003).

Because of the need of identifying respondents in order to match questionnaire data with language proficiency tests data, and with other sources of information obtained about the same participants such as course marks, anonymity was not desirable. Confidentiality was, however, promised to respondents, and it was ensured by assigning codes to learners (and schools) prior to entering the data into a computer database.

Subjects completed the questionnaire in class at the beginning of the first session. The administrators tried to clarify all possible doubts learners might have and placed special emphasis on the answers relating to extracurricular exposure. On the basis of these answers, subjects were divided into a group that had had only school exposure and whose number of instructional hours could be experimentally controlled, and a group with extracurricular exposure, mainly through out-of-school classes. The latter was later divided into sub-groups on the basis of the amount of extracurricular exposure they had had. Subjects were also assigned to different language sub-groups on the basis of their responses to the questions concerning the languages they used to talk to their family and friends: balanced bilinguals, Spanish-dominant bilinguals, Catalan-dominant bilinguals.

Oral data (interviews, picture-elicited narratives and role-plays) were first transcribed orthographically and introduced in a computer file. Later they were double-checked at the phase of code insertion following the conventions of the CHAT sub-programme in CHILDES (Child Language Data Exchange System). Written and oral/aural data were analysed and scores were given for different language aspects. Scores were submitted to a variety of parametric and non-parametric statistical tests using the Statistical Package for Social Sciences (SPSS 11.5.0).

General results

Two comparative analyses are presented here in order to provide an overview of the results. The first comparison is concerned with longitudinal data from subjects who were assessed over two testing times, that is, for a total of 416 instruction hours distributed over three and two years, early and late starters respectively. They form part of the two main groups in this study: group A (AO = 8) and group B (AO = 11), respectively. The second comparison involves data from all the subjects in the cross-sectional design.

The tests chosen for this overview are the cloze test, the dictation test, the listening comprehension test, the oral interview (both measures of production and reception), and a measure of textual cohesion of the oral narrative. They are representative of different abilities and tap different language subcomponents. In addition, they complement the linguistic analyses presented in the other more specific chapters in this volume.

A comparison of longitudinal data from early and late starting school learners

Longitudinal data are considered to be the most valuable type of data but they are also very difficult to obtain in naturalistic studies. For this reason the longitudinal samples in the BAF Project are smaller than the cross-sectional samples. As is usually the case in studies that extend over long periods of time, a number of subjects were lost between test administrations and by the end the number of learners who could be followed over the whole period had fallen considerably with respect to the number of the first cohorts. Subject attrition was due to various reasons: mainly, at some point during the six to seven-year period some learners began extracurricular English classes; other subjects were lost when they changed from the primary school where they first completed the tests to a secondary school and for a variety of reasons were no longer available for study;

finally, some learners who had to repeat a course year also had to be excluded.

For this comparative analysis only subjects who were followed for the two first administration times are selected. As mentioned above, whereas early starters could be followed over a period of seven years to include the three times of the study (and even for a fourth testing time on the following year), late starters could only be followed longitudinally from Time 1 to Time 2 (over a period of two years). Learners with age of onset 11 and 726 tuition hours (B3) would not be available because of the gradual disappearance of the curriculum in which they had begun English instruction, and data were collected from a different cohort. Therefore, the comparisons involving B3 are always cross-sectional, or with independent subjects, and there were no learners from that group available for longitudinal comparison with A3.

Tables 1.2 and 1.3 display the number of longitudinal subjects, and the mean and standard deviation for each test. The descriptive data show that the late starters (group B) always obtained higher scores than the early starters (group A), even when the sample size is too small to be submitted to robust statistical tests, as in the case of the oral tests.

Table 1.2 Group A longitudinal subjects

Group A (AO = 8)	N	Mean A1	SD A1	Mean A2	SD A2
Cloze	52	7.05	5.58	18.52	14.48
Dictation	54	13.96	9.81	36.88	17.74
Listening comprehension	55	39.56	11.89	47.20	11.42
Reception interview	8	46.42	12.07	67.85	12.07
Production interview	8	34.82	8.90	56.24	8.04
Textual cohesion narrative	8	23.57	6.26	43.85	18.18

Table 1.3 Group B longitudinal subjects

Group B (AO = 11)	N	Mean B1	SD B1	Mean B2	SD B2
Cloze	25	14.80	13.94	51.73	31.58
Dictation	28	29.64	13.22	59.28	18.34
Listening comprehension	28	40.57	13.18	56.57	15.03
Reception interview	4	60.71	7.14	71.42	11.66
Production interview	4	48.21	10.71	67.85	21.42
Textual cohesion narrative	4	35.00	23.80	65.00	12.90

An analysis of variance (general linear model with repeated measures) was conducted for the three tests with a large enough sample size: the cloze, the dictation and the listening comprehension tests, with "time" as the within-subjects factor (two levels) and "group" as the between-subjects factor (early or late starters). The alpha level was set at 0.01 and

Bonferroni adjustments were made for the multiple contrasts. Time was shown to be a highly significant factor ($p < 0.001$).[4] Pair-wise comparisons of the mean differences at T1 and T2 show that the difference is always significant ($p < 0.001$; but $p < 0.01$ for the difference between A1 and A2 in the listening comprehension test).

Group was also a highly significant factor ($p < 0.001$) for the dictation and the cloze test, but only marginally significant for the listening comprehension test ($p = 0.025$).[5] Pair-wise comparisons show significant differences in favour of the older starters ($p < 0.001$ in all, except in the cloze test at Time 1, where $p = 0.001$, and the listening comprehension test at Time 2, where $p < 0.01$). The only exception is the comparison between the results on the listening comprehension test at Time 1, in which the inter-group difference is not significant. Summarising, the differences between the groups are highly significant at both times in the cloze test and the dictation test. In the listening comprehension test, the difference reaches significance after 416 hours.

The interaction of group and time is also significant. The biggest interaction is found for the cloze test, where the late starters appear to be improving much faster than the early starters. In the cloze and the dictation tests the rate of improvement after 200 hours seems to depend on the time of initial learning, and is much higher for the late starters. The early starters' rate is slower; at Time 2 they have only just reached the value obtained by the late starters at Time 1. Conversely, the rate of improvement on the listening comprehension skill does not seem to depend on the time of initial learning, for after 200 hours the two groups obtain similar scores. However, after the first test administration time the late starters appear to be increasing much faster (from age 12;9 to age 14;9) than the early starters (from age 10;9 to age 12;9). Figure 1.1, the results from the cloze test and the listening comprehension test, illustrates two different patterns in which age of initial learning and age at testing affect rate of improvement of a language skill.

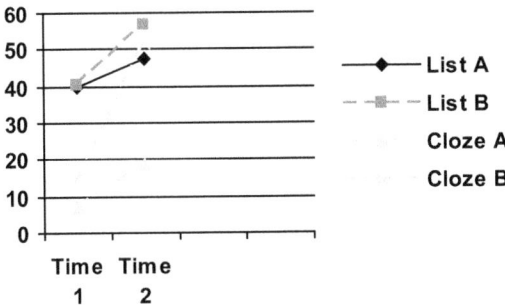

Figure 1.1 Rate of learning of groups A and B in the listening comprehension and the cloze tests

A general comparison of groups with different initial age of learning

In this analysis (non-longitudinal) subjects are distributed into groups according to initial age of learning (A, B, C, D) and according to the accumulated number of English instruction hours at testing (A1, A2, A3, B1, B2, B3, C1, C2, D1 and D2). Longitudinal subjects were randomly kept either at T1, T2 or T3, so that they appeared only once in their respective group, and thus can be considered cross-sectional subjects for the purpose of analysis. The same tests as in the analyses with longitudinal data were selected for comparison. Tables 1.4, 1.5 and 1.6 display descriptive data of test results of each group (number of subjects, mean score and standard deviation), as well as results from the inter-group comparisons. Although group C2 did not have enough subjects to be submitted to statistical analysis, the descriptive information in the table shows size differences and their direction.[6]

Table 1.4 Cross-sectional T1 data: Description and results

	A1		B1		C1		D1		F
	M	SD	M	SD	M	SD	M	SD	
Cloze	6.28 (n = 78)	6.44	11.47 (n = 68)	10.67	38.41 (n = 21)	26.94	72.63 (n = 48)	15.25	$F(3, 211) = 295.232$[a]
Dictation	15.02 (n = 83)	11.55	21.57 (n = 67)	13.16	54.19 (n = 21)	20.02	69.08 (n = 48)	15.19	$F(3, 215) = 187.666$[a]
Listening comprehension	34.21 (n = 86)	13.54	35.57 (n = 68)	12.56	52.57 (n = 21)	17.44	59.16 (n = 48)	12.83	$F(3, 219) = 44.243$[a]
Reception interview	42.41 (n = 16)	15.08	50.31 (n = 23)	12.64	69.92 (n = 19)	11.56	86.02 (n = 46)	8.77	$F(3, 99) = 85.450$[a]
Production interview	33.92 (n = 16)	9.22	42.85 (n = 23)	12.92	54.13 (n = 19)	15.48	81.67 (n = 46)	8.86	$F(3, 99) = 107.602$[a]
Textual cohesion narrative	21.00 (n = 15)	12.56	31.73 (n = 23)	15.27	51.05 (n = 19)	20.24	64.13 (n = 46)	8.58	$F(3, 98) = 59.208$[a]

Note: [a] $p < 0.001$.

Table 1.5 Cross-sectional T2 data: Description and results

	A2		B2		C2		D2		F*
	M	SD	M	SD	M	SD	M	SD	
Cloze	15.23 (n = 77)	12.37	57.87 (n = 88)	25.30	76.66 (n = 5)	12.24	88.42 (n = 19)	5.81	$F(2,181) = 157.225$[a]
Dictation	29.45 (n = 77)	16.67	67.29 (n = 88)	14.66	80.80 (n = 5)	15.27	88.84 (n = 19)	9.73	$F(2,181) = 185.152$[a]
Listening comprehension	46.00 (n = 78)	12.05	57.21 (n = 89)	12.18	76.00 (n = 5)	14.69	81.26 (n = 19)	10.24	$F(2,183) = 69.486$[a]
Reception interview	59.44 (n = 31)	8.52	69.45 (n = 29)	13.75	85.71 (n = 3)	0	92.85 (n =19)	6.73	$F(2,76) = 60.847$[a]
Production interview	50.00 (n = 31)	9.22	68.22 (n = 29)	14.73	90.47 (n = 3)	8.25	83.83 (n = 19)	8.85	$F(2,76) = 53.024$[a]
Textual cohesion narrative	42.50 (n = 20)	16.50	63.67 (n = 34)	14.10	80.00 (n = 3)	10.00	70.55 (n = 18)	5.66	$F(2,69) = 24.076$[a]

Notes: * Only A2, B2 and D2 were submitted to statistical analysis; [a] $p < 0.001$.

Table 1.6 Cross-sectional T3 data: Description and results

	A3		B3		F
	M	SD	M	SD	
Cloze	64.55 (n = 63)	24.37	82.74 (n = 51)	10.40	F (1,112) = 24.737[a]
Dictation	72.73 (n = 65)	15.54	83.49 (n = 51)	9.41	F (1,114) = 18.926[a]
Listening comprehension	66.46 (n = 65)	13.63	74.66 (n = 51)	10.75	F (1,114) = 12.409[b]
Reception interview	82.60 (n = 39)	12.13	84.98 (n = 39)	10.07	F (1,76) = 0.889
Production interview	68.86 (n = 39)	12.09	82.05 (n = 39)	8.49	F (1,76) = 31.042[a]
Textual cohesion narrative	56.02 (n = 39)	14.42	73.07 (n = 39)	7.91	F (1,76) = 41.875[a]

Notes: [a] $p < 0.001$; [b] $p = 0.001$.

The comparison between the different age groups after the same number of instruction hours (by means of analysis of variance tests) shows that the older-starting learners obtain higher scores at the three comparison times (see Tables 1.4, 1.5 and 1.6). However, the contrasts between groups do not yield identical results for all tests and times. The comparison of the scores obtained at Time 1, after 200 instruction hours, shows that the difference between A1 and B1 is not significant on the cloze test and the listening comprehension test, but is marginally significant on the dictation test (Tukey test, $p = 0.024$). Nor is the difference between C1 and D1 on the listening comprehension test significant. All other contrasts indicate a significant advantage in favour of the older starters ($p < 0.001$). It is important to note that when the number of subjects is increased (by, for example, applying less stringent criteria and including learners with small amounts of extracurricular exposure), the differences become significant. For all the tests, the order of the groups from highest to lowest scores is D1, C1, B1, A1.[7]

The comparison of the scores obtained in those same tests by learners after 416 instruction hours shows the same linear increase with age. Differences between groups are significant on all the tests, except on the textual cohesion measure between the group of learners who began at age 11 and the adult group (B2–D2). As at the previous testing time, the order of the groups from most to least proficient was: D2, B2, A2. The comparison after 726 hours shows significant differences on all the tests in favour of the older learners (B3) except on the measure of reception in the oral interview (see Table 1.6).

Figures 1.2 through 1.7 display the results of each group on the six tests at the different testing times. Results from C2 are only indicative due to the very small sample size. It can be clearly observed that significantly higher scores are obtained with increasing starting age (and biological age at testing).

Discussion

These results confirm that there exists an age-related difference in rate of learning a foreign language in a school setting. As hypothesised in relation to the first research question, older learners of foreign language

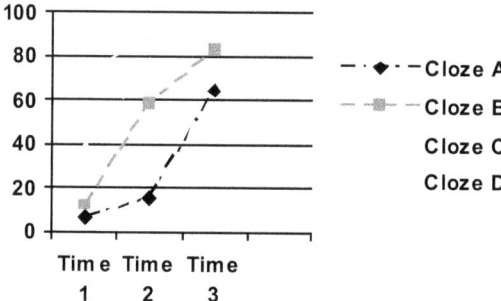

Figure 1.2 Cloze test results across groups (A, B, C, D) and testing times

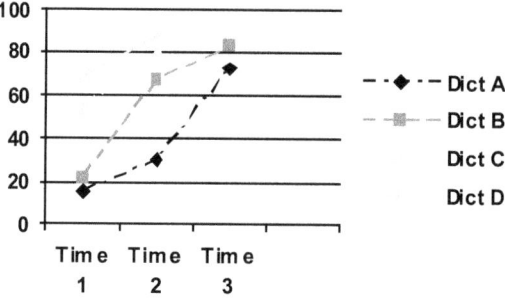

Figure 1.3 Dictation test results across groups (A, B, C, D) and testing times

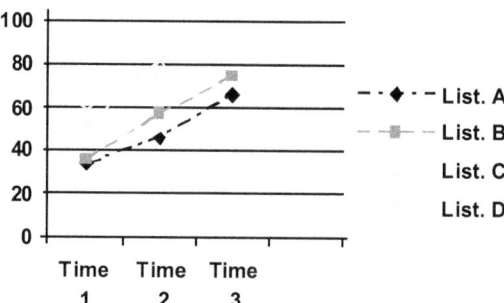

Figure 1.4 Listening comprehension test results across groups (A, B, C, D) and testing times

The Effects of Age

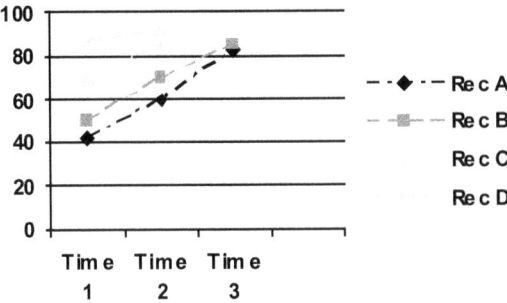

Figure 1.5 Reception measure on the interview. Results across groups (A, B, C, D) and testing times

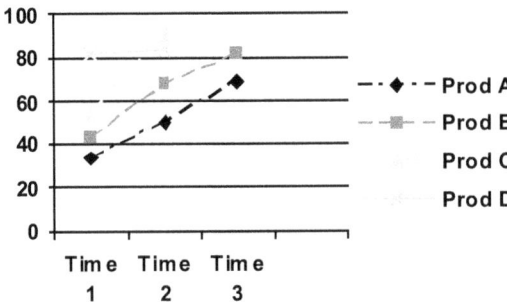

Figure 1.6 Production measure on the interview. Results across groups (A, B, C, D) and testing times

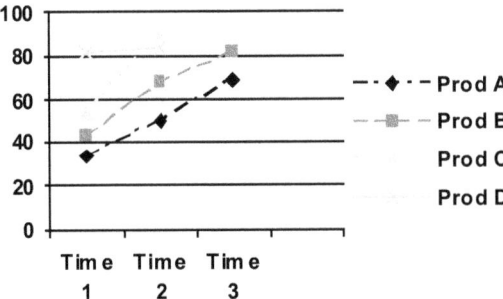

Figure 1.7 Textual cohesion on the narrative. Results across groups (A, B, C, D) and testing times

progress faster than younger learners. The adults showed the most rapid initial acquisition, with significantly higher scores than all the younger groups at Time 1, but they improved relatively slowly between Time 1 and Time 2, particularly on the two measures of aural comprehension (listening comprehension and the reception measure on the interview). The group of learners who began at age 14 (C1) obtained significantly higher scores than the younger groups as well, showing a more rapid initial rate of learning than the younger groups. The group of learners who began at age 11 (B) had higher scores than the group with the youngest initial age (A); the difference did not reach significance at Time 1 in most tests, but it was highly significant at Time 2. At Time 3, scores of the older group were also significantly higher than those of the younger group on all tests except the reception measure of the interview. The youngest group showed the slowest rate in the first 416 hours, but a rapid increase from Time 2 to Time 3.

The answer to the second research question, whether younger foreign language learners eventually surpass older learners, is negative. In the time span covered by this study, younger learners do not obtain higher scores than older learners. As seen in the figures above, the largest differences are found at T2, and the differences diminish at T3, when distances in age and grade are also smaller (learners are only one year and one grade apart, as opposed to two years and two grades apart at Time 2). But the differences do not diminish homogeneously for all the tests analysed here, a fact that leads us to consider the issue of the relationship between age and progress in different language skills. Indeed this was the issue involved in the third research question, that is, whether evidence could be found in these data of different age effects for different language subcomponents. The comparison between the different tests at different times has indeed suggested that age effects are not uniform across measures of language abilities. Two findings will be brought to bear here in order to illustrate this argument: first, differences between older starters and younger starters vary in size in the different tests; second, distinct patterns of development characterise the acquisition of different language subcomponents.

The largest inter-group differences are observed in the cloze and the dictation test. The shortest distance between groups is seen in the listening comprehension test in the initial stages of language acquisition and in the reception measure on the oral interview; in the latter, learners who started at age 8 catch up with learners who started at age 11 after 726 tuition hours. The disappearance of the older learners' advantage is also observed in other tests from the BAF Project. On the phonetic discrimination test the difference becomes non-significant after 726 hours (see Fullana, this volume). Similarly, the analysis of the written productions of groups A and B, using a number of fluency, complexity and accuracy measures, indicates that the former catch up with the latter after 726 hours in some fluency measures (see Torras *et al.*, this volume for a complete account). In addition, on the imitation test no clear age-effects are observed in the degree of accentedness of learners' productions (see Fullana, this volume, for a complete account).

In sum, younger learners are seen to catch up with older starters, or not to differ significantly, in aural perception (reception skills on the interview task, and phonetic discrimination test), oral production (phonetic imitation test), as well as in some fluency measures on the written composition task. It is important to note that the production measure on the interview task had a strong morphosyntactic component (i.e. it assessed clause structure and morphological agreement in oral speech) therefore, it is not surprising that this measure is not included in the group above but patterns in a similar way as the cloze, the dictation and the textual cohesion measure in the picture-elicited narrative (see also Muñoz, 2003a). A distinction emerges then between the latter tests and measures with a strong morphosyntactic component (more cognitively-demanding tasks), and the former group of tests which tap speech perception and production, and fluency skills (that is, less cognitively-demanding tasks).

A second related finding is a more precise age-effect in the evolution of different language skills, which is particularly visible in the comparison of morphosyntactic and listening comprehension abilities, in both in the longitudinal and the cross-sectional data. The observation of the pattern of the results in tests with a strong morphosyntactic component (see Figures 1.2, 1.3 and also 1.6 and 1.7 above) indicates a notable increase in development around puberty. Interestingly, very similar findings were obtained in a study of the acquisition of morphosyntactic aspects (the verb *to be*, subject pronouns and inflections) in formal Basque-Spanish learners of English (see Lázaro, 2002). As seen previously, three learner groups were compared at two different times. In addition to the finding that the late starters outperformed the early starters after similar amounts of instructional hours, the study revealed very different paces of learning: the youngest learners were the slowest, and a speeded progression could be seen between the ages of 11 and 13, much faster than that between ages 14 and 16.

In the BAF Project data, the pattern of morphosyntactic development also shows age-related rate differences, contrasting with the more homogeneous development in listening comprehension skills. The comparison of Figures 1.2 and 1.4 (as representative examples of the tests with an important morphosyntactic component, and of the measures of aural comprehension skills, respectively) shows the contrast in the performance of the different age groups in the two tests.[8] Although in both types of abilities older learners are seen to progress faster than younger learners, the contrast between the two patterns indicates that in the initial 200 hours the effect of age on learning rate does not affect listening comprehension skills as much as morphosyntactic skills. In addition, while the former seem to evolve in parallel fashion in the four groups, the latter show a less homogeneous development, suggesting a further age-related effect on rate of learning. The comparison of groups A and B shows that the greatest increase in this morphosyntactic measure takes place between Time 1 and Time 2 in group B, that is, between the ages of 12;9 and 14;9, and between Time 2 and Time 3 in group A, that is, between the ages of 12;9 and 16;9. In other words, independently of the amount of hours of instruction (much higher in the latter than in the former), morphosyntactic learning seems to boost at around age 12, coinciding with the cognitive growth associated with puberty. Important changes around that age have also been observed in the analyses of other data in the BAF Project: in relation to the development of writing skills (Torras & Celaya, 2001; Torras *et al.*, this volume) and narrative skills (Álvarez, this volume), as well as in relation to the development of interactional skills (Grañena, this volume), and of learning strategies (Tragant & Victori, this volume).

In contrast, listening comprehension skills may be less affected by age than morphosyntactic skills. Instead, amount of exposure may be the most important determinant of the development of listening comprehension abilities. As seen above, listening comprehension was the only ability in which early starters in the *Pilot Scheme* in Britain succeeded in maintaining an advantage over late starters. Similar findings are reported in immersion studies that have compared early and late immersion students (Lapkin *et al.*, 1980, Turnbull *et al.*, 1998). Likewise, in the study by Snow and Hoefnagel-Höhle (1978) in a naturalistic context, differences on the pronunciation, auditory discrimination, story comprehension and spontaneous speech fluency tests diminished earlier than on the morphology and sentence translation tests.

Further evidence in this direction comes from a previous study of the younger and older children starters in the BAF Project (groups A and B), in which a multiple regression analysis was conducted with the results from the listening comprehension, dictation, cloze and grammar tests as dependent variables. The independent variables included L1 proficiency (Spanish and/or Catalan), socio-cultural class, grade, school, and degree of extracurricular exposure. The findings showed that L1 proficiency, associated with children's cognitive development, was the factor with the strongest weight on the English scores of all the tests with the exception of the listening comprehension test (Muñoz, 2001b, 2003b; see also Sparks *et al.*, 1995). The degree of extracurricular exposure showed a moderate influence on listening comprehension, higher in the first 200 hours than later.

In sum, differences in cognitive development play an important role in explaining why older learners in a formal foreign language situation are faster and more efficient than younger learners, especially in tests in which the morphosyntactic component is important. The older learners' superior cognitive development also allows them to take greater advantage of explicit teaching processes in the classroom. In contrast, young learners seem to favour and to be favoured by implicit learning. Implicit learning improves with practice, but occurs slowly and requires massive amounts of exposure. In other words, learners need to be exposed to multiple instances of a feature before it is acquired. In a typical school syllabus, very little time is devoted to the foreign language (usually no more than three one-hour periods), and target language input is very limited (and part of it is usually accented). As a consequence, exposure is very scarce and probably insufficient for children to be able to make use of implicit learning mechanisms (DeKeyser, 2000; DeKeyser & Larson-Hall, 2005), and hence younger learners may not have enough time and exposure to benefit from the alleged advantages of implicit learning.

The point has been made from a slightly different perspective by Kirsner (1994: 308), noting that in the absence of an immersion programme the L2 learner will never enjoy the use of pattern recognition or production procedures which remotely approach the levels reached with L1 problems. Also from a neurolinguistic perspective Perani and his associates (2003) have highlighted the importance of exposure. On the basis of their study on the effects of age of acquisition and intensity or usage of exposure, these authors have argued that intensive use of a language leads to a lower activation threshold (Green, 1986) and therefore to a higher degree of automaticity, that is, decreased dependence on controlled and attentional processing which appear to be reflected in decreased activity in the prefrontal region. The authors therefore conclude that language exposure is a crucial factor for the neural representation of multiple languages (Perani *et al.*, 2003: 180).

The age-related differences between the various language subcomponents that have been observed in this study may also be interpreted in the light of the distinction between implicit and explicit learning mechanisms (see e.g. Ellis, 1994; Fabbro, 1999, 2002; Paradis, 1994, 1997). In fact, although the tasks in this study were not specifically designed to assess implicit and explicit knowledge (see Ellis, 2004), they may be tentatively ordered along a continuum of greater or lesser involvement of implicit and explicit processes, with the aural comprehension tasks nearer the implicit end, and the cloze task nearer the explicit end. There are greater inter-groups differences in the former and smaller differences in the latter.

Conclusion

This study has suggested that age differences in a foreign language context favour older learners in the short term due to their superior cognitive development and probably to the advantages provided by explicit learning mechanisms, which also develop with age. That is, in contexts where opportunities for implicit learning and practice are minimal, older learners may be quicker to acquire language aspects that involve above all declarative or explicit learning and memory. Conversely, younger learners may be greatly deprived of their potential advantage when there is not enough exposure and contact with the language for L2 to proceed in the same way as L1 learning.

The comparison of different groups has revealed age-related differences in learning rate. Adolescents and adults showed a very rapid initial rate of learning in the first third of the period (after 200 hours); learners with initial age of learning at the beginning of puberty (11 yrs) made the most progress in the second third of the period (between 200 and 416 hours); and learners with the earliest initial age of learning (8 yrs) showed the most rapid learning in the last third of the period (between 416 and 726 hours). In the last two groups the increase in learning rate was observed when learners reached the age of 12.

It has been suggested that the time span needed for the younger learners to catch up with (or eventually surpass) the older starters in a foreign language learning context will necessarily be longer than that needed in a naturalistic language learning context. After nine years of formal learning of English (and seven years after the first data collection time), the younger learners in this study reduced the distance with respect to older learners on tests with a greater involvement of implicit learning mechanisms. However, from there it does not follow that younger learners will necessarily outperform older learners in the longer term. On the contrary, if the older learners' advantage is mainly due to their superior cognitive development, no differences in proficiency are to be expected when differences in cognitive development also disappear with age.

In other words, the findings from this study lead to the following prediction for age effects in the long term: when younger learners attain a state of cognitive development that is similar to that of the older learners with whom they are being compared, and are given the same conditions of time and exposure (and instruction), the differences should disappear. This runs counter to earlier predictions that were based on evidence from naturalistic second language acquisition at a time when there was a lack of previous studies conducted over periods that were long enough to observe younger starters overtaking older starters (Singleton, 1995). The present study covers a considerably longer time period than most previous studies in this area, reaching the end of secondary education, which for the majority of students represents the end of foreign language learning as well. Because of its external validity, important educational implications may be drawn from its results.

In sum, these findings suggest that second language learning success in a foreign language context may be as much a function of exposure as of age. Exposure needs to be intense and to provide an adequate model. Initial age of learning seems more relevant for skills that can be acquired implicitly, whereas age at learning can be seen as a factor explaining the rate of learning of most skills. The fact that this distinction has not been sufficiently highlighted goes some way towards explaining the somewhat confused ideas that have prevailed in relation to age effects in second language acquisition.

Acknowledgements

This study was carried out with the assistance of the research grants PB94-0944, PB97-0901, and BFF2001-3384 of the Spanish Ministry of Education. I would also like to express my appreciation to Immaculada Miralpeix and Gisela Grañena for their help with the preparation of this chapter.

Notes

1. The comparisons between the groups after 40, 80 and 120 hours (different subjects in each comparison) showed that the older learners were superior on all skills tested.
2. A map task was also performed in pairs, but the results are still under analysis and have not been included in this volume.
3. EPT stands for English–Second Language Placement Test. The two lower level forms were produced by D. Ilyin, and the two higher level forms by D. Illyn, J. Best and V. Biagi.
4. The eta-squared values were 0.62 for the cloze test, 0.75 for the dictation, and 0.34 for the listening comprehension test.
5. The eta-squared values were 0.33 for the cloze test and the dictation, and 0.37 for the listening comprehension test.
6. Due to their late start, learners in group C were already near the end of secondary education after Time 2. As for group D, the research conditions were so restrictive that it was very difficult to find adults that after such a long period of instruction had not engaged in some sort of extracurricular exposure, such as English summer courses, or significant contacts with English native-speakers.
7. It is evident that the conditions under which teaching-learning processes among adult learners and school learners take place are very different, mainly in terms of teachers' training and characteristics, the proportion of class time that constitutes actual 'learning time' (affected by time consumed for classroom management needs among school learners), and the amount and quality of time spent doing homework.

    The design tried to account for this by adding some extra time to the actual class hours adult learners had received when establishing comparison times (30 minutes more per week).
8. The same pattern was followed by the longitudinal data above.

References

Abutalebi, J., Cappa, S. and Perani, D. (2001) The bilingual brain as revealed by functional neuroimaging. *Bilingualism: Language and Cognition* 4, 179–190.

Álvarez, E. and Muñoz, C. (2003) Las habilidades narrativas en inglés (LE) y su evolución con la edad. In G. Luque, A. Bueno and G. Tejada (eds) *Languages in a Global World* (pp. 3–10). Jaén: Universidad de Jaén.

Asher, J. and Price, B. (1967) The learning strategy of the total physical response: Some age differences. *Child Development* 38 (4), 1219–1227.

Bialystok, E. (1994) Representation and ways of knowing: Three issues in second language acquisition. In N. Ellis (ed.) *Implicit and Explicit Learning of Languages* (pp. 549–569). San Diego, CA: Academic Press.

Bialystok, E. (1997) The structure of age: In search of barriers to second language acquisition. *Second Language Research* 13 (2), 116–137.

Bialystok, E. and Hakuta, K. (1999) Confounded age: Linguistic and cognitive factors in age differences for second language acquisition. In D. Birdsong (ed.) *Second Language Acquisition and the Critical Period Hypothesis* (pp. 161–181). Mahwah, NJ: Erlbaum.

Birdsong, D. (1992) Ultimate attainment in second language acquisition. *Language* 68, 706–755.

Birdsong, D. (1999) Introduction: Whys and why nots of the critical period hypothesis for second language acquisition. In D. Birdsong (ed.) *Second Language Acquisition and the Critical Period Hypothesis* (pp. 1–22). Mahwah, NJ: Erlbaum.

Birdsong, D. (2005) Interpreting age effects in second language acquisition. In J. Kroll and A. de Groot (eds) *Handbook of Bilingualism: Psycholinguistic Perspectives* (pp. 109–127). Oxford: Oxford University Press.

Birdsong, D. and Molis, M. (2001) On the evidence for maturational constraints on second-language acquisition. *Journal of Memory and Language* 44, 235–249.

Bley-Vroman, R. (1989) What is the logical problem of foreign language learning? In S. Gass and J. Schachter (eds) *Linguistic Perspectives on Second Language Acquisition* (pp. 41–68) Cambridge: Cambridge University Press.

Bongaerts, T. (1999) Ultimate attainment in L2 pronunciation: The case of very advanced late L2 learners. In D. Birdsong (ed.) *Second Language Acquisition and the Critical Period Hypothesis* (pp. 133–159). Mahwah, NJ: Erlbaum.

Bongaerts, T., Van Summeren, C., Planken, B. and Schils, E. (1997) Age and ultimate attainment in the pronunciation of a foreign language. *Studies in Second Language Learning* 19, 447–465.

Broeder, P., Extra, G. and van Hout, R. (1993) Richness and variety in the developing lexicon. In C. Perdue (ed.) *Adult Language Acquisition: Field Methods* (pp. 145–163). Cambridge: Cambridge University Press.

Burstall, C. (1975) Primary French in the balance. *Foreign Language Annals* 10 (3), 245–252.

Celaya, M.L., Pérez, C. and Torras, M.R. (2001) Matriz de criterios de medición para la determinación del perfil de competencia lingüística escrita en inglés (LE). *RESLA* 14, 87–98.

Cenoz, J. (2002) Age differences in foreign language learning. *ITL Review of Applied Linguistics* 135–136, 125–142.

Chaudron, C. (2003) Data collection in SLA research. In C. Doughty, and M. Long, (eds) *The Handbook of Second Language Acquisition* (pp. 762–828). London: Blackwell.

Colombo, J. (1982) The critical period concept: Research, methodology, and theoretical issues. *Psychological Bulletin* 91, 260–275.

Coppieters, R. (1987) Competence differences between native and near-native speakers. *Language* 63, 544–575.

Cummins, J. (1980) The cross-lingual dimensions of language proficiency: Implications for bilingual education and the optimal age issue. *TESOL Quarterly* 14 (2), 175–187.

Cummins, J. (1981) Age on arrival and immigrant second language learning in Canada. A reassessment. *Applied Linguistics* 11 (2), 132–149.

Cummins, J. (1982) Tests, achievement, and bilingual students. *FOCUS* February (9), 1–7.

Cummins, J. (1983) Language proficiency, biliteracy and French immersion. *Canadian Journal of Education* 8 (2), 117–138.
Cummins, J. and Swain, M. (1986) *Bilingualism in Education*. London: Longman.
Curtiss, S. (1977) *Genie: A Psycholinguistic Study of a Modern-day 'Wild Child'*. New York: Academic Press.
DeKeyser, R. (2000) The robustness of critical period effects in second language acquisition. *Studies in Second Language Acquisition* 22 (4), 499–533.
DeKeyser, R. (2003) Implicit and explicit learning. In C.J. Doughty and M.H. Long (eds) *Handbook of Second Language Acquisition* (pp. 313–348). London: Blackwell.
DeKeyser, R. and Larson-Hall, J. (2005) What does the critical period really mean? In J.F. Kroll and A.M.B. de Groot (eds) *Handbook of Bilingualism: Psycholinguistic Approaches* (pp. 88–108). Oxford: Oxford University Press.
Diller, K. (1981) 'Natural methods' of foreign language teaching: Can they exist? What criteria must they meet? In H. Winnitz (ed.) *Native Language and Foreign Language Acquisition* (pp. 75–86). New York: The New York Academy of Sciences.
Dörnyei, Z. (2003) *Questionnaires in Second Language Research. Construction, Administration, and Processing*. Mahwah, NJ: Lawrence Erlbaum Associates
Doughty, C. (2003) Instructed SLA: Constraints, compensation, and enhancement. In C. Doughty and M.H. Long (eds) *The Handbook of Second Language Acquisition* (pp. 256–310). London: Blackwell.
Ekstrand, L.H. (1976) Age and length of residence as variables related to the adjustment of migrant children, with special reference to second language learning. In G. Nickel (ed.) *Proceedings of the Fourth International Congress of Applied Linguistics*. Stuttgart: Hochschul-Verlag. Reprinted in S.D. Krashen, R.C. Scarcella and M.H. Long (eds) (1982) *Child-Adult Differences in Second Language Acquisition* (pp. 123–135). Rowley, MA: Newbury House Publishers.
Ellis, N. (1994) Vocabulary acquisition: The implicit ins and outs of explicit cognitive mechanisms. In N. Ellis (ed.) *Implicit and Explicit Learning of Languages* (pp. 211–282). London: Academic Press.
Ellis, R. (2004) The definition and measurement of L2 explicit knowledge. *Language Learning* 54 (2), 227–276.
Elman, J.L. (2001) Connectionism and language acquisition. In M. Tomasello and E. Bates (eds) *Language Development* (pp. 295–306). Oxford: Blackwell.
Fabbro, F. (1999) *The Neurolinguistics of Bilingualism. An Introduction*. Hove: Psychology Press.
Fabbro, F. (2002) The neurolinguistics of L2 users. In V. Cook (ed.) *Portraits of the Second Language User* (pp. 197–218). Clevedon: Multilingual Matters.
Felix, S. (1985) More evidence on competing cognitive systems. *Second Language Research* 1, 47–72.
Gálvez, L. and Hernández, E. (1998) El inglés como lengua extranjera en niños de 2 a 6 años. Unpublished research paper, Universitat de Barcelona.
Green, D.W. (1986) Control, activation, and resource: A framework and a model for the control of speech in bilinguals. *Brain and Language* 27, 210–223.
Grinder, R., Otomo, A. and Toyota, W. (1962) Comparisons between second, third, and fourth grade children in the audio-lingual learning of Japanese as a second language. *The Journal of Educational Research* 56 (4), 463–469.
Harley, B. (1986) *Age in Second Language Acquisition*. Clevedon: Multilingual Matters.
Harley, B. and Wang, W. (1997) The critical period hypothesis: Where are we now? In A. de Groot and J. Kroll (eds) *Tutorials in Bilingualism: Psycholinguistic Perspectives* (pp. 19–51). Mahwah, NJ: Erlbaum.
Heaton, J.B. (1966) *Composition through Pictures*. London: Longman (reprinted 1972).

Holmstrand, L.S.E. (1982) *English in the Elementary School*. Stockholm/Uppsala: Almqvist & Wiksell International.

Hughes, A. (1989). *Testing for Language Teachers*. Cambridge: Cambridge University Press.

Hyltenstam, K. and Abrahamsson, N. (2000) Who can become native-like in a second language? All, some, or none? On the maturational controversy in second language acquisition. *Studia Linguistica* 54 (2), 150–166.

Hyltenstam, K. and Abrahamsson, N. (2003) Maturational constraints in SLA. In C.J. Doughty and M.H. Long (eds) *Handbook of Second Language Acquisition* (pp. 539–588). London: Blackwell.

Ioup, G., Boustagui, E., El Tigi, M. and Moselle, M. (1994) Reexamining the critical period hypothesis: A case study of successful adult SLA in an naturalistic environment. *Studies in Second Language Acquisition* 16, 73–98.

Johnson, J. and Newport, E. (1989) Critical period effects in second language learning: The influence of maturational state on the acquisition of English as a second language. *Cognitive Psychology* 21, 60–99.

Johnson, J. and Newport, E. (1991) Critical period effects on universal properties of language: The use of subjacency in the acquisition of a second language. *Cognition* 39, 215–258.

Jones, P.E. (1995) Contradictions and unanswered questions in the Genie case: A fresh look at the linguistic evidence. *Language & Communication* 15 (3), 261–280.

Kellerman, E. (1995) Age before beauty. Johnson and Newport revisited. In L. Eubank, L. Selinker and M. Sharwood-Smith (eds) *The Current State of Interlanguage* (pp. 219–231). Amsterdam/Philadelphia: John Benjamins Publishing Company.

Kim, K.H.S., Relkin, N.R., Kyoung-Min, L. and Hirsch, J. (1997) Distinct cortical areas associated with native and second languages. *Nature* 388, 171–174.

Krashen, S., Long, M. and Scarcella, R. (1979) Age, rate and eventual attainment in second language acquisition. *TESOL Quarterly* 9, 573–582. Reprinted in S.D. Krashen, R.C. Scarcella and M.H. Long (eds) (1982) *Child-adult Differences in Second Language Acquisition* (pp. 161–172). Rowley, MA: Newbury House Publishers.

Lapkin, S., Swain, M., Kamin, J. and Hanna, G. (1980) Report on the 1979 evaluation of the Peel County late French immersion program, grades 8, 10, 11 and 12. Unpublished report, University of Toronto, OISE.

Lázaro, A. (2002) *La adquisición de la morfosintaxis del inglés por niños bilingües euskera-castellano: una perspectiva minimalista*. Unpublished PhD thesis, Universidad del País Vasco.

Lenneberg, E.H. (1967) *Biological Foundations of Language*. New York: Wiley.

Long, M. (1990) Maturational constraints on language development. *Studies in Second Language Acquisition* 12 (3), 251–285.

McNamara, T. (2000) *Language Testing*. Oxford: Oxford University Press.

Molfese, D. (1977) Infant cerebral asymmetry. In S. Segalowitz and F. Gruber (eds) *Language Development and Neurological Theory* (pp. 22–35). New York: Academic Press.

Muñoz, C. (1998) Informe de resultados del proyecto 'Los efectos de la edad en la adquisición de una lengua extranjera (inglés), con especial atención a la edad 2–6'. Unpublished report, Universitat de Barcelona.

Muñoz, C. (2001a) The effects of age on rate of acquisition of a foreign language. In P. Gallardo and E. Llurda (eds) *Proceedings of the XXII International Conference of AEDEAN* (pp. 567–572). Universitat de Lleida, December 2000.

Muñoz, C. (2001b) Factores escolares e individuales en el aprendizaje formal de un idioma extranjero. In S. Pastor and V. Salazar (eds) *Tendencias y líneas de investigación en ASL. Estudios de Lingüística*. Volumen monográfico (pp. 249–270). Universidad de Alicante.

Muñoz, C. (2003a) Le rythme d'acquisition des savoirs communicationnels chez des apprenants guidés. L'influence de l'age. *Acquisition et Interaction en Langue Étrangère* 18, 53–77.

Muñoz, C. (2003b) Variation in oral skills development and age of onset. In M.P. García Mayo and M.L. García Lecumberri (eds) *Age and the Acquisition of English as a Foreign Language: Theoretical Issues and Fieldwork* (pp. 161–181). Clevedon: Multilingual Matters.

Muñoz, C. (2005) Trilingualism in the Catalan educational system. *International Journal of the Sociology of Language* 171, 75–93.

Newport, E. (1990) Maturational constraints on language learning. *Cognitive Science* 14, 11–28.

Oller, J.W. (1972) Scoring methods and difficulty levels for cloze tests of ESL proficiency. *The Modern Language Journal* 56, 151–157.

Oller, J.W. (1979) *Language Tests at Schools*. London: Longman.

Oller, J.W. (1983) *Issues in Language Testing Research*. Rowley, MA: Newbury House.

Oller, J. and Nagato, N. (1974) The long-term effect of FLES: An experiment. *Modern Language Journal* 58, 15–19.

Paradis, M. (1994) Neurolinguistic aspects of implicit and explicit memory: Implications for bilingualism and SLA. In N. Ellis (ed.) *Implicit and Explicit Learning of Languages* (pp. 393–419). San Diego, CA: Academic Press.

Paradis, M. (1997) The cognitive neuropsychology of bilingualism. In A.M.B. de Groot and J.F. Kroll (eds) *Tutorials in Bilingualism. Psycholinguistic Perspectives* (pp. 331–354). Mahwah, NJ: Lawrence Erlbaum Associates Publishers.

Patkowski, M. (1980) The sensitive period for the acquisition of syntax in a second language. *Language Learning* 30, 449–472.

Patkowski, M. (2003) Laterality effects in multilinguals during speech production under the concurrent task paradigm: Another test of the age of acquisition. *International Review of Applied Linguistics* 41 (3), 175–200.

Penfield, W. and Roberts, L. (1959) *Speech and Brain Mechanisms*. New York: Atheneum.

Perani, D. and Abulatebi, J. (2005) The neural basis of first and second language process. *Current Opinion in Neurobiology* 15, 202–206.

Perani, D., Abulatebi, J., Paulesu, E., Brambati, S., Scifo, P. et al. (2003) The role of age of acquisition and language usage in early, high-proficient bilinguals: An fMRI study during verbal fluency. *Human Brain Mapping* 19, 170–182.

Perani, D., Paulesu, E., Galles, N.S., Dupoux, S., Dehaene, S. et al. (1998) The bilingual brain: Proficiency and age of acquisition of the second language. *Brain* 121, 1841–1852.

Pulvermüller, F. and Schumann, J.H. (1994) Neurobiological mechanisms of language acquisition. *Language Learning* 44, 681–734.

Savignon, S.J. (1997) *Communicative Competence: Theory and Classroom Practice*. (2nd edn.). New York: McGraw-Hill.

Schachter, J. (1996) Maturation and the issue of universal grammar in second language acquisition. In W.C. Ritchie and T.K. Bahtia (eds) *Handbook of Second Language Acquisition* (pp. 159–193). New York: Academic Press.

Scovel, T. (1988) *A Time to Speak. A Psycholinguistic Inquiry into the Critical Period for Human Speech*. Rowley, MA: Newbury House.

Seliger, H. (1978) Implications of a multiple critical periods hypothesis for second language learning. In W. Ritchie (ed.) *Second Language Acquisition Research: Issues and Implications* (pp. 11–19). New York: Academic Press.

Singleton, D. (1995) A critical look at the Critical Period Hypothesis in second language acquisition research. In D. Singleton and Z. Lengyel (eds) *The Age Factor in Second Language Acquisition* (pp. 1–29). Clevedon: Multilingual Matters.

Singleton, D. and Ryan, L. (2004) *Language Acquisition: The Age Factor* 2nd edn. Clevedon: Multilingual Matters.

Skehan, P. (1998) *A Cognitive Approach to Language Learning*. Oxford: Oxford University Press.

Slavoff, G.R. and Johnson, J.S. (1995) The effects of age on the rate of learning a second language. *Studies in Second Language Acquisition* 17 (1), 1–16.

Snow, C. (1983) Age differences in second language acquisition: Research findings and folk psychology. In K.M. Bailey, M.H. Long and S. Peck (eds) *Second Language Acquisition Studies* (pp. 141–150). Rowley, MA: Newbury House Publishers.

Snow, C. and Hoefnagel-Höhle, M. (1978) The critical period for language acquisition: Evidence from second language learning. *Child Development* 49, 1114–1128.

Sparks, R., Ganschow, L. and Patton, L. (1995) Prediction of perfomance in first-year foreign language courses: Connections between native and foreign language learning. *Journal of Educational Psychology* 87 (4), 638–655.

Swain, M. (1981) Time and timing in bilingual education. *Language Learning* 31 (1), 1–13.

Swain, M. (1984) A review of immersion education in Canada: Research and evaluation studies. In B. Honig (ed.) *Studies on Immersion Education* (pp. 87–111). Sacramento, CA: California State Department of Education.

Tomasello, T. (2003) *Constructing a Language. A Usage-based Theory of Language Acquisition*. Cambridge, MA: Harvard University Press.

Torras, M.R. and Celaya, M.L. (2001) Age related differences in the development of written production. An empirical study of EFL learners. Special issue edited by R.M. Manchón, *Writing in the L2 classroom: Issues in Research and Pedagogy. International Journal of English Studies* 1 (2), 103–126.

Torras, M.R., Tragant, E. and García, M.L. (1997) Croyances populaires sur l'apprentissage précoce d'une langue étrangère. In C. Muñoz, L. Nussbaum and M. Pujol (eds) *Acquisition et Interaction en Langue Étrangère* 10, 127–158.

Turnbull, M., Lapkin, S., Hart, D. and Swain, M. (1998) Time on task and immersion graduates' French proficiency. In S. Lapkin (ed.) *French Second Language Education in Canada: Empirical Studies* (pp. 31–55). Toronto: University of Toronto Press.

van Wuijtswinkel, K. (1994) Critical period effects on the acquisition of grammatical competence in a second language. Unpublished Ph.D. thesis, Katholieke Universiteit, Nijmegen, The Netherlands.

Wattendorf, E., Westermann, B., Zappatore, D., Franceschini, R., Lüdi, G. *et al.* (2001) Different languages activate different subfields in Broca's area. *NeuroImage* 13, 624.

White, L. and Genesee, F. (1996) How native is near-native? The issue of ultimate attainment in adult second language acquisition. *Second Language Research* 12 (3), 233–265.

Chapter 2

The Development of English (FL) Perception and Production Skills: Starting Age and Exposure Effects

NATALIA FULLANA

Introduction

Second language (L2) phonological research has been conducted under either one of two broad hypotheses, as noted by Flege (2003): the Critical Period Hypothesis (CPH) (Lenneberg, 1967) and an alternative hypothesis to the CPH.

According to the CPH, adult and older adolescent learners' failure to attain native-like phonological skills in the target language (TL) results from a loss of neural plasticity after the passing of a critical period (CP) for language learning. In addition, and based on evidence of the emergence of accented pronunciation in the TL as early as age 6 (e.g. Asher & García, 1969; Oyama, 1976; Tahta *et al.*, 1981; see also Long (1990) and Piske *et al.* (2001) for comprehensive reviews of accent studies), supporters of the CPH indicate that the first linguistic area to be influenced by a CP[1] is L2 phonology. Furthermore, even some researchers claim that phonology is the only linguistic domain subject to a CP (Scovel, 1988).

However, recent findings of adult and adolescent L2 learners' mastery of the L2 phonology at native-like levels (e.g. Bongaerts, 1999; Bongaerts *et al.*, 1997; Ioup *et al.*, 1994; Moyer, 1999) run counter to the premises of the CPH. Thus, an alternative account has been put forth, which highlights the importance of the learners' first language (L1) phonological system and their stage of L1 phonological development when they start learning the TL, rather than neurophysiological maturation. This alternative hypothesis takes the form of various models of speech learning such as the Native Language Magnet (NLM) model (Kuhl, 1993), the Perceptual Assimilation Model (PAM) (Best, 1995), and the Speech Learning Model (SLM) (Flege, 1995), all of which examine learners acquiring the TL largely in L2 immersion settings.

In particular, a number of studies have looked at non-native speakers' (NNSs) perception and production of L2 segments within the framework of the SLM. As Flege (1995) points out, the basic assumption of the SLM is that phonetic learning ability remains intact across the lifespan, contrary to what the CPH predicts. The model also proposes an account of the differences observed in perception and production of L2 sounds by early and late learners. Thus, varying degrees of success in non-natives' perception and production of L2 sounds will depend upon whether learners identify L2 sounds as new or similar to a category in their L1 phonetic inventory (Flege, 1991a, 1995). What is more, Flege's model points to age 5–7 as the age at which L1 phonetic categories are established. Consequently, if L2 learning begins after that age, L2 learners will tend to identify TL vowel segments based on their L1 phonetic categories, while successful perception of TL consonant sounds might not be dependent on starting age of L2 learning. Although the SLM confers age of onset of L2 learning a significant role in determining the nativeness of perception and production of TL sounds, the relevance of starting age is directly related to the formation of L1 phonetic categories, and not related to the passing of a CP of any kind. Furthermore, based on the fact that learners maintain their phonetic learning ability, the SLM predicts that as non-natives' experience in the L2 increases, they may be able to discern phonetic differences between L1 and new L2 sounds, whereby a phonetic category for a new L2 sound may be established. The formation of an additional phonetic category, in turn, may lead to a more native-like perception and production of L2 segments, as shown by Flege *et al.* (1997).

As noted above, the SLM and other models of L2 speech learning focus on learners who have acquired the TL mostly in an L2 naturalistic setting. Besides, in the case of the SLM, the subjects under examination have reached their ultimate attainment in the L2 (Flege, 1995). In spite of this, the still incipient research in strictly formal instructional settings makes use of the hypotheses and premises of these models – mainly, the SLM and the PAM – to account for the foreign language (FL) learners' various degrees of native-like perception and production of TL sounds (e.g. Cebrian, 2002a, 2003; Cortés, 2002, 2003; Rallo, 2003).

Studies conducted in FL instruction environments have a common trait in that the subjects examined began learning the TL after the establishment of L1 phonetic categories (Bongaerts, 1999; Bongaerts *et al.*, 1997; Cortés, 2002; Elliott, 1995a, 1995b; Moyer, 1999; Rallo, 2003; cf. García-Lecumberri & Gallardo, 2003). While this fact could lead one to hypothesise that perception and production of TL sounds in a native-like fashion would be unattainable in a formal learning setting, studies such as Bongaerts *et al.* (1997) have shown that FL learners can attain native-like phonological skills in the TL despite a late starting age of FL learning.

One likely explanation for the latter findings has to do with the variable of exposure to (or experience in) the TL, which is often understood as the number of hours (or years) of instruction in the FL that the subjects have received in a classroom setting. Thus, FL learners' successful perception and/or production of certain FL sounds (in addition to their accent-free pronunciation of the TL) are thought to arise from explicit (phonetic) instruction in the FL.[2] This is particularly evident in studies looking at subjects who have pursued a university degree in the FL in question; for example, Spanish/Catalan native speakers (NSs) doing a degree in English Philology in their home country (Cebrian, 2003; Rallo, 2003)[3] and Dutch NSs studying or teaching English at the university level (Bongaerts et al., 1997).

On the other hand, in those investigations where exposure to the FL is even more limited – that is, research where subjects have not benefited from extra-curricular exposure to the FL and/or from spending time in the TL country – the effects of experience in the TL on the attainment of native-like perception and production skills in the FL are still inconclusive. For instance, García-Lecumberri and Gallardo (2003) found that after 6–7 years of instruction in English, Basque/Spanish NSs differing in starting age of FL learning (4, 8 and 11 years) did not perceive the FL vowel and consonant sounds at native-like levels. Nor were they successful in producing the English sounds accent-free. The authors go on to suggest that the lack of a clear beneficial effect of formal instruction emphasises the differences between formal learning and L2 immersion settings in the amount of input learners receive, being far much greater in the latter context. To be more precise, García-Lecumberri and Gallardo (2003) quote Singleton's (1995) estimation that 18 years of instruction in the FL in a formal setting would be needed to attain the same amount of exposure to the TL that is achieved after one year in an L2 naturalistic setting. Based on all this, they conclude that exposure to the TL has not been large enough to provide clear-cut evidence as to the attainment of native-like perception and production of FL sounds.

Another relevant aspect of the García-Lecumberri and Gallardo (2003) study to the present chapter is the finding of a late starting age advantage in the foreign accent (FA) and intelligibility scores learners obtained. In that case, 11-year-old beginners were rated as producing FL speech as less accented and more intelligible (though not at native-like levels) than 8-year-old and 4-year-old starters. Interestingly enough, those learners who still have not formed their L1 phonetic categories performed at the lowest range. Thus, in accordance with the yet rather limited research in FL formal settings, it then seems that late starting age is more beneficial to the successful attainment of FL phonological skills. However, together with the exposure effects reported above, the authors indicate that six to seven years of instruction in the FL are not sufficient for age differences to surface in the expected direction. That is, in an instructed-classroom learning context younger beginners have not had the time required to catch up to older starters, as shown in the Snow and Hoefnagel-Höhle (1977) study carried out in an L2 naturalistic setting. In fact, Snow and Hoefnagel-Höhle found that only after a period of 10–11 months of naturalistic exposure in The Netherlands, native English subjects with an earlier age of onset of L2 learning (3–5 year olds and 6–7 year olds) produced several

Dutch vowel sounds at higher correct rates than older learners (12–15-year-old and adult starters); whereas late beginners had obtained less accented scores when their exposure to Dutch was minimal and after a few weeks in the host country.[4]

Furthermore, García-Lecumberri and Gallardo (2003) suggest that a lack of a clear effect of exposure on the results obtained might be the result of the NNS input the subjects had received. The negative effect of NNS input on learners' successful perception and production of TL sounds has also been observed in L2 immersion contexts and operationalised as the "accented L2 input hypothesis" (Flege, 1991a). Thus, according to this hypothesis, regardless of an early starting age of L2 learning, learners will not be able to perceive and produce L2 sounds accurately if they have received accented input in the L2.

To sum up, research on FL learners in formal learning contexts within the L1 community is still more limited than in L2 naturalistic settings. Consequently, findings of starting age and exposure effects on the native-like attainment of (or failure to attain native-like) perception and production of FL sounds are still inconclusive.

Thus, the aim of the present chapter is to examine learners of English as an FL, who had been exclusively exposed to the TL in a formal language learning context. More precisely, the study looked at Spanish and Catalan NSs' perception and production of English sounds in an attempt (1) to determine the effect of different starting ages of FL learning – 8, 11, 14, 18+ years – on FL sound perception and production; and (2) to assess the factor of varying degrees of exposure to the TL – 200, 416 and 726 hours (corresponding to 2.5, 4.5 and 7.5 years on average) – in the different age groups' perception and production of specific English segments.

Method

Subjects

Subjects (Ss) in this study are part of the BAF Project at the *Universitat de Barcelona*, but, as stated in Chapter 1, only a smaller number of participants performed the oral tasks. To be exact, 281 Ss participated in the phonetic tasks.

Ss were distributed in 11 learner groups that differed in terms of onset age of FL learning (8, 11, 14 and 18+ years or groups A, B, C and D, respectively) and in the amount of formal exposure to the TL (200, 416 and 726 hours, or exposure Time 1, Time 2 and Time 3, respectively). It should be further emphasised that participants in this study were exclusively exposed to English in a school setting and had not spent any time in an English-speaking country. As for the Ss' L1, they were classified into three language groups based on a questionnaire they filled out: Spanish-dominant speakers, Catalan-dominant speakers, and Spanish/Catalan balanced bilinguals (see Chapter 1, this volume). Since all Ss lived in Catalonia, they had been exposed to both Spanish and Catalan, and so they were familiar with the phonology of both languages. Moreover, previous studies (Fullana & MacKay, 2002, 2003, 2004) showed a very similar performance on the phonetic tasks across the various language dominance groups. For all these reasons, the three language dominance groups' results will be considered jointly in this chapter.

In addition, a control group consisting of 13 NSs of British English (Native English group, henceforth NE group) was examined along with learners' production of English sounds. It is worth noting that fewer learners – 148 Ss – were finally looked at in the production task, for the quality of some recording sessions made it necessary to select those recordings with a signal-to-noise ratio (S/N) above 10 decibels (dB) for further study.[5]

The characteristics of all participant groups are summarised in Tables 2.1 and 2.2 (participants in the perception task and participants in the production task, respectively).

Speech materials

An auditory discrimination task and an imitation task were designed in order to test for the effects of starting age and exposure to the TL on the learners' perception and production of English sounds, respectively.

The perceptual task was a same-different (AX) discrimination task (Beddor & Gottfried, 1995). It consisted of 20 tape-recorded pairs of words produced by a female native speaker of Standard British English, in which the second word in each pair could be either the same as or different from the first word presented in the pair. Thirteen different word pairs were minimal pairs (8 pairs concentrated on vowel sound oppositions and

Table 2.1 Characteristics of learner groups in the perception task. Standard deviations are in parentheses

Group	N	Onset age (in years)	Exposure (in hours)	Gender[a]	Chronological age (in years)[b]	Grade[c]
A1	29	8	200	m 14, f 15	10.91 (0.28)	KS2 – Year 6
A2	36	8	416	m 18, f 18	12.99 (0.32)	KS3 – Year 8
A3	27	8	726	m 9, f 18	16.53 (0.37)	6th Form
B1	28	11	200	m 16, f 12	13.04 (0.36)	KS3 – Year 8
B2	29	11	416	m 11, f 18	15.01 (0.31)	KS4 – Year 10
B3	40	11	726	m 16, f 24	17.95 (0.29)	6th Form
C1	22	14	200	m 11, f 11	16.07 (0.47)	KS4 – Year 11
C2	7	14	416	m 3, f 4	18.70 (0.86)	6th Form
D1	49	18+	200	m 13, f 36	28.74 (7.90)	Year 2*
D2	10	18+	416	m 2, f 8	27.55 (5.59)	Year 4*
D3	4	18+	726	m 0, f 4	37.68 (10.19)	Year 5/6*

Notes: [a] m: male, f: female; [b] mean chronological age at testing; [c] subjects' grade at testing, *adult language school.

Table 2.2 Characteristics of learner groups in the production task. Standard deviations are in parentheses

Group	N	Onset age (in years)	Exposure (in hours)	Gender[a]	Chronological age (in years)[b]	Grade[c]
A1	17	8	200	m 11, f 6	10.97 (0.31)	KS2 – Year 6
A2	27	8	416	m 13, f 14	12.92 (0.29)	KS3 – Year 8
A3	13	8	726	m 7, f 6	16.61 (0.36)	6th Form
B1	13	11	200	m 5, f 8	13.09 (0.43)	KS3 – Year 8
B2	14	11	416	m 8, f 6	14.92 (0.30)	KS4 – Year 10
B3	15	11	726	m 10, f 5	18.04 (0.27)	6th Form
C1	13	14	200	m 6, f 6	16.14 (0.54)	KS4 – Year 11
C2	4	14	416	m 2, f 2	18.45 (0.86)	6th Form
D1	23	18+	200	m 18, f 5	28.62 (7.9)	Year 2*
D2	7	18+	416	m 5, f 2	26.25 (5.74)	Year 4*
D3	2	18+	726	m 0, f 2	45.79 (6.42)	Year 5/6*
NE	13	–	–	m 7, f 23	11.62 (13.98)	–

Notes: a m: male, f: female; b mean chronological age at testing; c subjects' grade at testing, *adult language school.

5 pairs contained consonant sound oppositions), and the remaining 7 pairs were distractors that were made up of pairs of the same word repeated twice.

The imitation task consisted of repeating a list of 34 English words presented in isolation by the same taped female model voice as in the AX discrimination task.

The majority of the sound oppositions included in the AX task and segments in the words of the imitation task looked at features of the English sound system that have been reported to be difficult or problematic for Spanish and/or Catalan learners of English when it comes to their successful perceptual discrimination and production, such as the tense/lax vowel distinction, word-final consonant voicing and consonant clusters in both word-initial and final position (e.g. Cebrian, 2002b; Coe, 1987; Flege, 1991b; Kenworthy, 1990; Recasens, 1984).

Listeners

Seven female NSs of General Canadian English participated in a subsequent study to assess learners' production of English segments in the imitation task (see Procedure below). They were 26.14 years old on average and reported normal hearing. Listeners, or judges, were either undergraduate or graduate students in Linguistics at the University of Ottawa (Canada). All had taken courses in phonetics and communication disorders. As for Spanish and Catalan, none of the judges was fluent in either of the two languages. In fact, no judge had heard of Catalan. At the most, all of the seven judges had taken Spanish courses at some point (between two months and two years). And only one judge had spent time in a Latin American Spanish-speaking country (two months).

Procedure

The auditory discrimination and imitation tasks constituted about 6 minutes of a 30-minute oral session that Ss performed (see Appendix 3). The two tasks and their stimulus presentation were in the same fixed order for all participants. In both cases learners were not provided with any practice or training beforehand and they did each task only once. Both tasks were first explained by the interviewer and later presented via tape-recorder. As for the AX task, learners were asked to say whether the pairs they heard were "the same" or "different". Regarding the imitation task, learners repeated a word immediately after hearing it as delivered on the tape by a female NS of Standard British English. Participants were told to proceed in the event that they missed identifying a pair or producing a word. Subjects' responses to the AX task and their imitations of English words were tape-recorded on school premises.

Answers to the AX discrimination task were calculated and then analysed by means of SPSS (Statistical Package for the Social Sciences) 11.0. In order to assess learners' productions of English words (and their corresponding segments), a further study was undertaken that had English NSs rate the Ss' production of English sounds for degree of FA and later identify the same English sounds in a 15-response forced-choice identification task. Due to the huge quantity of data collected, the latter study focused on seven English vowel segments /i, ɪ, ɛ, æ, ɒ, u, ʌ/ in 11 words.

Therefore to carry out the FA study and vowel identification task, the 11 words that contained English /i, ɪ, ɛ, æ, ɒ, u, ʌ/ were presented twice, each in different random blocks, to each judge through headphones via computer.[6] The first presentation of words, done in 11 sessions (one session per word) involved assigning a FA rating to each vowel sound on a nine-point scale of FA,[7] where 1 meant *native-like accent in English* and 9 stood for *very strong accent in English*. The second presentation of words, also done in 11 sessions, consisted of identifying the vowels that the subjects had produced in the same words (all tokens of a single word were presented in a single session). In this case, listeners had to choose among 15 possible response options presented on the computer screen. In all cases, judges had to give a FA rating on the specific segments and identify the vowel that best characterised each subject's production of the sound in question. The inter-stimulus interval was 1.5 seconds, although judges could listen to an item as many times as needed. In both parts of the task, judges were given specific instructions as well as five or ten practice items (for the FA rating and vowel identification tasks, respectively) at the beginning of each session. Unknown to the listeners, a random 25% of the total subjects' productions was added once the 161 imitations (148 learners and 13 English NSs) had been presented.

Among the possible response options "good", "slightly distorted" and "very distorted" instances of the specific segments were considered as correct identifications (e.g. [ɪ] good, [ɪ] slightly distorted, and [ɪ] very distorted for target /ɪ/), whereas the remaining vowel responses were considered misidentifications (e.g. [i], [ɪj], [e], and [ɛ], among others, for /ɪ/).

Analysis

The statistical package SPSS 11.0 for Windows was used to analyse the Ss' responses to the AX task and the judges' FA ratings and vowel identifications assigned to the learners' productions.

For three-group (or higher number of group) comparisons, Kruskal-Wallis analyses were performed on the correct discrimination scores, accent ratings and percent vowel identification scores (as dependent variables); and with onset age of FL learning and exposure to English as factors (one factor at a time). In the event of significant differences among groups, Mann-Whitney U tests were computed to locate between which two groups the differences occurred. For the accent and vowel identification results, inter-rater and intra-rater coefficients were also calculated prior to the statistical study of groups' performance on the production of English vowel segments.

For all the statistical analyses performed, the significance level was set at 0.05. Moreover, due to the large number of tests with the same subject-group comparisons, a rather conservative alpha level was adjusted accordingly, so that the experiment-wise error was held constant at 0.05.[8]

Results

AX task

Total correct discrimination scores on the AX task, in addition to correct discrimination scores on each vowel and consonant contrasts and distractors, are presented in Table 2.3.

A first look at the results shows that younger beginners, 8-year-old starters, discriminated sound contrasts at lower correct rates than the remaining age groups. In fact, starting age was found to be a significant factor in the overall discrimination scores and discrimination scores for vowel contrasts, according to Kruskal-Wallis analyses ($p < 0.05$). In all cases, 8-year-old starters with 200 and 416 hours of instruction in English obtained significantly lower correct discrimination scores than the other starting age groups. However, age differences became nonsignificant when all age groups' exposure to the FL amounted to 726 hours. As for the identification of consonant contrasts, a similar nonsignificant tendency was observed: younger starters with 200 hours of instruction discriminated consonant sound oppositions at lower rates. Unlike the discrimination of vowel contrasts, correct scores were fairly similar across the various age

Table 2.3 Overall mean correct discrimination scores on AX task, vowel and consonant sound contrasts, and distractors. For each type of contrast, both mean raw scores and mean per cent scores are provided

Group	All 20 pairs		Vowel contrasts (max: 8)		Consonant contrasts (max: 5)		Distractors (max: 7)	
	raw	%	raw	%	raw	%	raw	%
A1	13.97	69.85	5.34	66.75	1.86	37.20	6.76	96.57
A2	14.28	71.14	5.61	70.12	2.28	45.60	6.39	91.28
A3	16.04	80.20	6.56	82.00	2.85	57.00	6.63	94.71
B1	15.39	76.95	6.07	75.87	2.54	50.80	6.79	97.00
B2	15.28	76.40	6.62	82.75	2.24	44.80	6.41	91.57
B3	15.58	77.90	6.53	81.62	2.60	52.00	6.45	92.14
C1	15.36	76.80	6.68	83.50	2.23	44.60	6.45	92.14
C2	15.57	77.85	6.29	78.62	2.57	51.40	6.71	95.85
D1	15.90	79.50	6.73	84.12	2.53	50.60	6.63	94.71
D2	16.60	83.00	7.10	88.75	2.80	56.00	6.70	95.71
D3	15.00	75.00	6.50	81.25	2.50	50.00	6.00	85.71

groups when groups had received 416 hours of formal instruction. In other words, younger starters appeared to have caught up with older starters on consonant sound discrimination with less amount of formal exposure to English than on vowel sound discrimination. In any event, each learner group's overall discrimination scores on the task, as well as those of consonant and vowel contrasts, were for the most part non-native-like.

As for the effect of exposure on correct sound discrimination, it was barely noticeable, with the exception of 8-year-old beginners. That is, older starters discriminated the various types of sound contrasts on the AX task at similar rates regardless of their amount of experience in English. By contrast, learners with an onset age of 8 and with 726 hours of exposure to English obtained significantly higher correct discrimination scores on vowel contrasts than learners with 200 and 416 hours of instruction matched for starting age of FL learning. The same starting age group did also obtain higher correct discrimination scores on consonant contrasts along with an increase in experience, though differences in scores approached significance only ($p = 0.022$, adjusted $p > 0.05$).

Finally, it should be mentioned that all learner groups coincided with their rates of correct discrimination scores on each of the sounds examined: first, distractors were discriminated at higher rates than vowel and consonant contrasts. Vowel contrasts were, in turn, better discerned than consonant contrasts (see per cent columns in Table 2.3 above). Therefore, while all subject groups tended to concur with what type of contrast was discriminated correctly at higher rates, learners disagreed about the number of pairs and the specific contrasts that they found easy to discriminate in relation to other contrasts included in the task. Based on the criteria put forth in García-Lecumberri (1999) in order to classify sound contrasts according to their perceptual difficulty, a taxonomy of different degrees of difficulty by Spanish/Catalan NSs in the discrimination of English sounds included in the AX task (together with the results of the Cochran Q test as well as the frequencies computed) may be characterised in the following tentative way:[9]

(1) Sound contrasts that present no difficulty: 100% correct discrimination.
(2) Sound contrasts that present little difficulty: correct discrimination rate higher than 80% (and just below 100%).
(3) Sound contrasts that present some difficulty: correct discrimination rate between 65% and 80%.
(4) Sound contrasts that present a great deal of difficulty: correct discrimination rate below 65%.

Table 2.4 shows the distribution of the sound contrasts in the AX task into these four categories based on the perceived difficulty of 8- and 11-year-old beginners with differing degrees of exposure to English.

Table 2.4 Classification of sound contrasts by 8- and 11-onset age groups with 200 hours, 416 hours and 726 hours of formal exposure to English

Degree of perceived difficulty in discerning sound contrasts	8-year-old beginners (group A) sound contrasts		11-year-old beginners (group B) sound contrasts	
No difficulty: 100% correct discrimination	/æ/-/ɛ/[8,12]	A3	/æ/-/ɛ/[8,12]	B1[12], B2, B3
			/ɒ/-/ʌ/[7]	B2, B3
			/ɒ/-/ɑ/	B2
Little difficulty: 81%–99% correct discrimination	/æ/-/ɛ/[8,12]	A1, A2	/æ/-/ɛ/[8]	B1
	/ɒ/-/ʌ/[7,14]	A1, A2, A3	/ɒ/-/ʌ/[7,14]	B1, B2[14], B3[14]
	/ɒ/-/ɑ/	A2, A3	/ɒ/-/ɑ/	B1, B3
	/ɪ/-/ɛ/	A2, A3	/ɪ/-/ɛ/	B1, B2, B3
	/ɪ/-/i/[11]	A3		
	/b/-/v/	A3	/b/-/v/	B1, B3
Some difficulty: 65%–80% correct discrimination	/ɪ/-/ɛ/	A1	/ɪ/-/i/[11]	B3
	/ɒ/-/ɑ/	A1		
	/b/-/v/	A1	/b/-/v/	B2
	/ʒ/-/dʒ/	A2, A3	/ʒ/-/dʒ/	B1, B2, B3
High difficulty: below 65% correct discrimination	/i/-/ɪ/[1,11]	A1, A2, A3[1]	/i/-/ɪ/[1,11]	B1, B2, B3[1]
	/ʒ/-/dʒ/	A1		
	/b/-/v/	A2		
	/t/-/d/	A1, A2, A3	/t/-/d/	B1, B2, B3
	/b/-/p/	A1, A2, A3	/b/-/p/	B1, B2, B3
	/s/-/z/	A1, A2, A3	/s/-/z/	B1, B2, B3

Notes: 1 pair # 1 seat-sit; 7 pair # 7 gone-gun; 8 pair # 8 man-men; 11 pair # 11 still-steal; 12 pair # 12 bad-bed; 14 pair # 14 cop-cup.

As a whole, it can be seen that common to both age groups was the difficulty in perceiving the consonant voicing distinction in word-final position (/t/-/d/, /b/-/p/, and /s/-/z/ were correctly identified in less than 65% of instances), whereas they were better able to discern the voicing contrast in initial-word position (/b/-/v/) – in particular when both 8- and 11-year-old starters had reached 726 hours of formal instruction. As for vowel contrasts, two sound oppositions deserve further attention. On the one hand, the tense/lax vowel distinction /i/-/ɪ/ posed learners with the highest difficulty for their successful identification. And, on the other hand, /ɛ/-/æ/ sound opposition was by far the easiest contrast to perceive, as illustrated by the near-perfect (and often perfect) correct discrimination scores.

Imitation task

FA rating task

About 14,350 FA scores were obtained. Results reported in this section will focus on accent ratings on vowel sounds that have been most often studied in L2 phonological acquisition research, namely /i, ɪ, ɛ, æ/.[10] Moreover, due to the few subjects comprising some learner groups after the selection of recordings based on S/N values, the effects of onset age and exposure will be mainly discussed concerning two age groups: 8-year-old and 11-year-old starters.

First, intra-listener reliability was examined. It was found that intra-class coefficients were fairly high, frequently ranging from 0.75 to 0.85. Thus, judges were consistent within themselves in the ratings they assigned to those Ss' productions that were heard twice. However, inter-listener agreement was not always strong enough to allow for averaging judges' accent scores over a single mean accent rating. Despite this, the seven listeners always identified the control NE group accurately. In fact, FA ratings were significantly lower (less accented, or native-like in this case) than those of learner groups (mean range = 1.16–2.42 for NE group vs. 1.90–6.14 for learner groups[11]).

As far as FL learner groups are concerned, differences in accent scores as a function of starting age were nonsignificant, even though most judges tended to rate 8-year-old beginners' productions as more foreign-accented than 11-year-old starters.

With regard to the effects of instruction in English on learners' FA scores, an increase in formal exposure to the FL resulted in a higher (though not significant) degree of FA in 8-year-old starters' vowel productions. However, judges differed in their accent scores assigned to 11-year-old beginners as a result of an increase in experience. Thus, while some judges rated those Ss' productions as less foreign-accented along with an increase in experience, the other remaining judges considered that 11-year-old beginners produced vowel sounds as more foreign-accented as they gained experience in the FL.

When looking at the FA scores on the four English vowels /i, ɪ, ɛ, æ/ (Table 2.5), it can be observed that age of onset and exposure had no conclusive effects (see Figures 2.1 and 2.2). Two findings are worth mentioning here. First, all learner groups' vowel productions were generally rated as medium foreign-accented. Second, ratings on /ɛ/[12] and /æ/ were nearly always higher (more foreign-accented) than those of /i/ and /ɪ/, which somehow contradicts the perceptual discrimination scores obtained for these two sound contrasts.

Table 2.5 Ss' FA ratings on English /i, ɪ, ɛ, æ/ (averaged over 7 judges)

Groups	/i/	/ɪ/	/ɛ/	/æ/
A1	3.67	3.57	4.14	3.92
A2	4.07	4.13	4.12	4.64
A3	3.73	4.14	4.31	5.21
B1	3.62	4.57	4.18	4.85
B2	4.10	3.96	4.56	4.26
B3	3.95	3.77	4.01	4.46
NE	1.46	1.27	1.53	1.73

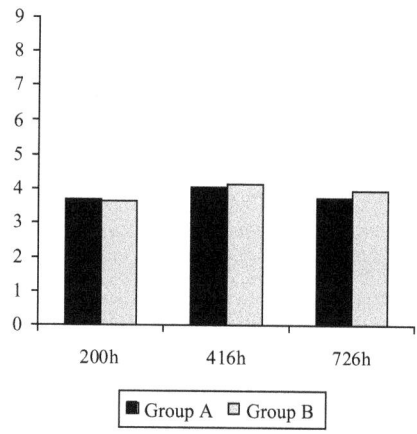

Figure 2.1 FA Ratings on /i/ is a function of onset age and exposure

Vowel identification task

As in the FA rating task above, about 14,350 vowel identifications were collected, of which only those of 8-year-old and 11-year-old beginners on /i, ɪ, ɛ, æ/ will be presented.

Intra-listener consistency was computed, mostly resulting in acceptable coefficients (about 0.70) for each judge. Based on the procedure followed

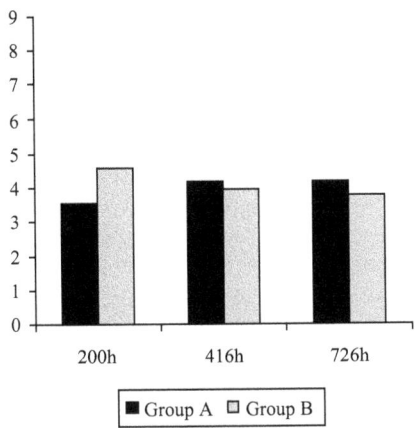

Figure 2.2 FA ratings on /ɪ/ as a function of onset age and exposure

in Flege *et al.* (1997), vowel identification scores derived from the percentage of times each target vowel was identified correctly by the seven judges. By the same token, misidentification patterns (or sound substitutions or mispronunciations) for each /i/, /ɪ/, /ɛ/, and /æ/ were obtained by counting the number of times other responses than the target vowel were chosen (heard) instead, which were then converted to percentage scores.

The NE group obtained significantly higher vowel identification scores than learners (mean range = 89.01%–98.35% for the control group vs. 38.46%–89.67% for FL learner groups). In this case, learners' /ɛ/s were identified at high correct rates and very similar to those of English foils; hence the high mean range endpoint (89.67%), though still significantly lower than that of native English participants (98.35%) (see also Table 2.6).

Table 2.6 Ss' per cent correct identification scores on English /i, ɪ, ɛ, æ/ (see also note 13)

Groups	/i/	/ɪ/	/ɛ/	/æ/
A1	69.74	60.5	83.61	61.76
A2	64.54	56.87	89.67	55.55
A3	64.28	55.16	88.45	46.70
B1	69.22	51.64	86.26	47.79
B2	64.53	68.82	89.28	69.38
B3	61.90	57.14	89.04	60.47
NE	92.85	97.80	98.35	89.01

As far as Ss' starting age is concerned, no significant differences were found in correct vowel identification scores between 8- and 11-year-old beginners. Nor were there any significant differences between groups as a function of exposure to the FL. Moreover, no clear effects of either age of onset of FL learning or exposure to English could be observed, for different results were obtained depending on the sound examined. For instance, in Figure 2.3 it can be seen that starting age was not a significant factor in the production of /ɛ/, as both groups obtained correct vowel identification scores at high frequency rates (83.61%–89.28%). In contrast, divergent exposure effects were found in learners' production of /æ/: 8-year-old starters produced /æ/ at lower correct rates as they gained experience in English; whereas 11-year-old starters' /æ/s tended to be progressively identified as the target sound at higher rates as a result of an increase in formal instruction (Figure 2.4).

Lastly, the misidentification patterns obtained for /i, ɪ, ɛ, æ/ were consistent with previous findings (e.g. Cebrian, 2003; Flege *et al.*, 1997). Therefore, it was observed that for target /i/ subjects often produced [i] and [ɪ]; for /ɪ/ learners pronounced [i] and [ij]; [a] and [ɑ] were common substitutes for /æ/; while [i] and [e] substituted to a lesser extent for target /ɛ/.

Discussion and Conclusions

The present chapter aimed to determine the effects of onset age of FL learning and exposure to the TL on the perception of both English vowel and consonant segments and the production of English vowel sounds, specifically /i, ɪ, ɛ, æ/, by Spanish/Catalan learners of English as an FL in an instructed-classroom learning setting. Therefore, it was examined

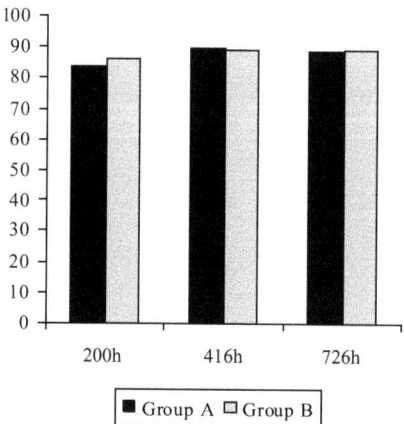

Figure 2.3 Per cent correct identification scores on /ɛ/ as a function of onset age and exposure

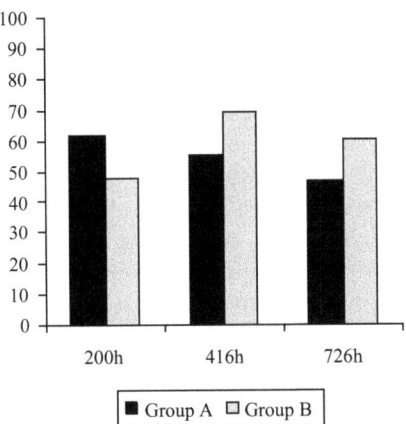

Figure 2.4 Per cent correct identification scores on /æ/ as a function of onset age and exposure

whether the factors of starting age and experience in the TL as characterised by the SLM would prevail in a situation where subjects are not immersed in the L2-speaking community. That is, even if Ss had been first exposed to English after the formation of L1 phonetic categories, it was hypothesised that early starters (age 8) would perceive and produce English segments better than late starters (ages 11, 14 and 18+). Moreover, based on the SLM's postulates, it was expected that an increase in formal instruction would lead to a better discernment of English segments, and, in turn, to their more native-like production. Taking all this into account, the present study was undertaken to further investigate the factors of starting age and exposure in a formal learning environment. Finally, as mentioned above, learners were not considered separately according to their language dominance (Spanish-dominant, Catalan-dominant, and Spanish-Catalan balanced bilinguals), for they performed on a similar basis.

Age and exposure effects on the perception of FL sounds

Results on the AX task showed that generally older starters (11- and 14-year-old and adult beginners) discriminated English vowel and consonant contrasts at higher correct rates than younger learners (8-year-old starters), which is in agreement with findings of a late starting age advantage in FL learning contexts (e.g. García-Lecumberri & Gallardo, 2003). Likewise, the lack of a significant effect of exposure on older starters' discrimination of English sound contrasts – namely, learner groups varied (improved) very little in their discrimination scores as instruction increased – is in line with García-Lecumberri and Gallardo's (2003) observations. All these results would not seem to support the predictions of the SLM as applied to a different learning context. However, younger learners discriminated both vowel and consonant sound contrasts at increasingly higher rates as they gained experience in the FL. Particularly, 8-year-old starters were reported to have caught up with the remaining older beginner groups on the discrimination of consonant contrasts when they had received 416 hours of instruction, and they even discerned consonant contrasts at slightly (nonsignificant) higher rates than older learners when exposure to the FL amounted to 726 hours (see Table 2.3 above). The finding of younger learners' catching up and even surpassing older starters after a longer period of exposure to the TL agrees with Snow and Hoefnagel-Höhle's (1977) naturalistic study. Moreover, this result partly corroborates the experience effect as predicted by SLM – only "partly" as younger learners did not perceive TL sound contrasts at native-like levels, nor did the gain in experience result in significant differences in the discrimination scores between learners with the same onset age of FL learning and varying degrees of experience.

Failure to discriminate FL segment contrasts at native-like levels was noted not only for younger starters but also for older starters. As shown in Table 2.4 above, all learner groups had a great deal of difficulty perceiving the consonant voicing distinction in word-final position, regardless of starting age and amount of exposure. In any case, this finding is consistent with results of studies conducted on Spanish and Catalan learners of English in L2 naturalistic settings (e.g. Flege *et al.*, 1992; Cebrian, 2000).

As for the discrimination of vowel sounds, learners exhibited different degrees of successful discernment of English vowels according to specific vowel contrasts. Thus, like findings of NNSs of English in L2 immersion settings, such as those Flege *et al.* (1997) reported on native Spanish subjects, and Cebrian (2002a) on Catalan learners of English, Ss in this study correctly discriminated /ɛ/–/æ/ nearly in 100% of instances. This result also agreed with studies examining Catalan NSs with a higher amount of exposure in a formal setting (Cebrian, 2003; Rallo, 2003). In spite of this, results on /ɛ/–/æ/ might alternatively be interpreted as in Flege (1991b) – i.e. learners successfully identified /ɛ/–/æ/ not because they had previously formed a new phonetic category for these two sounds, but because they identified them with Spanish /e/ and /a/ vowels, respectively (see results on production of /ɛ/ and /æ/ above, as well). Likewise, the same argument (Flege, 1991b) might account for FL learners' high successful discrimination rates for the /ɪ/–/ɛ/ contrast – that is, English /ɪ/ and /ɛ/ were likely to have been identified with Spanish/Catalan /i/ and /e/, respectively, hence the high correct discrimination scores obtained (see also Cebrian, 2002a). At the other end of the scale, Spanish/Catalan learners of English had difficulty in discriminating the tense/lax vowel contrast /i/–/ɪ/, no matter their starting age of FL learning or amount of exposure. In this case, the per cent correct discrimination rate in all learner groups was below 65%, which might as well suggest that FL learners identified both /i/ and /ɪ/ as Spanish/Catalan /i/, based on the misidentification patterns the same subjects displayed on the vowel identification task (see Results section above), in addition to the various findings of learners acquiring the L2 in immersion settings that have reported on Spanish learners' non-native-like perception of English contrast /i/–/ɪ/ (e.g. Flege, 1991b; Flege *et al.*, 1997). On a more positive note, it should be noted that a longer exposure to the FL seemed to help older learners perceive the tense/lax vowel distinction /i/–/ɪ/ at better correct rates (11-year-old beginners with 726 hours of instruction discriminated /i/–/ɪ/ between 65% and 80% of the time, whereas with less amount of exposure the same age group, as well as younger learners, scored below 65% correct discrimination rates). This improvement in the discrimination of difficult English vowel contrasts seemed to be consistent with findings of FL learners that have received a larger amount of (and often explicit phonetic) instruction in the TL, such as the undergraduate students of English examined in Cebrian (2003) and Rallo (2003). In the same way, younger learners (with an onset age of 8) benefited from an increase in formal instruction as after 726 hours of instruction they were better able to discriminate English vowel contrasts /ɒ/–/ʌ/ and /ɒ/–/ɑ/ that from the start posed little problems or no difficulty whatsoever to older beginners (see Table 2.4).

In summary, starting age did not provide clear-cut evidence as to the perception of FL sounds in a formal learning context by Spanish and Catalan learners of English. Thus, while older starters tended to discriminate English sounds more accurately in the short- and mid-term, younger learners discerned sound contrasts at slightly better rates in the long-term. Besides, in neither case did any age group perform within the NS range. Exposure effects were inconclusive as well, as far as discrimination of English vowel and consonant contrasts were concerned.

Age and exposure effects on the production of FL sounds

Based on the FA ratings obtained (Table 2.5 above), a first preliminary conclusion that might be drawn is that late starting age in a formal learning context results in a less accented production of English vowels. However, this observation should be taken with caution for a number of reasons. First, 11-year-old starters did not produce English /i, ɪ, ɛ, æ/ with a significant lower degree of FA than 8-year-old beginners. Rather, in those instances where age groups' scores happened to differ by a point on the FA scale, it was to the younger learners' advantage (e.g. 3.57 and 4.57 on /ɪ/ for A1 and B1, respectively). Second, as in García-Lecumberri and Gallardo (2003) and Snow and Hoefnagel-Höhle (1977), none of the age groups' vowel productions were rated as native-like, which in turn did not favour any firm conclusion as to a late starting age advantage in the learning of an FL phonology. Third, listeners varied in the accent ratings assigned to each learner group, which was consistent with previous studies conducted in L2 naturalistic settings (e.g. Munro *et al.*, 1996). While judges' failure to reach a high degree of inter-listener agreement might question the validity of their ratings on learners' vowel productions, it did not seem to be the case in this study.[13] On the one hand, all seven judges performed as expected in that they identified the control group at native-like rates. On the other hand, this variability in accent ratings assigned to a given age group might result from the own Ss' characteristics. It has been reported that six to seven years of instruction in a formal setting do not equal the amount of exposure that a learner receives for six to seven years in an L2 immersion setting (García-Lecumberri & Gallardo, 2003; Singleton, 1995). Thus, the largest amount of instruction the subjects in the present study had received (726 hours, which corresponded to an average of 7.5 years of school instruction), together with subjects' starting ages – 8 and 11 (past the age at which L1 phonetic categories have been formed) – was not large enough to bring about noticeable differences (if any) in accent scores, and therefore the nine-point scale of FA listeners were asked to use might have been too detailed.

As was the case of onset age of FL learning, exposure to English did not yield conclusive results. Mixed exposure effects were particularly evident when /ɪ/ and /æ/ (often tentatively classified as new TL sounds in Flege *et al.*'s research) were considered. Therefore, while 11-year-old beginners produced both vowels with a lower degree of FA as their exposure to English increased, 8-year-old beginners' /ɪ/ and /æ/ productions were rated as more foreign-accented along with an increase in experience.

A final comment about accent ratings has to do with the more foreign-accented ratings that learner groups obtained for /ɛ/ and /æ/ in contrast to those of /i/ and /ɪ/, which came as a surprise based on the perceptual findings mentioned above and elsewhere (e.g. Cebrian, 2002a, 2003). As was hypothesised earlier, this finding might indicate that learners had not established an additional phonetic category for /ɛ/ and /æ/; hence, perception and production were not based on the same parameters as those of English NSs. However, assuming that new phonetic categories had been formed, the results might be interpreted in light of the SLM, as well, since successful perception of L2 sounds does not necessarily entail their native-like production. This is especially relevant in those cases where learners have received accented L2 input (Flege, 1991a, García-Lecumberri & Gallardo, 2003). Similarly, learners in this study had likely received accented input in the FL,[14] which then might have led them to pronounce the vowel sounds with an inevitable degree of FA.

Much of the same inconclusive evidence as to starting age and exposure effects on FL learners' production of English vowels resulted from the correct identification scores the seven judges assigned to subjects on the vowel identification task. That is, no learner group consistently obtained higher or lower per cent identification scores as a function of onset age of

FL learning or exposure to English, corroborating findings of studies conducted within the same type of learning context (García-Lecumberri & Gallardo, 2003). Moreover, under no circumstances were the differences in vowel identification scores between the two age groups significant. Despite this, the identification rates and misidentification patterns for /i, ɪ, ɛ, æ/ found were consistent with findings of either Spanish or Catalan learners of English acquiring the TL in an L2 naturalistic setting (e.g. Cebrian, 2002a; Flege *et al.*, 1997).

Finally, the identification scores Spanish and Catalan learners obtained on /ɛ/ should be taken as further evidence about the lack of clear-cut effects of starting age and exposure on the production of English vowels by FL learners in a formal learning context. In this case, both age groups produced /ɛ/ at similar high rates, closely resembling those of the control group. While this would be an expected result, based on previous research (e.g. Cebrian, 2002a; Flege *et al.*, 1997; Rallo, 2003) and findings of the AX task reported above, these results are difficult to reconcile with the same Ss' results obtained on the accent rating task.

To sum up, age of onset of FL learning (in particular, starting ages of 8 and 11) and exposure (200, 416 and 726 hours) were not conclusive determinants for perceiving and producing English sounds in a native-like manner in a formal language learning context. At the most, late starting age tended to result in a somewhat better perception and production of English segments in the short, mid, and long term of the present study, as noted by García-Lecumberri and Gallardo (2003) and Snow and Hoefnagel-Höhle (1977). Moreover, the lack of a definite effect of exposure on the attainment of native-like perception and production of FL sounds should not be regarded as an irrelevant factor in FL phonological acquisition. Rather, it should be considered along with observations stated between the differences in quantity and quality of input delivered in L2 immersion settings and formal instruction contexts (Singleton, 1995). Furthermore, an increase in exposure to NS input, especially in the form of explicit phonetic instruction, has proven to be beneficial in formal language learning contexts (Piske *et al.*, 2001; Rallo, 2003). Thus, further research should be conducted to assess how larger amounts of instruction in the TL and of exposure to native-like input influence Spanish/Catalan NSs' perception and production of English sounds in the final stages of FL acquisition. In addition, these differences in quantity and quality of exposure should be examined in order to determine whether they favour a late starting age of FL learning in formal instruction learning settings, as the available findings to date seem to suggest.

Acknowledgements

The author would like to thank Professor Ian R.A. MacKay of the University of Ottawa for his suggestion to conduct a pilot study of FA when data collection had yet to be completed, as well as providing guidance and resources to carry out all the subsequent accent and vowel identification studies reported in this chapter and Fullana (2005). Thanks are also due to N. Rivera and M. Alambillaga for help collecting the English control group data. This work was supported by doctoral research grant *Beca de Formació en la Recerca i la Docència (Universitat de Barcelona)* and "la Caixa" and the Canadian Studies Foundation Scholarship (Spain) to the author; and Grants PB94-0944, PB97-0901, and BFF2001-3384 from the Ministry of Education in Spain to the BAF Project (*Universitat de Barcelona*).

Notes

1. As in Birdsong (1999) and Patkowski (1994), in this chapter the term *critical* is used in a broad sense that includes other (and perhaps more accurate) notions such as *sensitive* period and *optimal* period.
2. Other variables investigated that appear to play a role in the native-like attainment of FL phonological skills are learners' motivation and the fact that learners' L1 is typologically related to the TL under study (e.g. Dutch and English in the Bongaerts *et al.* study, 1997, and German and English in Moyer, 1999).
3. In addition, subjects in those studies had spent at least a few months (range = 3 months–1 year) in an English-speaking country, which entails a larger amount of exposure to the TL and in an L2 naturalistic setting.
4. It is also worth noting that, in Snow and Hoefnagel-Höhle's (1977) laboratory study, 15–17-year-old and adult English NSs with no prior exposure to the TL received lower accent scores (less accented) on the production of the same Dutch segments included in the naturalistic study than 5- to 7-year-old participants.
5. See Fullana (2005) for how the actual measurements of signal and noise present in the recordings were made and reasons why taking this course of action was necessary.
6. The design and implementation of the FA study and vowel identification task via computer were possible thanks permission to use WNSPARCS (Smith, 1997). This software was developed for use in James E. Flege's laboratory and those of his coinvestigators, including Ian R.A. MacKay.
7. Southwood and Flege (1999) (see also Piske *et al.*, 2001) recommend using FA scales of 9 to 11 points, based on the findings of their study in which listeners successfully partitioned nonnatives' production of TL speech into 9 degrees of foreign accent.
8. For more details on the adjustment of alpha levels, see Fullana (2005).
9. The classification of degree of perceptual difficulty of English sound contrasts should be considered on a tentative basis, since each specific sound contrast was presented in very few instances of the AX task. Therefore, further studies examining a larger number of the various sound contrasts delivered within the same task would be desirable to deem the taxonomy outlined above to be conclusive.
10. Results for other vowel sounds examined (/ɒ, u, ʌ/) are reported elsewhere (Fullana, 2005).
11. In general, judge 2 tended to rate both foils' and learners' vowel productions with a lower degree of FA (most frequent points used on the accent scale ranged from 1 to 5) than the remaining six judges. Thus, the mean accent rating of 1.90 observed for learner groups (B1, to be exact) corresponds to judge 2's

averaged rating on B1's production of English vowels. Even then, judge 2's differences in accent ratings on vowel sounds between B1 and NE (control group) (M = 1.90 and 1.28, respectively) were significant.
12. For the sake of clarity, accent ratings on /ɛ/ (produced in the words *red* and *tests*) have been averaged into one single rating in Table 2.5, though the differences in accent scores between /ɛ/ in *red* and /ɛ/ in *tests* were significant (the latter being rated as significantly more foreign-accented than the former). Similarly, the correct vowel identification scores on /i/ and /ɪ/ presented in Table 2.6 have been averaged, in spite of being statistically different: /i/ in *speak* was correctly identified at significantly higher rates than /i/ in *tea*; while /ɪ/ in *it* was identified at significantly higher correct rates than /ɪ/ in *this*. These differences might be the result of the part the surrounding phonetic context might have played in FL learners' production of target vowel sounds (Cebrian, 2002a; Fullana, 2005).
13. Recall the finding of high intra-listener consistency coefficients (about 0.75 and 0.85). In addition, on many occasions inter-listener correlation analyses yielded acceptable coefficients (about 0.70).
14. See Naves and Muñoz (1999) for an account of training characteristics common to teachers of English in the Spanish educational system.

References

Asher, J.J. and García, R. (1969) The optimal age to learn a foreign language. Reprinted in S.D. Krashen, R.C. Scarcella and M.H. Long (eds) (1982) *Child-adult Differences in Second Language Acquisition* (pp. 3–12). Rowley, MA: Newbury House.

Beddor, P.S. and Gottfried, T.L. (1995) Methodological issues in cross-language speech perception research with adults. In W. Strange (ed.) *Speech Perception and Linguistic Experience: Issues in Cross-language Research* (pp. 207–232). Timonium, MD: York Press.

Best, C.T. (1995) A direct realist view of cross-language speech perception. In W. Strange (ed.) *Speech Perception and Linguistic Experience: Issues in Cross-language Research* (pp. 171–204). Timonium, MD: York Press.

Birdsong, D. (1999) Introduction: Whys and why nots of the Critical Period Hypothesis for second language acquisition. In D. Birdsong (ed.) *Second Language Acquisition and the Critical Period Hypothesis* (pp. 1–22). Mahwah, NJ: Lawrence Erlbaum.

Bongaerts, T. (1999) Ultimate attainment in L2 pronunciation: The case of very advanced late learners. In D. Birdsong (ed.) *Second Language Acquisition and the Critical Period Hypothesis* (pp. 133–159). Mahwah, NJ: Lawrence Erlbaum.

Bongaerts, T., van Summeren, C., Planken, B. and Schils, E. (1997) Age and ultimate attainment in the pronunciation of a foreign language. *Studies in Second Language Acquisition* 19, 447–465.

Cebrian, J. (2000) Transferability and productivity of L1 rules in Catalan-English interlanguage. *Studies in Second Language Acquisition* 22, 1–26.

Cebrian, J. (2002a) Acquiring a new vowel contrast: The perception of English tense and lax vowels by native Catalan subjects. In A. James and J. Leather (eds) *New Sounds 2000. Proceedings of the Fourth International Symposium on the Acquisition of Second-language Speech* (pp. 48–57). Amsterdam: University of Klagenfurt.

Cebrian, J. (2002b) Phonetic similarity and acoustic cue reliance in the perception of a second language contrast. In M. Barrio, M.H. Cuenca, J. Díaz, L.F. Rodríguez and J.A. Vidal (eds) *Actas del II Congreso de Fonética Experimental* (pp. 124–128). Sevilla: Universidad de Sevilla.

Cebrian, J. (2003) Input and experience in the perception of an L2 temporal and spectral contrast. In D. Recansens, M.J. Solé and J. Romero (eds) *Proceedings of the 15th International Congress of Phonetic Sciences* (pp. 2297–2300). Barcelona/Australia: Causal Productions.

Coe, N. (1987) Speakers of Spanish and Catalan. In M. Swan and B. Smith (eds) *Learner English* (pp. 72–89). Cambridge: Cambridge University Press.

Cortés, S.M. (2002) Acquisition of two sounds by Catalan speakers. In A. James and J. Leather (eds) *New Sounds 2000. Proceedings of the Fourth International Symposium on the Acquisition of Second-language Speech* (pp. 67–71). Amsterdam: University of Klagenfurt.

Cortés, S.M. (2003) Transfer in L2 sound production. In D. Recansens, M.J. Solé and J. Romero (eds) *Proceedings of the 15th International Congress of Phonetic Sciences* (pp. 1097–1100). Barcelona/Australia: Causal Productions.

Elliott, A.R. (1995a) Field independence/dependence, hemispheric specialization, and attitude in relation to pronunciation accuracy in Spanish as a foreign language. *The Modern Language Journal* 79, 356–371.

Elliott, A.R. (1995b) Foreign language phonology: Field independence, attitude and the success of formal instruction in Spanish pronunciation. *The Modern Language Journal* 79, 530–542.

Flege, J.E. (1991a) Perception and production: The relevance of phonetic input to L2 phonological learning. In T. Huebner and C.A. Ferguson (eds) *Crosscurrents in Second Language Acquisition and Linguistic Theories* (pp. 249–290). Philadelphia: John Benjamins.

Flege, J.E. (1991b) The interlingual identification of Spanish and English vowels: Orthographic evidence. *The Quarterly Journal of Experimental Psychology* 43, 701–731.

Flege, J.E. (1995) Second language speech learning: Theory, findings and problems. In W. Strange (ed.) *Speech Perception and Linguistic Experience* (pp. 229–273). Timonium, MD: York Press.

Flege, J.E. (2003) Assessing constraints on second-language segmental production and perception. In A. Meyer and N. Schiller (eds) *Phonetics and Phonology in Language Comprehension and Production: Differences and Similarities* (pp. 319–355). Berlin: Mouton de Gruyter.

Flege, J.E., Bohn, O.-S. and Jang, S. (1997) Effects of experience on non-native speakers' production and perception of English vowels. *Journal of Phonetics* 25, 437–470.

Flege, J.E., Munro, M. J. and Skelton, L. (1992) Production of the word-final English /t/–/d/ contrast by native speakers of English, Mandarin, and Spanish. *Journal of the Acoustical Society of America* 92, 128–143.

Fullana, N. (2005) Age-related effects on the acquisition of a foreign language phonology in a formal setting. Unpublished PhD dissertation, Universitat de Barcelona, Spain.

Fullana, N. and MacKay, I.R.A. (2002) A study of foreign accent in Spanish and Catalan speakers production of English words: Preliminary evidence. In M. Barrio, M.H. Cuenca, J. Díaz, L.F. Rodríguez and J.A. Vidal (eds) *Actas del II Congreso de Fonética Experimental* (pp. 198–203). Sevilla: Universidad de Sevilla.

Fullana, N. and MacKay, I.R.A. (2003) Production of English sounds by EFL learners: The case of /i/ and /I/. In D. Recansens, M.J. Solé and J. Romero (eds) *Proceedings of the 15th International Congress of Phonetic Sciences* (pp. 1525–1528). Barcelona/Australia: Causal Productions.

Fullana, N. and MacKay, I.R.A. (2004) FL learners' production of English vowel sounds: Effects of starting age and formal instruction on the degree of FA. Paper presented at the XIV EUROSLA Conference, San Sebastián, Spain.

García-Lecumberri, M.L. (1999) Influencia del tratamiento fonético en la percepción de vocales inglesas en una situación de L2. In J. de las Cuevas and D. Fasla (eds) *Contribuciones al Estudio de la Lingüística Aplicada* (pp. 181–188). Logroño: Gráficas Ochoa.

García-Lecumberri, M.L. and Gallardo, F. (2003) English FL sounds in school learners of different ages. In M.P. García-Mayo and M.L. García-Lecumberri (eds) *Age and the Acquisition of English as a Foreign Language* (pp. 115–135). Clevedon: Multilingual Matters.

Ioup, G., Boustagui, E., Tigi, M.E. and Moselle, M. (1994) Reexamining the critical period hypothesis: A case study of successful adult SLA in a naturalistic environment. *Studies in Second Language Acquisition* 16, 73–98.

Kenworthy, J. (1990) *Teaching English Pronunciation.* London: Longman.

Kuhl, P.K. (1993) Early linguistic experience and phonetic perception: Implications for theories of developmental speech perception. *Journal of Phonetics* 21, 125–139.

Lenneberg, E.H. (1967) *Biological Foundations of Language.* New York: Wiley.

Long, M.H. (1990) Maturational constraints on language development. *Studies in Second Language Acquisition* 12, 251–285.

Moyer, A. (1999) Ultimate attainment in L2 phonology. *Studies in Second Language Acquisition* 21, 81–108.

Munro, M.J., Flege, J.E. and MacKay, I.R.A. (1996) The effects of age of second language learning on the production of English vowels. *Applied Psycholinguistics* 17, 313–334.

Naves, T. and Muñoz, C. (1999) The implementation of CLIL in Spain. In D. Marsh and G. Langé (eds) *Implementing Content and Language Integrated Learning* (pp. 145–157). Jyväskylä: Continuing Education Centre.

Oyama, S. (1976) A sensitive period for the acquisition of a nonnative phonological system. Reprinted in S.D. Krashen, R.C. Scarcella and M.H. Long (eds) (1982) *Child-adult Differences in Second Language Acquisition* (pp. 20–38). Rowley, MA: Newbury House.

Patkwoski, M.S. (1994) The Critical Age Hypothesis and interlanguage phonology. In M. Yavas (ed.) *First and Second Language Phonology* (pp. 205–221). San Diego, CA: Singular.

Piske, T., MacKay, I.R.A. and Flege, J.E. (2001) Factors affecting degree of perceived foreign accent in an L2: A review. *Journal of Phonetics* 29, 191–215.

Rallo, L. (2003) Learning a second language influences perception of L1 sounds. In D. Recansens, M.J. Solé and J. Romero (eds) *Proceedings of the 15th International Congress of Phonetic Sciences* (pp. 1517–1519). Barcelona/Australia: Causal Productions.

Recasens, D. (1984) *Estudi Comparatiu de la Fonètica Segmental del Català i de l'Anglès.* Barcelona: Edicions ICE.

Scovel, T. (1988) *A Time to Speak. A Psycholinguistic Inquiry into the Critical Period for Human Speech.* Rowley, MA: Newbury House.

Singleton, D. (1995) A critical look at the Critical Period Hypothesis in second language acquisition. In D. Singleton and Z. Lengyel (eds) *The Age Factor in Second Language Acquisition. A Critical Look at the Critical Period Hypothesis* (pp. 1–29). Clevedon: Multilingual Matters.

Smith, V. (1997) *Windows Stimulus Presentation and Response Collection System (WNSPARCS).* University of Alabama, Birmingham

Snow, C. and Hoefnagel-Höhle, M. (1977) Age differences in the pronunciation of foreign sounds. Reprinted in S.D. Krashen, R.C. Scarcella, and M.H. Long (eds) (1982), *Child–adult Differences in Second Language Acquisition* (pp. 84–92). Rowley, MA: Newbury House.

Southwood, M.H. and Flege, J.E. (1999) Scaling foreign accent: Direct magnitude estimation versus interval scaling. *Clinical Linguistics & Phonetics* 13, 335–349.

Tahta, S., Wood, M. and Loewenthal, K. (1981) Foreign accents: Factors relating to transfer of accent from the first language to a second language. *Language and Speech* 24, 265–272.

Chapter 3

Age Effects on Oral Fluency Development

JOAN C. MORA

Introduction

The notion of fluency as an essential aspect of the oral performance of second and foreign language (L2) learners is a complex one, as suggested by the fact that native speakers' fluency ratings of learner speech are not based on a single invariant measure, but rely, according to raters' self-reports, on a variety of interacting factors, such as speed of delivery, the presence of hesitation phenomena, lexical variety and accuracy, and proficient use of syntactic and semantic resources (Kormos & Dénes, 2004; Riggenbach, 1991). From the perspective of L2 teaching, fluency is a notion often identifying a type of language learning task oriented towards spontaneous language use, as opposed to accuracy-oriented learning activities that focus on the correctness of the linguistic structures used (Brumfit, 2000). Within the communicative approach to language teaching that became widespread in the 1970s and 1980s (Wesche & Skehan, 2002), this notion of fluency has become such a prevailing aspect of language learning that L2 fluent speech often becomes equated with learners' success in L2 acquisition.

The complex nature of fluency was captured by Fillmore's (1979: 93) multi-dimensional definition of the term, which comprises a speakers' ability to "fill time with talk", "talk in coherent, reasoned and 'semantically dense' sentences", "have appropriate things to say in a wide variety of contexts" and "be creative and imaginative in their language use". The four dimensions of fluency Fillmore identified (uninterrupted delivery of speech, coherence, appropriateness and creativity) are implicitly included in comprehensive as well as specific approaches to fluency evaluation and may manifest themselves independently in speakers, who may be fluent in one way but not in another. Lennon's (2000: 26) working definition of fluency as "the rapid, smooth, accurate, lucid and efficient translation of thought or communicative intention into language under the temporal constraints of on-line processing", provides us with one further assertion of the variety of factors oral fluency is built on. Although these broad-focus definitions of fluency are meant to characterise L2 spoken language performance, they could be equally applied to characterise L2 learners' written production or speakers' oral and written fluency in their first language (L1), as they do not make any explicit assumptions as regards the type of language or language user whose speech is being characterised. This chapter, however, is mainly concerned with the analysis of the oral productions of learners of English as a foreign language (EFL) and the assessment of L2 oral fluency development through a quantitative analysis of their temporal properties.

Approaches to L2 Oral Fluency Analysis

The multi-faceted nature of oral fluency allows for a diversity of qualitative and quantitative analyses of speech production from multiple perspectives: linguistic as well as psycholinguistic and sociolinguistic. Approaches to second language oral fluency analysis have focused on a great variety of fluency-predicting phenomena (see the overviews in Chambers, 1997; Kormos & Dénes, 2004; and Riggenbach, 2000), and have done so from two main interrelated perspectives: a psycholinguistic approach and what might be referred to as a *linguistic* approach. The former analyses the characteristics of fluent spoken production (i.e. fluency in performance) as a reflex of the underlying cognitive mechanisms involved in spoken language production; the latter is mainly concerned with the investigation of how quantitative aspects of speech, such as temporal variables (pause length and frequency, articulation and speech rates) and various other hesitation phenomena, contribute to hearers' perception of speech as nonfluent and correlate with native speakers' fluency ratings of nonnative speech. Both these approaches are closely related and, in naturally occurring conversational speech, interact with sociolinguistic variables rooted in culturally accepted communicative behaviour.

Within the psycholinguistic approach to oral fluency analysis, research has mainly focused on the optimisation of automatic and controlled information processing (Segalowitz, 2000), automisation of speech production processes through procedural linguistic knowledge (de Bot, 1992; Pawley & Syder, 1983, 2000; Raupach, 1987; Schmidt 1992; Towell, 1987 Towell & Hawkins, 1994; Towell *et al.*, 1996;) and the use of formulaic speech and ready-to-use speech chunks as a means of explaining fluent speech production (Ejzenberg, 2000; Oppenheim, 2000; Pawley & Syder, 1983; Rehbein, 1987; Towell *et al.*, 1996). The evidence stemming from these studies suggests that speech production is severely constrained by limitations imposed by speech planning mechanisms. Several studies (e.g. Chafe, 1987; Pawley & Syder, 1983; Raupach, 1987; Towell *et al.*, 1996) demonstrate that oral fluency is largely dependent on speakers' ability to encode a message in a single planning act resulting in a clause-sized uninterrupted short stretch of speech of about six words on average. This "one-clause-at-a-time" constraint, as Pawley and Syder (2000: 163) have called it, is consistent with pausological research (e.g. Griffiths, 1991; Raupach, 1980; Riazantseva, 2001) in that pauses, as well as other dysfluency markers (repetitions, restarts, rephrasings, hesitations, etc.) seem to cluster at clause boundaries in the speech of competent fluent L2 speakers, a context in which pause frequency is relatively high even for native speakers. Within-clause silences, therefore, are normally perceived as unnatural pauses and constitute a strong indicator of nonfluent speech and a reflex of a subjects' difficulty and/or failure to encode the content of a clause in a single planning act. This is also consistent with findings from oral fluency research concluding that the mean number of syllables uttered between short pauses (ranging from 0.25 to 0.4 seconds, depending on researcher) or *mean length of run*, is one of the temporal variables that best correlates with native speakers' perception of fluency in nonnative speech (e.g. Ejzenberg, 2000; Freed, 1995, 2000; Freed *et al.*, 2004; Kormos & Dénes, 2004; Lennon, 1990; Riggenbach, 1991; Towell *et al.*, 1996). Proceduralisation of linguistic knowledge resulting in automaticity is often difficult for even the most advanced foreign language learners, who do not only have to strive to access and retrieve the right word from their limited L2 lexicon, but also need to properly encode their message under the time constraints of spoken language. Several studies (e.g. Oppenheim, 2000; Pawley & Syder, 1983; Rehbein, 1987) have investigated the relationship between fluency and formulaic speech and have shown that recourse to set phrases and expressions and memorising whole speech chunks for immediate retrieval are two of the most effective communicative strategies foreign language learners can use to make their nonnative speech sound more fluent. Appropriate use of formulaic speech and lexicalised sentences ("form-meaning pairings", in Pawley and Syder's words (1983: 192)) often requires, however, knowledge of language use that comes with extensive exposure in real communicative situations. In a foreign language setting, where exposure to the L2 is limited to the two/three-hours-per-week foreign language class, there is little opportunity for developing realistic language use and for exposure to authentic conversational speech; consequently, the use of formulaic speech is occasional and does not significantly affect learners' performance in terms of fluency.

Research within the "linguistic" approach to oral fluency analysis has mainly investigated the relationship between the temporal properties of speech and native speakers' fluency ratings in an attempt to identify a set of reliable fluency predictors that could be used to quantitatively assess oral fluency in nonnative speech as a measure of overall L2 proficiency. Lexical and syntactic accuracy and appropriacy have been reported by native judges as one of the factors they rely on in rating nonnative speech (i.e. different oral fluency ratings for two nonnative speakers may be based on the better grammar and vocabulary of one of the speakers, rather than on temporal variables), but such variables are certainly not the best predictors of oral fluency. In fact, virtually all linguistic aspects present in the speech signal may be shown to vary according to how fluent the nonnative speaker is in his/her L2, and this variation may therefore be used to characterise different levels of fluency in the speech of nonnative speakers. Wennerstorm (2000), for example, has shown how fluent nonnative speakers differ from less fluent speakers in the use they make of pitch to highlight relevant information contained in lexical words and to signal the information structure of utterances, thus facilitating the turn-taking process in conversational exchanges. There have also been a few attempts at characterising oral fluency on the basis of the phonetic and phonological processes that operate in connected speech. There is a whole host of contextual assimilation and linking phenomena occurring in connected speech in conversational speech styles taking place both word-internally and across word boundaries that normally pass unnoticed by native speakers but must somehow be perceived as oral fluency indicators. Assimilation phenomena originate as articulation adjusts to reduce the magnitude of articulatory gestures under the time constraints imposed by conversational speech, whereas linking phenomena serve to re-organise segmental sequences in newly created syllable units when words are strung together in utterances and word boundaries disappear. Hieke analysed these phonetic and phonological aspects of oral fluency in a series of studies (Hieke, 1984, 1985, 1987) and, not surprisingly, observed significant differences in the amount of *linking* (consonant attraction in syllabic restructuring, hiatus-breaking epenthesis) and *absorption* (assimilation and elision phenomena: lenition, consonant cluster reduction, place assimilation, degemination, etc.) used in native and nonnative speech. Hieke (1984: 353) suggests that linking and absorption are features of fluent speech that may be used as variables in fluency assessment. This approach to oral fluency analysis, however, has neither been incorporated nor pursued by subsequent research, which has focused on more easily quantifiable variables with greater fluency-predicting power.

Temporal variables such as *speech rate* (syllables uttered per second including pause time), *articulation rate* (syllables uttered per second without pause time) and *pauses*, are among the properties of nonnative speech that have received most attention (e.g. Chambers, 1997; Freed, 1995, 2000; Griffiths, 1990, 1991; Lennon, 1990; Raupach 1980; Riggenbach, 1991 Towell, 2002;). Silent pause duration, distribution and frequency, in particular, have been widely used as dysfluency markers in combination with other fluency measures such as *speech rate, hesitations* (restarts, repairs and repetitions) and *mean length of speech run* (average number of syllables between pauses). Pause duration, for example, has been found to be affected by L2 proficiency, so that less proficient speakers produce longer pauses; L2 speakers have also been found to pause more frequently in their L2 than in their L1 (Riazantseva, 2001). Pauses are perceived as unnatural and make speech dysfluent when clause-internal, but are not perceived as speech-disruptive provided they are not too long and occur at clause junctures or the end of word groups constituting a semantic unit, a context where pauses are very frequent in native speaker speech. Although it is generally agreed that proficient nonnative speakers produce shorter pauses than less advanced learners, there is no general consensus among researchers as to how long a pause should be for it to be considered dysfluent. Riggenbach (1991, 2000) makes a distinction between micropauses (0.2 sec.), which are not normally an indicator of lack of fluency, hesitations (0.3–0.4 sec.), and unfilled pauses (0.5–3.0 sec.), which function as dysfluency markers. Various other cut-off points distinguishing dysfluent from natural-sounding pauses, however, have been proposed: 0.25 sec. (Grosjean & Deschamps 1972, 1973, 1975; Raupach, 1987; Towell, 1987), 0.28 sec. (Towell, 2002), 0.30 sec. (Raupach, 1980), 0.4 sec. (Freed *et al.*, 2004). This lack of agreement stems from the fact that pause frequency and duration do not only vary as a function of phonostylistic factors such as individual speech style, speed of delivery and situational context, but may also vary substantially according to the speech processing requirements of different elicitation tasks and techniques (e.g. read speech is normally faster than spontaneous speech). Skehan & Foster (1999), for example, found that whereas complexity and accuracy measures did not differ across tasks, fluency did vary significantly as a function of task structure: tasks containing a clearer sequential structure generated more fluent language. The effects of task structure on oral fluency, however, may vary greatly as a function of the speakers' L2 proficiency level. Riazantseva (2001) compared the performance of native and nonnative speakers in a topic narrative and a cartoon description, and found a significant effect of task type on pause frequency: in the cartoon description task, which is a more highly structured task than a topic narrative, the subjects produced speech that was more halting, with higher pause frequency, because this type of task necessarily imposes a limit on the speakers' freedom of lexical and grammatical choice. Thus, pausological research has shown that pause duration and frequency, besides being dysfluency markers in nonnative speech, are good indicators of L2 learners' difficulties in speech processing, lack of automaticity in speech production and overall L2 proficiency.

In general, the quantitative fluency measures that have been found to better predict native speakers' ratings of nonnative speech in oral fluency analyses are *speech rate* and *length of run* (Kormos & Dénes, 2004: 4). Most of these analyses, however, have dealt with the speech of highly proficient nonnative speakers, normally young adults and university students, and have mainly focused on finding out what temporal variables best predict native speakers' fluency ratings of nonnative speech or more substantially contribute to native speakers' judgements of nonnative speech as nonfluent (e.g. Kormos & Dénes, 2004; Lennon, 1990; Riggenbach, 1991). A few studies have investigated oral fluency gains after a stay-abroad period as a measure of overall improvement in spoken language performance, as opposed to gains in written competence. It is precisely in spoken language fluency that stay-abroad programmes are supposed to exert greater positive effects, and unsurprisingly fluency gains (at least for some fluency measures) have been reported (e.g. Freed, 1995, 2000; Freed *et al.*, 2004; Segalowitz & Freed, 2004; Towell, 2002; Towell *et al.*, 1996).

The study reported on in the next section examines oral fluency in the speech of two groups of Catalan/Spanish EFL learners differing in the age at which they first started studying English, but matched with respect to exposure to the language and amount of instruction received in a formal learning context. The aim of the study is twofold. On the one hand, the quantitative approach to the data analysis seeks to explore the viability of well-established analytical procedures and widely used oral fluency measures in the analysis of spoken language. The spoken texts analysed were elicited through a series of pictures in a storytelling task produced by low-proficient young EFL learners. Some of the oral fluency measures used for highly proficient learners may prove troublesome or non-applicable to the subjects in our experimental context. On the other hand, we wish to investigate possible age effects on oral fluency in the two subject groups by testing the hypothesis that an earlier onset age of learning will have positive effects on learners. This hypothesis would predict better oral fluency scores for early starters than for late starters. Differential gains in oral fluency explainable in terms of the age factor have received little attention in the second language acquisition literature (Dewaele, 1998; Towell, 2002); other factors, such as L2 proficiency or amount of L2 use in stay-abroad contexts, have been invoked to explain individual differences in oral fluency. Towell (2002), for example, in a four-year longitudinal study into the acquisition of French by English learners, reports inter-subject differences in oral fluency development: learners beginning at a lower point increased their scores on temporal variable measures the most. However, because of group homogeneity (proficiency level and years of formal instruction, presumably also onset age of L2 learning), such differences in oral fluency are tentatively attributed to individual differences based on short-term memory capacity (Towell, 2002: 139). One study that does address the relationship between onset age of L2 learning (determined by age of arrival or AOA) and a fluency-related variable is Guion *et al.* (2000), who measured the duration (in milliseconds) of L2 utterances consisting of fluent sentences (without dysfluencies or pauses greater than 200 ms) elicited through a sentence-repetition task. A strong positive correlation was found between sentence duration and age of first exposure to English for a large group of Italian and Korean immigrants: subjects who were first exposed to English later in life pronounced sentences with a slower speech rate. Since speaking rate is normally higher in the L1 than in the L2 (Munro & Derwing, 1995), Guion *et al.* (2000: 225) account for their findings by suggesting that the more established the L1 is at the time of L2 learning, the more it interferes with L2 production. That study suggests that there may be an effect of onset age of L2 learning on one speech rate measure in favour of early starters; but can the same effect also be obtained for other speech rate measures or oral fluency variables? And are such effects observable in the speech of relatively nonfluent learners acquiring the L2 in a formal learning context that has been elicited through a storytelling task? These are the issues the following section addresses by reporting on a study of oral fluency temporal variables in the speech of L2 learners of English.

Temporal Variables in the Speech of Spanish/Catalan EFL Learners: A Quantitative Analysis of Oral Fluency

None of the studies cited in the approaches to oral fluency reported on above have investigated oral fluency in the speech of low proficiency L2 learners. This may be due to the fact that their speech is typically so halting that may be straightforwardly characterised as nonfluent. However, it is worth investigating the oral fluency features of the speech of such learners, as they relate to their overall spoken language ability. Besides, results obtained through quantitative measures may be worth correlating with other proficiency measures in other areas of linguistic competence, such as complexity and fluency measures in writing, or degree of phonetic accuracy in pronunciation. Previous research by Freed *et al.* (2004), for example, has revealed that variables such as out-of-class hours per week spent writing, presumably because it qualifies as an "output-generating type" activity, significantly predicted gains in speaking rate.

Research on L2 oral fluency suggests that it is possible to evaluate oral fluency through the detailed analysis of the temporal properties of nonnative speech and the presence of fluency and dysfluency markers. The reasoning underlying such an approach to oral fluency analysis is that variation within the temporal domain of speech production is the direct consequence of the variety of individual developmental stages in learners' speech planning processes and their skill to make this procedural knowledge automatic. Lack of automaticity in message encoding due to limited experience with the target language and poor use of syntactic and semantic resources results in nonnative-like pausing and a host of dysfluency markers such as repetitions, restarts, repairs and frequent long clause-internal pauses. To our knowledge no previous research has attempted to measure oral fluency in the speech of low-proficiency young learners, so little is known about the adequacy of the fluency measures that are normally used in research with advanced learners to the type of population we are investigating. The question of how finely grained the analysis of temporal phenomena should be in the analysis of nonfluent speech remains an important issue research should address. A widely used temporal variable of oral fluency, such as pause duration may be a reliable measure of oral fluency for proficient L2 speakers, but may be unreliable in the case of learners whose oral production is essentially dysfluent and contains many pauses. In such cases, the number of clause-internal pauses may be a more reliable measure of oral fluency than mean pause duration, a variable that may not be sensitive enough to capture differences in oral fluency in the speech of low-proficiency L2 speakers. Unfortunately, pausological research (e.g. Griffiths, 1991) has not addressed this issue and pausing time has largely been used as a variable in the oral fluency rating of the speech of proficient L2 speakers who are immersed in their L2 environment (e.g. Riazantseva, 2001).

The experimental research design of the study we report on here is exploratory with respect to the oral fluency measures used and their relative success in uncovering differences between the speech of the two groups of subjects we examined. The speech samples examined were obtained by means of a storytelling task intended to elicit a narrative. This was one of the oral tasks the subjects were asked to perform in the Barcelona Age Factor (BAF) Project as part of a whole battery of tests designed to measure their overall level of linguistic competence in English (see Muñoz, Chapter 1, this volume, for a comprehensive description of this large-scale project).

The use of a picture-elicited narrative task has the advantage of producing highly structured language and eliciting a number of syntactic and lexical forms, which may be very useful in assessing the learners' L2 productive grammatical knowledge, but it presents two main shortcomings for oral fluency assessment that need to be discussed briefly and be taken into account in the analysis of the results. The first one is that the researchers occasionally intervened when lower proficiency learners were at a loss for words and completely stuck, unable to carry out the task. On such occasions, researchers often intervened by asking questions that allowed subjects to proceed and complete the task, which allowed researchers to gather larger speech samples and to obtain a more substantial range of grammatical structures for subsequent analysis. This is clearly a drawback for a quantitative analysis of oral fluency because interviewers' elicited language, such as answers to a question (irrespective of whether it directly relates to the story or not), affects the lexical counts and time measures on which many temporal variables are based. This problem was avoided by carefully excluding any language triggered by researchers' interventions from the analysis. The second possible shortcoming of the picture-elicited narrative task is that lexical and grammatical choice is severely limited by the story itself, and this, as Riazantseva's (2001) study has shown, results in greater pause frequency than in other oral production tasks. A topic narrative, for instance, would have allowed the learners to make use of fluency-enhancing strategies such as lexical and syntactic avoidance or the use of ready-to-use lexicalised phrases directly drawn from memory. It is important to bear these task-structure conditioning factors in mind when interpreting the results of the quantitative oral fluency analysis, since the type of speech analysed is probably not too far from the bottom end of a fluency continuum determined by the type of speech elicitation task.

Subjects

Speech samples of 60 subjects were analysed using quantitative measures of oral fluency. These participants were selected from a much larger pool of Spanish/Catalan EFL learners (see Muñoz, Chapter 1, this volume, for a detailed description) on the basis of two essential criteria. The first criterion was the subjects' overall level of competence in English, which should be advanced enough for them to be able to produce sufficiently long and complex stretches of speech in the picture-elicited narrative task for it to be analysed in terms of quantitative oral fluency measures. Very low-level L2 learners unable to be productive orally in English beyond the one-word phrase stage would be unsuitable for the purposes of finding out significant oral fluency differences between subject groups. It was then decided to carry out the oral fluency analysis on speech samples of 60 subjects, when they had received the greatest amount of exposure to English (Time 3): 726 hours of formal instruction in English as a foreign language (Time 1 = 200 h; Time 2 = 416 h).

The second criterion used in subject selection was that subjects belonged to two different groups in terms of different onset age of foreign language learning (AO). Thirty of the subjects, Group A (mean age at testing 16;9), were randomly selected from those who were first exposed to formal EFL instruction at 8 years of age (AO = 8). The onset age of EFL learning of the other 30 subjects, Group B (mean age at testing 17;9), also randomly selected from the larger pool, was 11 years of age (AO = 11). Although there was a slight difference in intensity of exposure between groups (it was higher for Group B: the amount of exposure was distributed in seven years as opposed to the almost nine years in Group A), amount of formal EFL instruction at the time of testing was 726 hours for both groups. We did not consider the one-year difference between the mean ages of both groups at the time of testing a factor that could possibly lead to robust differences in oral fluency.

Unlike the type of populations taking part in oral fluency studies reported on in previous research, our participants' exposure to English was limited to a formal language learning context; subjects who had been exposed to English in contexts other than the school context, such as language schools or stay-abroad periods, were not included. The formal learning context determined to a certain extent the type of input received, which was not native-like. Learner-teacher interaction in the classroom seldom occurred in English and teachers were nonnative speakers of

English and spoke English with varying degrees of nativeness. There was little opportunity for subjects to be exposed to realistic native or nativelike conversational exchanges, and this was restricted to the use of audiovisual material in the classroom. The fact that most productive interactional language practice occurs between nonnative student peers may have consequences for oral fluency development. In an L2 immersion context, nonnative speakers' fluency development is enhanced by their involvement in daily conversational exchanges with native speakers in real situations (Morales-López, 2000; Riggenbach, 1991), which is the basis for improvement in conversational fluency (turn-taking, appropriate pausing and overlapping and other interactive phenomena and features). Although opportunity to interact with native speakers would seem to be an advantage in oral fluency development, empirical research is not conclusive in this respect. Segalowitz and Freed (2004), for example, who had initially hypothesised that interactional activities would lead to cognitive gains in lexical access that would result in oral fluency gains, found that, in a stay-abroad context, learners' fluency benefited only weakly and indirectly from out-of-class interaction with native speakers in real communicative situations. The participants in our study did not have the chance of taking advantage of communicative interaction with native speakers and could obtain no type of benefit from the exposure to the type of enriching conversational input available in an immersion learning context.

Procedure

The participants in this study were asked to take part in a storytelling task. They were given a simple six-picture cartoon and asked to look at it and tell the story in it (there was no time limit). The task was performed individually and tape-recorded in the presence of the researcher. The recorded narrative was digitised at a 22.050 kHz sampling rate and 16-bit resolution using a speech editor and then transcribed orthographically. This computer-edited version of the narrative allowed us to use the speech sample waveform (amplitude-time graph) to segment the speech samples precisely when necessary and to obtain accurate duration measures that were used in the analysis of the temporal variables of the speech samples, which were conveniently labelled.

The labelling of the orthographic transcription of the speech samples included a variety of labels for dysfluency markers: *pause, filled pause, silent pause, repetition, restart, rephrasing*. Subsequent dysfluency and lexical counts were then carried out on the basis of this labelling: *words, syllables, speech runs, L1 words, lengthened syllables*. The total duration (in seconds) of the speech sample was measured (disregarding silences at the beginning and ending of the task) and any speech material not belonging to the cartoon-elicited narrative (researchers' interventions and subjects' questions to the researcher) was not included in the analysis. Both the labelling and the dysfluency and lexical counts were independently carried out by two researchers with the help of a speech analysis tool (*Speech Analyzer 2.4.* SIL International, 2001) and then thoroughly revised. Table 3.1 lists the dysfluency and lexical counts, and the oral fluency variables created. The variables in Table 3.1 constitute the oral fluency measures on which the two groups of EFL learners taking part in this study were compared.

Fluency measures and data analysis

The fluency measures used in the present study (see Table 3.1) conform to fluency variables used in previous studies of oral fluency and pausological research and aim at characterising nonnative oral productions by means of temporal properties of speech. The storytelling task used to elicit the nonnative speech samples and the type of highly dysfluent narratives obtained did not allow for a complex fluency analysis including linguistic proficiency variables such as lexical variety and richness, grammatical complexity or linguistic accuracy. Research aiming at identifying a set of temporal variables that can reliably predict native listeners' judgements of fluency in nonnative speech (Freed, 1995; Lennon, 1990; Riggenbach, 1991) has generated a large number of measures capable of predicting oral fluency with varying degrees of success depending on the focus of the study and its approach to oral fluency analysis. Thus, the variables of pause frequency, duration and distribution have been thoroughly exploited in studies investigating the relationship between oral fluency and procedural knowledge and automaticity in speech production (e.g. Towell *et al.*, 1996). The temporal variables used in the present study are a subset of the variables that have been widely used in the literature and have proved to be good predictors of nonnative oral fluency.

Table 3.1 Dysfunctional and lexical counts and oral fluency variables

Counts	Variables	
	Name	Label
Words	Speech Rate in Words	SRW
L1 words	Speech Rate in Syllables	SRS
Syllables	L1-Word Ratio	L1WR
Lengthened syllables	Mean Length of Run in Words	MLRW
Speech runs	Mean Length of Run in Syllables	MLRS
Speech sample duration	Speech Run Rate	SRR
Dysfluencies	Longest Fluent Run	LFR
Pauses (Ps)	Dysfluency Rate	DYSR
Clause-internal (CI) Ps	Pause Frequency (1 & 2)	PF (1 & 2)
CI-filled Ps	Internal Pause Frequency (1 & 2)	IPF (1 & 2)
	Internal Filled Pause Frequency (1 & 2)	IFPF (1 & 2)
	Internal Silent Pause Frequency (1 & 2)	ISPF (1 & 2)
	Lengthened Syllables	LS

The selection of temporal variables has also been made in accordance with a general principle of analytical suitability with respect to the speech samples that constitute the corpus of the present study. For example, besides the fact that pause duration has not always been found to be a good predictor of oral fluency (e.g. Towell, 2002), the use of this temporal measure did not seem advisable for the analysis of highly dysfluent speech containing many pauses. Pause frequency, rather than pause duration, appeared to be in this case a more sensitive variable. Another instance of a temporal variable that we discarded for use with our data was *Articulation Rate*, a fluency measure often used in oral fluency analyses consisting of the number of phones or syllables articulated per second, excluding silent pauses (Kormos & Dénes, 2004; Riggenbach, 1991; Towell, 1987). By not counting pause time, this particular variable measures the efficiency of gestural coordination and overlap in articulation leading to fluidity in speech production; the blending and hiding of articulatory gestures has long been recognised (e.g. Browman & Goldstein, 1989, 1990, 1992) as one of the features of fluent speech that enables a speaker to produce sequences of speech sounds fast enough to allow speech to adjust to the time constraints of spoken discourse. Learners have to acquire this type of overall L2 articulation fluency as part of their L2 pronunciation ability, usually by acquiring new articulatory habits and phonetic settings that will make their speech production sound more natural and native-like. Although this measure would capture differences in the speed of delivery of L2 syllables and sound sequences, the pronunciation ability of our L2 learners was generally not good enough to be able to use this pronunciation fluency measure.

The fluency measures used in the present study (see Table 3.1) have been listed below with a general description and a detailed explanation of how the measure was applied to our data. Due to huge inter-subject differences in the size of the narrative produced and in order to minimise the bias effect such differences may have on the lexical and dysfluency phenomena counts, the variables used represent in most cases a ratio of a particular fluency measure and either the total number of words produced in the speech sample or the total duration of the narrative. Thus, it was the number of dysfluencies per minute, rather than the total number of dysfluencies in the narrative, or the percentage of lengthened syllables, rather than the total number of lengthened syllables in the narrative, that were computed to obtain the means on which the group comparisons are based. The measures used constitute a selection of commonly used temporal measures in oral fluency analysis that have been shown in previous research to strongly correlate with native speakers' evaluation of oral fluency in the speech of nonnative speakers. They have been selected on the basis of, and adapted to, the speech samples produced by the subjects in the present study and have been used in the subsequent statistical analysis of the results to explore differences in oral fluency between the two groups of subjects taking part in the study. It is hoped that the selection is adequate enough for the type of data under analysis to be able to yield reliable results with respect to L2 oral fluency in the speech of relatively dysfluent learners of English.

Total Time of Speech Sample (TTSP)

TTSP is the duration (in seconds) of the whole narrative excluding the interviewer's turns. This temporal variable measured the duration of the narrative from the first to the last word including learner-produced utterances only and consistently excluding any occasional intervention by the researcher, which mostly consisted of questions of the type *"what happens/do you see in the next picture?"* or *"what are they doing?"* intended to help the participant proceed with the storytelling task after a long silence indicating that s/he was stuck. Sometimes, when the participant was at a loss for a word, the researcher opted for helping her/him by producing the right word. In both cases, the researchers' interventions were always preceded by long silences. These silences were included as part of the narrative, but the pause between the end of the researchers' intervention and the following participant's turn was not included in the time count. The initial silence before the first sound in the narrative is uttered is not included, nor is the period of silence after the last sound in the narrative computed. Any dialogue between the participant and the researcher, comments, questions addressed to the researcher such as *"How do you say this (or an L1 word) in English?"* and repetition of words or language directly taken from or suggested by the researcher's intervention was not considered when computing the duration of the narrative. Our aim was to measure the duration of the speech samples the participants produced as their own linguistic productions. The speech productions thus measured varied a lot in duration, from 9.61 to 198.76 sec. (mean 96.85 sec.). Duration measures were used to calculate speech rate and pause frequency variables, which are dependent on the duration of the whole narrative.

Speech Rate In Words (SRW)

SRW is the number of words per minute (wpm) including pause time. This is calculated by dividing the result of the word count by TTSP (in minutes). The word count on which this fluency measure is based exclude any stretches of speech that are not part of the participant's narrative (researchers' interventions and participants' questions and comments addressed to the researcher). In the case of repetitions of a word/phrase, words were counted once only. In the event of false starts and rephrasings, the same principle was applied and only the words in the final phrase/clause/sentence were computed. Contractions were counted as two words (Griffiths, 1990) and exclamations such as "Oh!" were computed as words when occurring as part of the oral narrative. Research in oral fluency analysis (Kormos & Dénes, 2004) has shown that speech rate, whether measured in *wpm* or syllables per second/minute (*sps/spm*), is a very robust predictor of perceived oral fluency. It is therefore included in all fluency analyses of nonnative speech.

Speech Rate in Syllables (SRS)

SRS is the number of syllables per minute including pause time. The syllable count on which this measure is based is the number of syllables in the words computed in the word count on which the SRW variable is based and therefore syllables belonging to words and stretches of speech that are excluded in SRW have not been computed for this variable either. Despite the fact that speech rate measured in syllables is normally reported in sps, it was found more convenient for descriptive purposes to report this variable in spm (as in Grosjean, 1980) due to our subjects' very low speech rates and short spoken productions. Although there is not much difference between word and syllable counts (e.g. Griffiths (1990: 322) gives an average syllable/word ratio of 1.15), such difference may produce more accurate estimates of speech rate in the speech of relatively nonfluent learners, whose mean wpm speech rate is very low when compared to that of native speakers.

L1 Word Ratio (L1WR)

L1WR is the number of words in the L1 (Spanish or Catalan) by total number of words in the narrative. Although most of the fluency measures used relate to temporal properties of speech, we decided to include this measure of lexical frequency in the form of a ratio between L1 and L2 words. The use of L1 words is here considered to be a strong indicator of nonfluent speech: L1 words are normally preceded by long silences resulting from the subject striving for a lexical item, and their occurrence indicate the subjects' failure in retrieving the intended L2 word from the L2 mental lexicon. Occasionally, participants created novel lexical forms by adding an English suffix to a Spanish base form and then gave the novel form an English-like pronunciation, as in the following examples (asterisks indicate incorrect form): **señaling* [seˈɲalivn̩] "pointing at" from Spanish *señalar* /seɲaˈlar/ "to point at"; **aliments* [ˈalimens] "food" (pl.) from Spanish *alimento* /aliˈmento/ or Catalan /aliˈmen/ "food" (sing.); **camp* [ˈkamp] "countryside" from Spanish *campo* /ˈkampo/ or Catalan /ˈkam/ "countryside"; **sorpresly* [sorˈpresli] "surprisingly" from Spanish *sorpresa* /sorˈpresa/ or Catalan /surˈprɛzə/ "surprise". These anglicised forms were all computed as L1 words.

Mean Length of Run in Words (MLRW)

MLRW is the average number of words between pauses of 0.4 sec. or longer. Every stretch of speech between pauses (0.4 sec. or longer) was considered a speech run. Fluent clause-sized speech runs consisting of five to seven words, which are indicative of encoding acts in language processing, are the norm in native-like speech (Pawley & Syder, 1983, 2000), but occurred very rarely in our data.

Mean Length of Run in Syllables (MLRS)

MLRS is the average number of syllables between pauses of 0.4 sec. or longer. This variable, therefore, measures the same as the MLRW variable in syllables instead of words. As with speech rate, the mean length of run is computed both in words (MLRW) and syllables (MLRS). Although mean length of run is normally given in words, syllables may provide a more accurate measure of the length of run because the same number of words may result in very different syllable counts. However, whereas syllable counts are more sensitive to phonostylistic features such as variation in articulation rate or speed of delivery, word counts are more stable as a measure of the mean length of run across different speech styles and more sensitive to inter-subject differences in language processing ability.

Speech Run Rate (SRR)

SRR is the number of speech runs (stretches of speech between pauses of 0.4 sec. or longer) per minute. This variable measures how fragmentary the speech sample is and at the same time is also an indicator of the mean length (in number of words) of speech samples: the higher the SRR, the more speech runs the subjects produced per minute and the more fragmentary the speech sample is, provided the speed of delivery in articulation does not differ greatly across subjects. Obviously, it is possible to think of a high SRR as an indicator of fluency if more speech runs are produced per minute while keeping the length of run constant and not increasing pause frequency; this, however, would necessarily affect the speech rate in words, which would also be higher. This is not the case in the speech samples analysed in the present study, where speech rate is relatively low and higher SRRs correlate with higher pause frequencies.

Longest Fluent Run (LFR)

LFR is the number of words in the longest run of speech without silent or filled pause dysfluencies. It is therefore a measure of a subjects' ability to successfully process and produce a clause-sized stretch of speech without internal dysfluencies.

Dysfluency Rate (DYSR)

DYSR is the number of dysfluencies per minute occurring in the speech samples, based on dysfluency counts that include a whole range of hesitation phenomena such as partial or complete *repetitions* (e.g. the (…) the basket; how (…) how are; sur- (…) sur- (…) surprised; Bob and Mary (…) [hmm] are:: (…) are:: preparing (…) preparing the:: (…) [hmm] the food);

restarts (e.g. the dog (…) [hmm] two children) and *repairs* (e.g. the (…) her mother (…) their mother). Filled and unfilled pauses, lengthened syllables and L1 words were not included here, as they were independently computed as different variables.

Lengthened Syllables (LS)

LS is the percentage of *lengthened syllables* and *drawls* (phonetic lengthening of segments) with respect to the total number of syllables in every speech sample. This type of hesitation phenomena (e.g. *and* [æːːːnd], *the* [ðəːːː]) helps keep the speech flow by substituting for a silent or filled pause, and in our data are often followed by a relatively long pause, indicating some type of processing difficulty in the act of formulating speech, such as the striving for a lexical item or the need of extra time for an encoding act (Pawley & Syder, 2000).

Pause Frequency (PF)

PF is the number of pauses per minute (PF1) or per word (PF2) occurring both clause-internally and at clause boundaries. Since this variable computes clause-internal as well as pauses occurring at word boundaries, it does not yield a reliable measure of oral fluency, nor does this variable accurately characterise the extent to which a speech sample is dysfluent with respect to pause frequency (in fluent native-like speech pauses typically occur at clause boundaries). Thus, this measure of oral fluency provides us with a general impression of the amount of time the subjects devote to pausing, irrespective of pause duration. It is the frequency of clause-internal pauses that will serve the purpose of capturing inter-subject differences in oral fluency.

Internal Pause Frequency (IPF)

IPF is the number of clause-internal pauses per minute (IPF1) or per word (IPF2). Clause-internal pauses are a well-established dysfluency marker (e.g. Griffiths, 1991; Raupach, 1980) and a common feature of nonnative speech. However, although IPF is normally reported in pauses per minute in oral fluency analyses, the time/unit ratio may present one important shortcoming in nonfluent speech: in the case of highly dysfluent speakers, pause frequency tends to be high, but pause duration may also be long. Thus, since speech rate measures include pause time, the presence of long pauses will imply lower pause frequency (fewer pauses per minute, i.e. higher oral fluency), which would not account for the fact that long clause-internal pauses are more dysfluent than short clause-internal pauses. In order to avoid this problem and obtain a more accurate description of the effect of pause frequency on oral fluency, a pause-word ratio (IPF2) was computed in addition to the pauses-per-minute measure (IPF1).

In order to classify a silence as clause-internal an operational definition of a clause in spoken discourse is necessary, but there is no complete consensus among grammarians as to what qualifies as a clause (Pawley & Syder, 2000: 174). In the present study, pauses were considered clause-internal if occurring within the limits of grammatical unit larger than a phrase and consisting of a verb and its dependent elements (subject, object, complement, adverbial). The clause-internal pauses computed by this variable include filled as well as silent pauses, for which two independent measures (IFPF and ISPF, respectively) have also been calculated.

Internal Filled Pause Frequency (IFPF)

IFPF is the number of clause-internal filled pauses per minute (IFPF1) or per word (IFPF2). The motivation for having computed a time-based as well as a lexical-count-based frequency is the same as that argued for IPF1 and IPF2. Pauses filled by lexical fillers (discourse markers) such as *well*, *you see, you know*, etc., which occur very rarely in our data, are to be counted as words because they are indicators of overall fluency in the speech of nonnative speakers, a strategy of compensatory fluency that is very useful to create the impression of fluency without actually being lexically fluent. Therefore, the filled pauses computed here consist exclusively of nonlexical fillers such as *mmm* [m:::], *ah* [ə:::] or *um* [əm] and are given the same value as silent pauses when computing internal pause frequency. These nonlexical fillers typically co-occur in our data with preceding and/or following silent pauses. Sequences of *silent pause + filled pause* without any intervening speech material were counted as a single (albeit long) pause when calculating clause-internal pause frequency (IPF).

Internal Silent Pause Frequency (ISPF)

ISPF is the number of silent (i.e. unfilled) clause-internal pauses per minute (ISPF1) or per word (ISPF2). Following Freed (1995) and Freed *et al.* (2004), only clause-internal pauses of 0.4 sec. or longer were computed. Long silent pauses tend to occur in combination with other dysfluency markers such as hesitation phenomena. Except in the case of a *silent pause + filled pause* sequence all these dysfluency markers were computed independently of silent pauses. The duration of silent pauses was not measured. The fact that the nonnative speech analysed was highly dysfluent and contained many pauses suggested that pause frequency rather than pause duration would be a much more sensitive measure when having to distinguish between the pausing behaviour of two highly nonfluent groups of subjects.

Results and discussion

Overall, the results obtained in the oral fluency measures computed for the speech samples analysed reflect the low fluency level of the subjects in a cartoon description task, which was well below native-like performance.

For example, native-like speech rate, which varies a lot according to contextual factors and individual speech styles, is approximately 150–200 wpm (de Bot, 1992; Griffiths, 1990) for American English, i.e. about 200 spm if we apply the 4–6 sps average suggested by Hieke (1985) or 180–240 spm if we apply the 1.23 syllable-per-word index of Kowal et al. (1983), cited in Griffiths (1991: 349). Griffiths (1990) established an average speed of 150 wpm (2.87 sps) as reading speed across different reading styles and text materials (range = 94–206 wpm; 1.79–3.94 sps). In the speech productions examined in the present study, speech rate (SRW) ranged from 17.25 to 91.33 wpm (mean = 54.15 wpm). The reason for this very low speech rate is to be sought in the highly dysfluent speech the learners in our study produced, which was generally very halting and contained many pauses. This generalises to many of the fluency measures examined. The speech rate values in syllables (SRS) range from 19.72 spm to 104.57 spm (mean = 65.19 spm), scores which fall well below the speech rate of native speakers. An average of 4–5 L1 words per speech sample (L1WR), representing 8.5% over the mean total number of words in the speech samples, was obtained, which gives an indication of the subjects' difficulty in accessing and retrieving words from the L2 lexicon.

The mean length of run (MLRW) was also very low, ranging from 1 to 5.8 words per speech run (the overall mean was 2.8 words per speech run). Longer speech runs (5–8 words) were uncommon and it was only occasionally that speech runs containing a whole clause were produced. The 2.8-word MLRW obtained (cf. 5–7-word MLRW typical of native speech) suggests that the learners had serious processing difficulties when encoding and producing the descriptive pieces of language the storytelling task was designed to trigger. The most frequent number of words in the longest speech run (LFR) the subjects produced was 7; 6-, 7- and 8-word speech runs were the longest for 63.3% of the subjects, longer speech runs containing more than 8 words were the longest for 21.6% of the subjects (range 9 to 14) and shorter speech runs were the longest for 15.1% of the subjects (range 1 to 5).

As far as DYSR is concerned, a mean of 7.3 dysfluencies per minute occurred in the speech samples analysed, which together with the considerable amount of time devoted to pausing and the very low speech rate, indicated that the speech samples analysed were highly nonfluent. This is also consistent with the mean number of LS, which was very high (17.9), approximately representing 17.6% of the syllables in the speech samples, and with the mean clause-internal pause frequency of 14.9 pauses per minute (IPF1), i.e. one pause occurring every 3.8 words (IPF2), which is clearly indicative of a low-proficiency language processing ability.

The oral fluency variables listed in Table 3.1 were computed for all subjects (N = 60) and entered in the SPSS (Statistical Package for the Social Sciences, 11.5) data editor for statistical analysis and their mean scores on

13 oral fluency values were compared. Independent-samples *t*-tests were used to assess whether the differences between the mean scores between the two groups of subjects was statistically significant. Since the participants differed in AO but had all received the same amount of formal instruction (FI) in English at the time of testing (FI = 726 h) differences between the mean scores of the two groups could be attributed to the different AO of the groups. Table 3.2 lists the mean scores obtained by both groups of subjects on the 13 oral fluency variables computed.

The independent-samples *t*-test conducted to compare the mean oral fluency scores for early (Group A) and late starters (Group B) has revealed significant differences in 4 of the 13 variables examined (those marked with an asterisk on Table 3.2). Significant differences in scores were found in the speech rate variables (SRW and SRS), which are one of the most robust measures of oral fluency, a good predictor of nonnative fluency that correlates with native speakers' fluency ratings of nonnative speech. The late starters (SRW M = 59.01; SRS M = 71.20) were found to significantly outperform the early starters (SRW M = 49.29; SRW M = 59.17) in speech rate, thus producing more words per minute. Late starters managed to produce more language in their L2 in the same amount of time than early starters. Early starters make use of L1 words significantly more frequently than late starters, produce less and shorter fluent speech runs, but produce

Table 3.2 Mean scores in oral fluency variables according to group and *t*-test results

Oral fluency variables	Subject groups (N = 60; FI = 726h, T3)				T-tests (*statistically significant differences, alpha level = 0.05)
	Group A (N = 30) Early starters (AO = 8)		Group B (N = 30) Late starters (AO = 11)		
	M	SD	M	SD	
Speech Rate in Words (SRW)	49.29	19.53	59.01	16.46	$t(58) = -2.08, p = 0.042$*
Speech Rate in Syllables (SRS)	59.17	21.67	71.20	20.07	$t(58) = -2.23, p = 0.030$*
L1-Word Ratio (L1WR)	12.57	16.40	4.38	8.89	$t(44) = 2.40, p = 0.042$*
Mean Length of Run Words (MLRW)	2.70	0.84	2.89	0.56	$t(58) = -0.982, p = 0.330$
Mean Length of Run Syllables (MLRS)	3.27	0.98	3.4	0.69	$t(58) = -0.949, p = 0.346$
Speech Run Rate (SRR)	18.41	6.04	20.23	3.75	$t(58) = -1.40, p = 0.167$
Longest Fluent Run (LFR)	6.73	2.34	7.67	2.59	$t(58) = -1.46, p = 0.149$
Dysfluency Rate (DYSR)	5.63	3.81	8.98	4.04	$t(58) = -3.30, p = 0.002$*
Lengthened Syllables (LS)	17.42	8.21	17.75	7.54	$t(58) = -0.163, p = 0.871$
Pause Frequency (PF1)	20.63	5.22	22.48	2.90	$t(45) = -1.69, p = 0.098$
Pause Frequency (PF2)	2.38	0.65	2.62	0.70	$t(58) = -1.40, p = 0.165$
Internal Pause Frequency (IPF1)	14.53	4.75	15.34	2.56	$t(44) = -0.823, p = 0.415$
Internal Pause Frequency (IPF2)	3.57	1.31	3.99	1.45	$t(58) = -1.16, p = 0.250$
Internal Filled Pause Frequency (IFPF1)	3.00	2.21	2.9	1.89	$t(58) = 0.198, p = 0.843$
Internal Filled Pause Frequency (IFPF2)	19.60	18.48	24.50	18.23	$t(49) = -0.962, p = 0.341$
Internal Silent Pause Frequency (ISPF1)	11.52	5.3	12.44	2.75	$t(43) = -0.842, p = 0.405$
Internal Silent Pause Frequency (ISPF2)	5.31	4.69	4.97	1.82	$t(58) = -0.370, p = 0.713$

less clause-internal silent pauses (though not significantly), i.e. less silent pauses per minute (ISPF1, $\underline{M}$ = 11.52; ISPF2, $\underline{M}$ = 5.31, i.e. one pause every 5.31 words) than late starters (ISPF1, $\underline{M}$ = 12.44; ISPF2, $\underline{M}$ = 4.97, i.e. one pause every 4.97 words). The percentage of lengthened syllables is almost identical for both groups of subjects. Early starters were found to obtain greater standard deviations in most variables than late starters: early starters' greater asymmetry of distribution may be due to the fact that many of them performed very poorly and obtained very low scores, particularly in variables based on lexical counts (L1WR, SRR).

The results obtained for speech rate are in accordance with some of the lexical and temporal measures obtained, but are apparently at odds with the outcome of the DYSR and PF variables. According to the DYSR and PF results, late starters produce significantly more dysfluencies (repetitions, restarts and repairs) per minute ($\underline{M}$ = 8.98) than the early starters ($\underline{M}$ = 5.63) and their speech contains a higher frequency of clause-internal silent pauses, even if such a difference does not reach statistical significance. This would seem to suggest that early starters are more fluent than late starters, since both DYSR and PF are good predictors of nonfluent speech. However, this interpretation is not consistent with the statistically significant results obtained for speech rate, which suggests that late learners are more fluent than early learners. The explanation of this apparent contradiction is to be sought in the fact that speech rate and DYSR and PF measures capture different dimensions of oral fluency in speech, and in the fact that the participants in our study produced highly nonfluent speech samples due to their low L2 proficiency level. In the nonnative speech samples analysed, subjects who produced more substantial narratives and obtained a higher speech rate (late starters) also produced more repetitions, restarts, repairs and clause-internal silent pauses, but the rest of variables examined suggest that this is due to the fact that they managed to complete the storytelling task more successfully. For example, late starters had a statistically significant lower rate of L1 words ($\underline{M}$ = 4.38) than early starters ($\underline{M}$ = 12.57), who had to resort to L1 words more often in order to proceed with the task. Late starters managed to produce (not significantly, though) more speech runs per minute and longer fluent runs. This interpretation is also supported by the results of the lexical counts and duration measures that were used to compute the variables in Table 3.2 (see Table 3.3): on average, late starters' speech samples contained more words and syllables, less L1 words, more speech runs and were longer in duration, but differences between subject groups did not reach statistical significance.

An estimate of the subjects' overall oral fluency based on the scores obtained in the variables examined suggest that, despite the higher pause frequency and dysfluency rates they obtained, late learners outperform early learners on the basis of their faster speech rate, much lower restricted use of L1 words and the use of longer fluent runs.

Table 3.3 Mean scores in oral fluency measures according to group and *t*-test results

Oral fluency counts in the speech samples	Subject groups (N = 60; FI = 726 h, T3)				T-tests (*statistically significant differences, alpha level = 0.05)
	Group A (N = 30) Early starters (AO = 8)		Group B (N = 30) Late starters (AO = 11)		
	M	SD	M	SD	
Words (number of words)	75.33	35.59	92.40	32.67	$t(58) = -1.95, p = 0.056$
Syllables (number of syllables)	90.63	40.94	111.8	41.34	$t(58) = -1.99, p = 0.051$
L1 words (number of L1 words)	6.37	7.88	3.27	5.59	$t(58) = 1.75, p = 0.084$
Speech runs (number of speech runs)	27.43	11.04	32.70	11.55	$t(58) = -1.80, p = 0.076$
Duration (in seconds)	94.81	40.37	98.89	34.02	$t(58) = -.423, p = 0.674$
Dysfluencies	9.97	14.53	20.23	3.75	$t(58) = -2.33, p = 0.023*$

Conclusions

Speech samples elicited through a picture-elicited narrative task produced by two groups of young EFL learners were evaluated for oral fluency as one aspect of their L2 oral competence. Crucially, the subject groups were matched with respect to L2 exposure (726 hours of formal instruction in the school setting) but differed in onset age of learning (AO = 8 for Group A vs. AO=11 for Group B). The mean scores groups A and B obtained on a set of well-established oral fluency variables based (mainly) on quantitative temporal measures were compared. It was initially predicted that an earlier start could have a positive effect on oral fluency development (the earlier the start, the more fluent the learner becomes), so that early starters would outperform late starters in oral fluency. Since groups A and B are matched with respect to L2 exposure, significant group differences in oral fluency may be attributed to AO. Groups A and B, however, are not a perfect match with respect to age at the time of testing (A = 16.9; B = 17.9). But it seems unlikely that the mean 1-year difference in age at the time of testing between the groups would result in differences in oral fluency due to chronological age explaining older participants' greater language processing ability to encode meaning.

The results reveal that late starters significantly outperform early starters on *speech rate* and *L1-word ratio* and obtain better results on other variables such as *mean length of run, speech run rate* and *longest fluent run*. Early starters, however, obtain higher fluency scores than late starters on *clause-internal silent pauses* and *dysfluency rate*. This apparently contradictory outcome may be due to the fact that in highly dysfluent nonnative speech, better performance on oral fluency variables associated with amount of oral production results in an increase in repetitions, restarts and pause frequency. These results suggest that in the analysis of highly dysfluent non-native speech, speech rate may be a more reliable oral fluency measure than pause frequency. We can conclude, therefore, that late starters outperform early starters in oral fluency, which is indicative of their higher oral L2 competence and strongly suggests that as far as oral fluency is concerned, the oral competence of the EFL learners in this study did not benefit from an early start.

The analysis of oral fluency in nonfluent L2 learner speech we have carried out has revealed a number of methodological considerations stemming from the type of learner speech analysed and the non-adequacy of some of the oral fluency measures employed in the analysis. In particular, further research is needed to determine what oral fluency variables are best discriminators of differences in the level of oral competence of nonfluent young EFL learners and whether the quantitative measures normally used in oral fluency analysis of advanced learner speech are also adequate for the analysis of the speech of less proficient learners. Further insights into the multi-faceted nature of oral fluency may be gained by looking into the relationship between the oral fluency variables examined in this study and related variables measuring other performance aspects of the same pool of learners in other domains of linguistic competence, such as lexical fluency in writing.

Acknowledgements

I would like to thank Laura Sánchez Pérez for painstakingly marking, labelling and computing the fluency variables in many of the subjets' oral productions. Special thanks are due to Carmen Muñoz, the editor of this volume, for being so kindly patient and for her useful comments on earlier drafts of this work.

References

Browman, C.P. and Goldstein, L.M. (1989) Articulatory gestures as phonological units. *Phonology* 6, 201–251.
Browman, C.P. and Goldstein, L.M. (1990) Tiers in articulatory phonology, with some implications for casual speech. In J. Kingston and M.E. Beckman (eds) *Between the Grammar and Physics of Speech. Papers in Laboratory Phonology I* (pp. 341–376). Cambridge: Cambridge University Press.
Browman, C.P. and Goldstein, L.M. (1992) Articulatory phonology: An overview. *Phonetica* 49, 155–180.
Brumfit, C. (2000) Accuracy and fluency: The basic polarity. In H. Riggenbach (ed.) *Perspectives on Fluency* (pp. 61–73). Ann Arbor: The University of Michigan Press.
Chafe, W. (1987) Cognitive constraints on information flow. In R. Tomlin (ed.) *Coherence and Grounding in Discourse* (pp. 21–51). Amsterdam: John Benjamins.
Chambers, F. (1997) What do we mean by fluency? *System* 25 (4), 535–544.
de Bot, K. (1992) A bilingual production model: Levelt's "Speaking" model adapted. *Applied Linguistics* 13 (1), 1–24.

Dewaele, J.-M. (1998) Speech rate variation in two oral styles of advanced French interlanguage. In V. Regan (ed.) *Contemporary Approaches to Second Language Acquisition in Context* (pp. 113–124). Dublin: University College Dublin Press.

Ejzenberg, R. (2000) The juggling act of oral fluency: A psycho-sociolinguistic metaphor. In H. Riggenbach (ed.) *Perspectives on Fluency* (pp. 287–313). Ann Arbor: The University of Michigan Press.

Fillmore, C.J. (1979) On fluency. In C.J. Fillmore, D. Kempler and W.S.-Y. Wang (eds) *Individual Differences in Language Ability and Language Behaviour* (pp. 85–101). New York: Academic Press.

Freed, B.F. (1995) What makes us think that students who study abroad become fluent? In B.F. Freed (ed.) *Second Language Acquisition in a Study Abroad Context* (pp. 123–148). Amsterdam: Benjamins.

Freed, B.F. (2000) Is fluency, like beauty, in the eyes (and ears) of the beholder? In H. Riggenbach (ed.) *Perspectives on Fluency* (pp. 243–265). Ann Arbor: The University of Michigan Press.

Freed, B.F., Segalowitz, N. and Dewey, D.P. (2004) Context of learning and second language fluency in French. *Studies in Second Language Acquisition* 26, 275–301.

Griffiths, R. (1990) Speech rate and NNS comprehension: A preliminary study in time-benefit analysis. *Language Learning* 40 (3), 311–336.

Griffiths, R. (1991) Pausological research in an L2 context: A rationale, and review of selected studies. *Applied Linguistics* 12 (4), 345–364.

Grosjean, F. (1980) Temporal variables within and between languages. In W. Dechert and M. Raupach *Towards a Cross-linguistic Assessment of Speech Production* (pp. 39–55). Frankfurt: Lang.

Grosjean, F. and Deschamps, A. (1972) Analyse des variables temporelles du français spontané. *Phonetica* 26, 129–156.

Grosjean, F. and Deschamps, A. (1973) Analyse des variables temporelles du français spontané II. Comparaison du français oral dans la description avec l'anglais (description) et avec le français (interview radiophonique). *Phonetica* 28, 191–226.

Grosjean, F. and Deschamps, A. (1975) Analyse contrastive des variables temporelles du français: Vitesse de parole et variables composantes, phénomènes d'hésitation. *Phonetica* 31, 144–184.

Guion, S.G., Flege, J.E., Liu, S.H. and Yeni-Komshian, G.H. (2000) Age of learning effects on the duration of sentences produced in a second language. *Applied Psycholinguistics* 21, 205–228.

Hieke, A.E. (1984) Linking as a marker of fluent speech. *Language and Speech* 27 (4), 343–354.

Hieke, A.E. (1985) A componential approach to oral proficiency evaluation. *The Modern Language Journal* 69 (2), 135–142.

Hieke, A. E. (1987) Absorption and fluency in native and non-native casual English speech. In A. James and J. Leather (eds) *Sound Patterns in Second Language Acquisition* (pp. 41–58). Dordrecht: Foris Publications.

Kormos, J. and Dénes, M. (2004) Exploring measures and perceptions of fluency in the speech of second language learners. *System* 32, 145–164.

Kowal, S.H., Wiese, R. and O'Connell, D.C. (1983) The use of time in storytelling. *Language and Speech* 26, 377–392.

Lennon, P. (1990) Investigating fluency in EFL: A quantitative approach. *Language Learning* 40 (3), 387–417.

Lennon, P. (2000) The lexical element in spoken second language fluency. In H. Riggenbach (ed.) *Perspectives on Fluency* (pp. 25–42). Ann Arbor: The University of Michigan Press.

Morales-López, E. (2000) Fluency levels and the organization of conversation in non-native Spanish speakers' speech. In H. Riggenbach (ed.) *Perspectives on Fluency* (pp. 266–286). Ann Arbor: The University of Michigan Press.

Munro, M.J. and Derwing, T.M. (1995) Processing time, accent, and comprehensibility in the perception of native and foreign-accented speech. *Language and Speech* 38 (3), 289–306.

Oppenheim, N. (2000) The importance of recurrent sequences for nonnative speaker fluency and cognition. In H. Riggenbach (ed.) *Perspectives on Fluency* (pp. 220–240). Ann Arbor: The University of Michigan Press.

Pawley, A. and Syder, F.H. (1983) Two puzzles for linguistic theory: Nativelike selection and nativelike fluency. In J. C. Richards and R. W. Schmidt (eds) *Language and Communication* (pp. 191–226). New York: Longman.

Pawley, A. and Syder, F.H. (2000) The one-caluse-at-a-time hypothesis. In H. Riggenbach (ed.) *Perspectives on Fluency* (pp. 163–199). Ann Arbor: The University of Michigan Press.

Raupach, M. (1980) Temporal variables in first and second language speech production. In H.W. Dechert and M. Raupach (eds) *Temporal Variables in Speech* (pp. 263–270).

Raupach, M. (1987) Procedural knowledge in advanced learners of a foreign language. In J. Coleman and R. Towell (eds) *The Advanced Language Learner* (pp. 123–157). London: AFSL/CILT.

Rehbein, J. (1987) On fluency in second language speech. In H.W. Dechert, and M. Raupach (eds) *Psycholinguistic Models of Production* (pp. 97–105). Norwood, NJ: Ablex Publishing Corporation.

Riazantseva, A. (2001) Second language proficiency and pausing. *Studies in Second Language Acquisition* 23, 497–526.

Riggenbach, H. (1991) Toward an understanding of fluency: A microanalysis of non-native speaker conversations. *Discourse Processes* 14, 423–441.

Riggenbach, H. (ed.) (2000) *Perspectives on Fluency*. Ann Arbor: The University of Michigan Press.

Schmidt, R. (1992) Psychological mechanisms underlying second language fluency. *Studies in Second Language Acquisition* 14, 357–385.

Segalowitz, N. (2000) Automaticity and attentional skill in fluent performance. In H. Riggenbach (ed.) *Perspectives on Fluency* (pp. 200–219). Ann Arbor: The University of Michigan Press.

Segalowitz, N. and Freed, B.F. (2004) Context, contact, and cognition in oral fluency acquisition. *Studies in Second Language Acquisition* 26, 173–199.

Skehan, P. and Foster, P. (1999) The influence of task structure and processing conditions on narrative retellings. *Language Learning* 49 (1), 93–120.

Towell, R. (1987) Approaches to the analysis of the oral language development of the advanced learner. In J. Coleman and R. Towell (eds) *The Advanced Language Learner* (pp. 157–183). London: AFSL/CILT.

Towell, R. (2002) Relative degrees of fluency: A comparative case study of advanced learners of French. *International Review of Applied Linguistics* 40, 117–150.

Towell, R. and Hawkins, R. (1994) *Approaches to Second Language Acquisition*. Clevedon: Multilingual Matters.

Towell, R., Hawkins, R. and Bazergui, N. (1996) The development of fluency in advanced learners of French. *Applied Linguistics* 17 (1), 84–119.

Wennerstrom, A. (2000) The role of intonation in second language fluency. In H. Riggenbach (ed.) *Perspectives on Fluency* (pp. 102–127). Ann Arbor: The University of Michigan Press.

Wesche, M. and Skehan, P. (2002) Communicative, task-based, and content-based language instruction. In R. Kaplan *The Oxford Handbook of Applied Linguistics* (pp. 207–228). New York: Oxford University Press.

Chapter 4
Age and Vocabulary Acquisition in English as a Foreign Language (EFL)

IMMACULADA MIRALPEIX

Introduction

The relationship between age and vocabulary acquisition in the first language (L1) is well documented. A growing number of studies analyses vocabulary development in children (D'Odorico *et al.*, 2001 -in Italian-; Hamilton & Plunkett, 2000 -in English-; Jackson-Maldonado *et al.*, 1993 -in Spanish-), late talkers, handicapped learners (Wachal & Spreen, 1973) or bilinguals (Engel & Whitehead, 1993; Vihman, 1985). As regards lexical acquisition in any second/foreign language (L2/FL), the literature covers both early and late vocabulary learning (for instance, Yoshida, 1978 in children; Altman, 1997; Broeder *et al.*, 1988, 1993; Service & Craik, 1993 in adults). There is also a number of studies looking for differences between younger and older learners as regards learning styles (Papalia, 1975; Turner, 1983), mnemonic strategies (Pressley & Dennis-Rounds, 1980; Pressley *et al.*, 1980), word associations (Sökmen, 1993), meaning production (Verhallen & Schoonen, 1993), transfer (Cenoz, 2003; Ringböm, 1987) and representation and access of words (Silverberg & Samuel, 2004).

However, as Singleton points out, "the age factor, as it relates to second language lexical acquisition is not a matter that receives a great deal of attention" (1995: 10). When it comes to the study of language learning and age-related constraints, most studies concentrate on phonology and morphosyntax. Harley and Wang (1997: 24) call attention to the fact that Lenneberg, who first posited the idea of a "critical period" for language acquisition, "seems to have viewed vocabulary learning as exempt from maturational constraints, or at least, that his primary concern was with syntax and phonology".

The emphasis on these areas and the overlooking of vocabulary may be due to two main reasons. First of all, aspects affected by age are thought to be learned mostly in an implicit way, and both phonology and morphosyntax seem to adhere to this condition better than vocabulary might seem to do. Ellis (1994) describes vocabulary acquisition as an implicitly acquired skill as regards learning of surface forms and as an explicit learning process as regards acquisition of meaning. Also Hulstijn (2003: 362) points out that "it is widely held that little vocabulary is acquired in an intentional fashion" and that "it is widely believed

[...] that most vocabulary, in L1 as well as in L2, is acquired in an incidental fashion, as a by-product".

The second explanation would come from the neurolinguistic field. There is evidence that suggests that semantic and grammatical functions are neurobiologically different (Neville & Lawson, 1992). The influence of age on these two systems also seems to be different. Paradis (1994: 398) explains that "patterns of cortical organisation associated with the processing of morphosyntax are altered as a function of age of acquisition to a greater extent than those associated with the processing of vocabulary". Fabbro (2002) reviews some studies that show that the lexicons of the L1 and L2 are represented in the same brain areas (declarative memory systems in the left cortical associative areas) regardless of the age of acquisition. This does not happen with other linguistic aspects: the representation of grammatical aspects, for example, is claimed to be different in the two languages if the L2 is acquired later than age 7.

In spite of this evidence, it is sometimes assumed that it is mainly pronunciation and vocabulary that children will learn more efficiently in the first stages of learning a language. In a study carried out by Burstall *et al.* (1974) about an earlier introduction of French in primary schools in the UK, most of the teachers considered that starting the second language when children were younger than 12 was positive, as an earlier start "would help pupils to acquire a *wider vocabulary*" and that it was the time "to get children speaking French quite naturally, assimilating *new words* and sounds *without difficulty*" (1974: 69–70; my emphasis).

A distinction has often been made between naturalistic settings and formal settings and, within each, short-term and long-term studies have been carried out. As regards naturalistic settings, most studies reveal that younger learners do not perform as well as older learners in the short term. Snow and Hoefnagel-Höhle's research in The Netherlands, with English learners of Dutch, shows that adolescent and adult learners' results in the Peabody Picture Vocabulary Test (Dunn, 1959) were better than those of the younger learners, thus suggesting an advantage for the older over the younger learners in vocabulary, as well as for aspects of the second language skill that depended strongly on rule acquisition such as syntax and morphology (Snow, 1983; Snow & Hoefnagel-Höhle, 1978). Also Cummins and Swain (1986) found that older learners would acquire cognitively demanding aspects of L2 proficiency more rapidly than younger learners; in lexis, older learners in an immersion context in Canada acquired more vocabulary in the same amount of time than did younger learners, as evaluated in a Picture Vocabulary Test. However, research has shown as well that Early Starters (ES) will most probably overtake Late Starters (LS) in the long run (Hyltenstam, 1992; Mägiste, 1987). Also Snow and Hoefnagel-Höhle's younger subjects began to catch up with the older ones after about a year.

Studies in formal settings also show that older learners outperform younger ones in the short-run (Asher & Price, 1967; Stankowski Gratton, 1980). An immediate advantage for younger learners is suggested in Yamada *et al.* (1980), although the nature of the task being performed, involving pair-associates of just four English concrete nouns, makes the results obtained difficult to generalise (see Harley, 1986 and Singleton, 1995, for a complete review of these studies). In the long term, younger learners do not seem to catch up with older learners either. Results in Burstall *et al.* (1974), indicate that an early start is not synonymous with better long-term performance. She explains that students who had been taught French from the age of 8 did not reveal, by the age of 16, any "substantial" gains apart from listening comprehension, the only test in which they were slightly better. Vocabulary in this study was assessed in different ways: in the reading comprehension test, students were asked to identify the pictures that corresponded to printed items and then to choose the words needed to complete sentences; in the oral test, the answers to questions referring to illustrations were scored for structure and vocabulary using four-point scales (Burstall, 1968). Oller and Nagato (1974) carried out a cross-sectional study at Grades 7, 9 and 11 of Japanese learners of English. Despite an advantage of six years in EFL for ES, LS outperformed them towards the end of high-school education. This fact led the authors to conclude that an early start does not necessarily mean a lasting benefit. However, lexical competence was assessed here only by means of cloze tests and both ES and LS were integrated into the same class from the 8th year on, which could have made it easier for LS to catch up with ES.

Singleton's study (1995, 1999) analyses the performance of a group of university students who started learning the foreign language before age 12 and a group who had started after this age. The study, which involves three data-collection times, seemed to reveal a long-term benefit of an early start by the time of the second data collection, but the differences in favour of the ES group did not persist in the third data-collection time. Here, the only measure of lexical performance that was taken into account was the *c*-test, and there is a question over whether *c*-tests are actually good tests of lexis (Chapelle, 1994). Moreover, neither in Oller and Nagato (1974) nor in Singleton (1995, 1999) was it possible to separate the age at which learners had begun the instruction in the FL from the amount of time it had been going on.

The present study is concerned with age effects on vocabulary acquisition. It has been conducted within the framework of the Barcelona Age Factor (BAF) Project. One of the aims of the BAF Project is to find out if an earlier introduction to English in a Catalan/Spanish bilingual context has any positive effects (linguistic, attitudinal ...) in the long run. This study analyses the productive vocabulary of two groups of students towards the end of secondary education. They all have received the same amount of formal exposure to English, but they have started instruction at two different ages. We want to know if those who started learning English earlier will have better productive vocabularies than those who started later. Both oral and written data have been analysed: oral free vocabulary was assessed from an interview, a storytelling task and a role-play; written free vocabulary from a composition. Written controlled vocabulary was tested in a cloze.

Measures to Assess Lexical Richness

Different measures have been used to assess learners' lexical knowledge: vocabulary scales, *c*-tests, and clozes, among the most frequent. Lexical richness has also often been measured by the Type-Token Ratio (TTR), that is, the number of different words as a ratio of the total number of running words in a text. This measure is supposed to show how likely it is for a learner to repeat the same words. However, one of the main problems that this measure presents is its sensitivity to text length (Daller *et al.*, 2003; Faerch *et al.*, 1984, Richards, 1987; Vermeer 2000, 2004), basically because the rate at which new word-types appear in a text decreases as the text size increases. There have been some attempts to overcome this problem. For instance, the use of adapted measures like the Guiraud Index, the Mean Segmental TTR or the Bilogarithmic TTR, which are just small variations of the TTR and therefore not feasible solutions in most cases. Another possibility has been to fix the length of all the samples to be analysed so as to keep length constant, but this also implies that data are lost when cutting the texts.

Apart from the TTR, Lexical Density (LD) has often been used to assess lexical richness. LD is the proportion of content words as opposed to function words (Ure, 1971), but it does not seem to be a good measure at low levels either, due to the fact that some students use telegraphic style, thus they do not make use of much function words. This would yield higher LD values while it would actually reflect the inability to construct a coherent text (Hyltenstam, 1988).

Recently, a new measure, D, has been proposed by Malvern and Richards (1997, 2002) and Malvern *et al.* (2004). D is an index that measures lexical diversity through a process of curve-fitting, which is the general problem of finding equations of approximating curves that fit given sets of data. It is claimed to be more informative than TTR, because, as opposed to the single value of the TTR, it represents how TTR varies over a range of token sizes for each speaker or writer. This measure also has two other advantages. Firstly, because it is not a function of the number of words in the sample, it uses all the data available in the text, so it is not necessary to standardise text length. Secondly, it is claimed to work with short texts (50 tokens are needed), which is especially relevant when working with low-level learners and oral data, since these learners do not normally produce much.

Jarvis (2002) compares the D formula with other indices of lexical diversity that can also be used in a curve-fitting approach. He concludes that D is accurate for analysing whole texts (with both content and function words), as opposed for instance to U,[1] which seems to be more reliable when carrying out the analysis with just the content words from each text. However, Jarvis points out that more evidence is needed to check whether the efficacy of D extends to other types of written and oral texts (he used written narratives in his study) produced by a greater variety of learners and native speakers.

It is difficult to say if D will actually become a standard measure for lexical richness but, up to now, and according to the studies carried out by Malvern and Richards, it seems to be one of the most reliable. Our study is also an attempt to provide the so-often requested evidence for or against the adequacy of this measure for vocabulary acquisition research, compared to other more traditional measures. Moreover, it would be of great interest to use D in age-related studies in particular, given the variety of measures that have been used in previous studies, which makes it difficult to generalise and compare the results obtained in different contexts.

Method

Subjects

The subjects of this study were two groups of Catalan/Spanish bilinguals who were learning English as an L3 in state-funded schools in Barcelona. The first group (ES, $N = 57$) started learning English at the age of 8 and was tested when their average age was 16.3.[2] The second group (LS, $N = 41$) began learning English at the age of 11 and was tested at the age of 17.9. The amount of exposure was the same for both groups: 726 hours (see Table 4.1), although distributed differently: seven school years for LS and eight to nine years for ES (see note 2). For the purpose of this study, we chose the students with curricular exposure only. Those with stays abroad, attending language schools and repeaters were not included in the sample. See Chapter 1 for a detailed account of the sample in the BAF Project.

Instruments

Background questionnaire

A questionnaire written in Catalan was used to elicit information about when students started receiving English classes and for how long instruction

Table 4.1 Participants

	N	Onset Age	Age at testing	Hours of instruction
Early Starters -ES-	57	8	16.3	726 h (8–9 school years)
Late Starters -LS-	41	11	17.9	726 h (7 school years)

had taken place, to make sure that the hours of exposure were kept equal for both groups. It also elicited information about extracurricular exposure, if any, and extensive biographical and linguistic information about the learners (see Appendix 4).

Oral tests

Free productive vocabulary

Learners were asked to perform three tasks (1) a semi-guided interview, where they were asked about their daily lives, hobbies, etc. by a researcher; (2) a storytelling where they had to tell a story given to them in six pictures with no text; and (3) a role-play, where two students (a father/mother and a son/daughter) talked about organizing a party (see Table 4.2).

Written tests

Free productive vocabulary

Students wrote a composition about themselves, the maximum time allowed for them to write was 15 minutes.

Controlled productive vocabulary

A cloze test was used to assess learners' written controlled productive vocabulary. Reliability of the cloze test was assessed by computing Cronbach's alpha for a group of ES ($N = 51$) and a group of LS ($N = 51$). The results, 0.8860 and 0.7832 respectively show that the test has internal consistency. It was also shown to have a good discrimination and difficulty rate in subjects with different proficiency levels in the BAF Project.

Procedure

As regards oral data, it became necessary to make a selection of the items that were going to be included in the analyses. Oral data were transcribed and revised at least two times by a different researcher and all the transcripts were checked and adapted in order to ensure that the learners' amount of types and tokens produced was neither overestimated nor underestimated: following Broeder *et al.* (1988) and Richards and Malvern (2000), immediate self-repetitions, false starts, laughter and fillers were not included in the final analyses. Both in the oral and written data non-

Table 4.2 Tests

Background questionnaire		
Oral tests	Free	Semi-guided interview Storytelling Role-play
Written tests	Free	Composition
	Controlled	Cloze

completed words, which normally occur in the shortened form (*disco-discotheque, vet-veterinary, cos-because*) were turned into their completed forms, mistakes (*childrens, nouse*) were corrected, lexical inventions (*impersonality, cistel*) and all words in L1 or languages different from English were excluded and words with more than one spelling (*programme-program*) were consistently changed into one.

Number of types, tokens and word-families were obtained using *VocabProfile* (Nation, 1995) and for the computation of D a new instrument was created: *D_Tools*[3] (Meara & Miralpeix, 2004), following Malvern and Richards. All the measures were calculated with and without standardising text length in all of the tasks. The reason for keeping length constant in one of the analyses is to control for a possible length effect in the results. Length was set at 50 tokens for the standardised tasks because it was the minimum number of tokens needed to calculate D and most of the tasks in our study were at least 50 tokens long. For the storytelling, role-play and composition, the first 50 tokens were chosen, for the interview we left out the first 20% of learners' production and counted the next 50 tokens, as the openings of the interviews were very similar in all cases (name, grade, age …).

T-tests for independent samples were performed to see if there were any significant differences between ES and LS. Alpha was set at 0.01 as the analyses involved multiple comparisons. Pearson correlations were carried out between D and the other measures (TTR, types and tokens). We performed these correlations with a twofold purpose: to check how this new measure was related to other measures of lexical richness and especially to see if D correlated with the number of tokens in each task and was therefore affected by text length.

Results

Tables 4.3 to 4.6 show the results for each group (ES and LS) in all of the tasks. The first five columns in the tables correspond to the means of the measures computed for each group without standardising length. The last three columns present the results when length is set at 50 tokens. Table 4.7 summarises the measures and tasks where the differences between the two groups are found, as well as the significance of these differences.

Results from the interview show that LS outperform significantly ES as regards the number of tokens, types and word-families when length is not

Table 4.3 Interview

	Non-standardised					Standardised		
	Tokens	Types	WF	TTR	D	Types	WF	TTR
ES N = 57	145.54	70.79	56.42	0.5340	40.36	31.96	26.80	0.6392
LS N = 41	207.85	91.83	72.46	0.4653	44.53	32.88	28.05	0.6566

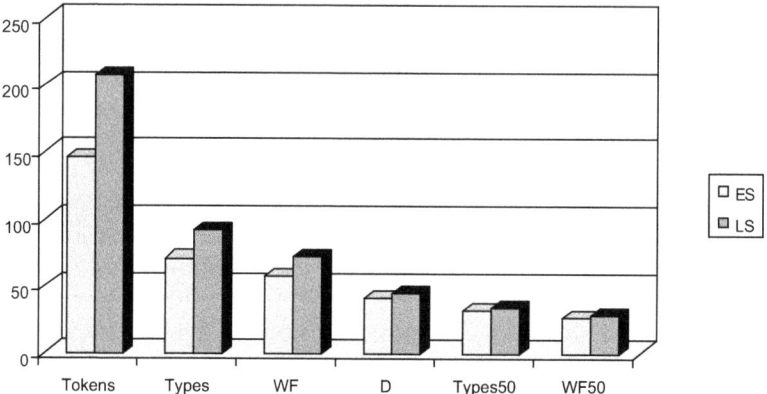

Figure 4.1 Interview

standardised. There is also a significant difference in TTRs between the two groups in favour of ES (see Tables 4.3, 4.7 and Figure 4.1).

In the storytelling task, we find significant differences between ES and LS in all measures except when TTR is calculated without standardising length (see Tables 4.4, 4.7 and Figure 4.2).

Table 4.4 Storytelling

	Non-standardised					Standardised		
	Tokens	Types	WF	TTR	D	Types	WF	TTR
ES $N = 57$	89.79	38.54	35.23	0.4570	18.90	26.81	24.72	0.5362
LS $N = 41$	110.78	49.46	43.90	0.4606	23.86	29.23	26.35	0.5845

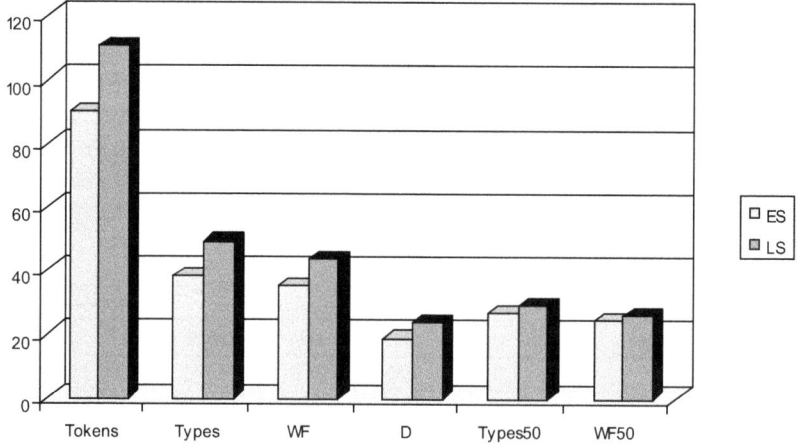

Figure 4.2 Storytelling

In the roleplay, ES and LS perform very similarly, there are no significant differences except for word-families when length is kept equal, in which LS significantly outperform ES (see Tables 4.5, 4.7 and Figure 4.3).

Table 4.5 Role-play

	Non-standardised					Standardised		
	Tokens	Types	WF	TTR	D	Types	WF	TTR
ES N = 54	65.06	35.61	31.06	0.6111	33.78	31.27	27.64	0.6255
LS N = 41	70.56	40.00	35.88	0.6214	38.85	32.89	29.96	0.6579

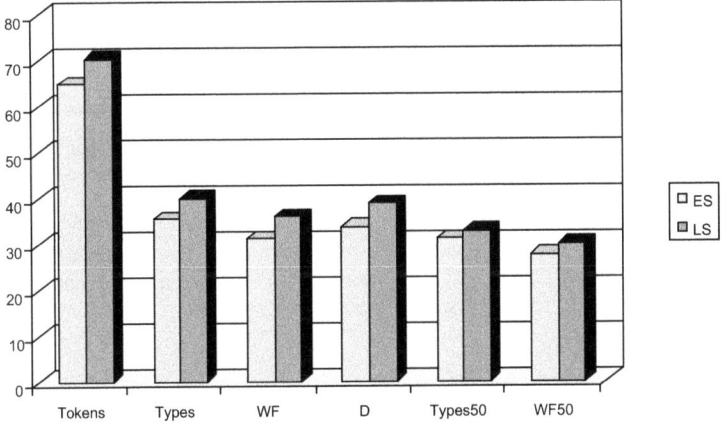

Figure 4.3 Role-play

Significant differences between ES and LS are found in the composition only when length is standardised in the amount of types, word-families and TTR (see Tables 4.6, 4.7 and Figure 4.4).

Table 4.6 Composition

	Non-standardised					Standardised		
	Tokens	Types	WF	TTR	D	Types	WF	TTR
ES N = 56	93.50	53.48	41.30	0.5979	40.80	33.20	25.56	0.6640
LS N = 35	96.54	54.34	45.69	0.5902	43.97	34.86	29.04	0.6971

In the English cloze, which was taken as a measure of controlled productive vocabulary, LS significantly outperformed ES: ES ($M = 58.53$, $SD = 27.59$); LS [$M = 82.52$, $SD = 10.46$; $t(70) = 5.814$, $p = 0.000$).

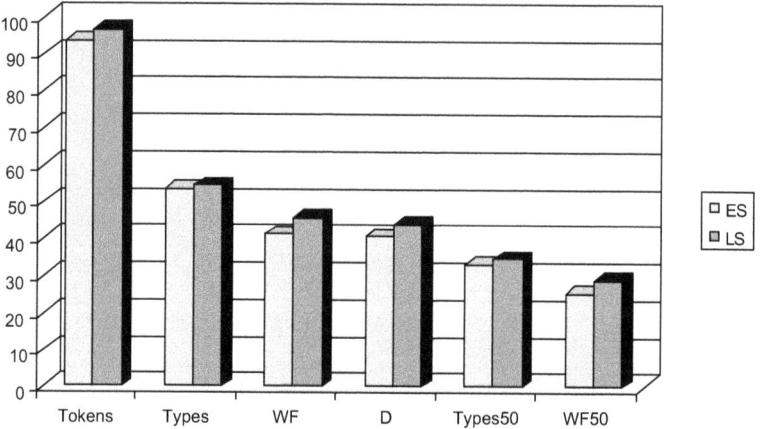

Figure 4.4 Composition

Table 4.7 Significant differences in the *t*-tests, when $p < 0.01$

	Tokens	Types	WF	TTR	D	Types	WF	TTR
Int.	0.000[a]	0.000[a]	0.000[a]	0.000[b]	–	–	–	–
Story	0.007[a]	0.000[a]	0.000[a]	–	0.000[a]	0.002[a]	0.037[a]	0.002[a]
Role	–	–	–	–	–	–	0.022[a]	–
Comp.	–	–	–	–	–	0.031[a]	0.000[a]	0.031[a]

Notes: a LS>ES; b ES>LS.

The correlations between D and the other measures in each task have a similar pattern. They are shown in Table 4.8. Positive moderate-strong correlations are found between D and the number of types (and word-families), especially when length is standardised, e.g. in the storytelling (r = 0.881 n = 98 $p < 0.001$). There are also positive (moderate-strong) correlations between D and TTR, most of the time when length is kept constant, e.g. in the

Table 4.8 Correlations between D and the other measures in each of the tasks

	Non-standardised				Standardised		
	Tokens	Types	WF	TTR	Types	WF	TTR
Dint N = 98	0.034	0.257*	0.252*	0.379**	0.537**	0.450**	0.537**
Dstory N = 98	0.223*	0.642**	0.625**	0.620**	0.881**	0.821**	0.881**
Drole N = 95	–0.032	0.365**	0.394**	0.608**	0.808**	0.733**	0.808**
Dcomp N = 91	0.134	0.383**	0.301**	0.565**	0.708**	0.347**	0.708**

Notes: * $p < 0.005$; ** $p < 0.001$.

composition (r = 0.708, n = 91, p < 0.001). Very small correlations are found between D and the number of types and word-families in the interview when length is not standardised. There is no correlation either between D and the number of tokens produced in any of the tasks, apart from a very small one in the storytelling.

Therefore, significant differences between the two groups are always in favour of the LS (both in free and controlled productive vocabulary), except for the TTR of the interview and composition, which is higher for ES when length is not fixed. While standardising length does not imply big differences in the significance of the results in the storytelling and the role-play, results vary in the interview and composition depending on whether we kept length equal in all texts. In addition, although D significantly correlates with other measures of lexical richness (number of types, word-families even with TTR), this is not so with the number of tokens and only in the storytelling is a very weak correlation between number of tokens and D found.

Discussion

In this study we set out to explore if, towards the end of secondary education, students who had been learning English from the age of 8 in a formal context outperformed the students who had started it at 11, as regards oral and written productive vocabulary. It was also our purpose to analyse how the D measure was related to other vocabulary measures and to check if it was useful to describe the vocabularies of our learners, who are not at an advanced level and produce short texts.

Results show that, as regards free productive vocabulary, after 726 hours of formal exposure, learners who started learning English earlier did not outperform those who started three years later. We have many instances in which the differences are not significant, although LS productive vocabulary is shown to be marginally more diverse. LS tend to obtain higher results in some of the tasks (for example, LS outperform ES in the storytelling). However, there is another task where the two groups performed similarly (the role-play), and two other tasks where the advantage of the older group is just shown in some of the measures (i.e. the interview and the composition). The differences in favour of the LS are obvious in controlled productive vocabulary, as they obtain significatively better results in the cloze test. Therefore, these findings are consistent with previous research in other formal contexts (Burstall *et al.*, 1974; Oller & Nagato, 1974; Singleton, 1999), which do not provide evidence in favour of the ES either.

Our results are also in line with other long-term studies carried out in the Basque Country. In a similar context to ours – where Basque/Spanish bilinguals learn English as an L3 – after six years of EFL instruction, LS (starting at 11 and being 16 when they were tested) significantly outperformed ES (starting at 8 and being 13 when they were tested). Vocabulary was assessed in an oral storytelling task, a cloze and a composition. In this last written task, Jacobs *et al.*'s profile (1981) was used in the ratings (see Cenoz, 2002). The older the students were, after a similar amount of English language instruction, the greater the lexical complexity found in their compositions (Lasagabaster & Doiz, 2003).

It can also be seen in our data that the interview and the composition show length effects. In the interview, differences are found between the groups in the amount of tokens, types and word-families when length is not set at 50 tokens, but there are no differences when length is kept equal. This might be due to the nature of the task: the interviewer introduces new topics, which may act as a trigger for more lexical variety in this oral data, something which cannot be shown when length is set at 50 tokens. With the help of the interviewer, who asks and provides topics to talk about, it is easier for students to talk more, which does not happen in a task where the interviewer is not present or does not have such an active role, as in the storytelling. Therefore, LS have more lexical variety that can only be shown in longer texts.

Unlike what happens in the interview, differences between the groups in the composition are only found when length is standardised. Given equal length to the texts of both groups, LS significantly outperform ES. Hence we see here the importance of standardising length in these two tasks so as not to obtain misleading results with traditional measures.

The results from the storytelling and role-plays are not so dependent on length as the ones obtained from the interview and the composition, as most of the measures do not give different results when length is not kept constant. Of all the oral tasks, the storytelling may be the most adequate to assess productive vocabulary knowledge. Firstly, the results do not vary according to length. Secondly, it elicits more words from the students than the role-play. Probably, the reason why the two groups performed in such a similar way in the role-play is that it is a dual task and they have to take into account the limitations not only of their own lexical resources but also those of their partners. Therefore, more proficient learners might adapt to the demands of a less-proficient partner (use of a less varied vocabulary, asking or answering using very short utterances ...). As they are not perfoming the task alone and they do not have any planning time, like in the composition or the storytelling, it is also more difficult for them to think just after their partner's turn of what they are going to say, which might also be the reason why it is the task where they produce fewer tokens.

As regards TTRs, there is variation in the results when length is not kept constant. Sensitivity to text length is clearly seen in the interviews, where LS have more types and tokens than ES (and where we find the biggest difference between the group means in these measures). However, it is ES who have a higher TTR. This finding is in line with what has been repeatedly shown in the literature, that is, the dependency of TTR on the number of tokens (Lenko-Szymanska, 2002; Richards, 1987; Vermeer, 2000). Nevertheless, we notice a resemblance between the results given by the TTR with length standardised and D values. This might seem to contradict Richards and Malvern's (2000) results, as they find no correlation between D and TTR. Our correlations between D and TTR without keeping length constant are moderate, but they get stronger if we correlate D and the TTRs computed after standardising length. This fact makes us wonder about the necessity of D and of a curve-fitting approach if the results given by TTRs and Ds are correlated. Actually, D itself might be also considered a variation of the TTR because at some point we do take into account the relationship between types and tokens, but it is theoretically more valid and, in addition, much more appropriate for practical purposes as we do not need to standardise text length and discard part of the data. Apart from this, the positive correlations between D and the number of types confirms its potential as a measure of lexical variation (maybe more useful at these elementary stages than LD). The lack of correlation between D and amount of tokens shows that this measure is not affected by text length as TTR is.

These results, however, cannot be taken in isolation, but interpreted together with other findings in the BAF Project. The fact that ES are not superior to LS in productive vocabulary has been gauged in this study only by some lexical measures. A more complete view of their competence emerges if we take into account that ES ask for assistance in the oral tests more often than LS do (see Grañena, this volume), which may also be seen as an indicator of their poorer lexical competence (i.e. asking for help in vocabulary they do not know). In the written data, Navés *et al.* (2003) also show that LS do normally produce more and that significant differences in favour of the ES are very rarely found (see also Torras *et al.*, this volume). An advantage of LS over ES in lexical knowledge (especially written) seems to be present since the first stages of learning the foreign language. In the compositions, for instance, LS lexical gains after 200 hours of school instruction are superior to those of ES after the same number of hours of exposure (Miralpeix, 2002). In the storytelling task, Muñoz (2000) finds significant differences between the verb/noun ratio of ES and LS, who were already performing better than their peers. Moreover, by Time 2 (after 416 hours of instruction), LS do not resort to the L1 as often as ES do (Muñoz, 2003), which would mean that LS have more vocabulary available in the L2. Taken together, these results would be an indication that, given similar opportunities, efficiency in second language learning increases with age as regards productive vocabulary knowledge as well.

Conclusion

In summary, we have seen that, regarding productive vocabulary, ES did not obtain better results than LS in spite of their earlier exposure to the foreign language. Differences in other lexical abilities (receptive vocabulary, speed of retrieval ...) may be shown by further research. From a pragmatic perspective, more information could be obtained that might also offer an account of lexical performance; i.e. speed at answering, silences or, as suggested in Lorenzo-Dus and Meara (2005), the time spent on the topics selected for conversation in the oral tasks.

In this study, we have used intrinsic measures, that is, the assessment has been carried out in terms of the words that appear in the text itself. This has given us a gross indication of learners' levels, which can be further explored by using extrinsic measures of vocabulary (Daller *et al.*, 2003; Laufer & Nation, 1995; Meara & Bell, 2001; Vermeer, 2004) i.e. classifying items according to criteria external to the text itself would help us to study the vocabularies of these two groups of learners (Miralpeix, in preparation).

As productive vocabulary knowledge is not always easy to assess, especially when we deal with oral production from low-level students, we find it worthy to explore new ways to analyse the data. D is a measure that has not been widely used, but the fact that it can become a standard index that can work in a variety of contexts and languages suggests that it can be a more adequate measure of lexical diversity than TTR. Thus, curve-fitting approaches can solve some of the problems that traditional lexical richness measures have been shown to have. We are also well aware of the limitations of a curve-fitting approach (Jarvis, 2003), but it can be regarded as a good start to explore how lexical diversity might be approached in the future.

Acknowledgements

This study was supported by grants 2001FI-0062 from Generalitat de Catalunya to the author and BFF2001-3384 from the Ministry of Education in Spain to the BAF Project. We would also like to thank Professor Paul Meara and the Centre for Applied Language Studies at University of Wales Swansea. Responsibility for the final version, however, rests with the author.

Notes

1. Uber index: A vocabulary measure: $\log^2 N / (\log N - \log V)$.
2. The subjects in the ES group belong to two different grades: Grade 4 (4Eso) and Grade 5 (1Batxillerat). They all started English at school when they were 8 (Grade 3) and received the same amount of exposure (726 h), but the first group received it along eight school courses and the second along nine. The average age of the first group at testing is 15.6 and for the second group 16.6. Average age for the whole ES group is 16.3. In spite of the intensity difference, no significant differences were found between the groups, which assured they can be merged.

3. *D_Tools* comprises two programmes: *D_0* and *D_1*, which can be downloaded from WWW at http://www.swansea.ac.uk/cals/calsres/lognostics.html. D is computed by selecting samples from the text of different token size (from 35 to 50 tokens). The program then calculates and averages TTRs at each point and matches the curve produced by our text with a theoretical curve produced by Malvern and Richards' formula: TTR = $D/N [(1+2N/D)^{1/2} -1]$, the best match between the two curves, which is calculated using a least-square algorithm, is the D value of our text.

References

Altman, R. (1997) Oral production of vocabulary: A case study. In J. Coady and T. Huckin (eds) *Second Language Vocabulary Acquisition* (pp. 69–97). Cambridge: Cambridge University Press.

Asher, J. and Price, B. (1967) The learning strategy of the Total Physical Response: Some age differences. *Child Development* 38, 1219–1227. Reprinted in S. Krashen, R. Scarcella and M. Long (eds) (1982) *Child-adult Differences in Second Language Acquisition* (pp. 76–83). Rowley, MA: Newbury House.

Broeder, P., Extra, G. and Van Hout, R. (1993) Richness and variety in the developing lexicon. In C. Perdue (ed.) *Adult Language Acquisition: Field Methods* (Vol. 1, pp. 145–163). Cambridge: Cambridge University Press.

Broeder, P., Extra, G., Van Hout, R., Strömqvist, S. and Voinmaa, K. (eds) (1988) *Processes in the Developing Lexicon. Final Report to the European Science Foundation* (Vol. 3). Strasbourg, Tilburg and Göteborg: European Science Foundation.

Burstall, C. (1968) *French Form Eight: A National Experiment* (Vol. 18). London: National Foundation for Educational Research in England and Wales.

Burstall, C., Jamieson, M., Cohen, S. and Hargreaves, M. (1974) *Primary French in the Balance*. Windsor: NFER Publishing Company Ltd.

Cenoz, J. (2002) Age differences in foreign language learning. *ITL Review of Applied Linguistics* 135–136, 125–142.

Cenoz, J. (2003) The influence of age on the acquisition of English: General proficiency, attitudes and code-mixing. In M.P. García Mayo and M.L. García Lecumberri (eds) *Age and the Acquisition of English as a Foreign Language: Theoretical Issues and Fieldwork* (pp. 77–93). Clevedon: Multilingual Matters.

Chapelle, C.A. (1994) Are C-tests valid measures for L2 vocabulary research? *Second Language Research* 10 (2), 157–187.

Cummins, J. and Swain, M. (1986) Linguistic interdependence: A central principle of bilingual education. In J. Cummins and M. Swain (eds) *Bilingualism in Education: Aspects of Theory, Research and Practice* (pp. 80–95). London: Longman.

Daller, H., Van Hout, R. and Treffers-Daller, J. (2003) Lexical richness in the spontaneous speech of bilinguals. *Applied Linguistics* 24 (2), 197–222.

D'Odorico, L., Carubbi, S., Salerni, N. and Calvo, V. (2001) Vocabulary development in Italian children: A longitudinal evaluation of quantitative and qualitative research. *Journal of Child Language* 28, 351–372.

Dunn, L. (1959) *Peabody Picture Vocabulary Test*. Circle Pines, MN: American Guidance Service.

Ellis, N. (1994) Vocabulary acquisition: The implicit ins and outs of explicit cognitive mediation. In N. Ellis (ed.) *Implicit and Explicit Learning of Languages* (pp. 211–282). San Diego, CA: Academic Press.

Engel, D. and Whitehead, M.R. (1993) More first words: A comparative study of bilingual siblings. *Early Years* 14 (1), 27–35.

Fabbro, F. (2002) The neurolinguistics of L2 users. In V. Cook (ed.) *Portraits of the L2 User* (pp. 199–218). Clevedon: Multilingual Matters.

Faerch, C., Haastrup, K. and Phillipson, R. (1984) Vocabulary. In C. Faerch, K. Haastrup and R. Phillipson (eds) *Learner Language and Language Learning* (pp. 77–102). Clevedon: Multilingual Matters.

Hamilton, A. and Plunkett, K. (2000) Infant vocabulary development assessed with a British communicative development inventory. *Journal of Child Language* 27, 689–705.

Harley, B. (1986) *Age in Second Language Acquisition* (Vol. 22). Clevedon: Multilingual Matters.

Harley, B. and Wang, W. (1997) The critical period hypothesis: Where are we now? In A.M.B. de Groot and J.F. Kroll (eds) *Tutorials in Bilingualism* (pp. 19–51). Mahwah, NJ: Lawrence Erlbaum.

Hulstijn, J.H. (2003) Incidental and intentional learning. In M.H. Long and C. Doughty (eds) *Handbook of SLA* (pp. 349–381). Oxford: Blackwell.

Hyltenstam, K. (1988) Lexical characteristics of near-native second-language learners of Swedish. *Journal of Multilingual and Multicultural Development* 9, 67–84.

Hyltenstam, K. (1992) Non-native features of near–native speakers: On the ultimate attainment of childhood L2 learners. In R.J. Harris (ed.) *Cognitive Processing in Bilinguals* (pp. 351–368) London: Elsevier.

Jackson-Maldonado, D., Thal, D., Marchman, V., Bates, E. and Gutiérrez-Clellen, V. (1993) Early lexical development in Spanish-speaking infants and toddlers. *Journal of Child Language* 20, 523–549.

Jacobs, H.L., Zinkgraf, S.A., Wormuth, D.R., Hartfiel, V.F., and Hughey, J.B. (1981) *Testing ESL Composition*. Rowley, MA: Newbury House.

Jarvis, S. (2002) Short texts, best-fitting curves and new measures of lexical diversity. *Language Testing*, 19 (1), 57–84.

Jarvis, S. (2003) Measuring lexical diversity through "exhaustive sampling". Personal communication, Second Language Research Forum, Tucson, AZ.

Lasagabaster, D. and Doiz, A. (2003) Maturational constraints on foreign-language written production. In M.P. García Mayo and M.L. García Lecumberri (eds) *Age and the Acquisition of English as a Foreign Language* (pp. 136–160) Clevedon: Multilingual Matters.

Laufer, B. and Nation, I.S.P. (1995) Vocabulary size and use: Lexical richness in L2 written production. *Applied Linguistics* 16 (3), 307–323.

Lenko-Szymanska, A. (2002) How to trace the growth in learners' active vocabulary? A corpus-based study. In B. Kettermann and M. Georg (eds) *Teaching and Learning by Doing Corpus Analysis. Proceedings of the Fourth International Conference on Teaching and Language Corpora, Graz 19–24 July 2000* (pp. 217–230). Amsterdam: Rodopi.

Lorenzo-Dus, N. and Meara, P.M. (2005) Examiner support strategies and test-taker vocabulary. *IRAL 43*, 239–258.

Mägiste, E. (1987) Further evidence for the optimal age hypothesis in second language learning. In J. Lantolf and A. Labarca (eds) *Research in Language Learning: Focus on the Classroom. Proceedings of the Sixth Delaware Symposium on Language Studies* (pp. 51–58). Norwood, NJ: Ablex.

Malvern, D. and Richards, B. (1997) A new measure of lexical diversity. In A. Ryan and A. Wray (eds) *Evolving Models of Language* (pp. 58–71). Clevedon: Multilingual Matters.

Malvern, D. and Richards, B. (2002) Investigating accommodation in language proficiency interviews using a new measure of lexical diversity. *Language Testing* 19, 85–104.

Malvern, D., Richards, B., Chipere, N. and Durán, P. (2004) *Lexical Diversity and Language Development*. New York: Palgrave Macmillan.

Meara, P.M. and Bell, H. (2001) P_Lex: A simple and effective way of describing the lexical characteristics of short L2 texts. *Prospect. A Journal of Australian TESOL* 16 (3), 5–19.
Meara, P.M. and Miralpeix, I. (2004) *D_Tools (Version 1. 0)*. Swansea: Lognostics.
Miralpeix, I. (2002) Lexis in free written production of learners of English as an L3 with different starting ages: A computational analysis. Unpublished manuscript, Universitat de Barcelona.
Miralpeix, I. (in preparation) The influence of age on vocabulary acquisition in EFL. Doctoral dissertation, University of Barcelona.
Muñoz, C. (2000) The effects of age on rate of acquisition in a foreign language. In P. Gallardo and E. Llurda (eds) *Proceedings of the XXII International Conference of AEDEAN* (pp. 567–571). Lleida: Universitat de Lleida.
Muñoz, C. (2003) Variation in oral skills development and age of onset. In M.P. García Mayo and M.L. García Lecumberri (eds) *Age and the Acquisition of English as a Foreign Language* (pp. 161–181) Clevedon: Multilingual Matters.
Nation, I.S.P. (1995) *VocabProfile*. Victoria: University of Wellington.
Navés, T., Torras, M.R. and Celaya, M.L. (2003) Long-term effects of an earlier start. An analysis of EFL written production. In S.H. Foster-Cohen and S. Pekarek (eds) *Eurosla Yearbook 3* (pp. 103–129) Amsterdam: John Benjamins.
Neville, H.J. and Lawson, D.S. (1992) Fractionating language: Different neural subsystems with different sensitive periods. *Cerebral Cortex* 2, 244–258.
Oller, J. and Nagato, N. (1974) The long term effects of FLES: An experiment. *The Modern Language Journal* 58, 15–19.
Papalia, A. (1975) Students' learning styles in ascribing meaning to written and oral stimuli. *Hispalia*, 58 (1), 106–108.
Paradis, M. (1994) Neurolinguistic aspects of implicit and explicit memory: Implications for bilingualism and SLA. In N. Ellis (ed.) *Implicit and Explicit Learning of Languages* (pp. 393–419). San Diego, CA: Academic Press.
Pressley, M. and Dennis-Rounds, J. (1980) Transfer of a mnemonic keyword strategy at two age levels. *Journal of Educational Psychology* 72 (4), 575–582.
Pressley, M., Levin, J.R., and McCormick, C.B. (1980) Young children's learning of foreign language vocabulary: A sentence variation of the keyword method. *Contemporary Educational Psychology* 5, 22–29.
Richards, B. (1987) Type/Token ratios: What do they really tell us? *Journal of Child Language* 14, 201–209.
Richards, B. and Malvern, D. (2000) Measuring vocabulary diversity in teenage learners of French. In B.E.R. Association (ed.) Cardiff: Education-line Electronic Database.
Ringböm, H. (1987) *The Role of the First Language in Foreing Language Learning*. Clevedon: Multilingual Matters.
Service, E. and Craik, F.I.M. (1993) Differences between young and older adults in learning a foreign vocabulary. *Journal of Memory and Language* 32, 608–623.
Silverberg, S. and Samuel, A.G. (2004) The effect of age of second language acquisition on the representation and processing of second language words. *Journal of Memory and Language* 51, 381–398.
Singleton, D. (1995) Introduction: A critical look at the Critical Period Hypothesis in Second Language Acquisition. In D. Singleton and Z. Lengyel (eds) *The Age Factor in Second Language Acquisition* (pp. 1–29). Clevedon: Multilingual Matters.
Singleton, D. (1999) *Exploring the Second Language Mental Lexicon*. Cambridge: Cambridge University Press.
Snow, C.E. (1983) Age Differences in second language acquisition: Research findings and folk psychology. In K.M. Bailey, M.H. Long and S. Peck (eds) *Second Language Acquisition* (pp. 141–150). London: Newbury House.

Snow, C.E. and Hoefnagel-Höhle, M. (1978) Age differences in second language acquisition. In E.M. Hatch (ed.) *Second Language Acquisition. A Book of Readings* (pp. 333–344). Rowley, MA: Newbury House.

Sökmen, A.J. (1993) Word association results: A window to the lexicons of ESL students. *JALT Journal* 15 (2), 135–150.

Stankowski Gratton, R. (1980) Una ricerca sperimentale sull'insegnamento del tedesco dalla prima classe elementare. *Rasegna Italiana di Linguistica Applicata* 12 (3), 119–141.

Turner, G. (1983) Teaching French vocabulary: A training study. Educational Review 35 (1), 81–88.

Ure, J. (1971) Lexical density and register differentiation. In G.E. Perren and J.L.M. Trim (eds) *Applications of Linguistics. Selected Papers of the Second International Congress of Applied Linguistics, Cambridge, 1969* (pp. 443–452). Cambridge: Cambridge University Press.

Verhallen, M. and Schoonen, R. (1993) Lexical knowledge of monolingual and bilingual children. *Applied Linguistics* 14 (4), 344–363.

Vermeer, A. (2000) Coming to grips with lexical richness. *Language Testing* 17 (1), 65–83.

Vermeer, A. (2004) The relation between lexical richness and vocabulary size in Dutch L1 and L2 children. In P. Bogaards and B. Laufer (eds) *Vocabulary in a Second Language* (pp. 173–189). Amsterdam: John Benjamins.

Vihman, M. (1985) Language differentiation by the bilingual infant. *Journal of Child Language* 12, 297–324.

Wachal, R.S. and Spreen, O. (1973) Some measures of lexical diversity in aphasic and normal language performance. *Language and Speech* 16, 169–181.

Yamada, J., Takatsuka, S., Kotake, N. and Kurusu, J. (1980) On the optimum age for teaching foreign language vocabulary to children. *IRAL* 18, 245–247.

Yoshida, M. (1978) The acquisition of English vocabulary by a Japanese-speaking child. In E.M. Hatch (ed.) *Second Language Acquisition. A Book of Readings* (pp. 91–100). Rowley, MA Newbury House.

Chapter 5

Accuracy Orders, Rate of Learning and Age in Morphological Acquisition

CARMEN MUÑOZ

In their oft-mentioned revision of studies concerned with the effects of onset age on second language (L2) acquisition, Krashen *et al.* (1979/1982) note that older learners proceed faster in the initial stages of second language acquisition, particularly of morphosyntactic aspects (among others, Ekstrand, 1976; Ervin-Tripp, 1974; for a recent revision see Singleton & Ryan, 2004). While most of those studies were conducted in naturalistic learning situations, findings from L2 immersion programmes have similarly shown late immersion students to catch up with and even outperform early immersion students, in spite of their lesser amount of exposure, on tests tapping literacy skills generally (among others, Swain, 1981; Turnbull *et al.*, 1998), and morphological features more specifically (such as the French verb system in the study by Harley, 1986).

Evidence from foreign language acquisition settings, that is, situations in which there is limited exposure to the target language and learners' exposure is limited to classroom input, is scarcer. The existing evidence also points to an older learners' superiority in morphological (as well as syntactic, semantic and sometimes also phonological) acquisition even after a number of years of instruction.[1] This chapter focuses on the accuracy orders of a set of morphemes or functors among learners of different ages in a formal language learning context, with the main aim of examining age-related effects on the development of morphological features. Important issues in that respect are the rate with which these functors seem to be acquired or at least used accurately by different-aged learners in an instructed setting, and also the way in which learners of various ages progress in their morpheme learning, as reflected in their respective accuracy rank orders. A second aim of the study is to compare data from purely instructed foreign language learners with data from previous studies in order to explore whether learning context bears an influence on learners' rank orders.

Morpheme Studies

In the investigation of the acquisition of grammatical morphology in English as a second language (ESL), a special role has been played by what came to be known following Krashen (1977) the "natural order" or "natural sequence" of grammatical morpheme acquisition. This order derived from the order of accuracy in which L2 learners were observed to produce English grammatical morphemes. According to Krashen, this order is uniform among subjects from a broad sampling of L2 studies, both cross-sectional and longitudinal, individual and group, child and adult, and among subjects of different first language (L1) backgrounds and different degrees of exposure to naturalistic input.[2]

The morphemes studies approached the analysis following Brown's (1973) obligatory contexts methodology that he first used in the study of L1 acquisition: learners' utterances are examined to determine the extent to which the grammatical morphemes in question are supplied in contexts where they are required. This is known as "suppliance in obligatory contexts" (hereafter also SOC).[3]

Dulay and Burt (1973, 1974) conducted the first studies of a series that revealed that the acquisition sequence of a subset of the functors studied by Brown was approximately the same for groups of children learning English with different first languages. However, the difficulty ordering found was not the same as that obtained in L1 acquisition studies (e.g. de Villiers & de Villiers, 1973), which was explained by the effects of the cognitive and conceptual development that L1 acquirers are simultaneously undergoing. Bailey *et al.* (1974) found that adults learning English also showed a high degree of agreement as to the relative difficulty of the set of grammatical morphemes studied, irrespective of amount of instruction, exposure to English, and first language. Furthermore, the relative accuracy of the adults correlated significantly with the relative accuracies shown by the children in the Dulay and Burt's (1973) study.

The "natural sequence" studies have been criticised on several fronts (for a review of the debate see, *inter alia* Cook, 1993; Ellis, 1986; Hatch, 1978; Long & Sato, 1984). From a conceptual point of view, the criticism has been made that accuracy is not to be equated with acquisition. In fact, evidence from some longitudinal studies tends to disconfirm the hypothesis that the relative accuracy that has been obtained in cross-sectional studies predicts the sequence of acquisition for groups of individuals (e.g. Rosansky, 1976). Consequently, this phenomenon is also referred to in the literature as an accuracy order (Larsen-Freeman, 1976), and also as a performance order (Andersen, 1977). This is related to the methodological criticism that most of the studies supporting the "natural sequence" were cross-sectional in design, and used the same task, a structured conversation based on the Bilingual Syntax Measure (Burt *et al.*, 1975), to elicit data from the subjects. Some researchers suggested that the sequence was an artefact of the Bilingual Syntax Measure (e.g. Larsen-Freeman, 1975). Krashen (1978) refuted this suggestion through his distinction between acquisition and learning, and proposed that the analysis of data from spontaneous language will always yield a morpheme accuracy order reflecting the "natural sequence", determined by unconscious acquisition processes. In contrast, data from discrete-point grammar tests, in which learners' formal knowledge is tapped, will show a different order, according to Krashen (1977). Research that used other tasks (e.g. the SLOPE test, Fathman, 1975) or language from oral communication found similar orders, but the similarities did not hold across language modalities. Larsen-Freeman (1975) used a battery of five tasks: reading, writing, listening, imitating and speaking, and found correlations among the morpheme sequences produced by the various language groups she studied for each task, but not when different tasks were compared. The morpheme sequences from the oral production tasks (speaking and imitating) did, however, correlate with Dulay and Burt's (1974) and with each other at both measurement times with an interval of two months.

Another problem with the accuracy order based on the obligatory contexts methodology is that it often leaves a substantial amount of data unaccounted for (Lightbown *et al.*, 1980: 171; Lightbown, 1983: 219). Learners may use a particular form correctly in obligatory contexts, and also incorrectly overuse it in other contexts (Andersen, 1977; Hatch, 1978). This led researchers to establish target-like use (TLU), besides or instead accuracy of use in obligatory contexts (Lightbown *et al.*, 1980). TLU takes into account both correct suppliance in obligatory contexts and incorrect suppliance in non-obligatory contexts. But both SOC and TLU studies have been criticised for focusing too strongly on the grammatical aspects of L2 acquisition and thus ignoring functional use of the language. The validity of SOC analysis of morphemes and any analysis conducted at the level of type, not token, have also been criticised (Long & Sato, 1984) for their unreliability in relation to assessing whether development of a particular item has ceased or stabilised (Long, 2003).

In spite of these criticisms, the hypothesis that learners follow some predictable sequence in their way towards language acquisition has been very attractive to researchers, and the wealth of studies produced provide an interesting "average order" (Long & Sato, 1983) against which to examine L2 learners' production. Goldschneider and DeKeyser (2001) remark that the revision of these studies may very well conclude, as Larsen-Freeman and Long (1991: 92) do, that the commonalities in these research findings cannot be ignored. The search for an explanation of these commonalities, that is, a theoretically motivated explanation for the L2 morpheme orders, has characterised much of the work in the past decades (see e.g. Gass & Selinker, 1994).

Beginning with the study by Dulay *et al.* (1982), a number of publications have suggested that the L2 morpheme acquisition order is indicative of some sort of innate blueprint. For example, Zobl and Liceras (1994) searched for a unified account for both L1 and L2 morpheme orders based on functional categories theory. Other explanations have appealed to properties of the functors themselves. J.D. Brown (1983) suggested that an explanation could be found in the systematic relationships between the qualities of the morphemes, such as free/bound distinction and the verb/noun phrase distinction. The explanation offered by Pienemann and Johnston (1987) and Pienemann (1998) called upon speech-processing constraints that are overcome sequentially allowing the sequential mastering of the morphemes.

Frequency in the input has often been examined in the search for an explanation, ever since the pioneer study by Brown (1973). Larsen-Freeman (1976) found that input frequency orders were related to accuracy orders for L2 learners of English, but in a related study Long and Sato (1983) did not find similar correlations. Long and Sato suggested that the discrepancy in the results could be due to the difference in proficiency levels of the learners in the two studies, intermediate in the former and beginner in the latter, and in particular to the great amount of distortion of the input (and the interactional structure of conversation) to which beginning ESL students were exposed. Neither did Lightbown (1983) find a direct relationship between input in the language classroom and frequency and accuracy of use of morphemes by beginner students. Larsen-Freeman (1976) concluded that, in spite of the frequency effect she found, there does not seem to be a single explanation for the phenomenon.

In a recent study, Goldschneider and DeKeyser (2001) have attempted to explain the "natural order" through a combination of features of the functors: perceptual salience, semantic complexity, morphophonological regularity, syntactic category, and frequency. Other factors, external to the functors, such as L1 transfer, may also contribute to the observed order, according to Goldschneider and DeKeyser, but the method of data analysis adopted in their study did not allow them to take this last factor into consideration. Through a meta-analysis of 12 studies selected from a pool of 25 candidate studies, Goldschneider and DeKeyser find that the five factors together account for a large portion of the variance ($R = 0.84$; $R2 = 0.71$), and conclude that they can all be subsumed under a more generic factor of salience, discarding the need of appealing to innate blueprints to explain the consistency in the morpheme rank orders found. From the perspective of language stabilisation, Long (2003: 517–518) also highlights perceptual saliency, frequency, semantic weight, and regularity, along with communicative value, as important characteristics of target structures that interacting with learners' input sensitivity may account for stabilisation of some structures.

Learning Context

Morpheme studies were in the great majority conducted in situations of naturalistic L2 acquisition (ESL, to be more precise). In fact, Krashen only claimed that the sequence he postulated was uniform across different degrees of exposure to naturalistic input. When learners were exposed to naturalistic input, formal language instruction did not seem to affect accuracy orders (Perkins & Larsen-Freeman, 1975). Likewise, Pica noted that the "natural order" was based on data from naturalistic and mixed L2 learners with access to "acquisition-rich" environments and native speaker input inside and out of the classroom (1983: 485). The claim that there could be an order common to both naturalistic and instructed language acquisition situations had been tested empirically, with mixed results. Makino (1979, cited in Goldschneider & DeKeyser, 2001) found no disturbance to Krashen's order in his data from Japanese children and adolescents enrolled in formal English classes. Sajavaara (1981, cited in Pica, 1983) found a disturbed order among instructed Finnish L1 students. What is more, while both the Japanese and Finnish do not have an article system, only Finnish learners of English showed a different rank order for article. In view of the conflicting claims made regarding the contribution of instruction to the spontaneous production of L2 learners, Pica (1983) conducted a study in which she examined the production of English morphology among three groups of adult native speakers of Spanish. The learner groups differed in their conditions of exposure to English: exposure only through instruction, naturalistic exposure only, and mixed exposure, a combination of both instructed and naturalistic exposure. Pica found that the SOC rank orders of the three groups were very similar to Krashen's "natural order", and all correlations between them were highly significant. A second interesting finding was that errors were also different among the groups. While morpheme oversuppliance in inappropriate contexts was significantly higher among the learners with instructed exposure only, omission errors were significantly higher among the learners with naturalistic exposure. This finding led Pica to suggest that instruction triggers oversuppliance of grammatical morphology, through the prevalent focus on formal aspects of the target language, as well as inhibiting use of ungrammatical but communicative constructions (i.e. omission of plural endings on nouns preceded by quantifiers). The general claim from Pica's study is that while learners do not differ with regard to percentages of accuracy, and hence learners are seen to contribute a great deal of "natural ability" to their acquisition of a second language, as suggested by Felix (1981), different conditions of L2 exposure have an effect on linguistic features of the interlanguage, indicating that they affect acquirers' hypotheses about the target language and their strategies for using it (Pica, 1983: 495).

The study by Lightbown (1983) extended beyond accuracy orders of functors to look at the relationship between the frequency with which certain forms appear in the classroom and the frequency or accuracy of use of these forms in the learners' language at the same point in time. The subjects ranged in age from 11 to 17 and completed an oral task twice in two consecutive years. They were instructed learners of English in Quebec with little exposure to the target language outside the English classes. The results of the study suggested that there is no direct relationship between input and frequency and accuracy of use of functors, as seen above, but the learners' first language was shown to have some influence on the (lack of) accuracy of the -s plural morpheme (which is not pronounced in French). In general, the learners' accuracy orders differed from those observed in previous studies, which may be due, according to the author, to the "distorted" version of the English language these learners were exposed to in the classroom (1983: 240). In addition, an important observation of the study was that there was relatively little improvement over time in the accuracy of learners' use of the set of six morphemes studied, which may have also been due to the lack of experience with communicative language, according to the author.

In sum, evidence of commonalities of accuracy orders among instructed learners in acquisition-poor settings is mixed and inconclusive. In fact, Goldschneider and DeKeyser (2001) excluded Andersen (1977), Makino (1979), Lightbown et al. (1980) and Lightbown (1983) studies from their meta-analysis because data came from English as a foreign language (EFL) situations. The present study with learners whose exposure comes exclusively from the foreign language classroom may throw some more light on the influence of the learning context on the accuracy order of these often-studied English grammatical units.

Age and Accuracy Orders

Krashen (1977) maintained that the natural order is not affected by learners' age, and in fact the sequence presented as the "natural order" was formed out of a heterogeneous group which comprised learners of different ages. As seen above, very early on Bailey et al. (1974) had reported a difficulty order for adult learners of English that was not different from that found for children (Dulay & Burt, 1973).

Fathman (1975) set out to specifically investigate the relationship between age and rate and order of acquisition of English structures. The subjects in her study were 140 children (ages 6–15), who had been in the United States for less than three years (70 for one year, 40 for two years, and 30 for three years) and were then all immersed in the verbal environment of the school. Subjects were divided into two age groups: a younger group from 6 to 10 years and an older group from 11 to 15 years. Fathman aimed at looking at changes between these two groups in the rate and in the order of acquisition of 20 morpheme categories or syntactic patterns. In addition, she elicited an oral description of a composite picture, and learners' oral production was rated for correctness of grammar, pronunciation and general fluency.

An analysis of variance test was run in order to determine the effect of age, years in the United States and language programme (ESL or regular programme) on the rate of learning of the 20 items. The results revealed that older learners did better in the production of correct morphological and syntactic structures, and that there were no differences in rate of learning due to language programme. No significant interactions were found between age, number of years and language programme. A *t*-test was used in order to look at the rating on pronunciation during the composite picture description, and it was found that the younger children did better than the older children when they were exposed to English the same period of time.

In contrast, no major differences were found in the order in which the children of different ages learned the structures in the test, as determined by the mean scores received by each group on the 20 subtests. The rank order correlation coefficient for the sequences attained was high (0.88; $p \leq 0.005$). Fathman concluded that the L2 acquisition process changes with age in terms of success in learning, with the younger children showing higher pronunciation abilities and the older children higher morphological and syntactic abilities. However, in terms of order of learning the L2 acquisition remains constant.

In a subsequent study, Krashen *et al.* (1976) further investigated age-related differences in relation to sequences of acquisition. The same test used by Fathman (1975) was administered to 66 adults of different L1 background, who also varied in the amount of English formal instruction they had had. The correlation coefficient between the group of children ($n = 120$) ranging in age from 6 to 14 and the group of adults was highly significant ($rho = 0.77; p < 0.01$). In addition, no differences were revealed between the adults with formal instruction and those without, nor among learners of different language background. The authors concluded that puberty does not represent an abrupt change in the operation of the language acquisition device, against the claims of the strong version of the Critical Period Hypothesis that the processes of language acquisition in children and adults are different. Also the study by Larsen-Freeman (1975) mentioned above found significant correlations between the morpheme sequences from two oral production tasks (speaking and imitating) of a group of adult learners and the morpheme sequences obtained by Dulay and Burt (1974) from child learners.

A very different type of study, concerned with rate of morpheme acquisition, was reported by Kessler and Idar (1979). In that study the morphological development in English of only two subjects, a Vietnamese woman refugee and her four-year-old daughter, recently arrived in the United States, was investigated. Their production of six grammatical morphemes was compared at two different stages, and the younger subject's rate of acquisition, as shown by the improvement on the accurate use of those morphemes, appeared to be much higher. The results cannot be taken as evidence of the influence of age on learning rate, however, since the study did not control for amount and type of exposure. For example, the period between the stages was longer for the child than for the mother, and the former enjoyed more intensive and extensive opportunities of interacting with English-speaking peers than the mother. In addition, the authors suggested that the slower rate observed for the mother could be due to affective and attitudinal variables arising from the difficulties of her refugee situation.

Finally, in a study of the acquisition of French by English L1 immersion students, Harley (1986) also compared the accuracy orders of a set of verb distinctions for early and late immersion students. The findings showed fundamental differences in the development of morphology (and syntax) by different-aged learners of the same L1 background.

The morpheme studies have been taken as evidence that there is not a qualitative difference in the way in which L2 learning progresses after a certain maturational point (Singleton & Ryan, 2004: 109). As seen above, however, the commonalities have been found (with the exception of Pica's study) in acquisition-rich environments, with or without instruction. In this chapter, morpheme or functor[4] accuracy orders will be investigated with the main aim of exploring whether different-aged learners in a foreign language setting also proceed in similar ways in morphological development, independently of age, and whether there are age-related differences in the rate of functor acquisition, as reflected (albeit partially) in the accuracy with which those functors are used.

Research Questions and Hypotheses

Three research questions and two hypotheses are posed in this study. The first research question is whether older and younger learners progress in similar ways in their accurate use of a set of grammatical morphemes or functors. Available evidence from different morpheme studies seems to indicate that age does not have a significant influence on the order of accuracy of grammatical functors. Therefore, the first hypothesis is that learners' age will not have a significant effect on the accuracy ranking of functors by younger and older learners.

The second research question is concerned with the effects of learners' age on the rate of functor acquisition, or, more precisely, on the rate with which different-aged learners come to use these grammatical units accurately in obligatory contexts. A hypothesis can be posed on the basis of previous findings from studies that have compared learners of different ages, and have found an advantage on the part of older learners, both generally in the first stages of morphosyntactic acquisition, and specifically in the difficulty orders of morphemes. Therefore, the second hypothesis is that older learners will show a more accurate use of grammatical functors in accordance with the general faster learning rate observed in previous studies. This will be seen in the older learners' higher SOC percentages. Furthermore, the advantage will be greater in the initial stages than in later stages.

The third research question addresses the issue of the influence on accuracy orders of learning context, and it asks whether there is a common order in both naturalistic and instructed contexts. Or, more precisely, whether there will be more similarities among the sequences obtained from learners in instructed foreign language settings than among those and the orders obtained from learners in naturalistic language learning settings. Given the existing mixed evidence, no hypothesis is presented for this research question.

Method

Subjects

The subjects in this study were six groups of instructed learners of English from the Barcelona Age Factor (BAF) Project database who had not had any extracurricular exposure to English (see Chapter 1). As shown in Table 5.1, the first group consisted of 30 pupils in Grade 5 (10;9 years on average) who had begun studying English in Grade 3 when they were 8 years old, and who had had 200 hours of previous instruction in English (group A1). The second group consisted of 30 pupils in Grade 7 (11;9 years on average) who had begun studying English in Grade 6 at the age of 11, and who had also had 200 hours of instruction in English (group B1). The third group was formed by 30 learners in Grade 11 (16;9 years on average) who had begun studying English at the age of 8, and who had had 726 hours of English instruction at the moment of testing (group A3). In the fourth group there were 30 learners in Grade 12 (17;9 years on average) who had begun studying English on grade 6 at the age of 11, and who had also had 726 hours of instruction of English (group B3). The fifth group consisted of 20 adult learners of English (28;9 on average) who had begun studying English after age 18, and who had had 200 hours of instruction in English (group D1). Finally, in the sixth group there were 15 adult learners (30;4 years on average) who had also begun studying English after age 18, and who had had 416 hours of instruction in English at the moment of testing (group D2). This group was comparable in proficiency to A3 and B3 (see Chapter 1).[5] Males and females were similarly distributed in all the groups.

Materials

Data from oral production tasks were analysed in order to compare with previous studies. Two different types of audiotaped data were chosen: data from an oral semi-structured interview and data from a picture-elicited story, a task that learners were asked to perform at the end of the conversation. Including the picture-elicited story together with the conversation provided contexts for appearance of functors which seldom appeared in the interview (for example, the third-person auxiliary *is*).

Table 5.1 Subjects

	Group AAO = 8		Group BAO = 11		Group DAO = 18+	
Time 1 200 h	A1	AT = 10;9 N = 30	B1	AT = 12;9 N = 30	D1	AT = 28;9 N = 20
Time 2 416 h	–	–	–	–	D2	AT = 30;4 N = 15
Time 3 726 h	A3	AT = 16;9 N = 30	B3	AT = 17;9 N = 30	–	–

The oral interview was a semi-structured interview in which researchers asked a set of questions to the learners about their family, daily life, hobbies and other non-cognitively demanding topics. The interviewer's questions created obligatory contexts for different morphemes, particularly for plural -s, articles, regular past, and copula *is*.

The oral narrative was elicited through a sequence of six pictures. The pictures themselves created contexts for obligatory use of some morphemes, such as the articles. The use of the auxiliary *is*, the -s third person, and the regular past would depend on whether learners simply described the pictures and the events in the story using the continuous present, or whether they had the ability to narrate the story through the use of the present simple or the past. As it happened, the learners with low levels of proficiency tended to describe the pictures (people and objects) rather than to narrate the story, while those with higher levels of proficiency tended to narrate the story but often mixing tenses, and then -*ing*, -s third-person singular, and -*ed* could all co-occur in the same narrative.

Procedures

Oral data were transcribed according to standard orthography and following the conventions of the CHAT sub-programme in CHILDES (Child Language Date Exchange System). Percentages of SOC were computed for the following morphemes: progressive -*ing*, plural -s, singular copula, progressive auxiliary, article, past irregular, past regular, and third person singular. Noun possession -s is not easily elicited in spontaneous speech nor was it frequently enough elicited by the story pictures, and hence it was excluded from the analysis (as was in Pica's (1983) analysis of data from spontaneous conversations). Other functors were excluded for a particular group if there fewer than ten obligatory contexts for them.[6]

SOC analyses were conducted according to guidelines from Brown (1973) and Dulay and Burt (1974), and following Pica (1983).[7] This entailed the use of weighted scores: two points when the correct functor was supplied; one point when an incorrect form was supplied and no points when no morpheme at all was supplied. The score values of all the learners' contexts for that morpheme were added and then the sum was divided by the product of twice the total number of contexts requiring suppliance of the morpheme in the subjects' speech. These group morphemes were used in determining rank order of functor accuracy for each group of subjects. The SPSS (Statistical Package for the Social Sciences) programme was used for statistical analyses.

Results

In order to explore the progression followed by learners with different onset age, comparisons were made between the accuracy percentages obtained by all the groups (see Table 5.2): A1 and A3 (onset age = 8; age at testing 10;9 and 16;9, respectively), B1 and B3 (onset age = 11; age at testing 12;9 and 17;9, respectively), and D1 and D2 (onset age = 18+; age at testing 28;9 and 30;4, respectively). Table 5.3 displays the Spearman correlation coefficients obtained.

Table 5.2 SOC percentages and rank orders

Functor	A1 SOC	A1 rank	B1 SOC	B1 rank	D1 SOC	D1 rank	A3 SOC	A3 rank	B3 SOC	B3 rank	D2 SOC	D2 rank
Progr. –ing	56	3	58	5	76	5	84	5	84	5	97*	4
Plural –s	86	1	86	1.5	96	2	96	2	98	1	99*	2
Sing. copula	82	2	86	1.5	99	1	97	1	96	2	99*	1
Progr. aux.	–	–	60	4	81	4	94	3	94	3.5	93	5
Article	50	4	74	3	95	3	92	4	94	3.5	97*	3
Past irregular	–	–	–	–	75	6	60	6	60	6	87	6
Past regular	–	–	–	–	57	7	59	7	49	7	83	7
Third p. sing.	7	5	21	6	25	8	39	8	42	8	74	8

Note: *Rank orders have been set before rounding up figures (ex.: 96.88 > 96.51).

Table 5.3 Spearman correlation coefficients

	B1	A3	B3	D1	D2
A1	0.87m.s.	0.80	0.90*	0.80m.s.	0.80
B1	–	0.93**	0.97**	0.99**	0.93**
A3		–	0.97**	0.98**	0.93**
B3			–	0.97**	0.93**
D1				–	0.98**
D2					–

Notes: ** Significant at 0.01 level (bilateral);
    * Significant at 0.05 level (bilateral);
    m.s.: Marginally significant (A1–B1: $p = 0.054$; A1–D1: $p = 0.072$).

All groups correlated significantly, independently of onset age and age at testing, except for the youngest and least proficient group, A1, whose rank order only correlated with B3 significantly, while in two other occasions the coefficient was marginally significant. In addition, correlation coefficients between A1 and the other groups were smaller than all other coefficients, but so was the sample ($n = 5$). Seemingly the very low proficiency level of A1 had an effect on these results.

The effects of learners' age on the rate of accurate use of these functors were investigated by means of comparing groups with similar amounts of exposure to the target language. As shown in Table 5.4, B1 scored higher than A1 on four of the five functors considered (also in past irregular and past regular, although the number of obligatory contexts did not reach ten and hence these do not appear in the table). The percentage differences between A1 and B1 showed a pronounced improvement in the accuracy rates of the last functors in the set analysed: article and third-person singular; in particular, the B1 group scored 24 percentage points higher on article than A1. The adult group scored always higher than the younger groups, and differences with the two younger groups' scores were generally larger.

Differences between SOC percentages of A3 and B3 (after 726 hours) were smaller than differences after 200 hours of instruction (see Table 5.5), although B3 still scored higher on three of the functors. In contrast, B3 scored 10 percentage points lower than A3 on the past regular, but the former also created many more contexts for using the past than the latter (45 vs. 22) and then omitted the functor more frequently (23 vs. 9). Differences between D2 and those two groups were also smaller for the easiest morphemes. Differences were still large for two functors that reached now ten obligatory contexts in A1 and B1, past irregular and past

Table 5.4 Comparison of SOC percentage scores for the three age groups. Low proficiency level

Functor	A1	B1		D1		
	SOC percentage	SOC percentage	Percentage difference	SOC percentage	Percentage difference	
Progr. -*ing*	56	58	+2	76	+20	+18
Plural -*s*	86	86	0	96	+10	+10
Sing. copula	82	86	+4	99	+17	+13
Progr. aux.	–	60	–	81	–	+21
Article	50	74	+24	95	+45	+21
Past irregular	–	–	–	75	–	–
Past regular	–	–	–	57	–	–
Third p. sing.	7	21	+14	25	+18	+4

Table 5.5 Comparison of SOC percentage scores for the three age groups. High proficiently level

Functor	A3	B3		D2	
	SOC percentage	SOC percentage	Percentage difference	SOC percentage	Percentage difference
Progr. -ing	84	84	0	97	+13	+13
Plural -s	96	98	+2	99	+3	+1
Sing. copula	97	96	−1	99	+2	+3
Progr. aux.	94	94	0	93	−1	−1
Article	92	94	+2	97	+5	+3
Past irregular	60	60	0	87	+27	+27
Past regular	59	49	−10	83	+24	+34
Third p. sing.	39	42	+3	74	+35	+32

regular, and for the third-person singular, which showed an important progress from D1 to D2, not yet paralleled by A3 and B3.

In order to examine the influence of learning context, the accuracy rank orders of the groups in this study were compared with those from other learner groups in similar and different learning contexts. In the first place, correlations were computed between the rank orders of A3, B3, D1 and D2, and those of Pica's instructed group, Pica's naturalistic group and Pica's mixed group (see Table 5.6, where Pica's SOC percentages for the three groups are also displayed). All these learners were adolescents or young adults with Spanish as the first language, so that they were all similar in terms of age and first language. In addition, the rank orders from the groups of the present study were correlated with Krashen's average order, corresponding to a heterogeneous group in terms of both age and first language, but from learners in naturalistic learning contexts with and without instruction.

Table 5.6 Comparison of rank orders for older instructed learners, Pica's groups, and Krashen's average order

Functor	Krashen's rank	Pica's I		Pica's N		Pica's M		A3 rank	B3 rank	D1 Rank	D2 rank
		SOC	rank	SOC	rank	SOC	rank				
Progr. -ing	1	97	1	94	1	98	1	5	5	5	4
Plural -s	2	93	3	74	5	74	4	2	1	2	2
Sing. Copula	3	95	2	92	2	97	2	1	2	1	1
Progr. aux.	4	85	5	76	4	66	6	3	3.5	4	5
Article	5	92	4	91	3	86	3	4	3.5	3	3
Past irregular	6	75	6	68	6	73	5	6	6	6	6
Past regular	7	51	8	58	7	44	7	7	7	7	7
Third p. sing.	8	63	7	25	8	22	8	8	8	8	8

The Spearman correlation coefficients displayed in Table 5.7 indicate that the rank orders of the four groups significantly correlated with Krashen's rank order. Also the correlations between D2 and the comparison groups were all significant at 0.05 level. Both the rank orders of D1 and A3 correlated significantly, at 0.05 level, with Krashen's rank order and with that of Pica's instructed group. B3 only correlated significantly, at 0.05 level, with Krashen's order, and the correlation with Pica's instructed group attained only a marginally significant *rho*. The fact that the correlations reached with Pica's instructed group were higher than those with Pica's naturalistic and mixed groups, might seem to indicate that the learning context has some effect here. But this effect disappears for the group with the highest accuracy percents, D2, which correlated with all groups independently of learning context. In addition, the instructed group is also the one that reaches the highest accuracy percentages of Pica's three groups.[8]

A second set of correlations were computed between the least proficient and youngest groups, A1 in Grade 5 and B1 in Grade 7, both with 200 hours of instruction, and Lightbown's (1983) Grade 6 learners. Krashen's heterogeneous group was also included in the comparison (see Table 5.8).

Table 5.7 Spearman correlations coefficients for older instructed learners, Pica's groups, and Krashen's average order

	Krashen's	Pica's I	Pica's N	Pica's M
A3	0.74*	0.71*	0.67	0.62
B3	0.75*	0.707 m.s.	0.61	0.61
D1	0.71*	0.74*	0.69	0.69
D2	0.79*	0.83*	0.76*	0.81*

Notes: * Significant at 0.05 level (bilateral);
m.s.: Marginally significant ($p = 0.05$).

Table 5.8 Comparison of rank orders for younger instructed learners, Lightbown's group, and Krashen's average order

Functor	Krashen's	L's Gr. 6 rank	A1 rank	B1 Rank
Progr. -*ing*	1	3.5	3	5
Plural -*s*	2	3.5	1	1.5
Sing. copula	3	2	2	1.5
Progr. aux.	4	5	–	4
Article	5	1	4	3
Past irregular	6	–	–	–
Past regular	7	–	–	–
Third p. sing.	8	6	5	6

Correlations between A1 and B1, in Grades 5 and 7 respectively, with Lightbown's Grade 6 learners were not significant (0.21 and 0.66, respectively). Language background may have played a role here in relation, most visibly, to the accuracy percents reached for the plural of nouns. The plural system of nouns in English and Spanish are morphologically alike and, in fact, the Spanish-speaking learners in this study show a very accurate use of the plural morpheme (possible errors of pronunciation of the English allomorphs were not taken into account). This contrasts with Lightbown's findings in which the accuracy of this functor was lower, because of the non-marking of plural in spoken French. In contrast, the instructed subjects in groups A1 and B1 found it more difficult to produce progressive *-ing* accurately. In fact, the largest difference between the ranks obtained in the present study and Krashen's average order, with which there were no significant correlations either (0.70 and 0.35, respectively), lies in the accuracy of use of progressive *-ing* (from three to four ranks lower). Again, low proficiency seems to underlie the general lack of significance among those groups. Also Lightbown (1983) found her group of school learners had a dissimilar ranking order from Krashen's.

Discussion

The first hypothesis in this study, that a similar ordering would be found independently of learners' age, has been confirmed. All correlations among the groups B1, A3, B3, D1 and D2, with different onset ages and ages at testing, are significant. But the analysis has also shown the influence of proficiency level, in that the rank order of A1 produces the lowest correlation coefficients. Furthermore, A1's correlation coefficients are incidentally higher with groups with different onset age and different age at testing, which excludes age as the determining functor of lack of correlation. The low correlations are also due to the fact that only five functors in A1 reach the criterion of ten obligatory contexts, which is in turn a consequence of the low proficiency level of learners in this group.

The second hypothesis postulated that older learners would show a faster rate of acquisition, or would reach higher accuracy percentages on those functors, than younger learners. This has been clearly confirmed, and the adult groups have always obtained higher scores than the two younger groups; differences between D2 and A3 and B3 are smaller in the easier functors but still very large in the difficult ones. Similarly, differences between A and B are clearly greater for A1–B1 than for A3–B3, and hence the second part of the hypothesis has also been confirmed for these two groups: the older learners' rate advantage is more marked in the first stages of language acquisition than in later stages. The reason for this levelling (up) may lay in the fact that learners from A3, now 16;9 years on average, have attained a similar cognitive development to that of learners from B3, now 17;9 years on average, and hence their rate of learning of morphological features in a formal learning context is now similar (see Chapter 1 for a discussion of this interpretation).

Finally, the third research question asked about the extent to which the orders found in this study would be similar to those of learners also in formal learning contexts, and different from those of learners in other learning contexts. The answer to that question may at first seem partly affirmative because the orders of the older groups significantly correlated with that of Pica's instructed group and only that of D2 significantly correlated with the orders from Pica's naturalistic and mixed groups. However, the fact that D2 and Pica's instructed group are those that present the highest functor accuracy percentages seems to indicate that proficiency or accuracy level is a stronger determinant factor than learning context.

At the other extreme, that of the comparison between the younger and less proficient learners, A1, B1, and Lightbown's Grade 6 French-speaking learners, no significant correlations were found. The divergence may partly be attributed to the influence of language background (Spanish vs. French). However, the claim weakens when considering the lack of total correspondence between the orderings from the learners in this study (Spanish-Catalan) and Pica's learners, with Spanish as the first language. Again, proficiency level may have played a bigger role than first language. Long and Sato (1983) suggested that the nonsignificant correlation they found was due to the general degree of "distortion" of classroom discourse at the beginner's level, and noted that other studies, and notably those on which Krashen's average order was based, dealt mostly with intermediate and advanced ESL speakers.

The importance of proficiency or accuracy level, at least when exposure is limited to classroom input, seems clear in this study. Correlations are higher and reach significance more often among the more proficient groups, while correlations among the less proficient groups are lower and do not always reach significance. As performance on morphemes improves with increased exposure to the target language, a commonality of ordering emerges, though not an invariant one. Hence, this study highlights the role of input, not with respect to the accuracy order of individual functors, but with respect to the whole set. In fact, if one of the determinant factors of the orderings found is frequency of occurrence (Goldschneider & DeKeyser, 2001; Larsen-Freeman, 1976), a certain amount of exposure will be needed to ensure accurate performance. In the same vein, perceptual saliency will interplay with frequency so that a particular feature will become more salient through repeated exposure. Also Long and Sato (1983: 283) speculated that perhaps the relative frequency of various structures in the input becomes a salient factor for learners once they have enough of the second language to "tune to the frequency", that is, beyond the very elementary level of the less proficient learners in this study.

In sum, this study has provided evidence against the existence of a qualitative difference in the way in which L2 learning of morphological functors in English as a foreign language progresses in different-aged learners. It has also provided evidence of an older learners' superior rate of learning to accurately use morphological features (in obligatory contexts) in comparison with younger learners, particularly in the initial stages of language acquisition. In addition, this study has shown that learning context does not affect accuracy orders as much as proficiency level does, and that foreign language learners present accuracy orders that approach the average order once they have had a certain amount of exposure to the target language and have progressed beyond the very elementary levels of proficiency.

Acknowledgements

This study was carried out with the assistance of the research grants PB94-0944, PB97-0901 and BFF2001-3384 from the Spanish Ministry of Education. I would also like to express my appreciation to Laura Sánchez and Catalina Gost for their help and enriching insights.

Notes

1. Concedingly, in absolute terms the exposure over those years may not amount to more hours than those provided by the initial stages of naturalistic language acquisition.
2. Krashen (1977) grouped the nine morphemes in four blocks in an alleged descending order of accuracy. He claimed that morphemes in each group typically cluster together and are unordered with respect to each other: progressive -*ing*/plural -*s*/copula > progr. auxiliary/article > irreg. past > regular past/third-person singular/possessive.
3. Another significant benchmark set by Brown was a standard for scoring and comparing data on morpheme acquisition order that set the cut-off point of "acquisition" at 90%, on the basis that once the curve of performance of a particular morpheme had passed above the 90% line for several consecutive samples, it tended to remain above 90%. Notwithstanding, he ordered all the morphemes he studied, as have done researchers after him, independently of whether morphemes reached or not the (arbitrary) acquisition point of 90% correct suppliance in obligatory contexts.
4. The term "functor" is largely used in this study with preference to the term "morpheme" to refer to the grammatical units considered in the analyses. As Goldschneider and DeKeyser (2001: 2) note, the term "morpheme" is not technically applicable to distinctions such as past regular vs. past irregular.
5. Besides, B3 had a very small sample. See Table 1.1 in this volume for a full account of the subjects in the BAF Project.
6. Studies vary in the number of obligatory occasions required. Krashen (1978) saw the need of having at least ten obligatory occasions for each morpheme analysed. Other authors used a less stringent criterion: Dulay and Burt (1974) and Andersen (1976; cited in Andersen, 1978) used 3, and Andersen (1978) used 5.
7. Also TLU scores were computed, but they are not used here because the possibilities of comparison with results from previous studies are not so rich (see Gost & Muñoz, 2004; Muñoz & Sánchez, 2003).
8. The mean of the instructed group is 81.4, whereas that of the naturalistic group is 72.3 and that of the mixed group is 70.

References

Andersen, R.W. (1977) The impoverished state of cross-sectional morpheme acquisition/accuracy methodology (or: The leftovers are more nourishing than the main course). *Working Papers on Bilingualism* 14, 47–82.

Andersen, R. (1978) An implicational model for second language research. *Language Learning* 28, 221–282.

Bailey, N., Madden, C. and Krashen, S. (1974) Is there a "natural sequence" in adult second language learning? *Language Learning* 21 (2), 235–243

Brown, J.D. (1983) An exploration of morpheme-group interactions. In K.M. Bailey, M.H. Long and S. Peck (eds) *Second Language Acquisition Studies* (pp. 25–40). Rowley, MA: Newbury House.

Brown, R. (1973) *A First Language*. Cambridge, MA: Harvard University Press.

Burt, M.K., Dulay, H.C. and Hernández, E. (1975) *Bilingual Syntax Measure*. New York: Harcourt Brace Jovanovich.

Cook, V. (1993) *Linguistics and Second Language Acquisition*. New York: St Martin's Press.

de Villiers, J. and de Villiers, P. (1973) A cross-sectional study of the acquisition of grammatical morphemes in child speech. *Journal of Psycholinguistics Research* 2, 267–278.

Dulay, H.C. and Burt, M.K. (1973) Should we teach syntax? *Language Learning* 23, 245–258.

Dulay, H.C. and Burt, M.K. (1974) Natural sequences in child second language acquisition. *Language Learning* 24, 37–53.

Dulay, H.C., Burt, M. and Krashen, S.D. (1982) *Language Two*. New York: Oxford University Press.

Ekstrand, L. (1976) Age and length of residence as variables related to the adjustment of migrant children, with special reference to second language learning. In G. Nickel (ed.) *Proceedings of the Fourth International Congress of Applied Linguistics*. Volume 3. Stuttgart: Hochschulverlag. Reprinted in S. Krashen, R. Scarcella and M. Long (eds) (1982) *Child-adult Differences in Second Language Acquisition*. Rowley, MA: Newbury House.

Ellis, R. (1986) *Understanding Second Language Acquisition*. Oxford: Oxford University Press.

Ervin-Tripp, S. (1974) Is second language learning like the first? *TESOL Quarterly* 8, 111–127.

Fathman, A. (1975) The relationship between age and second language productive ability. *Language Learning* 25, 245–253.

Felix, S. (1981) The effect of formal instruction on second language acquisition. *Language Learning* 31, 87–112.

Gass, S.M. and Selinker, L. (1994) *Second Language Acquisition: An Introductory Course*. Hillsdale, NJ: Erlbaum.

Goldschneider, J. and DeKeyser, R. (2001) Explaining the "Natural Order of L2 Morpheme Acquisition" in English: A meta-analysis of multiple determinants. *Language Learning* 51 (1), 1–50.

Gost, C. and Muñoz, C. (2004) El desarrollo de los morfemas gramaticales en aprendices adultos de inglés. Paper presented at the 22nd AESLA Conference, Universidad Politécnica de Valencia, April 2004.

Harley, B. (1986) *Age in Second Language Acquisition*. Clevedon: Multilingual Matters.

Hatch, E. (1978) Acquisition of syntax in a second language. In J.C. Richards (ed.) *Understanding Second and Foreign Language Learning: Issues and Approaches* (pp. 34–69). Rowley, MA: Newbury House.

Kessler, C. and Idar, I. (1979) Acquisition of English by a Vietnamese mother and child. *Working Papers on Bilingualism* 18, 65–79.

Krashen, S. (1977) Some issues relating to the Monitor Model. In H. Brown, C. Yorio and R. Crymes (eds) *TESOL '77* 144–158. TESOL, Washington, DC.

Krahen, S. (1978) Is the "Natural Order" an artifact of the bilingual syntax measure? *Language Learning* 28 (1), 187–191.

Krashen, S., Long, M. and Scarcella, R. (1979) Age, rate and eventual attainment in second language acquisition. *TESOL Quarterly* 9: 573–582. Reprinted in S.D. Krashen, R.C. Scarcella and M.H. Long (eds) (1982) *Child-adult Differences in Second Language Acquisition* (pp. 161–172). Rowley, MA: Newbury House Publishers.

Krashen, S., Sferlazza, V., Feldman, L. and Fathman, A. (1976) Adult performance on the SLOPE test: More evidence for a natural sequence in adult second language acquisition. *Language Learning* 26, 145–151.

Larsen-Freeman, D.E. (1975) The acquisition of grammatical morphemes by adult ESL students. *TESOL Quarterly* 9, 409–419.

Larsen-Freeman, D.E. (1976) An explanation for the morpheme acquisition order of second language learners. *Language Learning* 26, 125–134.

Larsen-Freeman, D.E. and Long, M.H. (1991) *An Introduction to Second Language Acquisition Research*. New York: Longman.

Lightbown, P. (1983) Exploring relationships between developmental and instructional sequences in L2 acquisition. In H. B. Seliger and M.H. Long (eds) *Classroom Oriented Research in Second Language Acquisition* (pp. 217–245). Rowley, MA: Newbury House.

Lightbown, P., Spada, N. and Wallace, R. (1980) Some effects of instruction on child and adolescent ESL learners. In R.C. Scarcella and S.D. Krashen (eds) *Research in Second Language Acquisition* (pp. 162–172). Rowley, MA: Newbury House.

Long, M.H. (2003) Stabilization and fossilization in interlanguage. In C.J. Doughty and M.H. Long (eds) *The Handbook of Second Language Acquisition*. Oxford: Blackwell Publishing.

Long, M.H. and Sato, C. (1983) Classroom foreigner talk discourse: Forms and functions of teachers' questions. In H.W. Seliger and M.H. Long (eds) *Classroom Oriented Research in Second Language Acquisition* (pp. 268–286). Rowley, MA: Newbury House.

Long, M.H. and Sato, C. (1984) Methodological issues in interlanguage studies: An interactionist perspective. In A. Davies, C. Criper and A.P.R. Howatt (eds) *Interlanguage* (pp. 253–279). Edinburgh: Edinburgh University Press.

Muñoz, C. and Sánchez, L. (2003) Morpheme development in two groups of EFL learners. Paper presented at the 27th AEDEAN Conference, Universidad de Salamanca, December 2003.

Perkins, K. and Larsen-Freeman, D. (1975) The effect of formal language instruction on the order of morpheme acquisition. *Language Learning* 25 (2), 237–243.

Pica, T. (1983) Adult acquisition of English as a second language under different conditions of exposure. *Language Learning* 33, 465–497.

Pienemann, M. (1998) *Language Processing and Second Language Development*. Amsterdam: Benjamins.

Pienemann, M. and Johnston, M. (1987) Factors influencing the development of language proficiency. In D. Nunan (ed.) *Applying Second Language Acquisition Research* (pp. 45–141). Adelaide: National Curriculum Resource Centre.

Rosansky, E. (1976) Methods and morphemes in second language acquisition research. *Language Learning* 26 (2), 409–425.

Singleton, D. and Ryan, L. (2004) *Language Acquisition: The Age Factor* (2nd edn) Clevedon: Multilingual Matters.

Swain, M. (1981) Time and timing in bilingual education. *Language Learning* 31, 1–15.
Turnbull, M., Lapkin, S., Hart, D. and Swain, M. (1998) Time on task and immersion graduates' French proficiency. In S. Lapkin (ed.) *French Second Language Education in Canada: Empirical Studies* (pp. 31–55). Toronto: University of Toronto Press.
Zobl, H. and Liceras, J. (1994) Functional categories and the acquisition orders. *Language Learning* 44 (1), 159–180.

Chapter 6
Rate and Route of Acquisition in EFL Narrative Development at Different Ages

ESTHER ÁLVAREZ

Introduction
Route of acquisition
One of the most robust findings in second language acquisition (SLA) research is the fact that learners proceed through a similar route, or series of sequences, in the acquisition of a second language (L2) irrespective of their first language (L1). In contrast, variation exists in the rate, or speed of progression through the sequences, and the level of L2 ultimately attained. Thus, both the rate of acquisition and L2 level ultimately attained vary across individuals, but the route is the same. Ellis (1994) points out that the term "route of acquisition" is used to refer to three different phenomena in the literature: a general developmental pattern, a fixed sequence in the acquisition of a single syntactic structure and a fixed order in the acquisition of morphological forms.

Paraphrasing Ellis (1984), the general developmental pattern posits an initial silent period followed by the use of formulaic speech. Learners become progressively more creative in use of structures, though use of morphology remains scarce. Syntax increases in complexity, but morphology is relegated to later use at more advanced levels of proficiency.

Studies centred on the acquisition sequence of single syntactic forms identify a series of stages towards mastery of the form and learners with different L1s have been shown to proceed in the same stages. An example is the acquisition of English personal pronouns, for which four sequential stages, correlated with the formal features of person, number, case and gender, are distinguished (Felix & Hahn, 1985).

A fixed order in the acquisition of L2 morphemes was first investigated by Dulay and Burt (1973, 1974) in child L2 acquisition, irrespective of L1, and it was corroborated by Larsen-Freeman (1975) in adult L2 acquisition. Krashen (1977) reviewed different morpheme studies and established the following order: progressive *-ing*, plural *-s,* copula, auxiliary progressive, article, irregular past, regular past, third-person singular and possessive *'s* (see Chapter 5). The studies on the natural order of morpheme acquisition have been criticised on several counts (see Cook, 1993), while various explanations of the posited natural order have also been attempted from different perspectives (see Goldschneider & DeKeyser, 2001 for a recent review).

A number of more current studies surpass the borders of the morpheme studies in their concurrent consideration of morphological and syntactic forms within a specific discourse context, the narrative, for example. Such studies have shown that, despite different L1s, L2 stages are determined to be identical in the results of narrative tasks. For example, both Klein *et al.* (1993) and Dietrich *et al.* (1995) in results from the European Science Foundation Project, describe the acquisition of second language narrative ability in adults who lack formal L2 instruction and whose source and target languages are in different combinations. The results reveal uniformity in early developmental stages and different rates of stage attainment. The authors describe the initial *pre-basic variety*, a stage in which narratives consist of noun phrases and adverbials and frequent omission of prepositions. In this stage if verbs appear, no syntax is built around them. Inflection is infrequent in the form of random appearances. The pragmatic principle of natural order, that the order of events corresponds to the order of utterances, is used to organise the narrative. In the second stage, the *basic variety*, utterances are organised around a verb, characteristically lacking inflection. Temporal adverbs, *yesterday, Sunday, often*, are used and local organisation of the story occurs in the form of a number of lexical devices to delimit the beginning and end of events, as exemplified by the phrase *"work finish"* to clarify the idea that work is over. Some but not all participants in the study were classified as going beyond the basic variety to use more language-specific elements.

The authors contend that participants may proceed beyond the basic variety because the stage is comprised only of transparent form-meaning mappings, simple linguistic forms and basic organising principles. The stage, while effective in the rudimentary sense that the listener will understand the story's content, is communicatively restricted. For example, the basic variety lacks third-person pronouns, verbal morphology and clausal subordination. The authors propose that what inspires certain participants to go beyond the communicative inadequacy of the basic variety is the desire to express more complex messages, which may contain, for example, alteration of the chronological order by means of aspect variation or subordination, and changes in the narrative perspective by means of the use of the passive. According to the authors, the basic variety represents universal narrative structure because its characteristics are shared by the majority of natural languages. In contrast, going beyond the basic variety means paying attention to the more language-specific ways of grammaticalisation.

In sum, data and conclusions reached thereof support the fact of a shared route of acquisition despite differences in L1 and acquisition context.

Rate and ultimate attainment

The distinction between rate of acquisition and ultimate attainment has been proven necessary in studies on the role of age in L2 acquisition. Since the early years of the decade of the 1960s, the question of whether children or adults are more successful language learners has generated a wealth of research, a question still relevant today. The results of studies in naturalistic settings suggest that age of initial exposure is a determining factor in predicting ultimate language proficiency. In other words, the younger children are first exposed to the L2, the more chances they have of coming to be considered native, or near native L2 speakers (see DeKeyser & Larson-Hall, 2005, for a review of the relevant studies). These findings corroborate the Critical Period Hypothesis (CPH) (Lenneberg, 1967), which, in the strong version, states that during the years leading up to puberty children can acquire an L2 more easily and also achieve native-like competence. After puberty, acquisition becomes more difficult and native-like competence impossible. The strong version of the CPH, however, can no longer be sustained in the face of cases in which learners first exposed to the L2 in adulthood become indistinguishable from native speakers (Bongaerts et al., 1997; Ioup et al., 1994), or, on the contrary, when young children fail to achieve native-like control (Hyltenstam & Abrahamsson, 2000; Thompson, 1991). The hypothesis' weaker version proposes instead a sensitive period during which L2 acquisition is simply more efficient.

Different learning mechanisms used by adults and children have been advanced as an explanation for the decline in ultimate attainment. The crux of the idea is that children use domain-specific procedures, while adults rely on general learning abilities (Bley-Vroman, 1988). In other terms, children acquire an L2 for the most part implicitly, whereas adults learn an L2 by means of explicit and declarative knowledge (DeKeyser, 2000; Harley & Hart, 1997). In fact, the explanation is consistent with the results of studies in which participants are exposed to the L2 for short periods of time, calculated as about ten months, in which adults are shown to have an advantage over children in the form of an initially faster rate of acquisition (Bialystok, 1997; Snow & Hoefnagel-Höhle, 1978). Under this view, adults employ explicit learning mechanisms that provide them with a head start, but that are less effective in the long run. Children, on the other hand, benefit from implicit learning, which is initially slower but more efficient in the long run. The empirical evidence necessary to support this view is however as yet unavailable.

The evidence to date for instructed language acquisition is consistent with the finding for naturalistic studies as regards the initial faster rate of adults and older children. No current study, however, with the foreign language classroom as learning context has shown that young children catch up with adults and older children in the long run. Singleton (1989) argues that the discrepancies result from variation in amount of exposure in the two contexts: to date, studies of the acquisition of a non-primary language in a formal context have not been conducted over a time period sufficient to detect an advantage of younger learners. Studies such as Burstall (1975), Ekstrand (1978), Cenoz (1997), and those within the Barcelona Age Factor (BAF) Project such as Pérez-Vidal *et al.* (2000), Muñoz (2003), Álvarez and Muñoz (2003), which examined the initial stages of acquisition, consistently report an advantage of the older subjects, but it remains to be seen whether within a longer time period in an instructional setting children might surpass older language learners.

A number of issues are thus open to research in the area of the route and rate of L2 acquisition and appear herein formulated as the research questions of our study. As regards the question of route, SLA research very often focuses on the acquisition of individual forms, measuring accuracy as compared with target language use, but not within discourse. This approach is represented by the morpheme studies and by studies which trace the development of a single feature outlined above. On the other hand, studies that have considered the acquisition of forms in discourse, for example in a narrative, have focused on adult L2 learners in a naturalistic setting. A second area of investigation, that of rate of acquisition, brings the age factor in the instructional setting to the forefront since previous studies have either focused on L2 learners in a naturalistic setting or have not allowed a sufficiently long period of time for a possible advantage of the early starters to manifest itself.

The central aim of our study is to determine if, when considering concurrently syntactic, morphological and discourse features, foreign language learners of different ages (children and adults) proceed in their development in clearly identifiable stages. We predict both that individual learners will transit through stages at different paces and that adult learners will proceed faster than their child counterparts. Finally, we intend to determine whether younger children eventually catch up with older children and adults after a long span of time. The research questions to encompass all of the issues to be addressed are postulated as follows:

(1) Do foreign language learners transit through identifiable stages in the development of oral narrative ability and, if so, how can these stages be characterised?

(2) How do the components of the narrative, morphology, syntax and discourse interact at each stage?

(3) Do individuals with the same number of instructional hours and different ages of first exposure attain the same stage?

(4) If not, do school-aged students catch up eventually with adult learners given a long span of time?

(5) Do adults follow the same route of acquisition as school-aged students?

Method

Participants

As can be seen from Table 6.1, the participants number 45 adults and 180 school-aged students. The school-aged students are learning English as a foreign language in the Barcelona state school system (primary and secondary education), selected from a variety of schools in one of the city's middle-class neighborhoods. Both school-aged students and adults' first languages are Catalan and Spanish. English is thus the foreign language of all participants.[1] The participants were screened to factor out those who study or have studied English outside of school or who have English-speaking parents or close relatives or who have spent time in English speaking countries. The school-aged participants, a total of 180, consist of 30 individuals in 6 different groups, each divided according to age of first exposure and testing times. There are, thus, respectively, a group who began instruction in English at an average age of 8 years, the early starters, (group A), and whose narrative performance has been tested at three different time periods: data collection Time 1 (T1) after 200 instructional hours and at an average age of 10;9 years, data collection Time 2 (T2) after 416 instructional hours and at an average age of 12;9 years and data collection Time 3 (T3) after 726 instructional hours and at an average age of 16;9 years. The data are cross-sectional, however, so the sets of individuals at each data collection time are not the same. The late starters (group B), those that begin instruction at an average age of 11 years, comprise three groups as well. A modification in the nationally mandated curriculum, which changed age of first exposure to foreign language from an average age of 11 to an average age of 8, made possible data collection times of different age groups. Their narrative abilities are tested after the same number of hours, which do not necessarily correspond to the same number of courses since there is a different distribution of instructional hours in the two curriculums. The late starters tested after 200 instructional hours are on average 12;9 years old, after 416 instructional hours 14;9 years old on average and after 726 instructional hours 17;9 years old on average. The final two groups consist solely of adult participants who are respectively in their second year and their third year of English instruction (D1 and D2, respectively). One group is comprised of 30 individuals and the other of 15.

Table 6.1 Age and hours upon testing

	A AO = 8 years	B AO = 11 years	D AO = 18+
T1: 200 h	AT = 10 N = 30	AT = 12 N = 30	AT = 28;9 N = 30
T2: 416 h	AT = 12 N = 30	AT = 14 N = 30	AT = 30;4 N = 15
T3: 726 h	AT = 16 N = 30	AT = 17 N = 30	

Notes: AO = age of onset;
AT = age at testing.

Instrument and data collection

The data are the result of an oral narrative based on a series of six drawings. The drawings depict, respectively: (1) a mother and her two children preparing a meal or snack to be taken in a picnic basket; (2) the family's little dog getting into the basket unbeknownst to the children and the mother, who is showing the children on a map the way to the place they are to go; (3) the children saying goodbye to the mother; (4) the children arriving in the country; (5) the children opening the basket and the dog coming out of it; and (6) the children finding left only a few crumbs and the thermos. Each participant was shown the series of drawings and allowed several minutes to arrive at an understanding of what the drawings represent. Subsequently, each participant was instructed to narrate the story based on the drawings. Each narrative was audio-recorded and later transcribed into document form. The data collectors were instructed to intervene as little as possible.

Procedure

The aim of the study was to establish whether, in this narrative task, a series of stages through which individual learners appear to proceed in English as a foreign language (EFL) could be delimited. Two evaluators, working independently on a sample of 60 narratives, established the characteristics of each stage and, after arriving at a consensus about the characteristics of each stage, they applied the stages to the 225 narratives of the study. The same evaluators, again working independently, arrived at a 97% agreement on the stage to be assigned to each narrative. On discussion of individual cases, the evaluators arrived at a 99% agreement on stages assigned.

The evaluators followed the same procedure in applying the criteria established in the stages. First appearance of a characteristic, for example, the single instance of a bare verb form such as *play*, was considered to count as emergence of that characteristic. Emergence was taken as an initial phase in the process of acquisition, based on the idea that the student has noticed a particular item or structure and is able to incorporate it in oral production. Errors were eliminated from the stages as a criterion based on the concept that awareness of a feature need not imply accurate use. As illustration, the appearance of a string such as "the dog eating sandwich" was considered to count as use of the present progressive, overlooking the error of the missing auxiliary.

Criteria used to analyse the discourse component

In L1 acquisition, two aspects of storytelling have been shown to be relevant in the study of the ability to narrate: story structure and the grammatical and lexical means employed to signal it, and textual cohesion.

As regards story structure, Labov's (1972) framework, posits four main components of the narrative: an orientation (who? when? what? where?), a complication (the events that lead to a crisis or high point), an evaluation (shows the point of telling the story), and the result (the resolution to the problem). The narrative proper, consisting of the complication and result, is composed of a set of clauses consisting of simple subjects, a perfective verb (a single event has to finish before the next event begins), and verbal complements and adverbials. These clauses constitute the foreground of the story (Hopper, 1979).

Evaluative sentences suspend the narrative and may contain (1) modals, (2) the progressive aspect; or (3) subordinate clauses. These clauses, as well as descriptive clauses in the orientation, constitute the background of the story (Hopper, 1979).

Used herein as a point of reference for narrative analysis, strict implementation of Labov's framework has not been possible in the present study for several reasons. First, Labov's data consist purely of personal narratives, whereas the data studied herein consist of a narrative elicited by narrator observation of a set of drawings. Fictional storytelling, in contrast to personal narratives, obviously lacks a degree of personal involvement and may result in less evaluation because both the motivation to make explicit the story's meaning as well as the purpose for telling it are weakened. A second and more important problem with strict application of Labov's framework is the fact that the present study's data have been elicited at very early stages of language development. As a result, in the majority of narratives the simple past, thus the perfective aspect, is not used, and therefore, under a strict application of Labov's criteria, the data do not contain narrative clauses, but consist rather of narratives in process. Therefore, clauses containing bare verbs or the present progressive have been accepted as belonging to the complication or the result components when the subject matter of the clause indicated as much.

As regards textual cohesion, Hickmann (2003) shows how this develops in children's discourse as they incorporate in their stories appropriate reference to person, time and space. In the present study, one fundamental distinction in the reference to person, the use of the indefinite/definite article to signal new introduction of a character versus maintenance of reference, will be considered, as illustrated in the following example:

> *The story starts with **a** mother, a boy and a girl who prepared sandwiches for a picnic. **The** mother said goodbye to her children.*

Furthermore, the development of reference to time will be considered in such aspects as tense maintenance throughout the story, aspectual distinctions to signal foreground versus background, and the use of temporal discourse markers, as illustrated in the following example:

> *While the children were looking at the map, the dog jumped into the basket with the sandwiches.*

In addition to these two aspects of narrative development, a third criterion has been considered when examining the discourse component. Alvarez (2003), using data taken from the same pool of data as that of the present study, shows to what degree school-aged students with a low command of the foreign language, need the interviewer's intervention in order to complete orally the task of telling the story. At these lower stages of command of the foreign language, the interviewers are sensitive to the age and the language problems and offer their help to such an extent that the task becomes a joint conversation about a story. Therefore, the ability to tell the story independently from the interviewer has been taken as related to the development of other discourse features.

Results

Description of stages

The following section addresses the first and second research questions and provides evidence of a series of developmental stages for oral narrative capabilities and the manner of interaction of the morphosyntactic and discourse components.

Stage 1 contains narratives completed in one of the L1s, which therefore contain no evidence of L2 morphological, syntactic or discourse narrative features.

Stage 2 is characterised by the emergence of bare nominal content words, as in (1), which may be accompanied by an L1 determiner, as in (2):

(1) *child, boy, dog*
(2) *el* [the] *picnic, un* [a] *dog*

Thus, Stage 2 narratives contain minimal L2 morphosyntactic structure, so that head nouns are used to name characters in the drawings and there is no evidence of the discourse component.

Stage 3 contains the emergence of nominally related functional categories, specifically the L2 definite article or an ordinal number employed to name characters, of which the examples below are characteristic:

(3) (a) *the child, the boy, the mother*
    (b) *one girl, one boy*

Bare nouns may still occur in a more limited number than in the previous stage. The plural *-s* emerges:

(4) *the boys, two boys, the brothers*

The first prepositions appear, characteristically *in*, and therefore prepositional phrases as well. The object of the preposition is realised as a determinerless noun or a noun determined by an L1 form:

(5) *at basket*
(6) (a) *in cesta* (basket)
   (b) *in la* (the) *cesta*

In conclusion, Stage 3 includes further noun phrase development and the emergence of prepositions and prepositional phrases. Still, there is no evidence of the use of verbs nor of the discourse component.

Stage 4 is characterised by further development of prepositional phrases, which contain objects with appropriate determiners, as illustrated in the examples:

(7) (a) *in the room*
   (b) *in the mountain*

The main characteristic of this stage is that narratives contain one or several verbs, very often the copula. Lexical verbs are, characteristically, transitive verbs. Clauses very often lack one obligatory constituent, as in the examples:

(8) (a) *is a mountain*
   (b) *the dog look*
   (c) *prepare sandwich*

The SVO[2] structure thus makes an incipient emergence, as do SVA structures, also often lacking constituents:

(9) (a) *go to excursion*
   (b) *the children on mountain*

The form *-ing* emerges as the token of verbal morphology:

(10) *the cows eating*

Negation of noun phrases also emerges, as does the coordinator *and* between noun phrases and lexical verb forms:

(11) *the brother and sister no breakfast*
(12) (a) *one dog and the mother*
    (b) *look a basket and play*

Furthermore, possessive adjectives appear, marked inappropriately for person and gender:

(13) (a) *your mother* (in context, their mother)
    (b) *his boy* (in context, her boy or son)

Thus, this stage is characterised by syntactic and morphological developments. With respect to syntax, at the clausal level there are incipient SVO and SVA structures with missing constituents and at the phrasal level prepositional phrases are adequately formed, negation and phrasal coordination emerge and nouns are determined by possessive adjectives with inappropriate features. A significant morphological development is the emergence of the *-ing* form. No evidence of the discourse component is present yet.

Stage 5 is characterised by the emergence of the first discourse properties and further development of clausal syntax. SVA structures appear in their complete form:

(14) (a) *The children is at the mountain*
     (b) *In the basket is dog*

The present progressive emerges, alternating between appropriate and inappropriate forms, although most typically in isolated clauses as descriptions of what the participant observes to be happening in the pictures, rather than linked to an appropriate discourse distinction:

(15) *the family is preparing the sandwich*

Other occurring verbal forms are bare lexical verbs that lack inflectional markers. Refinements in phrasal syntax include nouns consistently modified by L2 determiners with an infrequent use of contextually inappropriate bare nouns. Possessive determiners carry for the most part contextually appropriate person features though inappropriate gender features. A broader variety of prepositions, *into*, *on*, *under* or *for*, appear in prepositional phrases.

An incipient discourse organisation can be observed. The narrative text is structured using spatial deictics, allowing the participant to indicate to which picture reference is being made:

(16) (a) *in the second* (picture)
     (b) *in the third*

Stage 6 contains further development of clausal syntax with the emergence of SV, SVC, SVOO and SVOA structures. The conjunction *but* may occur to coordinate clauses:

(17) *She look a dog in the ... cesta* (basket) *but don't have a ... any dinner.*

In the area of phrasal morphosyntax bare nouns no longer appear. Possessive determiners still appear with inappropriate features of gender and number. Subject pronouns carry the correct case, number and person features, although object pronouns often carry contextually inappropriate case, number and gender features. Verb morphology undergoes some refinement. For example, in existential structure verbal concord is very often correct and the use of the present progressive form increases. Other verbal inflectional forms, for example, the third person present singular *-s*, future *will*, may occur randomly or sporadically. The examples below are from a single Stage 6 narrative:

(18) (a) *The mum helps the children*
    (b) *The mum read the map*
    (c) *They will going to the mountain*

An important discourse feature, the use of the L2 indefinite article marking first mention of inanimate nouns, emerges:

(19) *they have a breakfast*

In conclusion, phrasal and clausal morphosyntax undergoes further sophistication, seeming to provide a 'spring board' for the development of the discourse component.

Stage 7 includes further development of L2 clausal and phrasal syntax. Quantifiers, such as *all*, *many* and a broader variety of determiners appear. Subject and object pronouns tend toward appropriate usage in terms of case, number and gender features. There is evidence of awareness of the L2 verbal inflectional system. Some narratives contain the present progressive throughout and in others there is a combination of bare lexical verbs and verbs marked with third-person present singular *-s* or irregular simple past forms. Phrasal syntax is further refined with the appearance of post-nominal modification in the form of a prepositional phrase:

(20) *a place for a picnic*

The discourse component undergoes further development. The first usage of temporal discourse markers, such as *then* or *after*, occurs. The indefinite article is used to introduce animate characters, although not consistently. A significant development is the emergence of complex sentences, including adverbial and nominal clauses, which are used to mark the high point of the story, when the children realise that the dog has eaten their food:

(21) *When the children open the basket they see that the dog eat the food*

In Stage 7, however, subordinate clauses do not appear in other parts of the story yet. Thus, the emergence of subordination as a syntactic development is exclusively linked to a specific discourse function.

In conclusion, at Stage 7, L2 simple clause order is complete, while phrasal syntax is in the process of completion with the addition of word categories and features. The narratives of this stage reveal greater awareness of the L2 verbal morphology system, although accuracy is still quite problematic. Finally, the emergence of subordination, linked to a discourse function, is an important characteristic.

Stage 8 includes further developments in the complexity of the verb phrase in the form of modals and infinitive constructions, as illustrated by the examples below:

(22) (a) *the children must go*
    (b) *they want to go to breakfast*

Verbal inflection is more abundant and varied than in the previous stage and may include appropriate forms for present and past progressive, third-person present singular -s or past -ed. The use of *have* as a perfect auxiliary occurs, thus allowing a change in the chronological order of the narrative's events:

(23) *the dog has eat the sandwiches*

Furthermore, the expression of simultaneity of actions by means of the temporal conjunction *while* emerges as a new characteristic:

(24) *while the children are watching the plan, the little dog is watching something.*

Both subordination and post-modification become more complex and come to include a variety of both nominal and adverbial clauses:

(25) *After, her mother teaches him where is the road that he have to take you go to the mountain.*
(26) *Here, they arrive to the place where they want to go and they see that their dog has gone with them and they see that the dog has eaten all their food.*

Finally, with respect to the discourse component, there is now a clear orientation part where characters are introduced frequently with existential sentences showing correct agreement. Very often students at this stage include descriptions of the scenery which serves as background where the story takes place. There is also more evaluation in the form of causality: the purpose and the cause of events are stated by means of the infinitive of purpose and adverbial subordinate clauses of reason:

(27) *They prepare sandwiches because to go to a picnic.*

Stage 9 is characterised, at the morphosyntactic level, by the complexity of embedding, which may include the use of relative clauses:

(28) *there is the dog who is searching for some sandwiches*
(29) *and when the mother is telling what is the street they have to go, the dog came into the basket.*

As is evident from example (29), students at Stage 9 can successfully use grammatical aspect alternations to mark the discourse distinction of foreground (perfective) and background (progressive). Moreover, students at this stage also make use of aspectual verbs, especially inceptive verbs:

(30) *they get out of the house and they began to walk.*
(31) *they started to eat.*

In contrast with other stages, Stage 9 is characterised by the fact that the participant becomes an independent narrator, requiring no assistance on the part of the interviewer to complete the story successfully.

Despite the degree of sophistication of Stage 9 narratives, none of the stories, no matter the age of the participant, are anchored in a single tense. The observed trend shows random vacillation between present and past forms. Narratives told strictly in the present tense lack, for the most part, use of third-person present singular -s, an indication that the story is not really marked for tense, but rather that the student recounts the story by means of bare lexical verbs.

In this section, which addressed the first two research questions, nine stages have been identified to describe learner development of oral narrative ability. It has also been established in this section that the morphosyntactic and discourse component interact and that a certain level of morphosyntactic skills are essential to the emergence of the discourse component.

Narrative development and learners' age

In order to consider research questions 3, 4 and 5, average stages have been assigned to all the groups. Stages were independently validated by calculating the relationship between the narrative stages and the results of two other tests from the same group of students, an oral interview and a cloze test. A Pearson correlation showed a strong positive correlation for both: $r(217) = 0.876$, $p < 0.001$, for the interview, and $r(216) = 0.895$, $p < 0.001$ for the cloze. Figure 6.1 displays the comparison between the groups in terms of the stages assigned to them.

The group that takes the most advantage of the initial 200 hours of instruction is the adult group, followed by the late starters, the early starters

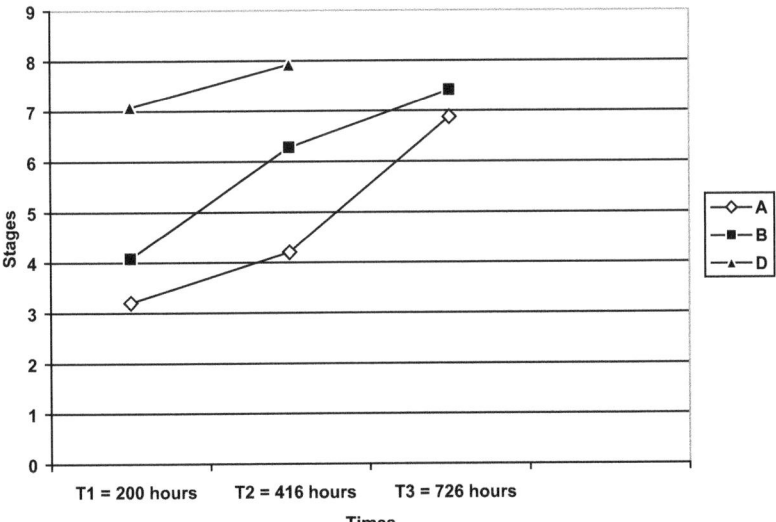

Figure 6.1 Development of the three groups

being the group that advances the least. This group, however, experiences a spurt in their results from T2 to T3 almost catching up with the late starters. In contrast, the adult group seems to have made little headway after the initial 200 hours. An analysis of variance (ANOVA) reveals significant differences among the average stages ($F(7,217) = 82,054$, $p < 0.000$). A post hoc Tukey test indicates significant differences in the results of the three groups at each time of testing, except between D1 and D2, where the level of significance is $p = 0.149$.

In Table 6.2 the results are set out in a way to facilitate the answer to research question 3, whether the stages correlate better with age of first exposure or with hours of instruction.

The results provide a definite answer: clearly, the factor hours of instruction shows little correlation with the average stage for each group. For example, at T1, after 200 instructional hours, the early starters attain an average stage of 3.2, so their production consists of noun phrases including determiners and some bare nouns, whereas the late starters attain an average stage of 4.08, so their narratives begin to be organised around a verb with many utterances still consisting of nouns and prepositional phrases. Only the adults' narratives, where average performance is at stage 7.08, contain consistent use of verbal morphology, some forms with a discourse function and syntax complex enough to organise the story

Table 6.2 Results stage assignment to groups

		School-aged early starters (A)	School-aged late starters (B)	Adults (D)
T1 (200 hours)	Group	A1 N = 30	B1 N = 30	D1 N = 30
	Average age	10;9	12;9	28;9
	Average stage	3.2	4.08	7.08
	SD	1.13	1.07	0.73
	Range	1–5.5	1–6.5	6–9
T2 (416 hours)	Group	A2 N = 30	B2 N = 30	D2 N = 15
	Average age	12;9	14;9	30;4
	Average stage	4.2	6.28	7.93
	SD	1.15	0.90	0.59
	Range	2–6	4–7	7–9
T3 (726 hours)	Group	A3 N = 30	B3 N = 30	–
	Average age	16;9	17;9	–
	Average stage	6.88	7.42	–
	SD	1.48	0.60	–
	Range	2–9	7–9	–

around a high point. A Tukey test shows the following levels of significance: for A1 and B1, $p = 0.020$, for B1 and D1, $p = 0.000$.

At T2, after 416 instructional hours, results of the Tukey test show the following levels of significance: for A2 and B2, $p = 0.000$ and for B2 and D2, $p = 0.000$. The narratives of the group who began instruction at 8 contain incipient use of verbs and therefore clause level constituents begin to be related at the average stage of 4.2. The narratives of the group who began instruction at 11 show organisation of utterances around a verb and the stories contain a variety of clause types at the average stage of 6.3. The adult narratives, on average almost at Stage 8, show more sophistication with the use of clausal subordination and tense and aspect morphology.

For the averages at T3, after 726 instructional hours, a Tukey test reveals a level of significance between A3 and B3 of $p = 0.474$. These results suggest that group A is beginning to catch up with group B. Worth stressing, however, is the fact that at T3 there is only a single year of age difference between the two groups, while at T2 and T1 the age difference is two years. This may be a significant factor given that Table 6.2 also shows that the A2 and B1, two groups coinciding in the biological age of 12 but with a different number of hours of exposure, have similar average stages, 4.2 and 4.0, respectively, and the difference between the two groups is not significant ($p = 1,000$).

This similarity between the two groups of 12-year-olds is so striking that it is worth exploring. The nature of the similarity becomes clearer by dividing the stages into three broad developmental levels: (1) the word-level syntax (Stages 1 and 2) in which only head nouns are used, (2) the phrase-level syntax (Stage 3) in which syntactic relations emerge at the level of the phrase, and (3) clause-level syntax (Stages 4 to 6) in which clause constituents are related syntactically. The information appears in Table 6.3 below.

The percentages between the two groups are strikingly similar with the main difference being that the developmental level of 'clause syntax' consists

Table 6.3 Comparison of stages T1 and T2, at 12;9 years of age

Developmental level	Stage*	A2 (N = 30) 416 hours		B1 (N = 30) 200 hours	
		No. of students	% of total number	No. of students	% of total number
Word-level syntax	1	0	6.67	1	6.67
	2	2		1	
Phrase-level syntax	3	7	23.33	5	16.67
Clause-level syntax	4	10	70.0	16	76.66
	5	7		5	
	6	4		2	

Note: * Half stages are rounded down to the nearest number

of a large number of narratives at Stage 4 in the group that has received 200 hours of instruction (B1). With 416 hours of instruction, there are more students able to use a wider selection of verbs and more inflections appear (Stages 5 and 6), although the difference is minimal between the two groups.

In order to answer research question 4, whether school-aged students eventually catch up with adult learners, the stages were divided into the same developmental levels as above. As Table 6.4 and Figure 6.2 show, there is almost no overlap between school-aged students' and adult's achievement after 200 hours of instruction.[3]

After 200 instructional hours, in 40% of school-aged students' narratives at Stages 1, 2, 3 not a single verb appears but rather constructions built on nouns and prepositions at the phrasal level. Morphology is scarce consisting only of a possible plural -s on a noun. The remaining 60% of narratives contain a verb or two, so the syntax consists of a combination of phrases and a clause or two, mainly SVA and SVO structures. Verbs appear for the most part in their base form with an incipient verbal morphology including a verb or two marked with progressive -*ing*.

In contrast, in the adult narratives syntax is shown to be more complex, including prepositional phrases as post-modifiers of noun-heads and adverbial clauses of reason or purpose. More importantly, there is frequent use in more than half of the adults' narratives of an adverbial clause of time which serves to order the story around a high point, a fact which indicates a higher degree of sophistication in the use of syntax.

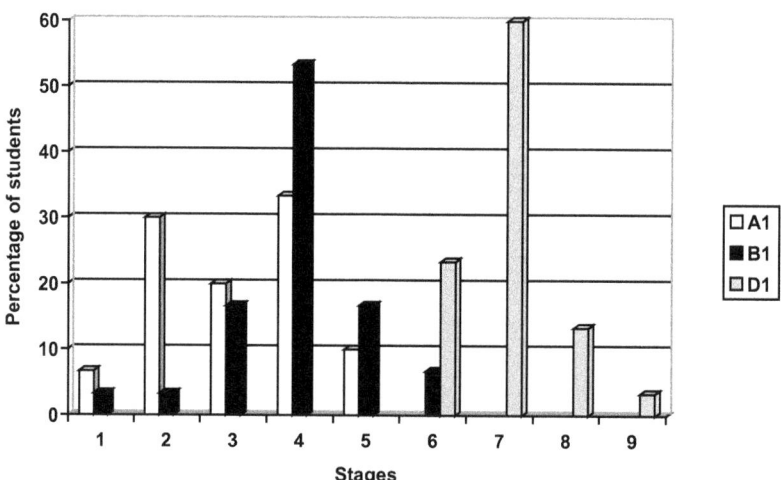

Figure 6.2 Percentage of students at each stage – Time 1

Rate and Route of Acquisition in EFL 143

Table 6.4 Comparison of stages between school-aged students and adults at T1

		School-aged students (N = 60)		*Adults* (N = 30)	
		Groups A1 and B1		Group D1	
Developmental level	Stage	No. of students	% of total number	No. of students	% of total number
Word-level syntax	1	3	21.67		
	2	10			
Phrase-level syntax	3	11	18.33		
Clause-level syntax	4	26	60.0		23.33
	5	8			
	6	2		7	
Syntax for discourse organisation	7			18	76.67
	8			4	
	9			1	

Similarly, at T2, after 416 instructional hours, the narratives of school-aged students and adults show different performance levels, as Table 6.5 and Figure 6.3 show.

These results illustrate that adults proceed more quickly through the stages than school-aged children. Given an identical number of instructional hours, adults construct a syntactically and morphologically more complex story with a higher degree of discourse organisation. Nevertheless, after 416 instructional hours more overlap between the narratives of school-aged students and adults can be observed than at T1. The 16 child

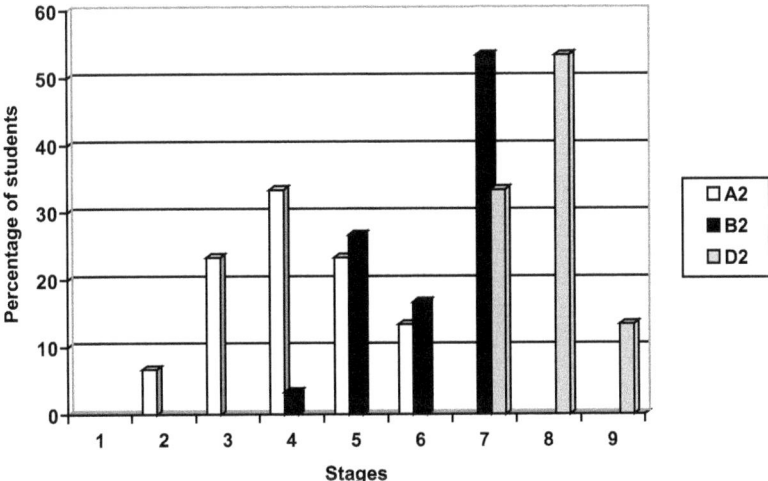

Figure 6.3 Percentage of students at each stage – Time 2

Table 6.5 Comparison of stages between school-aged students and adults at T2

Developmental level	Stage	School-aged students (N = 60)		Adults (N = 30)	
		Groups A2 and B2		Group D2	
		No. of students	% of total number	No. of students	% of total number
Word-level syntax	2	2	21.67		
	3	7			
Clause-level syntax	4	11	60.0		
	5	15			
	6	9			
Syntax for discourse organisation	7	16		5	100.00
	8			8	
	9			2	

narratives classified as Stage 7 correspond exclusively to group B2 (average age 14;9), representing 26.67% of child narratives in contrast to 33.33% adult narratives (five adults). Comparison of these results with those at T1 demonstrates that the distance between the two groups, adults and older children, has shortened. From another perspective, the results demonstrate that adults proceed faster than school-aged students after 200 instructional hours, but their pace slows down after an initial spurt. In contrast, school-aged students begin slower, but the pace picks up so that the distance between their performance and the adults' is shortened.

Research question five, whether school-aged students and adults follow the same route, can be answered only partially due to the very fast initial advance of the adults. At T1, after 200 instructional hours, the majority of adult narratives were already at Stage 6 or beyond. Child and adult narratives from Stages 6 to 9 can however be compared to establish similarities and differences.

For the most part, the differences relate to greater use of evaluation and description in the adult narratives. Beginning with Stage 6, a clear difference between adult and child narratives is that the former incorporate evaluative elements not typical of child narratives at the same stage. The following examples serve to facilitate comparison between a Stage 6 child narrative (1) and an adult narrative at the same stage (2):

(1) **A2:** in the first a mother is putting the tea on the ….
A2: *un* [a] dog, the dog is moving the *la cua* [the tail]. The girl is *tallando* [cutting] the bread and the boy is putting the sandwiches in the bag. The mother and the boys are looking the map and the dog is looking the bag. Then the mother is *está saludando a sus hijos* (is greeting her children), and the boys *saludan a* [greet] to his mother.

Four, the boys are going to the hill. *¿Cómo se dicen 'vacas'*? [How do you say 'cows'?]
RE(searcher): cow
A2: and the cow are eating. The fifth, the boys are looking the bag and in the bag is the dog. There are trees and ...
RE: birds
A2: birds. Six, the boy are looking the bag and it's *vacía* [empty].
RE: empty, why? why is it empty? what has happened?
A2: he are eating the breakfast
RE: but who has eaten the breakfast, who?
A2: the boys, and the dog
A2: are you sure?
A2: ah! not the boy and the girl, no, no, the dog!

(2) **D1:** is preparing tea for her childrens. In picture number two the table XXX the mother and the children preparing a map and the way to go to school. The dog is looking the ...
RE: basket
D1: the basket and in picture number three the mother say goodbye to the children, and in picture number four the children arrive at the mountain, and in picture number five sitting in the grey.
RE: and in the last picture, what do you see?
D1: the childrens looking with surprise that in this basket your breakfast se *lo ha comido el perro* [the dog has eaten it].

The adult narrator (D1) includes use of slightly more complex structures to post-modify a noun, such as *the way to go to school*, thus creating a noun phrase with more information. Moreover, this adult narrative contains a nominal *that*-clause as object at the story's high point when the children are surprised to discover that the dog has eaten their food. Despite word order and morphological inaccuracies, it is clear that in the adult example an attempt is made to highlight the story's crucial point by syntactic means.

Child and adult narratives at Stage 7 also exhibit similarities and differences. The first example represents a child narrative (B2) at Stage 7 and the second corresponds to an adult narrative at the same stage:

(1) **B2:** there are a boy and a girl. They are preparing a picnic and their mother are putting coffee in a *termo* [thermos flask]. The mother are showing them a map and the dog are looking what are in the bag. The boy and the girl are saying goodbye to her mother and they arrive in a mountain. There are two cows and when they are going to have lunch, they discover that the dog are inside the bag and he did eat all the lunch.

(2) **D1:** in the morning they are a boy, a girl, and they make a sandwich for to eat in the excursion in the country, and her mother make a tea and she put the tea in the *termo* [flask]. After that, in the picture

number two, the mother explain with a map the street for our walk on the country. In the picture three the boy and girl say bye a some mother. In the picture four they in the forest *y* [and] they are next to the, in the little ...
RE: house?
D1: the little house in the country. In the number five when the boy put the tea, see the dog. They are a dog in the basket, but they are surprised because the dog eat all the food. The boy and girl don't eat.

Both narratives include characteristic features of Stage 7. First, an indefinite article is used to mark both animate and inanimate referents. Second, a temporal adverbial clause is used to mark the story's high point, although the high point is indicated at slightly different moments in the story. Third, the majority of utterances are complete clauses and a variety of clause structures is employed. Fourth, subject and object pronouns appear correctly marked for features of case, person, number and gender. Possessives usually lack the appropriate person feature. Finally, narrative structure is emerging.

Again, the central difference between the two narratives lies in the fact that the adult incorporates more evaluation, stating purpose by means of post-modification, as in *a sandwich for to eat in the excursion in the country*, and states of mind, as in the example *they are surprised because* .... Furthermore, the adult includes temporal adverbials such as *in the morning, after that*, uncharacteristic of child narratives at the same stage. As Labov (1972) asserts, the most complex grammar is contained in the evaluation part of the story. Perhaps adults, with evidently more advanced cognitive levels than school-aged students, stretch to find the syntactic structures necessary to express evaluation.

Likewise, Stage 8 adult narratives show more complex syntactic structures to express evaluation by means of post-modification, by inclusion of more elaborate descriptions, or by statement of the purpose of things or actions, as the example below from an adult demonstrates:

(1) **D2:** In the picture I can see two young sons that they are preparing the food **for a walk, to eat outside**, and a dog is watching them and the mother was behind the tea or coffee. And next the children and the mother are looking a map and the dog are looking inside the bag. Well, next the sons saying goodbye to the mother and then take climb over a mountain and the two cows eating. And next they discover that inside the bag there is the dog and the dog go outside and then they can see that the dog have eaten all the food **that they has been preparing for their eating**, and that's all I think.

In contrast, at a similar point in the story, a school-aged student's narrative (A3) at the same Stage 8 lacks these features:

(2) **A3:** picture one there is a boy and a girl and his mother and the boy is putting two sandwich into the basket and the girl is cutting a bread. Now in the picture two the dog is looking into the basket and the children are looking to a map. In the picture three, the mother says goodbye to the children. In the picture four the children are in a hill and the boy is carrying the basket and they are climbing the mountain. In the picture number five the children are very surprised because in the basket there is the dog. And in the picture six they are looking to the basket and they *'descubrir', no sé* ('discover' I don't know)
RE: what do they discover?
A3: *això* (that's it), they discover that there aren't any food in the basket. The dog has eaten the sandwich and the bread.

The fundamental difference between the D2 and A3 narratives is the expression in the first of a more advanced notion of purpose shown by the use of more complex post-modification. Whereas in the child narratives causation may be expressed by means of an adverbial clause of reason, it is expressed for the most part only at the story's high point, where the children of the story notice that no food is left. In contrast, adult narratives at Stage 8 may contain both nominal and adverbial clauses at different points in the story as the examples below taken from a series of different narratives demonstrate:

> **D2:** the two boys they are doing the lunch **because they will go to the mountain**.
> **D1:** they stop **for drink and eat something**
> **D1:** they are looking for a plane (= a map), **they need to know where are they going**
> **D1:** they think is good time **for have the meal**
> **D1:** they are very happy **because they are coming out to the mountain**

Furthermore, the expression of causation in adult narratives means that narrative elements not present in the drawings are included. Adult narratives often contain invented or imagined circumstances, so probability adverbs and comment clauses such as *I think* or *I suppose* are included, as shown in the examples below:

> **D1 (Stage 7): naturally, I think** the dog is the guilty
> **D1 (Stage 8.5):** we can see a woman who must be their mother and two childrens, a boy and a girl, who are preparing some food and put it in a basket **maybe** for have a lunch away

> **D2 (Stage 9):** this is a family, a mother with two children, a girl **who is six years old more or less** and a boy.

In keeping with the characteristics stated above, adult narratives contain more elaborate orientations than child narratives:

> **D1 (Stage 6):** there is a house, *bueno* [well] a living-room I think or a kitchen, there is a boy and a girl and his mother *bueno* their mother I suppose, they are prepared a sandwich.
> **D1 (Stage 8):** is very warm day, it's hot with the sun shine and I can see the trees, the birds and they are very happy.
> **D1 (Stage 7):** once upon a time there are a family. In this family the mother early in the morning today it's cooking or preparing the meals for two child and probably her daughter and her son.

In conclusion, it is clear that adult and school-aged students' narratives share the established characteristics for Stages 6 to 9. What sets them apart, however, is that adult narratives contain more non-narrative material in the form of evaluation and orientations.

Discussion

Based on analysis of the contents of the stages posited, a series of generalisations can be drawn. First, a clear relation exists between the development of morphosyntactic components and the development of the discourse component. In other words, narrative elements emerge systematically at specific points in grammatical development. For example, not until Stage 6, at the point where English canonical subject verb plus complement order begins to stabilise, does the first narrative feature emerge: use of the L2 indefinite article to introduce previously unmentioned inanimate objects. Similarly, the use of subordination is tightly linked to a discourse function, that of signalling the high point of the story. The second generalisation concerns the interaction between syntactic and morphological development. Not until Stage 8, at which the L2 order of clausal constituents is consistently appropriate, does the morphological component undergo steady development in the area of verbal inflection.[4] In sum, the stages posited herein show the interaction among the different components of the grammar and discourse, and support the view that the communicative goal of achieving more adequate discourse drives the development of linguistic forms (Dietrich *et al.*, 1995).

The stages posited, which demonstrate a clearly identifiable route of development, confirm the general developmental pattern summarised in Ellis (1994): silent period, syntactic development, morphological development. Likewise, the stages coincide with those elaborated for adult L2 learners (Dietrich *et al.*, 1995). However, formal learning of a language is characterised by a slower developmental pace (Bley-Vroman, 1988) and therefore the stages have been further subdivided into five basic levels corresponding to the interaction of linguistic phenomena. The silent period or L1 period corresponds with Stage 1. The second level, however, is the level of incipient syntax where narratives consist of nouns designating objects or characters (Stage 2). At the third level, phrasal syntax emerges in the form of nominal and prepositional phrases (Stages 3). The fourth level, which has been subdivided into three stages (Stages 4, 5 and 6), sees the emergence of clausal syntax and the morphological component, where verbs may include subjects and complements or both, and verbal morphology is incipient. The final stages comprise the discourse level in which narrative functions are performed by complex syntactic relations and lexical items are used at the clausal level to achieve a temporal structure in the narrative (Stage 7). Stages 8 and 9 include the use of syntactic relationships and verbal morphology characteristic of narratives: aspect alternations to distinguish the foreground from the background; present perfect to alter the chronological order of events, post-modification and subordination to provide evaluative elements.

Next, according to the data analysed in this study, the emergence of morphemes reflects the following order: definite article; plural -s, the copula; present participle -*ing*; irregular past; third-person singular present -s; regular past -*ed*.[5] It should be emphasised, however, that the order found occurs within the framework of a narrative task and therefore the discourse function of the morphemes should be considered (see also Muñoz, Chapter 5, this volume). Initial development revolves around a free lexical morpheme, such as the definite article, although this item has first a local determining function at the level of the phrase. Emergence of the indefinite article, which is also a free morph with the discourse function of signaling given versus new information in both the L1s and the L2, occurs much later. Our study shows that discourse functions are not incorporated in narratives until Stage 7, correlating with emergence of certain morphological and syntactic features.

The use of free lexical morphemes is followed by the emergence of inflectional morphemes such as plural -s or -*ing*, morphemes that correspond to relatively transparent concepts. Yet, their use in the narrative has a very local function, that of indicating that in one of the drawings an action appears to be in process (Stage 4). Not until Stage 9 is grammatical aspect used to mark a discourse function, for example, the progressive aspect to mark the background of the story.

Lastly, morphemes expressing tense distinctions are incorporated at later stages, although only randomly. None of the narratives in the present study are anchored in the present or past tense consistently. The appearance of irregular past forms occurs before regular past forms, but both are used only sporadically. Third-person singular present-s and regular past -*ed* alternate with base verb forms even throughout the last stage.

The results support previous findings on the initial faster rate of adults (Snow, 1983) and older children in narrative development (Álvarez & Muñoz, 2003). After the same number of instructional hours, children whose initial exposure occurred at an average of 8 years attain a lower average stage than those whose average age of initial exposure is at 11, and these in turn attain a lower average stage than that of the adult participants. The explanation for these differences may lie partially in the different learning mechanisms of each age group. Some authors (DeKeyser & Larson-Hall, 2005; Skehan & Foster, 1999) suggest that adults rely on analytical skills to infer general patterns in the L2 and are then able to apply this explicit knowledge consciously in the performance of an L2 task. Children are believed to rely fundamentally on a form of effortless implicit learning, consequent only to enormous amounts of exposure, a condition missing in the EFL context. The contrast explains in part the different results obtained in the correlation between number of instructional hours and attainment of school-aged students and adults. However, another factor to take into consideration when explaining different rate and attainment is motivation. The adult participants have made a personal decision to enroll in an EFL course, while the school-aged participants simply follow the curriculum outlined for them. Likewise, the adult participants may perceive a need for improvement in EFL for the purpose of career advancement. Factors such as these have been proposed as strongly influencing L2 achievement (Masgoret & Gardner, 2003; Tragant, this volume). In conclusion, the faster rate of adult participants versus child participants should be viewed in light of such factors as explicit or implicit learning mechanisms and also instrumental motivation and a more self-determined type of attitude towards the target language.

The corollary of implicit versus explicit learning and age predicts an advantage for younger learners given a longer period of exposure. The data do not contradict the claim that children, given an earlier onset age and sufficient exposure may exceed adults and children with a later onset age in ultimate attainment. Clearly, the late starters progress further than the early starters after 416 instructional hours, although after 726 instructional hours, the difference is not always statistically significant (see Muñoz, Chapter 1 and also Fullana, and Torras *et al.*, this volume).

The last research question, whether adults follow the same developmental route as school-aged students, remains partially unanswered due to the subjects' unequal learning rate. At T1, after 200 instructional hours, the adult participants had already entered the discourse level, so whether the earlier development stages coincide with those established for adult development is not verifiable. Nevertheless, from Stage 7 onwards it is clear that the developmental pattern coincides with that of the child participants' developmental pattern. However, the adult narratives are perceived to be qualitatively 'better' than the child narratives, which may be explained by the fact that adults include more evaluation in the syntactic form of post-modification and subordination. Although Labov's (1972) narrative framework considers events that are not expressed in temporally ordered clauses, as for example, those expressed by means of subordination, not to form part of the narrative proper, Thompson (1987: 451) claims that events considered important for the narrative are expressed in subordinate clauses because of the double function performed by subordinate clauses in a narrative: "the use of subordinate clause allows the writer to accomplish a text-creation goal in addition to the obvious one of maintaining the temporal line". From this perspective, adult contributions are "richer" in the narrative sense because they go beyond the mere task of recounting what the pictures show. This difference between school-aged students and adult narratives is well attested in L1 narratives (Berman & Slobin, 1994).

The data also support the fact that the effect of cognitive maturity on the narrative task is an important issue. There is no statistically significant difference between the results of the narratives of the two groups of 12-year-old participants despite a difference of more than double instructional hours on the part of the younger students. These findings support the results of other studies on oral communicative tasks. Muñoz (2003), for example, in a study on oral interviews from a similar population of subjects, reports the use of similar strategies on the part of both early and late starters of the same age, findings which support Scarcella and Higa's (1982) claim that adolescent learners are more efficient interviewees than younger learners due to their more active role in communicative tasks (see Grañena, this volume). In the present study, comparison of the results of the two groups of 12-year-old participants shows that most of them reach Stage 4, where initial emergence of verbs occurs. The implication of this fact is significant. What it suggests is that these age-level participants all surpass the stage of simply designating characters and objects by means of bare nouns to make a conscious effort to actually tell a story.

Moreover, a methodological implication arises from the results. The oral texts collected cannot be said to constitute true narratives until Stage 7 with the incipient emergence of discourse features. The initial development focuses on the acquisition of morphosyntactic features and on developing vocabulary. Use of grammatical and lexical means to structure narrative discourse does not emerge until phrases are organised into well-formed clauses with incipient subordination and post-modification. These factors should be given due consideration in the design of elicitation instruments involving the production of a narrative, with or without pictorial support. Our results suggest that participants who have not yet attained a specific level of L2 development cannot be expected to produce a story, even if the story is very simple and presented in picture form. The pictures used for narrative elicitation in the present study lack complexity, do not represent a lengthy story or contain a large number of protagonists or unequivocal situations. However, despite the instruction to narrate a story, narratives assigned to initial stages are actually reformulated picture-description tasks as evidenced, for example, by the high number of progressive forms. These narratives are describing what is happening in the pictures rather than telling what happens or happened in the story.

Thus, our findings suggest that a substitute narrative genre, one with fewer cognitive demands, might be advisable in initial stages of foreign language learning, delimited perhaps by the moment just prior to usage of subordination. For example, in L1 child narrative development Hudson and Shapiro (1991) cite scripts or a general description of typical occurrences in a given situation as tasks requiring more basic cognitive, linguistic and communicative abilities. In fact, the first narrative genre that pre-school children master in L1 is a script in answer to questions such as *What happens when you go to the doctor?* The script's structure follows the chronological order of the sequence of events in the real world, and scripts are also linguistically simple in that the timeless present and *you* as a default pronoun are used. It remains clear that only further research could prove whether or not at early developmental stages in L2 a different type of oral narrative task would yield a different mastery of morphosyntactic and discourse features on the part of the storyteller.

Finally, there is a clear pedagogical application with respect to the results. Both child and adult participants show significant narrative improvement after periods of instruction of approximately 200 instructional hours, thereby indicating that the measurement instrument devised is sensitive to instructed language development. The consistent consensus between two evaluators in assigning a stage to each narrative demonstrates the accuracy of the stages posited for describing route of acquisition and suggests their usefulness as an evaluation instrument. To this effect, a formal scale based on the stages might be designed to measure levels of narrative oral proficiency.

Conclusion

The central purpose of this study was to determine whether child and adult foreign language learners follow the same route of acquisition in the development of their narrative abilities. The results have confirmed that it is feasible to outline the order in which learners of different ages proceed in the use of a variety of linguistic elements in discourse. A contribution of this study is the finding that certain levels of syntactic development correlate directly with the emergence of specific discourse features. The latter finding lays the foundation for future research about how the development of syntax and discourse interact.

A second objective of the investigation was to establish whether or not a difference exists in the level of attainment after the same instructional hours by three groups of learners with varying initial exposure ages. The results confirm the initial faster rate of acquisition of adults and older school-aged students, but also confirm that after a longer time span, the children that started learning English at an earlier age begin to catch up with those that started at a later age. Thus, the results of this study are in line with results in natural language acquisition and support the claim that young children do most of their L2 learning implicitly needing, therefore, more exposure than adults. The implication for foreign language policy planning is that advancing the age of first exposure to the foreign language does not by itself guarantee a higher level of attainment at the end of compulsory schooling. In order to achieve a higher level in foreign language attainment, it would be necessary both to advance the age of first exposure and to increase the amount of exposure.

Acknowledgements

This study was supported by grants PB94-0944, PB97-0901 and BFF2001-3384 of the Spanish Ministry of Education. I would like to thank Dr Corinne Helland for her valuable contribution to this chapter.

Notes

1. We have classified the participants as bilinguals learning a foreign language, although alternatively we might consider English the L3 (Cenoz, 2000; Muñoz, 2000).
2. We assume Quirk *et al.* (1985) description of basic English syntactic structures including S (subject) V (verb), SVO (direct object), SVO (indirect object), SVC (complement of the subject), SVOC (complement of the object, SVA (adverbial), SVOA.
3. The two students that are shown in the table to have reached Stage 6 belong to group B.
4. The finding is consistent with Lardière (1998) who shows that syntactic and morphological development are not intimately linked in the L2 process as they are in the L1 process.
5. The order found varies slightly from the accuracy order proposed in the morpheme studies outlined in the introduction, most probably due to the difference in methodology.

References

Alvarez, E. (2003) The role of the interviewer in the oral narratives of EFL students of different ages and proficiency level. In I. Palacios, M.J. López, P. Fra and E. Seoane (eds) *Fifty Years of English Studies in Spain (1952–2002). A Commemorative Volume* (pp. 341–348). Santiago de Compostela: Universidade de Santiago de Compostela Publicacións.

Alvarez, E. and Muñoz, C. (2003) Las habilidades narrativas en inglés (LE) y su evolución con la edad. In G. Luque, A. Bueno and G. Tejada (eds) *Languages in a Global World* (pp. 3–10). Jaén: Universidad de Jaén.

Berman, R.A. and Slobin, D.I. (1994) *Relating Events in Narrative: A Crosslinguistic Developmental Study.* Hillsdale, NJ: Lawrence Erlbaum Associates.

Bialystok, E. (1997) The structure of age: In search of barriers to second language acquisition. *Second Language Research* 13, 116–137.

Bley-Vroman, R. (1988) The fundamental character of foreign language learning. In W. Rutherford and M. Sharwood-Smith (eds) *Grammar and Second Language Teaching. A Book of Readings* (pp. 19–30). Rowley, MA: Newbury House.

Bongaerts, T., Van Summeren, Ch., Planken, B. and Schils, E. (1997) Age and the ultimate attainment in the pronunciation of a foreign language. *Studies in Second Language Acquisition* 19, 447–465.

Burstall, C. (1975) Primary French in the balance. *Foreign Language Annals* 10, 245–252.

Cenoz, J. (1997) L'acquisition de la troisième langue: Bilinguisme et plurilinguisme au pays basque. In C. Muñoz, L. Nussbaum and M. Pujol (eds) *Acquisition et Interaction en Langue Étrangère. Appropiation de Langues en Contact. Aile* 10, 159–175.

Cenoz, J. (2000) Research on multilingual acquisition. In J. Cenoz. and U. Jessner (eds) *English in Europe. The Acquisition of a Third Language* (pp. 159–175). Clevedon: Multilingual Matters.

Cook, V. (1993) *Linguistics and Second Language Acquisition*. New York: St Martins Press.

DeKeyser, R. (2000) The robustness of critical period effects in second language acquisition. *Studies in Second Language Acquisition* 22, 499–533.

DeKeyser, R. and Larson-Hall, J. (2005) What does the critical period really mean? In J. Kroll and A. de Groot (eds) *Handbook of Bilingualism: Psycholinguistic Approaches* (pp. 88–108). Oxford: Oxford University Press.

Dietrich, R., Klein, W. and Noyau, C. (1995) *The Acquisition of Temporality in a Second Language*. Amsterdam: Benjamins.

Dulay, H. and Burt, M. (1973) Should we teach children syntax? *Language Learning* 23, 245–248.

Dulay, H. and Burt, M. (1974) You cant learn without goofing. In J. Richards (ed.) *Error Analysis* (pp. 95–123). London: Longman.

Ekstrand, L. (1978) English without a book revisited: The effect of age on second language acquisition in a formal setting. *Didakometry*, 60. Department of Educational and Psychological Research, School of Education, Malmö. Reprinted in S. Krashen, M. Long and R. Scarcella (eds) (1982) *Child-adult Differences in Second Language Acquisition* (pp. 136–158). Rowley, MA: Newbury House.

Ellis, R. (1984) *Classroom Second Language Development*. Oxford: Pergamon.

Ellis, R. (1994) *The Study of Second Language Acquisition*. Oxford: Oxford University Press.

Felix, S. and Hahn A. (1985) Natural processes in classroom second language learning. *Applied Linguistics* 6, 223–238.

Goldschneider, J. and DeKeyser, R. (2001) Explaining the natural order of L2 morpheme acquisition in English: A meta-analysis of multiple determinants. *Language Learning* 51, 1–50.

Harley, B. and Hart, D. (1997) Language aptitude and second language proficiency in classroom learners of different starting ages. *Studies in Second Language Acquisition* 19, 379–400.

Hickmann, M. (2003) *Children's Discourse: Person, Space and Time across Languages*. Cambridge: Cambridge University Press.

Hopper, P. (1979) Aspect and foregrounding in discourse. In T. Givón (ed.) *Syntax and Semantics: Discourse and Syntax* 12 (pp. 213–241). New York: Academic Press Inc.

Hudson, J. and Shapiro, L. (1991) From knowing to telling: The development of childrens' scripts, stories, and personal narratives. In A. McCabe and C. Peterson (eds) *Developing Narrative Structure* (pp. 89–136). Hillsdale, NJ: Lawrence Erlbaum Associates.

Hyltenstam, K. and Abrahamsson, N. (2000) Who can become native-like in a second language? All, some or none? On the maturational constraints controversy in second language acquisition. *Studia Lingüística* 54 (2), 150–166.

Ioup, G., Boustagui, E., Tigi, M. and Moselle, M. (1994) Reexamining the critical period hypothesis: A case study of successful adult SLA in a naturalistic environment. *Studies in Second Language Acquisition* 16, 73–98.

Klein, W., Dietrich, R. and Noyau, C. (1993) The acquisition of temporality. In C. Perdue (ed.) *Adult Language Acquisition: Crosslinguistic Perspectives. Vol. II. The Results* (pp. 73–118). Cambridge: Cambridge University Press.

Krashen, S. (1977) Some issues relating to the Monitor Model. In H. Brown, C. Yorio and R. Crymes (eds) *On TESOL '77* (pp. 144–158). Washington, DC: TESOL.

Labov, W. (1972) The transformation of experience in narrative syntax. In *Language in the Inner City. Studies in the Black English Vernacular* (pp. 354–398). Philadelphia: University of Pennsylvania Press.

Lardière, D. (1998) Case and tense in the fossilized steady state. *Second Language Research* 14 (1), 1–26.

Larsen-Freeman, D. (1975) The acquisition of grammatical morphemes by adult ESL students. *TESOL Quarterly* 9, 409–419.

Lenneberg, E. (1967) *Biological Foundations of Language*. New York: Wiley and Sons.

Masgoret, A.M. and Gardner, R.C. (2003) Attitudes, motivation and second language learning: A meta-analysis of studies conducted by Gardner and associates. *Language Learning* 53 (1), 167–210.

Muñoz, C. (2000) Bilingualism and trilingualism in school students in Catalonia. In J. Cenoz and U. Jessner (eds) *English in Europe. The Acquisition of a Third Language* (pp. 157–178). Clevedon: Multilingual Matters.

Muñoz, C. (2003) Variation in oral skills development and age of onset. In M.P. García Mayo and M.L. García Lecumberri (eds) *Age and the Acquisition of English as a Foreign Language: Theoretical Issues and Fieldwork* (pp. 161–181). Clevedon: Multilingual Matters.

Pérez-Vidal, C., Torras, M.R. and Celaya, M.L. (2000) Age and EFL written performance by Catalan/Spanish bilinguals. *Spanish Applied Linguistics* 4, 267–290.

Quirk, R., Greenbaum, S., Leech, G. and Svartvik, J. (1985) *A Comprehensive Grammar of the English Language*. Harlow: Longman.

Scarcella, R. and Higa, C. (1982) Input and age differences in second language acquisition. In S. Krashen, R. Scarcella and M. Long (eds) *Child-adult Differences in Second Language Acquisition* (pp. 175–201). Rowley, MA: Newbury House.

Singleton, D. (1989) *Language Acquisition: The Age Factor*. Clevedon: Multilingual Matters.

Skehan, P. and Foster, P. (1999) The influence of task structure and processing conditions on narrative retellings. *Language Learning* 49, 93–120.

Snow, C. (1983) Age differences in second language acquisition: Research findings and folk psychology. In K. Bailey, H. Long and S. Peck (eds) *Second Language Acquisition Studies* (pp. 141–150). Rowley, MA: Newbury House.

Snow C. and Hoefnagel-Höhle, M. (1978) The critical age for language acquisition: evidence from second language learning. *Child Development* 49, 1114–1128.

Thompson, I. (1991) Foreign accents revisited: The English pronunciation of Russian immigrants. *Language Learning* 41, 177–204.

Thompson, S.A. (1987) Subordination and narrative event structure. In R.S. Tomlin (ed.) *Coherence and Grounding in Discourse. Typological Studies in Language* (Vol. 11, pp. 435–454). Amsterdam: John Benjamins Publishing Co.

Chapter 7

Age and IL Development in Writing

M. ROSA TORRAS, TERESA NAVÉS, M. LUZ CELAYA AND
CARMEN PÉREZ-VIDAL

Overview of Research into Writing

It is widely acknowledged that writing is a relevant activity from a very early age in the foreign language classroom. However, the study of second language acquisition through the analysis of written production has often been restricted to the analysis of accuracy. The present study offers a wider perspective, since it focuses on interlanguage (IL) development through the analysis of writing in instructed English as a foreign language (EFL) learning. It seeks to contribute to the field where "few large-scale projects have accounted comprehensively for grammatical or rhetorical development in second-language writing" (Cumming, 2001: 9).

According to Archibald and Jeffery (2000), current research into writing is in four areas – teaching, context, process and product. Before the 1970s, the teaching of writing was mainly approached as the practice of structures and vocabulary (see Nystrand *et al.*, 1993). Nowadays, although also associated with proficiency, the area has widened its scope to include issues such as genre, strategies and rhetorical aspects (Sengupta, 2000; Shaw & Liu, 1998, among others). Research on the social contexts of second language writing appears mainly in the form of case studies of learners studying at universities and colleges. This approach views writing as "a process of individual development in particular social contexts" (Cumming, 2001: 7). Recent studies have focused on the process of writing (see Chenoweth & Hayes, 2001; Leki, 2002; Manchón, 2001; Manchón *et al.*, 2000a; Manchón *et al.*, 2000b; Roca de Larios, 1999; Sasaki, 2000; Victori, 1997), an area where the use of the first language (L1) during the composing process has been one of the main issues in research (Manchón, 2001; Qi, 1998; Woodall, 2002). Studies that focus on the product have approached it from different perspectives and using various means of analysis (see Celaya & Tragant, 1997; Connor & Mbaye, 2002; Ishiwaka, 1995; Martín-Uriz *et al.*, 2000; Sasaki & Hirose, 1996). Research with beginner-level learners involving written production, especially instructed learners, is still needed (however, see Harley & King, 1989; Leki, 1996; Lightbown & Spada, 1997; Reichelt, 1999). Similarly, Matsuda and De Pew (2002) have claimed that although early second language (L2) writing research is now increasing rapidly, it has traditionally been under-represented due, among other reasons, to the ease of finding older participants.

Measuring development in writing

The idea that classroom foreign language attainment should not be compared with native-like competence has often been stressed, since exposure and the quality of input differ substantially between natural and formal classroom contexts (see Cook, 1997). In the same vein, important differences come to light if writing in L1 and in L2 are compared (see Foster-Cohen, 1999 for writing components in L1; Ferreiro & Pontecorvo, 2002 for word segmentation in L1 early written narratives). As a consequence, suggested by Torras *et al.* (1998), the indicators of students' achievement, i.e. the measurements used for the analysis of written production in a foreign language, should differ from those used to analyse native speakers' achievement. Polio (1997) argues that there seems to be a need to analyse written texts in the second language in a systematic, rigorous way in order to be able to provide valid indicators of students' achievement (see Connor-Linton, 1995; Hamp-Lyons, 1995).

The analysis of IL development through learners' written products entails taking decisions on how to describe the characteristics of the learner's interlanguage and how to measure linguistic change over time. Moreover, as stated by Kroll (1998), English as a second language (ESL) writing may be problematic as a whole when there are different levels of proficiency in different aspects of the product. Studies that use measures to analyse written products focus, on the one hand, on the training of raters (Cumming *et al.*, 2002; Sweedler-Brown, 1992) and the raters' performance (Lumley, 2002) and, on the other hand, on the analysis of the type of measures, with the main focus being on the comparison between holistic and analytic measures. From the premise that writing assessment is a procedure that takes place within a specific context, which can vary in multiple ways, Kroll (1998) aims to analyse both issues with her study of several variables in order to gauge both the written product and the scoring procedure.

Several studies have proved that holistic ratings of written products are not a reliable indicator of language development or change. Cohen (1994) used both types of measures and concluded that there are problems with holistic scoring. Bacha (2001) analyses issues for and against holistic and analytic scoring instruments. The study shows that in spite of the high inter- and intra-reliability coefficients, holistic scoring revealed little about the performance of the students in the different components of the writing skill (content, organisation, vocabulary, language and mechanics). When the analytic scores were compared, there were significantly high differences between the different writing components. Like Kroll (1998) (see above), the author concludes that holistic rating is not as informative as an analytic rating, because students may have different proficiency levels in the various writing components.

Previous findings in the BAF Project (see Chapter 1 for a presentation of the larger reseach project) also reveal that components of writing do not develop in tandem (see Navés *et al.*, 2003; Torras & Celaya, 2001). This may be the reason why the search for a single developmental index has not proved successful. Researchers have proposed a wide variety of measures that Wolfe-Quintero *et al.* (1998) classify in four major categories according to different aspects of development – fluency, lexical complexity, syntactic complexity, and accuracy. Among other objectives, Ishikawa (1995) aimed to find the best way to quantify change in low-proficiency EFL narrative writing. Since holistic ratings would not discriminate at such low proficiency levels, Ishikawa used 24 measures and concluded that "total number of words in error-free clauses" and "error-free clauses per composition" were the best measures for the objective of the study. In another context, at university level, Crerand and Lavin (1993) use six variables for quantitative analysis – the overall quality of the production, the number of *t*-units, the mean length of the *t*-unit, the number of error-free *t*-units, the mean length of error-free *t*-units, and, finally, the number of words. Also at university level, Arnaud (1992) analyses vocabulary and grammar using the following measures of vocabulary – lexical variation, lexical richness and lexical errors, and the following measures of grammar – *t*-unit length, error-free *t*-unit and error percentage. Laufer and Nation (1995) use a vocabulary measure, the LFP (Lexical Frequency Profile), to discriminate between two pieces of writing by the same learners and between different proficiency levels. The authors argue that in second language acquisition (SLA), this measure would show how vocabulary size is reflected in use. Ortega (2003) revises several syntactic complexity measures and their relationship to L2 proficiency. Her conclusion is that a year of college-level instruction is needed for substantial changes to be observed.

Age and written development

The issue of age and IL development, especially as measured through writing, in instructed learners as opposed to naturalistic learners, has not yet received enough attention (see, however, Archibald, 1994). Several relevant studies have recently been carried out in both the Basque Country and in Catalonia, in Spain. Among these, Lasagabaster and Doiz (2003) use a number of measures of fluency, complexity and accuracy, following on from Wolfe-Quintero *et al.* (1998) and Celaya *et al.* (1998) from the BAF Project as well as a holistic analysis, to analyse the production of school learners who had started their English learning at different ages. The older learners outperform the younger ones in all measures but the number of sentences.

In the BAF Project, the effect of age on the development of written competence in English as a foreign language has been investigated in the areas of Fluency, Lexical and Grammatical Complexity and Accuracy as components of this competence. The following research issues have thus been addressed:

(1) The effect of age of onset on rate in learners' written production of English in the short and mid-terms (200 and 416 hours).
(2) The comparison of rate of acquisition between learners with different instructional time but of the same age.
(3) A longitudinal analysis of the development of the four areas of written competence.
(4) The effect of age of onset on rate in the long run (726 hours).

In order to address these four research issues, four studies were undertaken that approached the data from different perspectives. The first study is a cross-sectional study of the differences and contrasts between the subjects in the BAF Project sample having a different onset time of instruction but the same number of hours in EFL, at two data collection times (T1 = 200 hours, T2 = 416 hours). This first study thus measures the short- and mid-term effects of an early start. It addresses the first issue stated above, i.e. whether learners starting their EFL instruction at earlier ages, namely the early starters (ES) of Group A, progress faster and achieve higher results than the Group B or late starters (LS). The study provides an intergroup analysis, i.e. a comparison of Groups A1 and A2, and Groups B1 and B2, or T1 and T2, respectively. The results show that age of onset has a clear influence on the scores obtained in the written compositions (Celaya *et al.*, 2001b; Pérez-Vidal *et al.*, 2000). At T1, the comparison of the variables obtained with a *t*-test (with a 0.95 confidence level) is significantly favourable to Group B1 (or LS, who are 12.9) in all measures in the areas of Fluency, Accuracy and Complexity, except for Lexical Density, Types of Adverbs and Types of Auxiliary and Modal Verbs, for which the effect of age was not significant. At T2, Types of Adverbs and Types of Auxiliary and Modal Verbs already yielded significant differences in favour of Group B2, who are now 14.9. It can be concluded that with the same number of hours of instruction, Group B (or LS) learn faster and achieve higher levels of attainment at T1 and T2. These results coincide with those of other studies (Cenoz, 2002; Doiz & Lasagabaster, 2001). It was hypothesised that differences in maturity or differences in teaching methodologies might account for these results. It remains to be seen whether Group A will catch up with Group B later on at T3 (= 726 hours), which is in fact what the fourth study reported below aims to find out.

The second study is a cross-sectional study of the two groups that share the same age (12.9), but have a different instructional time – Group B1 have had 200 hours at T1, and Group A2 have had 416 hours at T2. Results show that even with fewer hours of instruction, when measured at the same age, Group B1 still performs better than Group A2 in some variables, i.e. those in the area of Grammatical Complexity, and Modality, while Group A2 performs significantly better in those related to the acquisition of vocabulary (Lexical Complexity): Lexical Density, Types of Nouns,

Types of Adjectives, Types of Primary Verbs, Types of Lexical Verbs. As a consequence, Group A2 obtains markedly better results in the area of Fluency (Celaya *et al.*, 2001b; Pérez-Vidal *et al.*, 2000). It can thus be concluded that at the beginning stages of language acquisition, a higher number of hours of instruction together with an earlier age of onset may lead to an increase in Lexical Complexity and in Fluency, but not in Grammatical Complexity or Accuracy. It was hypothesised that the fact that Group B1 had their 200 hours of instruction concentrated over a shorter time span – one year, in contrast to the two years of Group A, with consequent higher intensity of the pattern of exposure – might be a key variable in explaining the results.

The third study (Torras & Celaya, 2001) is the analysis of the longitudinal data in the BAF Project, both developmentally at T1 and T2 (intra-group analysis) and then contrastively (inter-group analysis). Results for the intra-group analysis show that each area presents a statistically significant improvement between T1 and T2 for both Group A (the ES) and Group B (the LS), but with different patterns of development, i.e. they each proceed at a different rate in the following fashion. For both Group A and Group B, the mean single score calculated for Lexical Complexity is higher than that for Grammatical Complexity at both T1 and T2, which is something which may have influenced a faster development in the area of Fluency. By contrast, Grammatical Complexity and Accuracy behave differently for Group A than for Group B, in both rate and attainment. For Group B, they develop quite closely up to T1, only to diverge towards T2 with Complexity being higher than Accuracy. As for Group A, they develop separately from T1 onwards, with Complexity being higher than Accuracy at T1 but lower at T2. As for the inter-group comparisons, *t*-test results show that Group B significantly outperforms Group A at T1 in the four components of written competence, while differences in Accuracy are no longer statistically significant at T2. It can thus be concluded that the acquisition of written competence does not proceed linearly but shows different patterns of development within each of its four domains.

Finally, the fourth study is a cross-sectional study of the effect of age of onset in the long run, applying 39 indicators of development in order to analyse whether Group A (or the ES) would have caught up with Group B (the LS) at T3 (= 726 hours). It addresses the fourth of the issues stated above, i.e. the long term effects of an early start. The results of a *t*-test for the comparison of samples reveal that at T3, Group B still significantly outperforms Group A as far as Accuracy and Grammatical Complexity are concerned, while Group A seems to have caught up with Group B in the area of Fluency (Navés *et al.*, 2003). It can be concluded that as Group B starts developing in the area of Complexity and Fluency, Accuracy stabilises.

On the basis of the findings above, the study reported in this chapter seeks to further analyse the effect of differences in number of hours of instruction and age of onset on the written performance by learners of English, by focusing on the developmental patterns within each of the four domains of written competence. The following research questions are investigated:

(1) Do the age of onset and instructional time interact for each of the four writing areas (Fluency, Lexical Complexity, Grammatical Complexity and Accuracy)?
(2) Does the interlanguage of learners with different ages of onset follow the same pattern of development over time?

The Study

Participants

The participants in the study presented below consist of a sample of 495 EFL learners from the BAF Project. Table 7.1 presents how the sample was distributed in six groups according to age of onset (AO) and hours of instruction. The ES (Group A), or those who had begun at the age of eight (AO = 8), included three groups: the 10;9-year-old group who had had 200 hours of instruction when data were collected at T1; the 12;9-year-old group who had had 416 hours when data were collected at T2; and the 16;9-year-old group who had had 726 hours of instruction when data were collected at T3. The LS (Group B), or those who had begun at the age of 11 (AO = 11), also included three groups: the 12;9-years-old group with 200 hours of instruction when data were collected at T1; the 14;9-year-old group with 416 hours of instruction at T2, and, the 17-year-old group with 726 hours of instruction when data were collected at T3.

The hours of instruction that the subjects received are spread over unequal stretches of time for Group A and B, as shown in Table 7.2.

At T1, Group A received the 200 hours of instruction over three school years, while Group B received the same amount over two school years. At T2 both Group A and B received the additional 216 hours of instruction spread over two school years. At T3, the remaining 310 hours of instruction were distributed over four years in the case of Group A and three in the case of Group B. In other words, Group A received the 726 hours of instruction in nine academic years, while Group B received the same hours of instruction in seven school years.

Table 7.1 Participants, hours of instruction and data collection times

N = 495	Time 1 (200 hours)	Time 2 (416 hours)	Time 3 (726 hours)
GROUP A (AO = 8)	Age 10;9 N = 110	Age 12;9 N = 105	Age 16;9 N = 55
GROUP B (AO = 11)	Age 12;9 N = 108	Age 14;9 N = 67	Age 17;9 N = 50

Table 7.2 Distribution of hours of instruction

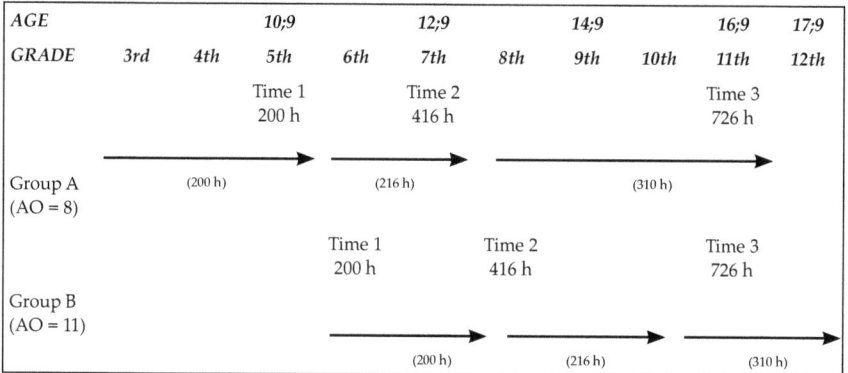

All the learners attended state-funded schools and their instruction in English took place exclusively during school hours, with no extra classes after school. The number of hours of instruction thus remained constant. The subjects had very little contact with the foreign language outside schools, with the exception of the Internet content, television and music that they might have been exposed to.

Procedure

As in the previous studies, the data were collected by an integrative test of written ability consisting of a composition task on a given topic. The task was administered in the classrooms by an external researcher in an exam-like situation, although the subjects were told it was not going to be assessed as an exam. All participants were given 15 minutes to write on the topic 'Introduce yourself' (time and topic held constant following Wolfe-Quintero *et al.* (1998)).

Analysis

Previous studies on writing within the BAF Project as summarised in the literature review informed the selection of analytical measures to describe and compare learners. Table 7.3 shows the 17 measures used to analyse the written tasks in this study. These measures were classified into four areas according to Wolfe-Quintero *et al.* (1998) and the suggestions by Ortega (2003) and Navés *et al.* (2003).

As in previous studies on writing in the BAF Project, we chose extensively used measures such as essay length, sentence and clause length, and subordinated clauses per sentence. Other extensively used measures, e.g. the coordination index and other ratios were disregarded because they could not be calculated for groups with a very low proficiency level. Some less-extensively used measures, such as those

Table 7.3 Measures for the analysis of EFL writing

Fluency	Lexical Complexity	Grammatical Complexity	Accuracy
1. W (total number of words)	6. NT (number of noun types)	10. Sub C (number of subordinate clauses)	15. EFS (number of error-free sentences)
2. S (number of sentences)	7. Adj. T (number of adjective types)	11. Coor C (number of coordinate clauses)	16. % EFS (percentage of error-free sentences)
3. C (number of clauses)	8. VT (number of verb types)	12. C/S (clauses per sentence)	17. B (number of borrowings)
4. W/S (words per sentence)	9. Adv. T (number of adverb types)	13. Sub/S (subordinate clauses per sentence)	
5. W/C (words per clause)		14. Coor/S (coordinate clauses per sentence)	

involving coordination and types of lexical words, were chosen because in our previous research studies they were seen to best reflect the development of interlanguage, especially at low levels and because they enable comparisons to be made between adjacent levels of proficiency.

The compositions were rated by the researchers according to previously established criteria that are described in detail in Celaya *et al.* (2001a). The analysis of the data was carried out by means of the Statistical Package for the Social Sciences (SPSS) 11.5, applying a series of four two-way between-group multivariate analysis of variance (MANOVAs), to investigate the impact of age of onset and instruction on the four areas of written competence (Fluency, Lexical Complexity, Grammatical Complexity and Accuracy). Preliminary assumption testing was carried out to check the normality and homogeneity of variance for the four areas, with no serious violations noted in any of them.

In each of the four two-way MANOVAs, the independent variables are age of onset and instructional time and the dependent variables are the measures of each writing area. This test will allow us to see whether each of the main factors, AO and instructional time, as well as the interaction between them, are statistically significant. If the results show that these two factors interact, a further analysis will be carried out to investigate how this interaction works, i.e. how the time of instruction received at different ages affects the development of the interlanguage of the two groups of learners.

Results and Discussion

Effect of age of onset and instructional time on Fluency, Lexical Complexity, Grammatical Complexity and Accuracy

The results of the series of two-way MANOVAs for the main factor – the AO – are shown in Table 7.4.

As the results show, there is a statistically significant main effect of the AO on each area (see F and p global values). When the results for the dependent variables are considered separately for each area (see the individual values for F and p), all of the measures with the exception of *number of sentences* (S) and *number of borrowings* (B) are statistically significant. Inspections of the mean scores of those variables that are statistically significant shows that learners in Group B, who started later, outperform the younger group (Group A) in the four areas. Group B learners write longer compositions, longer clauses and sentences and use more clauses, display a greater variety of content words and use more complex structures involving coordination and subordination, and also make fewer errors. In other words, Group B learners are more fluent, more accurate and write more lexically and syntactically complex compositions.

The results of the four two-way MANOVAs for the other main factor, instructional time, are shown in Table 7.5.

The results show that instructional time also has a major effect on the four areas (see the global values for F and p). In each area, when the results of the dependent variables are considered separately (see the individual values for F and p), all the dependent variables are statistically significant except for *number of borrowings* (B). An inspection of the mean scores reveals that learners who have received more hours of instruction obtain higher mean scores in the variables included in the areas of Fluency (the exception being *number of sentences*), Lexical Complexity and Grammatical Complexity i.e. learners at T3 (726 h) obtain higher mean scores than learners at T2 (416 h) who, in turn, outperform learners at T1 (200 h). Accuracy does not show the same tendency, since contrary to what could be expected learners at T3 do not write more accurately than learners who have received fewer hours of instruction. In this case, the group with 416 hours obtains higher means than the other groups in *number of error-free sentences* and *percentage of error-free sentences*. It is worth mentioning that these means show the effect of instructional time per se, irrespectively of the age of the learners; in consequence, these results have only to be considered as a necessary step to study the interaction between the two factors.

Interaction between the age of onset and instructional time on Fluency, Lexical Complexity, Grammatical Complexity and Accuracy

The results of the series of two-way MANOVAS for the interaction between the two main factors, AO and instructional time, are shown in Table 7.6.

Table 7.4 Impact of age of onset on Fluency, Lexical Complexity, Grammatical Complexity and Accuracy

	df	Error df	F	p	Eta squared	Group A M	Group A SD	Group B M	Group B SD
Fluency	5	485	18.615	0.000*	0.161	45.34	35.7	60.8	43.2
W	1	489	40.926	0.000*	0.077	6.25	3.73	6.89	3.68
S	1	489	4.398	0.036n.s.	0.009	8.12	5.64	10.3	6.48
C	1	489	27.965	0.000*	0.054	6.54	3.61	8.29	4.39
W/S	1	489	78.475	0.000*	0.138	5.23	1.73	5.54	1.34
W/C	1	489	6.900	0.000*	0.014				
Lex. Compl.	4	486	14.232	0.000*	0.105				
NT	1	489	12.707	0.000*	0.025	7.44	5.41	9.06	5.85
Adj T	1	489	20.063	0.000*	0.039	2.15	2.01	2.90	2.77
VT	1	489	46.881	0.009*	0.087	2.71	3.30	4.21	3.75
Adv. T	1	489	29.052	0.000*	0.056	0.85	1.83	1.48	2.25
Gra. Compl.	5	485	22.343	0.000*	0.187				
Sub C	1	489	79.337	0.000*	0.014	0.51	1.35	1.39	2.28
Coor C	1	489	17.737	0.000*	0.035	1.40	2.01	2.08	2.39
C/S	1	489	68.291	0.000*	0.123	1.25	0.40	1.46	0.54
Sub/S	1	489	103.613	0.000*	0.175	0.068	0.18	0.19	0.32
Coor/S	1	489	20.032	0.000*	0.039	0.19	0.28	0.28	0.32
Accuracy	2	487	5.366	0.001*	0.032				
EFS	1	489	12.389	0.000*	0.025	2.04	2.16	2.60	2.47
% EFS	1	489	9.552	0.002*	0.019	30.3	25.9	35.4	25.1
B	1	489	4.852	0.492n.s.	0.010	0.79	1.54	0.60	1.13

Notes: *Significant at alpha level $p < 0.01$; n.s. = not significant at alpha level $p < 0.01$; if the differences between Group A and Group B reach significance the higher mean score is highlighted.

Table 7.5 Effect of instructional time on Fluency, Lexical Complexity, Grammatical Complexity and Accuracy

	df	Error df	F	p	Eta squared	T1 (200 h) M	T1 (200 h) SD	T2 (416 h) M	T2 (416 h) SD	T3 (726 h) M	T3 (726 h) SD
Fluency	10	970	83.253	0.000*	0.462	25.24	18.90	62.79	36.53	91.80	37.39
W	2	489	227.900	0.000	0.482	4.83	3.12	8.30	3.97	7.20	2.79
S	2	489	59.072	0.000	0.195	5.38	3.64	10.90	5.87	13.94	6.01
C	2	489	137.958	0.000	0.361	4.72	1.81	7.22	2.71	12.95	3.72
W/S	2	489	420.904	0.000	0.633	4.52	1.46	5.61	1.21	6.73	1.20
W/C	2	489	109.634	0.000	0.310						
Lex. Compl.	8	972	77.522	0.000	0.390						
NT	2	489	101.887	0.000	0.294	4.98	3.85	10.12	5.8	11.6	5.17
Adj T	2	489	64.320	0.000	0.208	1.33	1.67	3.22	2.54	3.70	2.49
VT	2	489	247.319	0.009	0.503	1.20	1.52	3.59	3.16	7.60	3.44
Adv. T	2	489	213.160	0.000	0.466	0.08	0.29	0.91	1.49	3.68	2.70
Gra. Compl.	10	970	64.618	0.000	0.400						
Sub C	2	489	242.752	0.000	0.498	0.02	0.18	0.57	1.32	3.30	2.50
Coor C	2	489	128.847	0.000	0.345	0.50	0.95	2.02	2.33	3.72	2.28
C/S	2	489	266.751	0.000	0.522	1.09	0.17	1.30	0.33	1.96	0.56
Sub/S	2	489	294.072	0.000	0.546	0.00	0.02	0.06	0.16	0.47	0.35
Coor/S	2	489	126.750	0.000	0.341	0.08	0.16	0.23	0.27	0.54	0.34
Accuracy	6	974	14.272	0.000	0.081						
EFS	2	489	42.111	0.000	0.147	1.39	1.79	3.31	2.75	2.50	1.75
% EFS	2	489	12.168	0.000	0.047	26.6	27.59	38.08	23.93	36.20	21.65
B	2	489	0.711	0.492n.s.	0.003	0.77	1.40	0.68	1.28	0.60	1.45

Notes: * Significant at alpha level $p < 0.01$; n.s. = not significant at alpha level $p < 0.01$; if the differences among the learners for each instructional time reach significance the highest mean score is highlighted

Table 7.6 Interaction between age of onset and instructional time

	df	Error df	F	p	Eta squared
Fluency	10	970	8.596	0.000*	0.081
W	2	489	17.995	0.000*	0.069
S	2	489	5.810	0.003*	0.023
C	2	489	9.471	0.000*	0.037
W/S	2	489	15.779	0.000*	0.061
W/C	2	489	6.272	0.002*	0.025
Lex. Compl.	8	972	8.303	0.000*	0.064
NT	2	489	15.304	0.000*	0.059
Adj. T	2	489	4.416	0.001*	0.018
VT	2	489	17.453	0.000*	0.067
Adv.T	2	489	10.035	0.000*	0.039
Gra Compl.	10	970		0.000*	0.103
Sub C	2	489	21.685	0.000*	0.081
Coor C	2	489	15.934	0.000*	0.061
C/S	2	489	12.820	0.000*	0.050
Sub/S	2	489	34.099	0.000*	0.122
Coor/S	2	489	5.131	0.006*	0.021
Accuracy	6	974	2.477	0.022 n.s.	

Notes: * Significant at alpha level $p < 0.01$; n.s. = not significant at alpha level $p < 0.01$.

There is a statistically significant interaction effect between the AO and instructional time in all areas except for Accuracy (see the global values for F and p). When the results for the dependent variables are considered separately for the three areas showing interaction (see the F and p individual values), all are statistically significant.

These results allow us to answer the first research question, which focused on investigating whether there is any interaction between these two factors. It can thus be concluded that there is an interaction between the AO and instructional time in the areas of Fluency, Lexical Complexity and Grammatical Complexity, but not in Accuracy.

In order to answer the second research question, which aimed at investigating how the interlanguage of learners with different ages of onset develops over time, and in the light of the findings reported above, a series of one-way MANOVAs will be conducted for each data collection time. We will first report on the comparison of Group A and Group B for each data collection time (200, 416 and 726 hours) and then we will discuss the development of the interlanguage of each group of learners over time.

Development of learners' interlanguage

Table 7.7 shows the results of the series of the nine one-way MANOVAs to compare Group A and B learners at each data collection time in the areas of Fluency, Lexical Complexity and Grammatical Complexity. For the sake of clarity, the F values will only be reported for each global domain but not for each of the dependent variables. p values will nevertheless be reported for all of them.

These results show that the differences between Group A and B in the areas of Fluency, Lexical Complexity and Grammatical Complexity are statistically significant (see the global values for F and p) at each data collection time except for Grammatical Complexity at T1. In other words, in overall terms, Group A and B learners do not behave alike as far as their writing performance after either 200, 416 or 726 hours of instruction is concerned. At T1, after 200 hours of instruction, Group B learners significantly outperform their younger peers (Group A) in the areas of Fluency and Lexical Complexity but not in Grammatical Complexity. After 200 hours of instruction, Group B learners (aged 12;9, AO = 11) write more fluently than Group A learners (aged 10;9, AO = 8) as measured by *total number of words* (W), *number of sentences* (S) and *clauses* (C), as well as the average length of the sentence (W/S). Group B learners also display greater content word variety when it comes to the use of *noun types* (NT) and *verb types* (VT). However, no differences are found in Grammatical Complexity measures, which as reported in previous BAF Project studies (Navés *et al.*, 2003; Torras & Celaya, 2001) is probably due to the fact that learners need to be older in order to start using complex grammatical structures.

At T2, after 416 hours of instruction, Group B learners (aged 14;9, AO = 11) significantly outperform their younger peers from Group A (aged 12;9 AO = 8) in the three areas studied. Not only are they more fluent in writing their compositions as measured by the essay length, use of clauses and sentences and the average sentence and clause length, but their compositions are more complex both lexically and syntactically. Group B learners' Lexical Complexity is higher than that of Group A learners, as shown by their use of not only *noun* and *verb types* (NT, VT) (as in T1) but also in their use of *adjective* and *adverb types* (Adj. T, Adv. T). Group B learners at T2 significantly outperform their younger peers as far as Grammatical Complexity is concerned. They use significantly more subordination and coordination.

At T3, after 726 hours of instruction, Group B learners (aged 17;9, AO = 11) no longer systematically outperform their younger peers in Group A (aged 16;9, AO = 8). The differences between the learners in the two groups may be lessening if one examines the individual p values of the dependent variables. Although the global p and F values may suggest that there are, in overall terms, differences between the two groups, an examination of

Table 7.7 Comparisons of results of Group A and Group B at T1 (200 h), T2 (416 h) and T3 (726 h)

	Time 1					Time 2					Time 3				
	Group A		Group B		p	Group A		Group B		p	Group A		Group B		p
	M	SD	M	SD		M	SD	M	SD		M	SD	M	SD	
Fluency	$F(5, 212) = 3258$				0.007 *	$F(5, 166) = 23319$				0.000 *	$F(5, 99) = 3470$				0.006*
W	20.56	16.31	30.02	20.20	0.000 *	47.60	26.70	86.60	37.32	0.000 *	90.58	33.44	93.14	41.62	0.728 n.s.
S	4.21	2.93	5.46	3.20	0.003 *	7.64	3.99	9.36	3.72	0.005 *	7.67	2.65	6.68	2.87	0.069 n.s.
C	4.57	3.35	6.20	3.75	0.001 *	8.90	4.81	14.04	6.03	0.000 *	13.73	5.70	14.18	6.39	0.702 n.s.
W/S	4.44	1.87	5.01	1.71	0.021 *	5.93	1.78	9.26	2.68	0.000 *	11.92	3.56	14.08	3.60	0.0023 *
W/C	4.43	1.81	4.62	0.97	0.326 n.s	5.25	1.13	6.17	1.11	0.000 *	6.80	1.43	6.66	0.89	0.534 n.s.
Lexical Compl.	$F(4, 213) = 5027$				0.001 *	$F(4, 167) = 19.971$				0.000 *	$F(4, 100) = 3.729$				0.007*
NT	4.14	3.49	5.84	4.02	0.001 *	8.29	4.77	13.00	6.12	0.000 *	12.44	5.33	10.74	4.89	0.093 n.s.
Adj.T	1.12	1.35	1.56	1.92	0.052 n.s.	2.56	1.99	4.25	2.95	0.000 *	3.42	2.18	4.00	2.78	0.234 n.s.
VT	0.84	1.31	1.57	1.63	0.000 *	2.25	2.27	5.70	3.23	0.000 *	7.33	3.41	7.90	3.49	0.397 n.s.
Adv. T	0.09	0.29	0.07	0.30	0.671 n.s.	0.42	1.19	1.70	1.58	0.000 *	3.20	2.59	4.20	2.76	0.058 n.s.
Gram.Compl.	$F(5, 212) = 1.506$				0.189.n.s.	$F(5, 166) = 18.608$				0.000*	$F(5, 99) = 6,966$				0.000*
Sub C	0.00	0.00	0.05	0.25	0.055 n.s.	0.03	0.17	1.42	1.83	0.000 *	2.44	2.09	4.24	2.61	0.000 *
Coor C	0.35	0.78	0.65	1.08	0.019 n.s.	1.25	1.59	3.24	2.76	0.000 *	3.82	2.40	3.62	2.16	0.658 n.s.
C/S	1.06	0.14	1.12	0.20	0.019 n.s.	1.16	0.22	1.51	0.37	0.000 *	1.80	0.51	2.15	0.57	0.002 *
Sub/S	0.00	0.00	0.01	0.04	0.058 n.s.	0.01	0.10	0.16	0.20	0.000 *	0.31	0.26	0.65	0.36	0.000 *
Coor/S	0.06	0.13	0.11	0.18	0.026 n.s.	0.16	0.22	0.36	0.28	0.000 *	0.51	0.33	0.57	0.36	0.389 n.s.

Notes: * Significant at alpha level $p < 0.01$; n.s. = not significant at alpha level $p < 0.01$; if the differences between Group A and B for each instructional time reach significance the higher mean score is highlighted.

the *p* values of the individual dependent variables shows that there are few instances in which Group B learners still significantly outperform Group A learners – sentence length (W/S) and measures involving sentence complexity (C/S, Sub C and Sub/S). In other words, after 726 hours of instruction, it can be concluded that Group A learners may be catching up with Group B learners in all the areas examined, except those involving subordination.

In order to fully reveal the developmental patterns of each of the domains that show interaction between AO and instructional time, i.e. how the time of instruction received at different ages affects the rate of development of the interlanguage of the two groups of learners, a qualitative analysis of the development of the variables in the three domains (Fluency, Lexical Complexity and Grammatical Complexity) was carried out. To do this, we grouped the variables according to whether the differences between the two groups are significant at T3, i.e. whether the two age groups reach the same level after receiving the total amount of 726 hours. Once these two main categories were established, we then looked for common patterns of development in both groups according to whether the differences between the variables were statistically significant or not after 200 hours (T1), 416 hours (T2) and 726 hours (T3). We then analysed and compared the profiles of growth of the different patterns in both groups and over time, to compare the interlanguage development of Group A (AO = 8) and Group B (AO = 11).

Variables with no statistically significant differences between the means at T3

Three patterns can be identified when the results obtained by different sets of variables for the Group A and Group B at T1, T2 and T3 are compared.

Pattern 1.1

This pattern, shown in Figure 7.1, groups two Fluency variables, *total number of words* (W) and *number of clauses* (C) and one Lexical Complexity variable, *number of verb types* (VT).

This pattern is characterised by growth for both Group A and Group B from onset time to T3. However, when considering development over time, if Group B significantly outperforms Group A throughout T1 and T2, the differences decrease at T3 and the degree of significance is lost. This is interpreted as evidence for the gradual improvement of fluency, together with a greater variety of lexical verbs, which in a way are closely associated with Fluency, since the more learners write, the greater their need for different verbs to build clauses.

Although both groups reach the same level, i.e. they write with the same fluency after 726 hours of instruction, comparison of each group's development shows that the benefits of the hours of instruction are different

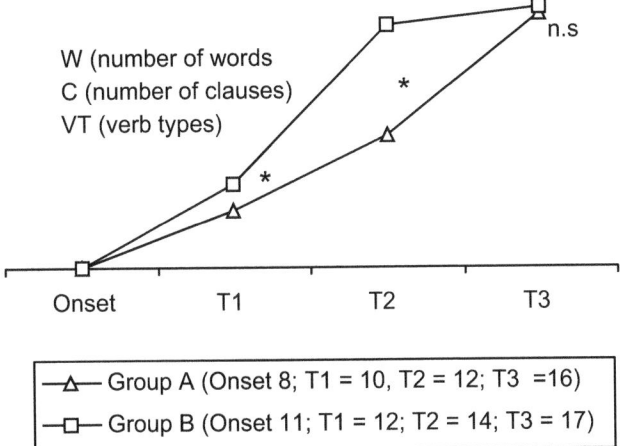

Figure 7.1 Pattern 1.1

Notes: *significant; n.s. = non significant; *p* < 0.01.

depending on the age at which they have been received. As Figure 7.1 shows, the younger group (Group A) distributes the gains more evenly over the three time periods than the older group (Group B); Group B presents a higher rate of development during the first 416 hours, especially in the age period between 12;9 and 14;9, and then slows down towards T3.

It can be concluded that the variables that conform to this pattern increase faster in older learners in the first stages of language acquisition. Younger learners, although slower at the beginning, are able to catch up with older ones in the long term. However, a word of caution is necessary here as the time limit on the writing task (15 minutes) may have influenced the results, since at T1 and T2 Group A presents lower fluency because their limited competence does not allow them to write more. One explanation for the levelling out of these two measures at T3 could be related to language processing constraints, since the results attained by both groups might indicate a ceiling effect in their attentional capacity to process language in a limited period of time. Group B, with more linguistic resources, would reach the maximum level at T2, whereas Group A, which is initially slower, continues acquiring resources until T3, when the ceiling effect appears as in Group B.

Pattern 1.2

This pattern, shown in Figure 7.2, groups one Fluency variable, *number of sentences* (S), and one Lexical Complexity variable, *noun types* (NT).

This pattern is characterised by growth between the onset time and T2 for both Group A and Group B, which is higher for Group B, although it largely takes place in parallel. However, when development at T3 is considered, the

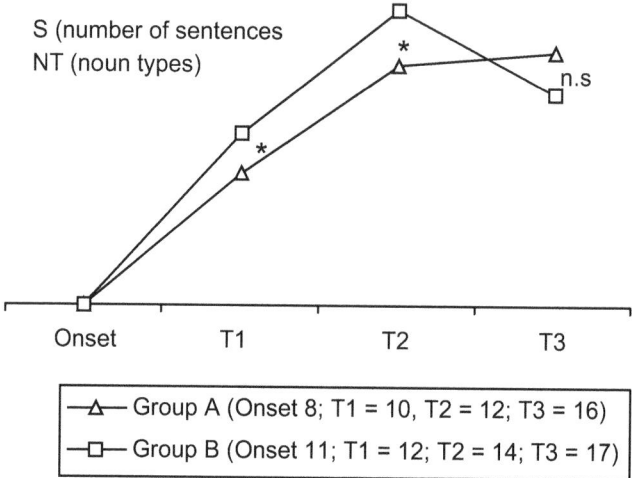

Figure 7.2 Pattern 1.2
Notes: *significant; n.s. = non significant; $p < 0.01$.

results are levelled out, as in Pattern 1.1. Nevertheless, at T3, unlike the previous pattern, the relationship is reversed and Group A shows a slight increase while Group B decreases. This can be interpreted as evidence that sentences may be a misleading indicator of development, as the differences between low proficiency and more advanced learners do not lie in the number of sentences but in their complexity (Wolfe-Quintero et al., 1998). Indeed, interpretation of this pattern must take into account the results for the following patterns (both 1.3 and 2.2), since the increase or decrease in the number of sentences is connected with development in other Grammatical Complexity variables. A similar interpretation can be made when considering *noun types* (NT), as their decrease for Group B at T3 and halt for Group A may be happening as a result of an increase in *verb types* (VT) (Pattern 1.1), *adjective types* (Adj. T) and *adverb types* (Adv. T) (Pattern 1.3 below).

Pattern 1.3

This pattern, shown in Figure 7.3, groups one Fluency variable, *words per clause* (W/C), two Grammatical Complexity variables, *number of coordinate clauses* (Coor C), *coordinate clauses per sentence* (Coor/S) and two Lexical Complexity variables, *adjective types* (Adj. T) and *adverb types* (Adv. T).

This pattern contrasts with the two above in that statistical significant differences are found only at T2. Figure 7.3 shows that the rate of growth in the profiles of both groups is clearly determined by age. Indeed, even if there is evidence of steady growth between the onset time and T1, after that point differences appear and Group B shows a dramatic improvement between the 11;9 and 14;9 age span, when compared to that of the

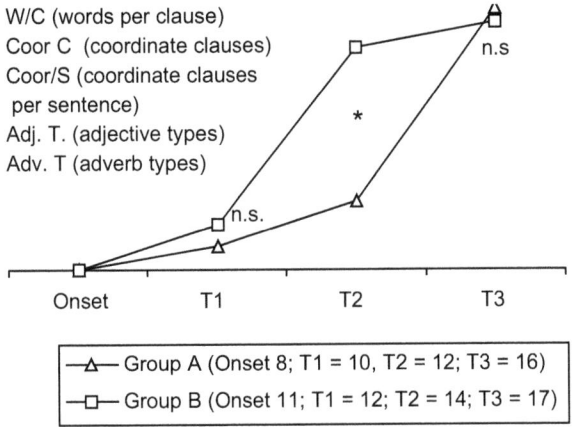

Figure 7.3 Pattern 1.3

Notes: *significant; n.s. = non significant; $p < 0.01$.

younger group (A), who are still around the age of 12 by T2. Nevertheless, like the pattern above, the lines converge at T3 since once the younger group (A) has reached the age of 12 at T2, they benefit most from the instructional time received after this age and catch up with the older group (Group B). Learners in Group B also benefit most from the hours received after 12 but they slow down between T2 and T3 and, in spite of their greater maturity, they do not seem to be able to sustain this advantage. In the case of coordination, these results can be easily interpreted as closely related to the development of subordination, as seen in Pattern 2.2 below.

The behaviour of the Lexical variables *adjective types* (Adj. T) and *adverb types* (Adv. T), and to a certain extent of *noun types* (NT) in Pattern 1.2. above might be explained by a combination of age factors and the learning context. These are on the one hand, maturity and memory constraints under the age of 12, and on the other, the limitations of the foreign language school context that cannot provide learners with a wide variety of authentic communicative situations that would foster the acquisition of new words and their use according to learners' real communication needs. These factors would explain the slow growth under the age of 12, whereas the lack of extensive real communicative situations might explain the stoppage of Group B.

From what can be seen thus far looking at the analysis and interpretation of Patterns 1.1, 1.2, and 1.3, we can conclude that an earlier start in a foreign language context does not make acquisition faster, since the learners in both groups reach a similar competence after the 726 hours of instruction in most of the variables. Nevertheless, what does make a difference is the age at which the hours of instruction are received, i.e. whether instruction takes place before or after the age of 12 years old plays a major role in the distribution of the gains between the onset time and T1, T2 and T3, as seen in the variables included in these three patterns.

Variables with no statistically significant differences between the means at T3

Two patterns can be identified when comparing the results obtained by different sets of variables for Group A and Group B, at T1, T2 and T3.

Pattern 2.1

This pattern only includes the variable *words per sentence* (W/S). The pattern shown in Figure 7.4 is characterised by growth at the three data collection times, for both Group A and Group B, yet is statistically higher for Group B, although they are largely parallel.

It is obvious that the increase that both groups present throughout the three times is due to the growth of sentence length, i.e. learners write more words per sentence. However, this variable does not indicate if this is the case because phrases are longer or because the sentence includes more clauses. Word/phrase ratio measures should have been used to give a more accurate explanation. In this study, we can only interpret this result in relation to the variable *clauses per sentence* (C/S) (see Pattern 2.2 below) and conclude that the lengthening of the sentences is the result of the increase of number of clauses.

Pattern 2.2

This pattern, shown in Figure 7.5, includes three grammatical complexity variables – *clauses per sentence* (C/S), *number of subordinate clauses* (Sub C) and *subordinate clauses per sentence* (Sub/S).

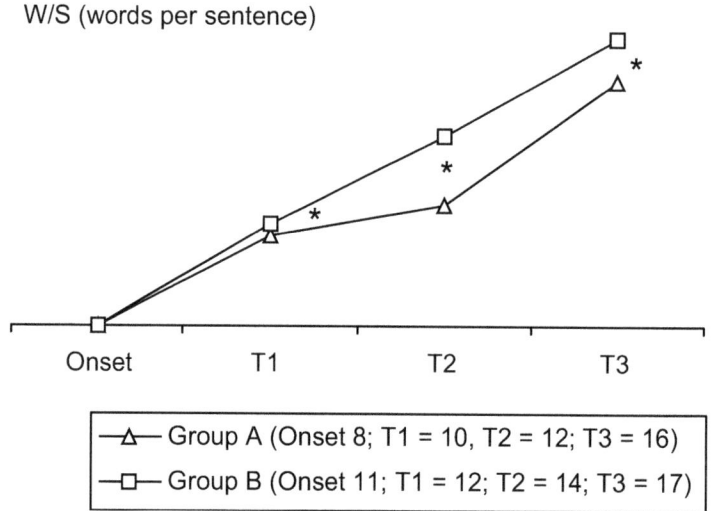

Figure 7.4 Pattern 2.1

Notes: *significant; n.s. = non significant; $p < 0.01$.

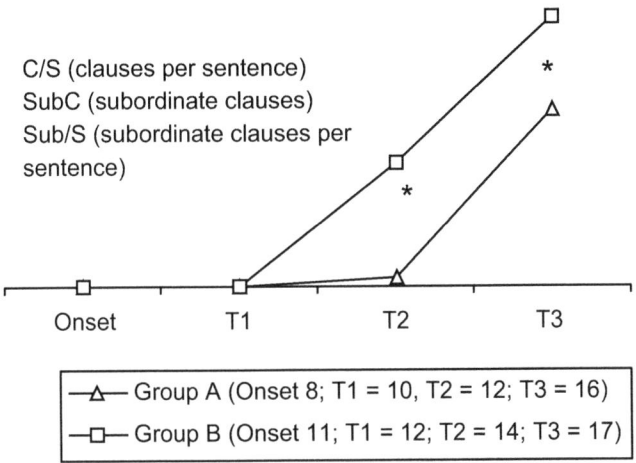

Figure 7.5 Pattern 2.2
Notes: *significant; n.s. = non significant; $p < 0.01$.

The pattern shown in Figure 7.5 is characterised by the fact that growth does not start in either group until they reach 12 years of age, regardless of the number of hours of instruction received. The younger group (Group A) therefore needs to have reached T2 (416 hours), whereas older learners (Group B) already present these features at T1 (200 hours). Group B therefore has an advantage, since after age 12, learners receive more hours of instruction (526, those between T1 and T3), whereas Group A only receives 310 (those between T2 and T3) (see Table 7.2). The pattern is similar to what we saw in Pattern 1.3. Neither group increases their *clauses per sentence* (C/S) at T1. Their ratio is 1 clause:1 sentence, and their production therefore exhibits a larger number of simple sentences, i.e. more fluency, but not more complexity. For Group A, the younger group, this ratio slightly increases between T1 and T2, meaning that learners continue to write simple sentences, whereas there is greater growth in the older learners (Group B), meaning that complexity is emerging and the internal characteristics of sentences are changing with it.

Interpretation of this emerging complexity in the older group requires consideration of two other ratio measures – *coordinate clauses per sentence* (Coor/S) in Pattern 1.3, and *subordinate clauses per sentence* (Sub/S) in this pattern. As can be seen, Group B increases both in coordination and subordination, and complexity is therefore due to both, and subordination in particular at T3. This explains the fall in the number of sentences in a time-constrained situation such as the written task, in favour of complexity. As far as Group A is concerned, it is not until the age of 12 that complexity starts developing, when coordinate clauses increase and subordinate clauses appear for the first time. These phenomena both appear at the same time as a decrease in the number of sentences.

As far as Patterns 2.1 and 2.2 are concerned, we can also conclude that an earlier start in a foreign language context does not make acquisition faster, but unlike the variables in Patterns 1.1, 1.2 and 1.3, learners in Group B (AO = 11) achieve better results after the same hours of instruction (726 h). In this case, the hours of instruction received after the age of 12 seem to have played a major role, with Group B receiving a larger amount of hours than Group A being a key factor, as shown in Table 7.2.

Conclusion

This study considers the issue of the development of EFL written competence as an effect of the interaction between age and instructional time, i.e. whether and how the number of hours of instruction affects rate of acquisition at different ages. Several features in this study stand out in contrast to previous research in the field of writing in SLA research. Firstly, the data are collected in a foreign language learning context, for which studies dealing with writing do not abound. Secondly, development is measured over a wide time frame, from 8 to 17 years of age. Last but not least, the large size of the sample, and the ages and proficiency spans covered in it, allow for new conclusions to be reached as far as foreign language acquisition is concerned.

Written production is analysed as consisting of four areas of competence – Fluency, Lexical Complexity, Grammatical Complexity and Accuracy. Each area was operationalised using a series of measures or variables, with their global values representing degrees of competence within the area in question. Firstly, the two-way MANOVAs showed that there is clear evidence of interaction for the areas of Fluency, Lexical Complexity and Grammatical Complexity but not for Accuracy, which was consequently excluded from subsequent analyses. Secondly, the study analyses the changes in the different variables for each of those three areas in order to ascertain whether the number of hours received at each data collection time has a different effect at different ages. In this regard, as shown by the results of the one-way MANOVAs for each area, it can also be concluded that an early start at 8 years of age does not involve higher levels of attainment at 16 years old, after 726 hours of instruction. By then, for 10 out of the 14 variables analysed included in the areas, results from Group A (AO = 8) do not present statistically significant differences from Group B (AO = 11). For the remaining four variables – one Fluency variable: *words per sentence* (W/S) and three Complexity Variables: *clauses per sentence* (C/S), *number of subordinate clauses* (SubC) and *subordinate clauses per sentence* Sub/S) – Group A is still weaker at T3. The reason for this, as further discussed below, seems to lie in the fact that the number of hours received after the age of 12 by Group A (T2 → T3 = 310 hours) is lower than that received by the older group (T1 → T3 = 216 + 310 hours), as Table 7.2 shows.

Thirdly, this study provides a ground-breaking, finely honed analysis of how each of the different variables in the three areas of Fluency, Lexical and Grammatical Complexity develop over time, as a result of the interaction between age and instructional time. To that end, five patterns of development are established according to both the ultimate attainment reached at T3, and also to the concomitances in the development of the variables measured. A qualitative analysis of such patterns of growth is provided, giving interesting proof of the differences between the two groups of subjects and the different development of the variables.

Analysis of the profiles of both groups shows that there are significant differences in the distribution of gains that affect the rate of acquisition of these variables in the different age spans. Some Fluency variables, such as *number of words* (W), *number of clauses* (C), *and number of sentences* (S) and two Lexical variables, *noun and verb types* (NT, VT) increase steadily from the beginning of instruction in both groups, although Group B presents higher levels in the early stages. By contrast, the age of 12 appears as a turning point for some other variables within Grammatical Complexity, such as *clauses per sentence* (C/S), *number of subordinate clauses* (Sub C) and *subordinate clause per sentence* (Sub/S), since it is then that these variables start increasing in both groups. This is also true, though to a lesser degree, of the other Grammatical and Lexical Complexity variables, i.e. *coordinate clauses* (Coor C), *coordinate clauses per sentence* (Coor/S) and *Adjective and Adverb types* (Adj. T, Adv. T). This means that this growth takes place when the subjects in Group A are at T2 (= 416 hours) but the subjects in Group B are at T1 (= 200 hours).

Another important conclusion in the context of this study is that neither the areas of language nor the variables included in them develop in tandem, whereas their rate of development seems to be affected by age. To be more precise, the age around 12 constitutes a turning point to develop Grammatical and Lexical complexity either triggering the development of subordination (see Pattern 2.2) or accelerating the rate of development of coordination and the increase of language variety (see Pattern 1.3). In short, these findings can be interpreted in the sense that an earlier start in a foreign language context does not mean reaching a higher level of ultimate attainment or a faster and more effective acquisition in the different subskills which form an integral part of the skill of writing. However, we do not know if the gains or benefits obtained by the younger group in fluency aspects and lexis before reaching the age of 12 might have a delayed effect in the long run, after a more extensive learning period than the one in this study.

Several key methodological issues must be mentioned at this point. Firstly, the selection of measures used in this study deserves some reflection. We have seen that measures hardly used in previous studies, such as types of word classes, have revealed themselves to be highly discriminatory in the early stages of language acquisition as far as written competence is concerned. We have also seen that *number of sentences* (S) is misleading evidence of the development of proficiency in writing, since differences seem to lie not in the number of sentences but in their internal complexity, which was analysed using three ratios (C/S, Coor/S and Sub/S). For the same reason, the measure *words per sentence* (W/S) showed that a larger number of words in the sentence was a result of coordination and subordination, i.e. it reflects complexity rather than fluency. In order to reflect the emergence of complexity in the interlanguage of beginners, we suggest the use of other measures, such as the number of simple and complex sentences as separate variables or the phrase/clause ratio, which would allow investigation of both the phrase and the clause from the point of view of constituents and their complexity. Secondly, the effect of the instructional context may have had an effect on the results in this study. Pattern 1.3 shows how the development of certain types of words (nouns and verbs) seems to come to a halt with Group B, whereas others (adjectives and adverbs) do not appear in the first stages in both groups, which is probably due to the type of classroom input, which is often impoverished and selective with forms, as several authors have remarked (see Han, 2004 for a recent review). These results should also be considered in the light of the methodology used by teachers. It is from age 11–12 onwards that explicit teaching of the linguistic system is introduced and more form-focused activities are developed in class. The superiority of adolescents therefore might be attributed not only to age, but also to methodological changes in the teaching approach, i.e. cognitive maturity inherent in age implies, in turn, changes in the pedagogical approach with the inclusion of metalinguistic activities and, consequently favours linguistic awareness. This is not the case with learners younger than 12, who seldom receive explicit instruction on the linguistic system of the foreign language.

The pedagogical implications therefore seem evident and worthy of mention, as they have a bearing on the controversy around when to start, the amount of instructional time and its distribution. Besides, since the benefits from the same hours of instruction at different ages may not be the same, the present study may have interesting implications for teachers' expectations in foreign language contexts. We have seen how the variables that are connected with complexity start growing at around the age of 12. Two learning profiles seem to emerge from the study – the fluency profile and the complexity profile – and the development of the former seems to precede that of the latter. In fact, even with low gains, ES start developing fluency in English by writing simple sentences thanks to the acquisition of nouns and verbs. There is therefore no reason to abandon the introduction of the foreign language at an earlier age, since there is some growth that has no negative effect. However, what this study has clearly shown is that after the age of 12, the group receiving the highest number of hours improves most in complexity. In this respect, it would be advisable to increase the number of hours that the younger group receives after this age, and not to reduce it as is the case in the sample of this study. Further research is thus needed to confirm whether the initial benefits in fluency and lexis together with programmes with a greater amount of instructional time, especially after the age of 12, would yield better results at the end of compulsory school or in the long run after school.

The conclusion that can be drawn from this analysis is that "early" does not mean "better" in written development, when the conditions of age and instruction are established as they are in this study where subjects undergo a "drip-feed", an impoverished low intensity type of programme and a low quantity of input over a relatively extended period of time.

Acknowledgements

This study was supported by grants PB94-0944, PB97-0901 and BFF2001-3384 of the Spanish Ministry of Education. The authors wish to express their most sincere gratitude to the following colleagues: Carmen Muñoz, for her patience and encouragement at all times and also for her insightful comments; Maribel Peró for her invaluable help with statistics; Craig Chaudron for his explanations and suggestions on statistical tests; and Mike Maudsley, for his careful proofreading. Any mistakes remain our own.

References

Archibald, A. (1994) *The Acquisition of Discourse Proficiency: A Study of the Ability of German School Students to Produce Written Texts in English as a Foreign Language*. Frankfurt: Peter Lang.

Archibald, A. and Jeffery, G.C. (2000) Second language acquisition and writing: A multi-disciplinary approach. *Learning and Instruction* 10 (1), 1–11.

Arnaud, P.J.L. (1992) Objective lexical and grammatical characteristics of L2 written compositions and the validiy of separate-component tests. In P.J.L. Arnaud and H. Béjoint (eds) *Vocabulary and Applied Linguistics* (pp. 133–145). London: Macmillan.

Bacha, N. (2001) Writing evaluation: What can analytic versus holistic essay scoring tell us? *System* 29, 371–383.

Celaya, M.L. and Tragant, E. (1997) Adquisición de lengua: Código escrito. In R. Ribé (ed.) *Tramas Creativas y Aprendizaje de Lenguas. Prototipos de Tareas de Tercera Generación* (pp. 237–251). Barcelona: Publicacions de la Universitat de Barcelona.

Celaya, M.L., Pérez-Vidal, C. and Torras, M.R. (1998) Writen performance by young bilingual lerarners of English as an L3. Paper presented at EUROSLA 9, University of Paris.

Celaya, M.L., Pérez-Vidal, C. and Torras, M.R. (2001a) Matriz de criterios de medición para la determinación del perfil de competencia lingüística escrita en inglés. *RESLA* 14, 87–98.

Celaya, M.L., Torras, M.R. and Pérez-Vidal, C. (2001b) Short and mid-term effects of an earlier start. An analysis of EFL written production. In S. Foster-Cohen and A. Nizegorodcrew (eds) *EUROSLA Yearbook* (Vol. 1, pp. 195–209). Amsterdam: John Benjamins.

Cenoz, J. (2002) Age differences in foreign language learning. *ITL Review of Applied Linguistics* 135–136, 125–142.

Chenoweth, N.A. and Hayes, J.R. (2001) Fluency in writing: Generating text in L1 and L2. *Written Communication* 18 (1), 80–98.

Cohen, A. D. (1994) *Assessing Language Ability in the Classroom* (2nd edn). Boston: Heinle & Heinle Publishers.

Connor, U. and Mbaye, A. (2002) Discourse approaches to writing assessment. *Annual Review of Applied Linguistics* 22, 263–278.

Connor-Linton, J. (1995) Looking behind the curtain: What do L2 composition ratings really mean? *TESOL Quarterly* 29 (4), 762–765.

Cook, V. (1997) L2 users and English spelling. *Journal of Multilingual and Multicultural Development* 18 (6), 474–488.

Crerand, M. and Lavin, E. (1993) From first language literacy to second language proficiency to second language literacy: The act of writing in a foreign language context. Paper presented at the Annual Meeting of American Educational Research Association (Atlanta, GA, 12–16 April, 1993) *EDRS – ERIC Document Reproduction Service* (ED376710).

Cumming, A. (2001) ESL/EFL instructors' practices for writing assessment: Specific purposes or general purposes? *Language Testing* 18 (2), 207–224.

Cumming, A., Kantor, R. and Powers, D. (2002) Decision making while rating ESL/EFL writing tasks: A descriptive framework. *Modern Language Journal* 86 (1), 67–96.

Doiz, A. and Lasagabaster, D. (2001) El efecto del factor edad en la producción escrita en inglés. In I. De la Cruz, C. Santamaría, C. Tejedor and C. Valero (eds) *La Lingüística Aplicada a Finales del Siglo XX. Ensayos y Propuestas* (pp. 63–68). Alcalá de Henares: Universidad Alcalá de Henares.

Ferreiro, E. and Pontecorvo, C. (2002) Word segmentation in early written narratives. *Language and Education* 16 (1), 1–17.

Foster-Cohen, S. (1999) *An Introduction to Child Language Development*. London: Longman.

Hamp-Lyons, L. (1995) Research on the rating process. Rating non-native writing: The trouble with holistic scoring. *TESOL Quarterly* 29 (4), 759–762.

Han, Z. (2004) *Fossilization in Adult Second Language Acquisition*. Clevedon: Multilingual Matters.

Harley, B.K. and King, M.L. (1989) Verb lexis in the written compositions of young L2 learners. *Studies in Second Language Acquisition* 11 (4), 415–439.

Ishikawa, S. (1995) Objective measurement of low-proficiency EFL narrative writing. *Journal of Second Language Writing* 4 (1), 51–69.

Kroll, B. (1998) Assessing writing abilities. *Annual Review of Applied Linguistics* 18, 219–240.

Lasagabaster, D. and Doiz, A. (2003) Maturational constrains on foreign-language written production. In M.P. García Mayo and M.L. García Lecumberri (eds) *Age and the Acquisition of English as a Foreign Language: Theoretical Issues and Fieldwork* (pp. 136–160). Clevedon: Multilingual Matters.

Laufer, B. and Nation, P. (1995) Vocabulary size and use: Lexical richness in L2 written production. *Applied Linguistics* 16 (3), 307–322.

Leki, I. (1996) L2 composing: Strategies and perceptions. In B. Leeds (ed.) *Writing in a Second Language* (pp. 27–37). London: Longman.

Leki, I. (2002) Second language writing. In R. Kaplan (ed) *The Oxford Handbook of Applied Linguistics*. Oxford: Oxford University Press.

Lightbown, P.M. and Spada, N. (1997) Learning English as a second language in a special school in Québec. *The Canadian Modern Language Review/La Revue canadienne des langues vivantes* 53 (2), 315–355.

Lumley, T. (2002) Assessment criteria in a large-scale writing test: What do they really mean to the raters? *Language Testing* 19 (3), 246–276.

Manchón, R.M. (2001) Trends in the conceptualizations of second language composing strategies: A critical analysis. *International Journal of English Studies* 1 (2), 47–70.

Manchón, R.M., Roca de Larios, J. and Murphy, L. (2000a) La influencia de la variable "grado de dominio de la L2" en los procesos de composición en la lengua extranjera: Hallazgos recientes de la investigación. In C. Muñoz (ed.) *Segundas Lenguas. Adquisición en el Aula* (pp. 277–297). Barcelona: Ariel.

Manchón, R.M., Roca de Larios, J. and Murphy, L. (2000b) An approximation to the study of backtracking in L2 writing. *Learning and Instruction* 10 (1), 13–35.

Martín-Uriz, A., Chaudron, C., Hidalgo, L. and Whittaker, R. (2000) El desarrollo del tema en la composición de estudiantes de secundaria: Medición y evaluación de la coherencia. Paper presented at XVIII Conference of the Spanish Association of Applied Linguistics, Universitat de Barcelona.

Matsuda, P.K. and De Pew, K.E.D. (2002) Early second language writing: An introduction. *Journal of Second Language Writing* 11 (4), 61–68.

Navés, T., Torras, M.R. and Celaya, M.L. (2003) Long-term effects of an earlier start. An analysis of EFL written production. In S. Foster-Cohen and S. Pekarek (eds) *EUROSLA-Yearbook. Annual Conference of the European Second Language Association* (Vol. 3, pp. 103–130). Amsterdam: John Benjamins.

Nystrand, M., Green, S. and Wiemelt, J. (1993) Where did composition studies come from? An intellectual history. *Written Communication* 10 (3), 267–333.

Ortega, L. (2003) Syntactic complexity measures and their relationship to L2 proficiency: A research synthesis of college-level L2 writing. *Applied Linguistics* 24 (4), 492–518.

Pérez-Vidal, C., Torras, M.R. and Celaya, M.L. (2000) Age and EFL written performance by Catalan/Spanish bilinguals. *Spanish Applied Linguistics* 4 (2), 267–290.

Polio, C. (1997) Replication and reporting. *Studies in Second Language Acquisition* 19 (4), 499–508.

Qi, D.S. (1998) An inquiry into language-switching in second language composing processes. *Canadian Modern Language Review/Revue canadienne des langues vivantes* 54 (3), 413–435.

Reichelt, M. (1999) Towards a more comprehensive view of L2 writing: Foreign language writing in the U.S. *Journal of Second Language Writing*, 8 (2), 181–204.

Roca de Larios, J. (1999) Cognitive processes in L1 and L2 writing. A cross-sectional study. PhD thesis, University of Murcia, Spain.

Sasaki, M. (2000) Toward an empirical model of EFL writing processes: An exploratory study. *Journal of Second Language Writing* 9 (3), 259–291.

Sasaki, M. and Hirose, K. (1996) Explanatory variables for EFL students' expository writing. *Language Learning* 46 (2), 137–174.

Sengupta, S. (2000) An investigation into the effects of revision strategy instruction on L2 secondary school learners. *System* 28 (1), 97–113.

Shaw, P. and Liu, E.T.K. (1998) What develops in the development of second language writing? *Applied Linguistics* 19 (2), 224–254.

Swedler-Brown, C.O. (1992) The effects of training on the appearance of holistic essay graders. *Journal of Research and Development in Education* 26 (1), 24–29.

Torras, M.R. and Celaya, M.L. (2001) Age-related differences in the development of written production. An empirical study of EFL school learners. Special issue edited by R.M. Manchón: Writing in the L2 classroom: Issues in research and in pedagogy. *International Journal of English Studies* 1 (2), 103–126.

Torras, M.R., Celaya, M.L. and Pérez-Vidal, C. (1998) Matriu de criteris de medició per a la determinació del perfil de competència lingüística escrita en anglès d'alumnes bilingües. Paper presented at II Congrès de les Llengües de l'Estat, Universitat de Barcelona.

Victori, M. (1997) EFL composing skills and strategies: Four case studies. *RESLA* 12, 163–184.

Wolfe-Quintero, K., Inagaki, S. and Kim, H.Y. (1998) *Second Language Development in Writing: Measures of Fluency, Accuracy and Complexity. Technical Report 17.* Manoa: University of Hawai'i Press.

Woodall, B.R. (2002) Language-switching: Using the first language while writing in a second language. *Journal of Second Language Writing* 11 (1), 7–28.

Chapter 8

Age, Proficiency Level and Interactional Skills: Evidence from Breakdowns in Production

GISELA GRAÑENA

Theoretical Background

The amount and nature of the input that different-aged learners are exposed to as well as the interactional processes they engage in are environmental factors that may contribute to explain age-related differences in second language (L2) learning. These factors, grounded on the well-accepted necessity for input in L2 acquisition, are generally referred to as input (Larsen-Freeman & Long, 1991) or linguistic environmental (Oliver, 2000) factors. Research has identified some differences in the interactional processes learners engage in according to their age. Oliver (1998) compared the interactional strategies used by young learners with those used by adults as reported by Long (1983). Her results showed that even though younger and older learners made use of the same interactional strategies, the child dyads in her study made more frequent use of other-repetition as an interactional strategy whereas the adult learners in Long (1983), especially those in NNS–NS (non-native speaker–native speaker) dyads, engaged in negotiation for meaning by using clarification requests and confirmation checks more often than the younger learners.

Other studies have drawn a connection between the interactional processes that different-aged learners get engaged in and the nature of the input they obtain (Muñoz, 2002; Scarcella & Higa, 1982). These studies contend that older learners are more efficient at drawing from their linguistic environment a type of input that addresses their learning needs in a more accurate way. Older learners are able to obtain this finely-tuned input through self-initiated behaviour in interactional processes in which they take an active part. These studies attribute older learners' more active engagement in conversation to their greater interactional skills.

One of the studies supporting older learners' greater advantage in learning the second language as a result of their more active involvement in conversation is Scarcella and Higa's (1982). Scarcella and Higa's experimental study with child and adolescent learners provided evidence of the various conversational management devices older learners used both to repair problems in comprehension and to keep the conversation going. As for those devices aimed at avoiding breakdowns in comprehension, the adolescent learners used a variety of signals such as questions and other-repetitions when they did not understand their NS interlocutor. These signals were followed by a response by their interlocutor aimed at modifying the trigger utterance. Scarcella and Higa argued that the NS modifications provided the older learners with finely-tuned input at those points where that was relevant for the learners. On the other hand, although the younger learners in their study were also getting comprehensible input from their interlocutors as a result of the special speech addressed to them, such input was not directed at problematic linguistic items identified by the learners themselves. Instead, the speech addressed to the younger learners included adjustments such as repetitions, questions, imperatives, prosodic and paralinguistic features. As for those devices to sustain conversation, age placed a greater burden on the adolescent learners, who were expected to keep up conversation even when lacking the resources to do so. The study showed that they were able to sustain discourse by means of conversational strategies such as topic initiations. Scarcella and Higa's study, in sum, showed how conversational involvement can help older learners' headstart in the language learning process by providing them with more finely-tuned input and with opportunities to stretch their linguistic competence in conversation.

As Singleton and Ryan (2004) argued citing Scarcella and Higa, although this input-based account assuming older learners' active involvement in conversation is well founded, evidence is still limited. A more recent study showing how the different interactional skills displayed by older and younger learners in a foreign language (FL) context can have an effect on the nature of the input addressed to them is Muñoz (2002). Muñoz observed that the frequency and type of interactional modifications in oral semi-structured interviews were influenced by the interviewers' accommodation to different proficiency levels as well as by the learners' interactional skills. Proficiency level had an effect on the pattern of interactional modifications by influencing the amount of interviewer linguistic accommodation. The interviewers' perception of a learner's low proficiency level led to a greater use of interactional modifications in order to sustain and involve the learner in the conversation. Qualitatively, some devices such as self-repetitions and reformulations were more sensitive than others to proficiency level. The use of accommodation devices took place both pre-emptively in order to avoid likely communication breakdowns and also reactively following learners' signals of lack of comprehension. Muñoz further reported that accommodation to proficiency level only could not account for the patterns observed. Her results showed that the frequency of the interviewers' modifications was also influenced by the different interactional skills displayed by the learners in conversation and that the different interactional skills were an effect of the learners' age. She observed that the groups of older learners avoided silences to a greater extent than their younger counterparts when they ran into comprehension problems and used more code-switching instead. This communicative behaviour influenced the interviewers' performance with regards to the abandonment and maintenance of topics and, ultimately, it also influenced the length of the interviews. Muñoz concluded that whereas the interviewers might have been dropping topics as a result of the younger learners' silences, they might have been maintaining them with the older learners by means of code-switching.

The Present Study

In both studies, the one by Scarcella and Higa and the most recent one by Muñoz, the focus is on breakdowns in conversation arising from comprehension problems. While engaged in interaction, the learners experienced and signalled some difficulty in understanding the message, which led to some kind of linguistic adjustment by their interlocutor. The present study approaches the issue of age, input and interactional skills from a different but related perspective by focusing on breakdowns in interaction arising from production problems. While interacting in the L2, learners may be confronted with problematic items and/or rules that they may attempt to overcome by means of a communication strategy (CS). Research within the CS framework has identified different types of strategies depending on whether the learner chooses to keep up the communicative goal (compensatory CSs) or drop/shift the goal (avoidance CSs) (Faerch & Kasper, 1983). One of the compensatory strategies learners may resort to is the *appeal for assistance*, a compensatory strategy which involves turning to an external source (e.g. speech partner, dictionary) to look for a solution.

Appeals for assistance can be distinguished from the rest of CSs in two respects that stand as relevant for the present study. The first respect that distinguishes appeals for assistance is that they operate both as a CS that keeps the communication channel open and as a learning strategy that may provide the learner with items available for incorporation at points where there is a need for them. This communicative need creates an opportunity for paying selective attention to the information provided in response to an appeal for assistance. In fact, several studies have brought up the issue of a connection between appeals for assistance and language acquisition (Cohen, 1998; Kasper & Kellerman, 1997; Willey, 2002). For example, Willey (2002) pointed out that this particular CS served several purposes in vocabulary acquisition as a means to recall known words, elicit unknown ones and test hypotheses about word usage.

The second respect that distinguishes appeals for assistance is that they are an interactional compensatory strategy that can be traced back in interaction through query–response episodes. Because the query is directed at a problematic item or rule in the L2 which arises spontaneously in a meaning-focused activity, appeals for assistance can be usefully examined within the theoretical framework of focus on form and form uptake as operationalised in Ellis *et al.* (2001a) and Williams (1999). In these studies, the traditional scope of focus on form was broadened to embrace form directed not only at grammar but also at any linguistic domain including vocabulary and addressed either by the teacher or another learner in response to a previous error (reactive focus) or by the teacher or the learner as self-initiation (pre-emptive focus). Following Ellis *et al.*'s (2001a) definition and operationalisation of focus on form, appeals for assistance can be seen as instances of preemptive student-initiated focus on form. As such, they further complement those breakdowns in comprehension studied by Scarcella and Higa (1982) and Muñoz (2002), which correspond to instances of reactive student-initiated focus on form.

The potentiality of appeals for assistance as acquisition devices is theoretically grounded on the role of attention in learning (Schmidt, 1990, 2001) and on Schmidt and Frota's (1986) notice-the-gap hypothesis according to which becoming aware of mismatches between ends and means in language production is essential for learning from input to take place. Swain (1998), citing Gass (1988), Schmidt and Frota (1986) and Doughty and Williams (1998), further distinguished three levels of noticing that may occur or co-occur in interaction: noticing a form in the target language (TL) ("noticing the form"), noticing an interlanguage (IL)/target language difference ("noticing the gap"), and noticing an IL deficiency ("noticing the hole"). According to these three levels of noticing, appeals for assistance can be considered as instances of noticing at the "noticing-the-hole" level.

Ellis *et al.* (2001a) highlighted the particular interest of student-initiated focus on form from the point of view of acquisition given that the students themselves are drawing attention towards a gap or hole that they have perceived in their IL. The possible role of student-initiated focus on form in acquisition pointed out by Ellis *et al.* ties in with Scarcella and Higa's hypothesis relating age-related learning differences with access to finely-tuned input.

Research Questions

The main purpose of this study was to examine the use of appeals for assistance by learners of different ages as a strategy to avoid breakdown in conversation and as a feature of their interactional skills. The role of L2 proficiency level was also examined. By focusing on a CS that is interactionally grounded, this study further aimed at exploring the effect of appeals for assistance on the provision of feedback and the linguistic environment of the students. Finally, by exploring appeals for assistance from the perspective of pre-emptive focus on form and form uptake, this study set out to examine the amount of feedback attended to and incorporated by learners of different ages and proficiency levels as a mechanism of potential acquisition.

In order to achieve these purposes, the following research questions were addressed:

(1) How often do learners of different ages and proficiency levels elicit help from their interlocutor in order to complete the task by means of appeals for assistance and to what extent that help is elicited by the learners in an explicit manner?
(2) What type of feedback does the learners' interlocutor provide and to what extent that can be related to the degree of explicitness of the learners' appeals for assistance?
(3) To what extent do the learners attempt to incorporate into discourse the feedback provided by their interlocutor in response to their appeals for assistance?

Methodology

Participants

The oral performance of 7 groups of 30 Spanish/Catalan bilingual learners of English as a FL ($n = 210$) was examined for this study. The data were drawn from the larger corpus in the Barcelona Age Factor (BAF) Project and the learners were selected according to their L2[1] exposure. No students with extra exposure to the L2 other than that received through the official state curriculum were included in this study.

The age of the learners in six of the seven groups ranged from 10 to 17. These six groups came from two different school curricula that for a short period overlapped in time in Spain. Three of these groups came from a former school curriculum in which FL learning started at the age of 11 (late starters) whereas the other three groups came from the present school curriculum in Spain in which FL learning starts at the age of 8 (early starters). In addition to these six groups of learners, an additional group of adult students was also examined. These students started learning English after the age of 18 at different language schools of English in Barcelona.

Data were collected at three different points in time: after 200 hours of English instruction and after 416 and 726 hours in the case of those groups of students belonging to the former and present curricula. Table 8.1 shows the number of students, the accumulated hours of instruction received, the students' age at the time they performed the task, and the school curriculum they belonged to.

In Table 8.2 the groups are ordered in increasing level of performance according to their mean scores on a series of language proficiency tests.[2]

The score difference between the groups with the same hours of instruction was statistically significant in Time 2 (T2) and Time 3 (T3) according to the one-way ANOVA and Tukey *post hoc* run, with the older learners in each of those two data collection times always attaining higher scores than

Table 8.1 Participants

	Present curriculum (A)	*Former curriculum (B)*	*Adult learners (D)*
Time 1 (T1) 200 hours	Group A1 10;9 years $N = 30$	Group B1 12;9 years $N = 30$	Group D1 +18 years $N = 30$
Time 2 (T2) 416 hours	Group A2 12;9 years $N = 30$	Group B2 14.9 years $N = 30$	
Time 3 (T3) 726 hours	Group A3 16;9 years $N = 30$	Group B3 17;9 years $N = 30$	

Table 8.2 Proficiency level

Group	Age	Hours of instruction	N	Mean[a]	SD
A1	10	200	30	20.58	6.16
B1	12	416	30	27.97	10.28
A2	12	200	30	37.03	9.25
A3	16	726	30	57.13	12.15
B2	14	416	30	61.93	13.05
D1	+18	200	30	72.43	13.36
B3	17	726	30	72.64	8.72

Note: [a] Mean standardised over 100.

the younger ones, $F = 143.112$ (6,200), $p < 0.001$. No significant differences were reported, however, in Time (T1) between the two age groups of learners belonging to the former and present curricula ($p = 0.256$),[3] only between those two groups and the group of adult learners.

Task and procedure

The participants carried out a narration task in which they were asked to tell the story depicted in a set of six pictures to an interviewer (researcher) with both participants having visual access to the pictures being described. The learners met one-on-one with one of the eight interviewers who took part in administering and audio recording the task, all of them members of the same research team.

The picture story narration as task

The picture story narration is a closed task (Long, 1990) in which learners are required to produce a predetermined right solution. The fact that learners are pushed to keep on with a topic even when trouble arises may facilitate the use of CSs. In fact, studies on CSs rely largely on closed tasks (e.g. Chen, 1990; Hyde, 1982).

The narration is also a monologic task intended to assess the learner's ability to narrate stories. However, the presence of an expert participant for data collection purposes and certain participant-related factors such as age and proficiency level may have an influence on the monologic nature of the task. In a study on the role of the interviewer in the narratives of learners of different ages and proficiency levels, Álvarez (2002) observed a co-construction of meaning that made the narration turn into a somewhat different task. This suggests that the narration task, as a result of participant-related factors, may share features of interactive tasks with the interviewer actively involved in the interaction. The interviewer can be seen as having access to linguistic information that the learner may require at some point to complete the task. Consequently, the learner may turn to his interlocutor for help and bring about learner-initiated exchanges as a result of communication breakdowns in production. The interviewer may also participate in interviewer-initiated episodes in order to scaffold, prompt or focus the learners' attention on relevant pieces of information in plot development to carry out the task successfully. This in turn may lead to communication breakdowns in comprehension.

Data analysis

The recordings of the narration task were transcribed verbatim and coded for episodes including (1) a signal by the learner appealing for assistance or indicating the presence of a problem, (2) a response by the interviewer providing some kind of feedback, and (3) an optional follow-up move, i.e. uptake by the learner reacting to the interviewer's feedback. A full description of each of the categories is provided below.

Raw frequencies were counted for each category. Also, relative frequencies of occurrence were calculated as mean percentages in order to correct for differences in number and see differing relative emphasis on different categories. In order to investigate the reliability of the coding, a trained second rater with background in Applied Linguistics coded a random sample of 15% of the data in each of the groups. Kappa reliability was 0.82 with a resulting agreement rate of 84%.

(1) Signal: Learners' appeals for assistance

The different categories of appeals for assistance were based on Faerch and Kasper's (1984) distinction between *direct appeals*, on the one hand, and *implicit* and *explicit signals of uncertainty*, on the other, all of which, they argued, can be interpreted as appeals for assistance from the interlocutor's point of view (see Table 8.3).

(2) Response: Interviewers' feedback

The interviewers' responses to the learners' appeals for assistance were coded according to whether they supplied the linguistic item(s) needed by

Table 8.3 Types of appeals for assistance

Category	Definition	Example
Direct appeals	Asking for help directly either through an explicit question or through rising intonation	*Example 1: Group A2* **Student 1 (S1):** boy and a girl i com es diu "menjar"? [Catalan: how do you say "eating"?] *Example 2: Group B1* **S2:** is a drink hmm "nens" "nens"? [Catalan: "children"]
Explicit indirect appeals	Asking for help indirectly. They express lack of a needed L2 item in a verbal way and correspond to Beneke's (1975) handicap signals or Palmberg's (1979) admission of ignorance	*Example 3: Group B1* **S3:** the children "preparan" no sé com es diu [Catalan: "they prepare", I don't know how to say that].
Implicit indirect appeals	Asking for help indirectly. They correspond to different types of hesitation phenomena (e.g. pauses, repeats, drawls) which function as non-verbal problem indicators[a] that may be interpreted as appeals for assistance by the interlocutor	*Example 4: Group A1* **S4:** looking looking at ... [unfinished utterance] **Interviewer (INT):** what's this? *Example 5: Group B* **S5:** the cows eating hmm... **INT:** what are they eating? What is this?

Note: [a]The category of implicit indirect appeals has been broadened in this study in order to includer learners' silences, which may have the same effect on the interlocutor as the different types of hesitation phenomena.

the learner or avoided supplying them. The categories were adapted from those developed by Ellis *et al.* (2001a) (see Table 8.4).

(3) Follow-up: Uptake

Uptake is defined in this study as the learner's exact repetition of the interlocutor's feedback or as the learner's incorporation of the interlocutor's feedback in a longer stretch of discourse after an appeal for assistance. This definition is based on the notion of *uptake* as operationalised by Ellis *et al.* (2001a). Their operationalisation differed from Lyster and Ranta's (1997), who studied uptake only in relation to reactive feedback. In the present study, like in Ellis *et al.*'s, the focus was on pre-emptive focus on form and student-initiated episodes. These episodes with a structure consisting of a trigger and a response may include a third optional move, i.e. uptake in which the learner reacts to the feedback provided.

Like Ellis *et al.* (2001a), the minimal version of uptake consisting of an acknowledgement was not considered an instance of successful uptake in this study. Although acknowledging may be relevant from a social perspective as appropriate communicative behaviour in conversation, it does

Table 8.4 Types of feedback

Category	Definition	Example
Provides	Providing the L2 item(s) that the learner requires	*Example 6: Group A1* **S6:** hmm "menjant" com has dit que era? [Catalan: "eating" how did you say that was?] **INT:** eat . **S6:** eat the dog s'ha menjat el sandwich. [Catalan: has eaten the]
Elicits and shifts	Avoiding the provision of the L2 item/s that the learner requires by means of elicitation in the learner's first language (L1), in the L2, or by means of topic shift	*Example 7: Group A2* **S7:** the cows eating hmm… **INT:** what are they eating? What is this? *Example 8: Group B1* **S8:** y hmm no sé "una montaña"? [Spanish: and hmm I don't know "a mountain"?] **INT:** say it in Spanish if you don't know *Example 9: Group A1* **S9:** and the dog "ai miran" … [Catalan: oh look at] **INT:** no? Ok number three now where are the children going?

not provide clear evidence of what Schmidt (2001) calls *noticing*, i.e. registering forms in the input so as to store them in memory. As a result, it does not provide enough evidence of attention to form and potential acquisition, the main reason for exploring uptake in this study. Absence of an overt response (i.e. silence) was not considered as successful uptake either. Unlike Ellis *et al.* (2001a), however, uptake consisting of an exact repetition of the interlocutor's feedback was tallied as an instance of successful uptake. It was considered in this study that repeating, unlike acknowledging or remaining silent, could provide more clear evidence that a form had been attended to and registered in short-term memory. Also, from a discourse point of view, it was considered that there could be grounds for a distinction between acknowledging and repeating. Loewen (2004), in order to explain the somewhat low level of successful uptake in his study, argued that there was the possibility that the discourse pattern of student-initiated episodes made it more usual to acknowledge by means of expressions such as *oh* or *yeah* than to repeat or incorporate the information provided in an utterance. If acknowledging was actually the unmarked follow-up move from a discourse point of view, repeating or incorporating feedback in a longer stretch of discourse could be both a sign of attention to form and potential acquisition, especially the correct incorporation of feedback into production like Ellis *et al.* (2001a) in fact argued. However, whether uptake can be actually considered a measure of acquisition or all together a mere discourse phenomenon is still a matter of debate (see Long, to appear).

In this study, uptake was further categorised according to whether it took place following a direct appeal, an explicit indirect appeal or an implicit indirect appeal for assistance. Examples of the three types of uptake are given in Table 8.5.

Results

Research question 1: How often do learners of different ages and proficiency levels elicit help from their interlocutor in order to complete the task by means of appeals for assistance and to what extent that help is elicited by the learners in an explicit manner?

A total of 674 appeals for assistance were identified in the data. Intra-group variation was frequent. The number of appeals per student ranged from 0 to 22 with an average of 3.16 (SD = 3.61) and a median of 2.00. Students who did not require any help at all were also present in all the groups. Out of 210 students, 40 (19%) did not signal for their interlocutor's help throughout the task.

Table 8.6 displays the raw frequency counts of the utterances produced by each of the groups as well as the raw and relative frequency counts of the utterances containing an appeal for assistance. Figure 8.1 shows the distribution of the proportional amount of utterances containing an appeal for assistance with respect to the total amount of talk produced by each of the groups. The groups are displayed and ordered throughout the study

Table 8.5 Types of uptake

Category	Definition	Example
Uptake following a direct appeal	Incorporating the feedback provided by the interlocutor in response to a direct appeal for assistance into discourse	*Example 10: Group B1* **S10:** hmm "les enseña" cómo se dice? [Spanish: "shows them" how do you say that?] **INT:** shows **S10:** shows the map
Uptake following an explicit indirect appeal	Incorporating the feedback provided by the interviewer in response to an explicit indirect appeal for assistance into discourse	*Example 11: Group A2* **S11:** es que no me acuerdo cómo se llama "comer" [Spanish: the thing is that I can't remember how to say "eating"] **INT:** eat **S11:** eat the dog
Uptake following an implicit indirect appeal	Incorporating the feedback provided by the interlocutor in response to an implicit indirect appeal for assistance into discourse	*Example 12: Group A2* **S12:** and the dog are eat the the … **INT:** the food the sandwich **S12:** the sandwich

Age, Proficiency Level and Interactional Skills 193

Table 8.6 Frequencies and proportions of utterances containing an appeal for assistance

Group	Utterances n	Appeals for assistance n	*Appeals for assistance Mean %*
A1	479	166	34.2
B1	615	177	28.6
A2	526	103	19.7
A3	378	69	17
B2	369	57	14.2
D1	507	69	11.8
B3	399	33	8.2

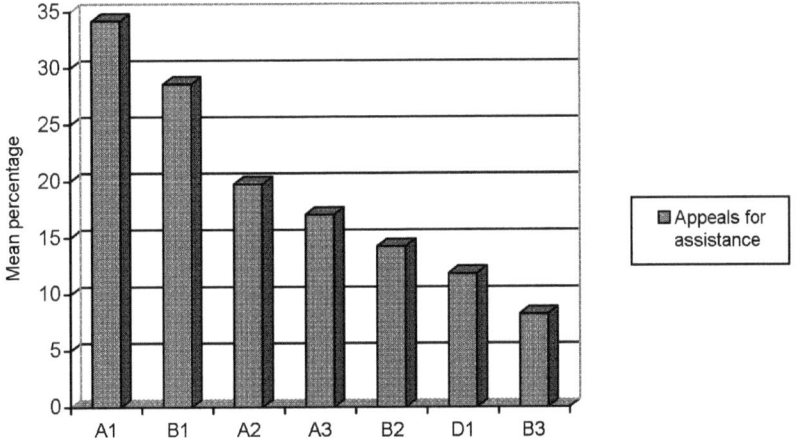

Figure 8.1 Mean percentage of appeals for assistance

in increasing level of performance according to their mean proficiency score.

The group whose performance was proportionally less dependent on the interlocutor's help was the most proficient group (Group B3). Only around 8% of the utterances they produced required some kind of assistance. On the other hand, the group that required help more often was the least proficient group (Group A1). Around 35% of the utterances they produced elicited some assistance from the interviewer. In fact, the decrease in the amount of help elicited by each group ran parallel to the increase in the students' overall score on the proficiency test administered to them. This suggested a proportionally inverse relationship between the two variables that was further supported by a significant moderate negative Pearson correlation (r (207) = –0.572, $p < 0.01$).

Table 8.7 presents the frequency counts of the different types of appeals for assistance and Figure 8.2 displays the frequencies as a mean percentage of the total number of appeals in each of the groups. Whereas the amount of help elicited by means of an appeal for assistance during task completion followed a linear pattern of decline with proficiency level, a qualitative analysis of the appeals for assistance from the point of view of their degree of explicitness showed that the distribution of the different types of appeals did not follow a linear pattern, even though there was a tendency toward a more balanced distribution of the different categories as proficiency level increased.

Overall, the proportion of help the learners obtained from their interlocutor by means of implicit non-verbal problem indicators such as pauses, repeats and drawls was greater than the help they obtained through direct or explicit indirect signals. According to the categorisation employed (i.e. Faerch & Kasper, 1984), implicit indirect signals were more frequent than direct or explicit indirect in almost all the groups. Only in Group B3, the

Table 8.7 Frequencies and proportions of types of appeals for assistance

Group	Direct appeals		Explicit indirect appeals		Implicit indirect appeals	
	n	Mean %	n	Mean %	n	Mean %
A1	11	12.3	15	12.5	140	75.2
B1	54	27.8	23	19.9	100	52.3
A2	27	18	25	24.1	51	57.9
A3	15	29.1	16	22.7	38	48.2
B2	21	36.8	12	21.1	24	42.1
D1	18	25.8	19	27.2	32	47
B3	11	33.3	13	39.4	9	27.3

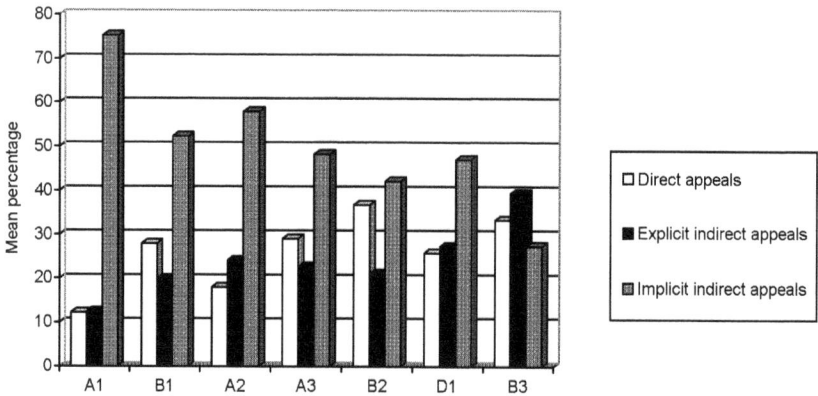

Figure 8.2 Mean percentage of types of appeals for assistance

most proficient group, was the frequency of both direct and explicit indirect signals proportionally higher.

Despite the lack of a linear pattern, the proportion of implicit indirect signals showed a tendency to drop with proficiency level, from 75% in the least proficient group down to 27% in the most proficient one, whereas the proportion of direct and explicit indirect signals showed the opposite trend. This overall tendency could be more clearly noticed when the individual categories of direct and explicit indirect appeals posed by Faerch and Kasper (1984) were merged together. Merging was justified on the grounds of the explicit and verbal nature that direct and explicit indirect appeals share in common. In both types of appeals, a trouble source has been identified and verbalised. In addition, from a communicative point of view, these two types of appeals impose a higher obligation on the interlocutor to assist. By means of a direct or explicit indirect signal, the offering of help becomes conditionally relevant and, therefore, both direct and explicit indirect signals can have a similar effect in interaction.

Figure 8.3 shows the proportional use of direct and explicit indirect signals in relation to the use of implicit ones. Some of the groups (Groups A3, B2 and D1) in which implicit behaviour was proportionally higher before merging the two categories of direct and explicit indirect appeals showed the inverse pattern with a greater proportion of explicit behaviour. In other groups, the two groups of 12-year-olds, the rearrangement of categories resulted in a more balanced distribution of explicit and implicit behaviour, even though implicit behaviour was still proportionally more frequent. Only in Group A1, the youngest and least proficient group, implicit indirect appeals continued to show a wide gap with respect to direct and explicit indirect appeals, a gap that mirrored the behaviour displayed by Group B3 with practically the opposite trend. A Wilcoxon Signed-Rank test was run to assess the significance of the difference between implicit and explicit behaviour in each of the groups. The test determined significant differences in the youngest and least proficient group, A1, between both types of behaviour ($z = 0$–3.331, $p < 0.001$) and non-significant differences ($p > 0.05$) in the rest of groups.

Although the merging of direct and explicit indirect appeals further supported that explicit behaviour tended to be more frequent with more proficient students, the resulting pattern was still not linear with respect to learner proficiency. The two groups of 12-year-olds, B1 and A2, displayed a similar pattern of use in spite of their significantly different proficiency scores and their different amount of hours of instruction. Although in both groups implicit behaviour was proportionally more frequent, the gap between implicit and explicit behaviour was not as wide as that observed in the younger group A1. In other words, the pattern shown by the group of 12-year-olds, B1, was closer to that of the group with twice as many hours of instruction, which scored significantly higher but which shared

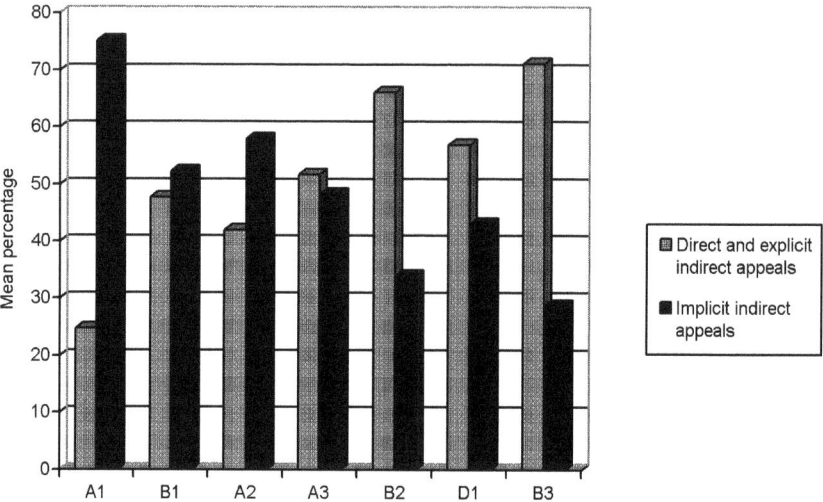

Figure 8.3 Mean percentage of direct/explicit indirect appeals and implicit indirect appeals

the same age, than to that of the group with the same hours of instruction, which did not score significantly lower and which was younger.

In the same fashion, the group of adult learners, Group D1, which scored practically the same as the most proficient group, B3, showed a greater preference for implicit behavior than the immediately preceding group in terms of proficiency level, Group B2.

Research question 2: What type of feedback does the learners' interlocutor provide and to what extent that can be related to the degree of explicitness of the learners' appeals for assistance?

The interviewers' responses to the learners' appeals for assistance were coded according to whether they provided the linguistic information needed by the learner or avoided providing it by means of elicitation either in the L1 or L2, or by means of topic shift. Table 8.8 displays the frequency counts of the two response types in each of the groups. *Provides* was the label used to refer to those responses that provided the linguistic information required by the learner and *Elicits and shifts* the label used to refer to those responses avoiding the provision of linguistic information.

Figure 8.4 shows the proportional amount of Provides, on the one hand, and Elicits and shifts, on the other, in each of the groups. All the instances of Provides identified in the data were aimed at bridging gaps in the learners' lexical knowledge. The interviewers supplied more items to those groups with a higher proficiency level, Groups A3, B2, D1 and B3. These groups were also the ones with a proportionally higher amount of direct and explicit indirect appeals (see Figure 8.3). On the other hand, the less proficient groups A1, B1 and A2 received a greater proportion of Elicits

Table 8.8 Frequencies and proportions of types of feedback

Group	Provides		Elicits and shifts		Total[a]
	n	Mean %	n	Mean %	n
A1	37	25.7	129	74.3	166
B1	74	44.8	103	55.2	177
A2	52	43.4	51	56.6	103
A3	35	69.8	27	30.2	62
B2	35	84.2	18	15.8	53
D1	45	73.8	13	26.2	58
B3	25	83.3	6	16.7	31

Note: [a] Learners' word checks followed by an interviewer's acknowledgement were eliminated from the count.

and shifts. These groups were the ones with a proportionally higher amount of implicit indirect appeals. Therefore, the distribution of the different types of feedback in each of the groups showed an effect of the different types of appeals for assistance. Group A1, the group with the greatest proportion of implicit appeals, was the group that proportionally received fewer Provides. The difference between Provides, on the one hand, and Elicits and shifts, on the other, in this group yielded in fact statistical significance ($z = 0$–3.017, $p < 0.005$).

The correspondence between the proportions of the interviewers' Provides and the learners' explicit behaviour in each of the groups could be further seen to follow a pattern of variation. In the younger and less

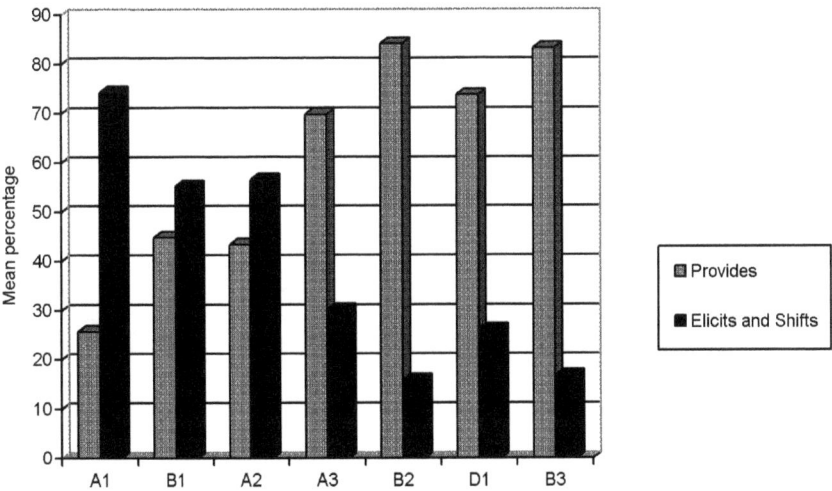

Figure 8.4 Mean percentage of the interviewers' response types

proficient groups, the proportions of Provides and explicit behaviour were very similar. Groups B1 and A2, the two groups of learners with the same age but different proficiency levels and which made a similar use of direct and explicit indirect appeals, received almost the same proportional amount of Provides responses from their interlocutors. As proficiency level increased, the proportional amount of Provides tended to be higher than the corresponding proportional amount of direct and explicit indirect appeals. In fact, whereas no significant differences were observed between implicit and explicit behaviour in the most proficient groups, Groups B2, D1 and B3, a significant difference was reported in the three of them between the Provides, on the one hand, and the Elicits and shifts, on the other, that they received ($p < 0.01$).

Research question 3: To what extent do the learners attempt to incorporate into discourse the feedback provided by their interlocutor in response to their appeals for assistance?

Table 8.9 presents the frequency counts of the instances of uptake in each of the groups and Figure 8.5 shows the frequency of occurrence of uptake as a mean percentage of the sum of the interviewers' Provides, that is, of the total amount of feedback that could be potentially incorporated into discourse as a result of learner initiation.

In general, uptake production was relatively high in this study. Uptake rate was over 60% in all the groups of learners analysed. This rate was higher among the most proficient groups, especially in the group of adult learners, D1, the group with the highest rate (100%). The groups that proportionally incorporated less feedback into their production after an appeal for assistance were the least proficient groups, Groups A1 and B1.

Table 8.9 also displays the frequency counts of the instances of uptake following each type of appeal for assistance and Figure 8.6 shows the amount of the different types of uptake as a percentage. The types of appeal for assistance that led to uptake more often within each of the groups were the direct appeal and the explicit indirect appeal. The Provides

Table 8.9 Frequencies and proportions of uptake

Group	Uptake						Total uptake	
	Direct appeal		Explicit indirect appeal		Implicit indirect appeal			
	n	%	n	%	n	%	n	Mean %
A1	7	100	5	100	12	57	24	60.9
B1	43	93.5	6	54.5	7	63.6	56	62.6
A2	21	95.5	8	88.9	15	83.3	44	80.3
A3	8	100	10	100	12	85.7	30	94.4
B2	16	91.1	8	100	8	80	32	90.5
D1	8	100	15	100	21	100	44	100
B3	7	100	10	90.9	6	85.7	23	94.4

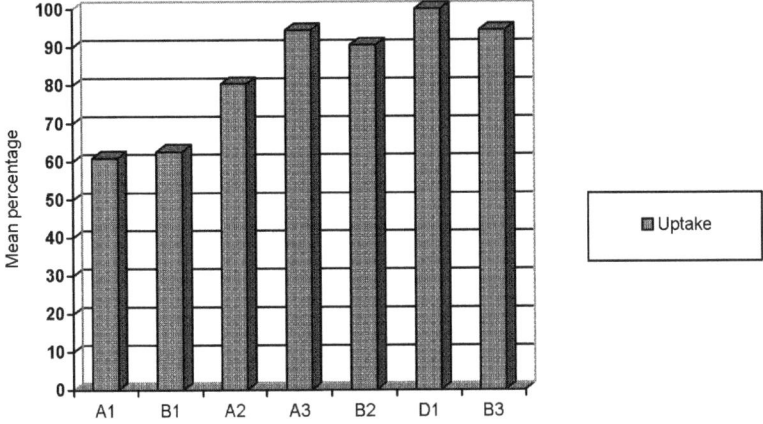

Figure 8.5 Mean percentage of uptake

the students received in response to implicit behaviour were not so readily incorporated. However, the degree of explicitness of the appeal played less of a role as proficiency level increased. More proficient learners incorporated the Provides in response to their implicit signals more often than less proficient ones. As a result, there was a more balanced distribution of the different categories of uptake in the most proficient groups.

Following Oliver (1995), in order to measure uptake rate, those interviewer turns containing a Provide but which gave no opportunity for the learner to take up the feedback were not taken into account. This methodological caveat eliminated from the analysis those cases in which the interviewer kept his turn by means of topic shift or continuation after the provision of feedback.

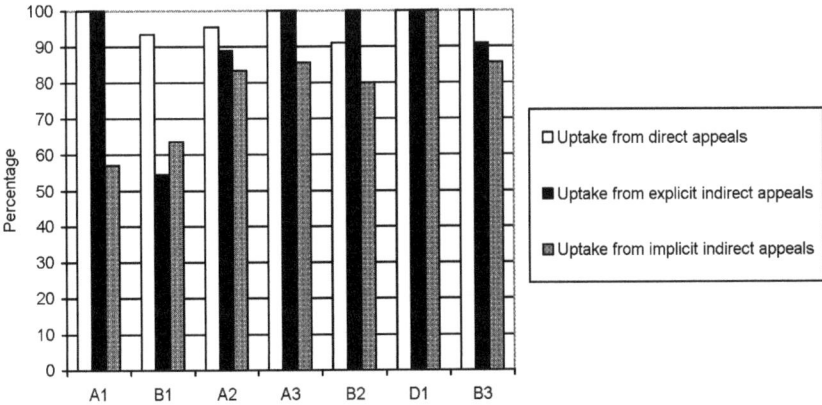

Figure 8.6 Percentage of uptake following each type of appeal for assistance

Example 13: Group A1
> **S13:** la madre aquí hmm mother look a map and dog hmm look a ...
> [Spanish: the mother here hmm]
> **INT:** it's a basket basket good and here what are they doing?

Table 8.10 displays the percentage of those instances where the learners were not given an opportunity to respond to feedback. The group that was given the fewest opportunities for uptake moves was the youngest and least proficient group A1.

Discussion

All the groups of learners in this study required and elicited the interlocutors' help at some point during task completion. However, variation was frequent within the groups. The number of appeals per student ranged from 0 to 22 with an average of 3.16 (SD = 3.61) and a median of 2.00. Students who did not require any help at all were also present in all the groups. Out of 210 students, 40 (19%) did not signal for their interlocutor's help throughout the task.

The groups that required the interviewer's help more often in order to carry out the task were the least proficient ones. Whereas the amount of help required for task completion decreased with proficiency level, a qualitative analysis of the degree of explicitness of the students' appeals for assistance showed that more proficient learners elicited help in a proportionally more explicit manner. When they experienced a breakdown in production, more proficient learners verbalised their problem and focused their interlocutor's attention on the linguistic information they needed rather than hesitating or remaining silent. This suggests a relationship between learner proficiency and an awareness of the linguistic needs to sustain discourse. The least proficient learners in this study, cognitively overloaded by those gaps in their L2, may have been unable to identify and specify L2 needs. The linguistic form of the appeals did not seem to interfere with the results since the students analysed appealed for help

Table 8.10 Proportions of *no-uptake-opportunity* moves

Group	No uptake opportunity (%)
A1	15.2
B1	8.1
A2	6.1
A3	8.6
B2	0
D1	2.3
B3	0

almost exclusively in their L1 irrespective of their proficiency level. Only seven out of the total raw count of appeals for assistance observed in the data ($n = 674$) were coded in the L2. The students' language use observed in the data would require further research. Relying on the L1 could be a feature of focus on form in FL learning contexts or, like Igarashi et al. (2002) pointed out, it could indicate lack of linguistic resources in dealing with breakdowns in L2 interaction.

Apart from proficiency level, the learners' age also seemed to contribute to the way the learners appealed for assistance. The influence of age could be observed in two respects. First, the two groups of 12-year-olds had a similar proportion of direct and explicit indirect appeals, even though their overall proficiency scores were significantly different. Whereas the amount of help required for task completion was greater in the 12-year-old group with the lowest proficiency level, the use of the different types of appeals for assistance in the two groups was qualitatively very similar. In both groups implicit signals were more frequent than direct or explicit ones, probably as a result of their overall low proficiency level like in the case of the younger and less proficient group of 10-year-olds. However, unlike in the group of 10-year-olds, the proportional occurrence of implicit and explicit behaviour was more balanced, a tendency more in line with the most proficient groups where explicit behaviour was more frequent than implicit. Second, results also showed that although adult learners elicited help more often in an explicit than implicit manner, they had a greater proportion of implicit behaviour than other groups that were less proficient. According to these results, age seemed to influence the type of signal given by the students to indicate the presence of a linguistic problem by favouring the use of explicit signals in both older children and teenagers and the use of implicit signals in younger children and adults. The increase in the proportion of implicit signals in the group of adult learners could have also been due to a greater amount of speech planning in this group to which the interviewers would have reacted with the provision of feedback. Fathman and Precup (1983) found that adults paused almost three times as often as children when speaking in the L2.

The type of feedback provided by the interviewers in this study was seen to be related to the degree of explicitness of the different types of appeals for assistance as shown by the correspondence between the pattern of use of the different types of appeals and the pattern of the interviewers' type of response. The proportional amount of interviewer responses including Provides and avoiding Provides mirrored the proportional amount of direct and explicit indirect appeals, on the one hand, and of implicit indirect appeals, on the other. The similarity among the proportions was greater in the youngest and least proficient groups whereas the oldest and most proficient ones received a greater amount of Provides than would have been expected according to their use of direct and explicit indirect appeals. This pattern suggested that Provides were mostly supplied when the interviewers were conversationally obliged to in the case of the youngest and least proficient groups whereas they were supplied both in response to explicit and implicit signals in the case of the oldest and most proficient groups.

Because the two groups of 12-year-olds had a proportionally greater amount of direct and explicit indirect appeals than the younger group of 10-year-olds, they also received a proportionally greater amount of Provides from their interviewers. Therefore, their behaviour in interaction when they experienced a problem in production had an effect on the type of feedback they elicited from their interlocutors. Conversely, the group of adult learners, as a result of the interviewers' behaviour with the oldest and most proficient groups, did not see the proportion of Provides affected by their greater use of implicit signals than other groups.

The level of uptake in this study was relatively high (over 60%) in all the groups of students. Other studies investigating the frequency of uptake reported levels such as 35% (Oliver, 1995), 55% (Lyster & Ranta, 1997), and 74% (Ellis *et al.*, 2001b). Uptake production in the two least proficient groups was around 60%, a similar rate to that reported by Lyster and Ranta (1997), whereas uptake production in the remaining five most proficient groups was higher (over 80%), a more similar rate to that reported by Ellis *et al.* (2001b). According to these results, learner proficiency might have been one of the factors contributing to the production of uptake. In fact, Mackey *et al.* (2000) suggested that the frequency with which learners perceive interactional feedback might be determined by learners' linguistic developmental stage. Group B1, which received the same proportional amount of provides as Group A2 (45% and 43% respectively), did not uptake to the same extent (63% vs 80%), even though the students in both groups shared the same age. Instead, the percentage of items Group B1 incorporated was more similar to that of the non-significantly less proficient group A1 (61%).

Apart from developmental readiness, age as a participant-related factor may also have contributed to the distribution of uptake production observed in this study (see Oliver, 2000 and Loewen, 2004 for the role of age in the production of uptake). Younger learners may be less likely to focus on form as a result of their more implicit approach to learning and, therefore, they may be less likely to produce uptake. Although in this study the most proficient groups showed a higher uptake rate than the least proficient ones, the results obtained suggest an interaction of proficiency level with other factors in some of the groups. The group of 16-year-olds showed a higher uptake rate than the more proficient but younger group of 14-year-olds and the same could be observed in the group of adult learners with a higher uptake rate than the more proficient but younger group of 17-year-olds.

Another factor to take into consideration in relation to student uptake is the instructional context as Ellis *et al.* (2001b) argued. The learners in this study belong to a FL learning context in which exposure to the L2 takes place mainly through explicit instruction in the L2 classroom. Ellis *et al.* (2001b) claimed that the extent to which learners focus on form may depend on the extent to which the L2 is learned in immersion or non-immersion contexts. Learners in non-immersion classrooms may be more able to approach the L2 as an object than learners in immersion classrooms. In fact, the overall high level of uptake reported in this study is in line with Ellis *et al.*'s claim, as well as with the levels of uptake they found, much higher than those in studies such as Lyster and Ranta (1997) with immersion students. However, further research would be needed which took a broader approach to focus on form than the current study in order to further examine the relationship between uptake production and instructional context.

This study also showed that participant-related factors such as age and proficiency level can play a role in the amount of uptake opportunities given to students, an important factor to take into account if uptake can actually be claimed to contribute to L2 acquisition. The results showed that the group which was denied the opportunity for uptake more often was the youngest and least proficient group. As a result, although the findings revealed that Group A1 showed the same capacity to uptake as the older group B1, they were not given an opportunity for uptake moves in 15% of the cases, almost twice as often as Group B1 (8%) or any other of the groups. A1 students' tendency towards more implicit and less co-operative behaviour at points of breakdown could contribute to explain the fact that their interlocutors held their turn after the provision of feedback as a device to sustain discourse and elicit further learner performance.

Uptake was operationalised in this study as including both exact repetitions and the incorporation of feedback in longer stretches of discourse. Acknowledgement tokens were not considered as instances of uptake. Taking into account the high levels of uptake reported in this study, this means that uptake in the form of repetition or incorporation into a longer stretch of discourse was more frequent than acknowledgement or silence in all the groups of learners and especially in the most proficient ones. From the point of view of the discourse structure of student-initiated focus on form (see Loewen, 2004), these results suggest that the students' most likely response to the provision of information in student-initiated focus on form may not be acknowledging for *all* the types of student-initiated focus on form as Loewen (2004) proposed.

The results in this study also showed that the higher the degree of explicitness of the appeal for assistance, the higher the chances for uptake to take place. The relationship between explicitness in addressing a linguistic item, noticing and uptake was also suggested by Basturkmen *et al.*

(2002). In the present study, however, explicitness played a greater role in the least proficient groups. Whereas in the most proficient groups uptake took place regardless of the type of signal that had triggered the interlocutors' response, in the least proficient groups, uptake took place more often as a follow-up to explicit signals. It seems that the fact of pre-empting attention to a gap they had identified, verbalised and were attempting to bridge facilitated the least proficient learners' uptake. Loewen's (2001) claim regarding the interest of student initiation in acquisition given that students themselves are drawing attention on items they find problematic would be of special relevance in the case of low-proficiency students according to the results in this study.

Finally, in line with other studies (Fathman & Precup, 1983; Loewen, 2001), which pointed out the high concern of L2 learners with language items during meaning-focused tasks, the linguistic focus of the appeals for assistance identified in this study was always lexical.

Conclusion

This study examined how learners of different ages and proficiency levels elicited help from their interlocutor when they experienced a breakdown in production during task-based interaction. Different types of appeals for assistance were identified according to their degree of explicitness. The results showed that more proficient learners elicited help in a more explicit manner. They verbalised and focused their interlocutor's attention on the language item(s) they required to sustain discourse. Age also played a role in the degree of explicitness of the learners' appeals. The groups of older children and teenagers used proportionally a greater amount of direct and explicit indirect signals. On the other hand, the group of youngest and least proficient students showed a clear preference for implicit signals such as hesitation, pauses and silence when they encountered a production problem. The proportion of implicit signals also increased in the group of adult learners with respect to the preceding group in terms of proficiency level, even though their overall behaviour was proportionally more explicit.

This study also examined the extent to which the different types of appeals for assistance had an effect on the interlocutor's type of response. The results showed that the degree of explicitness of the appeals had an effect on the type of feedback the learners obtained. The proportion of direct and explicit indirect appeals in each of the groups was similar to the proportion of Provides each of the groups received. On the other hand, the proportion of implicit indirect appeals was similar to the proportion of Elicits and shifts in each of the groups. Provides consisted in the provision of the language item/s required by the learner whereas Elicits and shifts consisted in either topic shift or in an attempt to elicit the language item(s) from the learner in the L2 or L1. The results further showed the interviewers' tendency to provide the linguistic item(s) needed by the learner only when conversationally obliged to by the learners' explicit signals in the case of the least proficient groups. In the case of the most proficient groups, the proportion of Provides was greater than the proportional amount of explicit signals they produced. As a result, those groups of less proficient but older learners, who made a greater use of explicit signals than less proficient and younger learners, obtained a proportionally greater amount of Provides due to the greater obligation that explicit signals imposed on the interlocutor to assist by means of a Provide response. The group of adult learners, whose proportion of implicit behaviour had increased with respect to less proficient learners, did not see the amount of Provides they received affected. On the contrary, in this group, like in the others with more proficient students, the intervie wers' feedback showed a tendency to include a Provide in response to both explicit and implicit signals.

The group of youngest and least proficient students was the group with the smallest proportion of Provides as well as the group with the greatest percentage of denied opportunities for uptake moves. However, their capacity to uptake was similar to that of the most similar group in terms of proficiency level.

This study provided some evidence about the influence that learners' behaviour in conversation can have on the type of feedback they elicit from their learning environment at points of breakdown. Older learners' more explicit behaviour contributed to create the conditions in conversation for finely-tuned feedback addressing those learners' linguistic needs.

Acknowledgements

This study was supported by scholarship to the author by the University of Barcelona as well as by grants PB94-0944, PB97-0901 and BFF2001-3384 to the BAF Project. The author also would like to thank M. Mar Suarez from the University of Barcelona for her invaluable help, Yucel Yilmaz from Florida State University for his useful suggestions, and the research team members of the BAF Project Carmen Muñoz and M. Luz Celaya for their insightful comments.

Notes

1. Although the students included in this study were bilingual learners of English, L2 will refer exclusively to English.
2. The mean score reported as an indicator of general proficiency in each of the groups was the result of the average performance of the students analysed on four language tests (cloze, dictation, grammar and listening tests), all of them administered to the participants in the BAF Project.
3. Although no significant differences were found in this study between the performance at T1 of the two samples of early and late starters belonging to the former and present curricula, larger samples analysed as part of the BAF Project did yield statistical significance.

References

Álvarez, E. (2002) The role of the interviewer in the oral narratives of EFL students of different ages and proficiency levels. Paper presented at the 26th AEDEAN Conference, University of Santiago de Compostela, Spain.

Basturkmen, H., Loewen, S. and Ellis, R. (2002) Metalanguage in focus on form in the communicative classroom. *Language Awareness* 11, 1–13.

Beneke, J. (1975) Verstehen und Missverstehen im Englischunterricht. *Praxis des neusprachlichen Unterrichts* 22, 351–362.

Chen, S.Q. (1990) A study of communication strategies in interlanguage production by Chinese EFL learners. *Language Learning* 40, 155–187.

Cohen, A.D. (1998) *Strategies in Learning and Using a Second Language*. London: Longman.

Doughty, C. and Williams, J. (1998) *Focus on Form in Classroom Second Language Acquisition*. Cambridge: Cambridge University Press.

Ellis, R., Basturkmen, H. and Loewen, S. (2001a) Preemptive focus on form in the SL classroom. *TESOL Quarterly* 35, 407–432.

Ellis, R., Basturkmen, H. and Loewen, S. (2001b) Learner uptake in communicative ESL lessons. *Language Learning* 51, 281–318.

Faerch, C. and Kasper, G. (1983) On identifying communication strategies in interlanguage production. In C. Faerch and G. Kasper (eds) *Strategies in Interlanguage Communication* (pp. 210–228). London: Longman.

Faerch, C. and Kasper, G. (1984) Two ways of defining communication strategies. *Language Learning* 34, 45–63.

Fathman, A.K. and Precup, L. (1983) Influences of age and setting on second language oral proficiency. In K.M. Bailey, M. Long and S. Peck (eds) *Second Language Acquisition Studies* (pp. 151–161). Rowley, MA: Newbury House.

Gass, S. (1988) Integrating research areas: A framework for second language studies. *Applied Linguistics* 9, 198–217.

Hyde, J. (1982) The identification of communication strategies in the interlanguage of Spanish speakers of English. *Anglo-American Studies* 2, 13–30.

Igarashi, K., Wudthayagorn, J., Donato, R. and Tucker, G.R. (2002) What does a novice look like? Describing the grammar and discourse of young learners of Japanese. *The Canadian Modern Language Review/La Revue canadienne des langues vivantes* 58, 526–554.

Kasper, G. and Kellerman, E. (1997) Introduction: Approaches to communication strategies. In G. Kasper and E. Kellerman (eds) *Communication Strategies. Psycholinguistic and Sociolinguistic Perspectives* (pp. 1–13). London/New York: Longman.

Larsen-Freeman, D. and Long, M. (1991) *An Introduction to Second Language Acquisition Research*. London: Longman.

Loewen, S. (2001) Variation in the frequency and characteristics of incidental focus on form. *Language Teaching Research* 7, 315–345.

Loewen, S. (2004) Uptake in incidental focus on form in meaning-focused ESL lessons. *Language Learning* 54, 153–188.

Long, M. (1983) Native speaker/non-native speaker conversation and the negotiation of comprehensible input. *Applied Linguistics* 4, 126–141.

Long, M. (1990) Task, group, and task-group interactions. In S. Anivan (ed.) *Language Teaching Methodology for the Nineties* (pp. 31–50). Anthology Series 24. Singapore: RELC.

Long, M. (to appear) Recasts in SLA: The story so far. In M. Long (ed.) *Problems in Second Language Acquisition*. Mahwah, NJ: Lawrence Erlbaum Associates.

Lyster, R. and Ranta, L. (1997) Corrective feedback and learner uptake: Negotiation of form in communicative classrooms. *Studies in Second Language Acquisition* 19, 37–66.

Mackey, A., Gass, S. and McDonough, K. (2000) How do learners perceive interactional feedback? *Studies in Second Language Acquisition* 22, 471–497.

Muñoz, C. (2002) Codeswitching as an accommodation device in L3 interviews. Paper presented at the 12th EUROSLA Conference, Basilea.

Oliver, R. (1995) Negative feedback in child NS-NNS conversation. *Studies in Second Language Acquisition* 17, 459–481.

Oliver, R. (1998) Negotiation of meaning in child interactions. *The Modern Language Journal* 82, 372–386.

Oliver, R. (2000) Age differences in negotiation and feedback in classroom and pairwork. *Language Learning* 50, 119–151.

Palmberg, R. (1979) Investigating communication strategies. In R. Palmberg (ed.) *Perception and Production of English: Papers on Interlanguage* (pp. 53–75). Publications of the Department of English. Abo: Abo Academy.

Scarcella, R. and Higa, C. (1982) Input and age differences in second language acquisition. In S. Krashen, R. Scarcella and M. Long (eds) *Child–adult Differences in Second Language Acquisition* (pp. 175–200). Rowley, MA: Newbury House.

Schmidt, R. (1990) The role of consciousness in second language learning. *Applied Linguistics* 11, 129–158.

Schmidt, R. (2001) Attention. In P. Robinson (ed.) *Cognition and Second Language Instruction* (pp. 3–32). Cambridge: Cambridge University Press.

Schmidt, R. and Frota, S. (1986) Developing basic conversational ability in a second language: A case study of an adult learner of Portuguese. In R. Day (ed.) *Talking to Learn: Conversation in Second Language Acquisition* (pp. 237–322). Rowley, MA: Newbury House.

Singleton, D. and Ryan, L. (2004) *Language Acquisition: The Age Factor*. Clevedon: Multilingual Matters.

Swain, M. (1998) Focus on form through conscious reflection. In C. Doughty and J. Williams (eds) *Focus on Form in Classroom Second Language Acquisition* (pp. 64–81). Cambridge: Cambridge University Press.

Willey, B. (2002) Vocabulary acquisition through interaction. Paper presented at the 13th AILA Conference, Singapore.

Williams, J. (1999) Learner-generated attention to form. *Language Learning* 49, 583–625.

Chapter 9
Reported Strategy Use and Age

ELSA TRAGANT AND MIA VICTORI

Introduction

Since the pioneering research undertaken by Rubin (1975), Stern (1975) and Naiman *et al.* (1978), in which they identify a set of what are apparently good language learning strategies insofar as they were reported as being used by successful learners, many studies have sought to describe the differences between successful and less successful learners on the basis of the learning strategies they display or report using. Chamot and El-Dinary (1999), Gu (2003) and Gan *et al.* (2004) are just a few recent examples of this prolific area of investigation. A complementary line of research is to be found in studies that examine the relationship between these learning strategies and levels of learner proficiency or the stages of learning. Such studies have identified differences both in the number and in the type of strategies used by learners at different proficiency levels (see Oxford & Burry-Stock, 1995).

Generally speaking, the mean reported frequency of strategy use in such studies has been found to be higher in advanced-level learners in studies involving adults (Griffiths, 2003), teenagers and adults (Chamot *et al.*, 1987) and children (Lan & Oxford, 2003). Differences have not only been observed in the frequency of use, but also in the types of strategy reported as being used by different groups of learners. Hence, the types of strategy found to be used by advanced-level adult learners in studies based on the Strategy Inventory for Language Learning (SILL, the most widely used instrument to date) seem to coincide: higher-level students report using the language more actively, adopting strategies that involve some type of interaction (Bremner, 1999; Green & Oxford, 1995; Griffiths, 2003). In contrast, lower-level students tend to make more use of strategies that involve isolated ways of learning the language with an emphasis on memorisation strategies and strategies involving vocabulary learning (Griffiths, 2003; Gu & Johnson, 1996).

A similar emphasis on vocabulary was observed by Leeke and Shaw (2000) among overseas students in Britain at the early or initial stages of learning, in a study based on semi-structured interviews. Results from another qualitative study (Takeuchi, 2003), based on a reading of "how I learned a foreign language" books in the Japanese foreign language (FL) context, also show several differences in strategy use among good adult language learners at the beginner, intermediate and advanced stages. Accordingly, beginners are described as being more concerned with fluency than with accuracy, and with increasing their vocabulary. In contrast, intermediate- and advanced-level learners appear to be more concerned with accuracy than fluency and seem to be ready to take steps to use the language while manifesting a concern for intensive language study. At the same time, students at different levels of proficiency are found to approach listening and reading tasks differently. Those at the beginner and intermediate stages show a preference for activities such as dictations (involving "deep listening") as opposed to activities involving strategies such as looking for the overall gist (involving "broad listening"). Similarly, for students at beginner and early-intermediate stages reading aloud, while focusing on phonological and semantic aspects of the language, is a particularly popular activity, while from the intermediate level on, references to analytical reading begin to appear in the data.

In spite of the evidence that points to a relationship between level of proficiency and strategy use, a number of authors (Bremner, 1999; Chaudron, 2003) have questioned the postulated linear correlation between these two variables after observing only low correlations, or even a curvilinear relationship, between them, that is, with intermediate-level students using certain learning strategies more often than low and high-level learners (Ehrman & Oxford, 1995; Gardner et al., 1997; Green & Oxford, 1995; Phillips, cited in Lan & Oxford, 2003; Yamamori et al., 2003). Other studies have only found significant correlations between some of the levels. For example, Politzer (1983) observed a closer association between the language learning behaviours of intermediate- and advanced-level students than those of elementary learners. On the other hand, in a university study involving Japanese and French learners in Singapore (Wharton, 2000), no significant main effect was found between elementary and intermediate learners as regards their strategy use nor was any effect for length of time spent studying English as a foreign language (EFL) reported. The findings of O'Malley et al. (1985) were also unclear as they found that beginner English as a second language (ESL) students were able to identify more strategies than intermediate-level students through retrospective interview data.[1] Finally, in Griffiths' study (2003), conducted in a private language school in New Zealand, it remains unclear as to why results are only reported for students at the elementary and advanced levels, since data was also collected from students in the other five levels taught by the language school. In view of these mixed results, care should be taken in establishing linear associations between proficiency levels and strategy use, and in assuming cause-effect relationships between these two factors.[2]

The absence of a systematic association between learner strategies and proficiency levels and, more generally language achievement, has recently led certain authors to claim that the effective use of language learning strategies depends on a complex and dynamic interplay of a range of factors (Gan *et al.*, 2004; Yamamori *et al.*, 2003). Hence, there would appear to be a need to approach this area of research by taking a holistic view of the real nature of strategy use. Quoting Yamamori *et al.* (2003: 382), "strategies are not "good" or "bad" in an absolute sense, and successful learners are not characterized by their use of special strategies that others do not use".

Rather, strategy effectiveness depends on various conditions including task knowledge, task purpose, the learner's style, background knowledge, prior experience, socio-cultural and educational context, sex, attitude, motivation and personality, among others (Wharton, 2000; Yamamori *et al.*, 2003).

While each of these variables has generally been found to account for a part of the variation in strategy use, few studies have attempted to analyse the degree to which such strategies form a systematic part of the learners' development, and hence the extent to which this variation can be attributed to differences in the learners' age. This present study seeks to shed some light on this neglected area.

Strategy Use and Age

A possible explanation as to why the association between age and strategy use has not been examined in any detail is related to the fact that most studies of language learning strategies have been undertaken with adults and university students. It would seem that at these levels age differences are not especially relevant when examined in association with proficiency levels. For this reason, we believe an examination of strategy use in learners of school age is required.

Among the few studies undertaken with primary school second language (L2) students, Lan and Oxford (2003) recently examined the learning strategy profiles of 379 6th grade students in Taiwan. Based on a criterion-referenced placement test, students were placed into three groups according to their proficiency level: high, medium and low, and significant differences were found in strategy use across the three groups. Similarly, Chamot and El-Dinary (1999) examined the strategies used for classroom reading and writing tasks by skilled and less skilled 3rd and 4th grade US learners of foreign languages. They report finding differences in some of the strategies used, particularly those that involve background-knowledge strategies, which were used more frequently by more skilled learners in both age groups. Purdie and Oliver (1999) also analysed the strategies used by children of school age by taking into account their cultural background, the number of years they had been living in the native country, their previous exposure to English instruction, their beliefs and their attitudes. They only found significant differences in the use of cognitive strategies according to the number of years living in the native country.

With secondary school students, the work conducted by García-López (2000), in which data were collected from 9th grade EFL students for three consecutive years, is worth noting. After examining the subjects' use of vocabulary strategies, he found a hierarchical order in the frequency of strategy use, whereby repetition and memory strategies were predominant, followed by semantic-based strategies and association strategies. Worthy of mention also is the study undertaken by Vandergrift (2003), who, after comparing the listening strategies used by 7th grade skilled and less skilled listeners, found significant differences between the two groups. A slightly different approach was adopted by Yamaori et al. (2003), who used cluster analysis in their design to categorise 7th grade EFL learners into different profiles based on three variables: strategy use, will to learn and English language achievement. The study identified four different groups, two high-achievers and two low-achievers, who had distinctive patterns of strategy use. These results led the authors to conclude that the relationship between strategy use and achievement is complex, multifactorial and not always linear, a conclusion that is in line with some of the studies undertaken with adults.

Although these findings have certainly helped broaden our knowledge of strategy use by learners in different school grades, the question as to just how these differences between students of different ages relate to their use of strategies is not addressed in these studies; nor do they trace the developmental pattern of strategic use across learners of different age groups. Answering these questions requires further research, using both cross-sectional (comparing learners of different age groups) and longitudinal designs (tracing strategic development over time). To date, however, only a few such studies have been undertaken and these have yielded mixed results.

Among cross-sectional studies, Zimmerman and Martínez-Pons (1990) analyse the use of self-regulating first language (L1) learning strategies as used by 5th, 8th and 11th grade learners. For some of the self-regulating strategies, they found that 11th grade students exceeded 8th graders, who in turn surpassed 5th graders. However, this increasing developmental pattern was not observed across subjects in all of their behaviours, and hence, their findings could not only be attributed to differences in students' age and grade. Similarly, Grenfell and Harris' (1999) case studies of three British adolescents aged 12, 15 and 17 attributed their variation in strategy use not only to differences in their developmental stages but also to variations in their competence, learning style, the nature of the task, and their motivation. On the other hand, Schoonen et al. (1998) compared several dimensions of 6th, 8th and 10th grade Dutch students' metacognitive knowledge as applied to EFL reading comprehension. Their results suggest a cross-sectional development across the three age groups, with older students obtaining higher scores than younger ones on one of the components of MK (knowledge of text characteristics), and with the "other components interchanging in their roles of relevant predictors" (1998: 97).

The general picture that emerges from these cross-sectional studies is that for some strategies there would seem to be a developmental trend across learners of different ages, which would explain some of the variation observed. The further exploration of this trend is one of the new challenges facing researchers in this field, a challenge that may require other research designs, such as longitudinal studies, but which, to date, have been little exploited (Bremner, 1999).

A rare exception is the study undertaken by Chesterfield and Chesterfield (1985) in which a developmental sequence was found in the range of strategies used by pre-school and 1st grade Mexican-American bilingual students. By using implicational scaling techniques, they showed that "the use of a specific strategy implied the ability to use the same set of strategies lying below it on the scale" (1985: 56), and therefore, a natural order of strategy acquisition could be established. Accordingly, strategies such as repetition and memorisation were used first, followed by strategies that facilitated interaction among learners. The monitoring of grammatical errors was last on the scale and was displayed by very few children at the end of the 1st grade. The results of this study are quite significant not only because they are suggestive of a natural order in the development of learning strategies but also because this order was found to be systematic regardless of the subjects' level of proficiency in English. That is not to say, however, that the level of proficiency did not play any role in such development. According to the authors, higher levels of proficiency in the second language would seem to imply a wider range of strategies as well as the ability to use language learning strategies in more demanding ways.

The existence of a developmental trend in the use of learning strategies finds support elsewhere. Nyikos (1987; cited in Oxford & Crookall, 1989), for example, reported finding a progression in the strategy use of university subjects from one semester to another over a two-year period; similarly, in Takeuchi's study (2003) of 67 autobiographical accounts, the subjects acknowledged "a shift in the strategies used according to their learning stages" (2003: 391), which leads the author to conclude that certain strategies seem to be connected to certain stages of learning. Yet, not all the evidence points in this direction. O'Malley and Chamot (1990), for example, failed to identify a clear pattern of strategy change in learners that were interviewed over a one-year period, with the exception of certain changes at the individual level. Similar conclusions can be drawn from Yamamori *et al.* (2003) who, after tracking the strategies used by 7th grade EFL beginner Japanese students for a year, reported the overall consistent use of strategies from one term to another. These latter findings seem to indicate that in a one-year period very few changes in strategic behaviour can be expected and, therefore, efforts should be made in future studies to trace learner development over longer periods of time.

With this purpose in mind, these authors (Victori & Tragant, 2003) conducted an earlier study based on cross-sectional data, involving learners who presented an age difference of more than three years, and longitudinal data, with subjects being monitored over a two-year period. The study sought to analyse differences between groups of EFL learners in different school grades and of different ages, namely, in the 5th (10;9-year-olds), 9th (14;9-year-olds) and 12th grades (17;9-year-olds). Our results from the cross-sectional study showed significant differences in reported strategy use across the three age groups, with older learners reporting a wider repertoire of strategies, which in turn varied in quality type. Accordingly, with increasing age, the complexity of the type of cognitive strategies used by learners also increased. Thus, the repertoire was expanded to include memorisation strategies, mnemotechniques, inferencing and more creative practice strategies, among others. This pattern, however, was not observed across the three groups with all types of strategy, which led us to conclude, that "variation does not seem to follow a regular pattern of development with increasing or decreasing age, but it fluctuates depending on the strategies reported" (2003: 195). These results were later confirmed in the longitudinal study involving 38 students, who were aged 12 when first assessed. The subsequent analysis enabled us to identify a framework comprising four stages of development, with which we were able to trace students' reported strategic changes over time. By examining the way in which students moved from one stage to another, common trends of development were identified in most students, though we also found evidence of individual variability. The variability observed, both in the cross-sectional and the longitudinal data, seemed to imply that the differences observed could be attributed to other intervening factors, such as cognitive maturity, learning style or metacognitive awareness. Furthermore, because of the fact that the amount of instruction these students received as they grew older differed – with the youngest learners receiving 200 hours of English instruction, 7th grade students receiving 400, and the oldest group 800 hours – we were unable to provide sufficient evidence to show that the differences observed could be exclusively attributed to differences in the learners' ages.

The present study seeks to tackle some of the questions left unanswered in the previous study, and to explore an area that has so far tended to be neglected, that is, the systematic analysis of language learning strategy use in learners of different ages. The objectives pursued here, therefore, are twofold: (1) to analyse whether there are any differences between the strategies reported by EFL learners of different ages, including children, teenagers and adults, after their having received the same amount of classroom instruction (cross-sectional data); and (2) to ascertain whether developmental changes in strategy use can be traced in two groups of teenagers over an extended period of time (longitudinal data).

The Study

The present study, which includes both cross-sectional and longitudinal data obtained through semi-open questionnaires, builds upon our previous investigation (Victori & Tragant, 2003) but introduces a number of important changes in design. The cross-sectional data were drawn from students of different ages, but from subjects who had received a similar number of hours of language instruction. This allowed us to isolate the effects of age from those of hours of instruction. On the other hand, the longitudinal data were obtained by tracing changes in the subjects' strategic development in more than one group and over a longer period of time.

The subjects

The cross-sectional data comprised 703 subjects distributed according to hours of instruction (Time 1, Time 2, Time 3) and age at onset of instruction (Groups A, B and D[3]), as shown in Table 9.1. Group A included 360 primary school students who started learning English at school at the age of 8;[4] Group B included 251 high school students who started learning English at the age of 11; and Group D included 92 adult students, with ages ranging from 19 to 49 (at T1), who started learning English after the age of 18. The students in Groups A and B were drawn from state-funded schools, while those in Group D were drawn from state-funded and university language schools.

As the students' exposure to English outside the classroom was varied, albeit somewhat limited, it was decided that for the purposes of the cross-sectional study, only those subjects who reported no exposure to English would be considered. This decision ensured that we were working with more homogeneous groups, since students had received similar amounts of formal instruction.

Table 9.1 Main subject groups in the cross-sectional study

	Group A *AoO = 8*	*Group B* *AoO = 11*	*Group D* *AoO = 18+*	*Total OSE*
T1 = 200 h	AT = 10;9 OSE = 152	AT = 12;9 OSE = 102	AT = 28;9 OSE = 68	322
T2 = 416 h	AT = 12;9 OSE = 147	AT = 14;9 OSE = 98	AT = 30;4 OSE = 21	266
T3 = 726 h	AT = 16;9 OSE = 61	AT = 17;9 OSE = 51	AT = 41;7 OSE = 3	115
Total OSE	360	251	92	703

Notes: AT = age at testing; OSE = only school exposure; AoO = age of onset; T1 = Time 1; T2 = Time 2; T3 = Time 3.

In the case of the longitudinal study, our data were drawn from a subsample of students from Groups A ($N = 48$; AoO = 8) and B ($N = 38$; AoO = 11), including both those who had only been exposed to English at school and those who had been exposed to other sources of the language. This decision was taken to avoid reducing the size of the subsample. In the case of Group A students, data were collected at three points in time: at the ages of 10;9 (T1), 12;9 (T2) and 16;9 (T3); while in the case of Group B students, data were collected at two points in time[5] (at the ages of 12;9 and 14;9).

Instruments

In order to elicit reported strategy use from our target population, an open-ended questionnaire was used, in which students reported on their use of strategies for learning vocabulary, pronunciation, spelling, reading and sentence writing. The questions, which students answered in their L1, were subsequently translated and are shown in Table 9.2. In addition to these, the questionnaire also included biographical questions, and questions concerning their use of communication strategies and their attitudes to learning English. The instrument comprised a total of 27 questions, which students answered in about 20 minutes during class time.

Analysis

A data-based procedure was adopted in classifying the students' answers, although we used Oxford (1990) and O'Malley and Chamot's (1990) inventories of strategies as a starting point. Preliminary codes were developed and subsequently refined while analysing a sample of these questionnaires. Once decided upon, two independent raters applied the final coding system to a number of questionnaires with a resulting inter-rater reliability percentage of 80.5%.[6] Table 9.3 shows the most frequently mentioned strategies, most of which are applicable to all five of the questions posed in the questionnaire (for example, the strategy of "practice"),

Table 9.2 The questionnaire

Question	Variable
Do you have any method to remember the meaning of English words? Which one(s)?	Vocabulary
Do you have any method to learn the pronunciation of English words? Which one(s)?	Pronunciation
Do you have any method to know how to spell new words in English? Which one(s)?	Spelling
Do you have any method to read in English? Which one(s)?	Reading
Do you have any method to write correct English sentences? Which one(s)?	Writing

Table 9.3 Classification of learning strategies

Strategy	Examples
Copying. Noting the words down in order to memorise them.	*I write them several times* (meaning)
Repetition. A range of methods for the memorisation of words (oral, visual, auditory and kinesthetic, involving repetition), other than copying.	*I say the words to myself* (pronunciation) *I spell out the word* (spelling)
Studying grammar. Formal study of rules and structures, including the memorisation of sentences.	*I learn sentences by heart* (writing) *I study orally* (writing)
Classifying. Organising words into some classification system.	*I have a notebook for vocabulary* (meaning)
Noting down. Annotating the pronunciation of words.	*I write the words the way they sound* (pronunciation)
Mnemotechniques. Auditory, visual and semantic associations.	*I play with words to memorise them* (meaning) *I learn the word in a context so that I can remember it* (meaning) *I make personal connections* (meaning)
Imagery. Using images to recall words.	*I memorise the words as images* (spelling)
Analysis and inference. Drawing relationships with L1, English and other languages and using context.	*I seek similarities with other words* (spelling). *I try to find the logic by thinking of words that I already know* (meaning)
Intuition. Using intuition to deduce or produce language.	*I focus on the words that I know and the ones I don't, I try to imagine what they mean* (reading) *I am guided by what sounds better* (pronunciation)
Practice. Self-initiated controlled and extended (non-interactive) practice.	*I try to write sentences with the new words* (meaning) *I speak to myself at home* (pronunciation) *I write lots of compositions* (writing)
Exposure to input in the L2. Listening (songs, films, TV, etc.), reading (books, storybooks etc.), paying selective attention to input (teacher, native speakers, etc.).	*I watch films in the original version* (meaning). *In class I pay attention to how the teacher pronounces new words* (pronunciation) *As I read in English, I gradually learn to write them (words)* (spelling).
Using reference materials. Looking up meaning, spelling and pronunciation.	*I look up my classnotes* (reading) *I use the dictionary* (meaning)
Imitating. Purposeful imitation of the pronunciation of an L2 speaker.	*I imagine I am a native speaker of English* (pronunciation) *I imitate the teacher* (pronunciation)
Using model sentences. Previously seen in class, textbooks or in grammar books.	*I try to follow this structure S + V + O* (writing) *I look up other sentences* (writing) *I have a look at the textbook* (writing) *I try to remember the structures we have learnt* (writing)
Social strategy. practicing with someone outside the classroom and getting help from the teacher or a relative.	*I practice them (the words) with someone who knows a lot of English* (pronunciation) *I ask someone who knows* (reading)
Translation. Translating from one language to another.	*I make the sentences in Catalan and then I translate them* (writing) *I need to know the translation* (meaning)

although others are more specific to one or more questions (for example, "annotation of pronunciation").

Upon analysing the data, we observed a relatively high number of students for whom no information could be retrieved concerning their use of learning strategies for one or more questions. In order to explore the reasons for these missing answers, a random sample of subjects was contacted. We found that a number of students had interpreted the term "method" as a formal systematic approach to learning rather than as a simple strategy; while others had not provided any information for some questions because they claimed not to do anything special or to use any method to learn English. Furthermore, the question regarding reading strategies was excluded from the final analysis because a good proportion of the youngest subjects either failed to answer it or interpreted it as a question about reading out loud.

When analysing the students' responses, all the strategies reported in each question were considered. Hence, our tables include the number of total *counts* of strategies reported by each group, which means that the total number of counts for each group and category do not coincide across the columns. This type of analysis, and the limitations imposed on us by the large number of missing answers, restricted the possibilities for running robust statistical tests on our data. Hence, intergroup comparisons are undertaken by considering the frequencies obtained.

In the case of the longitudinal study, the analysis consisted in first quantifying the number of questions answered over time by each student, and second in describing any changes in the types of strategy that students mentioned over time. This procedure enabled us to acquire detailed information about the changes that students undergo as they grow older and to identify common patterns of change over time.

Results

Cross-sectional data

In this section we present the strategies reported by each group and at each data collection point for the four questions included in the questionnaire. For each question, separate intergroup comparisons were undertaken for the three collection times. This analysis enabled us to observe whether subjects having received the same number of hours of instruction, but with different ages, report using similar or different strategies.

Vocabulary strategies

We can observe (Table 9.4) that the strategic behaviours reported by the three age groups (albeit having received the same amount of instruction) differ in a number of ways. At T1, when students have received 200 hours of instruction, there was a progressive increase in the reported percentage uses of "mnemotechniques", "analysis" and "classification strategies" with increasing student age, although the higher percentages reported by Group D for these strategies (30%, 17% and 11.3% respectively) indicates that these strategies were more prevalent among learners over 17. In contrast, these three strategies were barely mentioned by the two younger groups of learners (Groups A and B), among whom there appears to be a preference for other strategies, including those that involve asking, or working with, other people ("social strategies") – strategies which appear to become progressively less prevalent with age; the "use of reference materials" – the use of which (around 21% in both groups) declined beyond Group B; and "copying" – a strategy which became less prevalent beyond Group A (20.7%). Finally, the high percentage values obtained for "repetition" strategies across the three age groups (28, 38 and 22.6%) show that this was a popular strategy with learners of all ages, above all with those in Group B.

At T2, that is, when subjects have received 416 hours of instruction, we can see that some of the previously identified differences across the groups remained, whereas other strategic behaviours changed slightly or even completely. Hence, "analysis strategies" seem to become steadily more prevalent with age; "mnemotechniques" appear to be more popular with the oldest group of learners (32%), but no major differences can be identified between the two younger groups" (8% vs. 8.4%) reported use of these

Table 9.4 Vocabulary strategies

Strategy types	Time 1			Time 2			Time 3	
	GA	GB	GD	GA	GB	GD	GA	GB
Mnemo-techniques	1 (1.8%)	4 (9.5%)	16 (30%)	9 (8%)	7 (8.4%)	7 (32%)	8 (23.5%)	5 (16%)
Analysis	0	1 (2.3%)	9 (17%)	6 (5.3%)	8 (9.6%)	3 (13.6%)	2 (5.8%)	3 (9.3%)
Reference materials	11 (21%)	9 (21.4%)	0	49 (43.3%)	22 (26.5%)	3 (13%)	3 (8.8%)	0
Social	5 (9.4%)	1 (2.3%)	1 (1.8%)	10 (8.84%)	4 (4.8%)	0	0	0
Copying	11 (20.7%)	1 (2.3%)	2 (3.7%)	7 (6.1%)	7 (8.4%)	5 (22.7%)	8 (23.5%)	5 (15.6%)
Repetition	15 (28.3%)	16 (38%)	12 (22.6%)	19 (16.8%)	21 (25.3%)	1 (4.5%)	7 (20.5%)	6 (18.7%)
Classifying	1 (1.8%)	3 (7.1%)	6 (11.3%)	5 (4.4%)	3 (3.6%)	0	3 (8.8%)	5 (15.6%)
Other strategies*	9 (17%)	7 (16.6%)	7 (13%)	8 (7%)	11 (13.2%)	3 (13.6%)	2 (5.8%)	8 (25%)
Total counts	53	42	53	113	83	22	33	32

Notes: * Those strategies that obtained small percentages were grouped under this category; GA = Group A; GB = Group B; GD = Group D.

strategies. Similar to T1, the use of "social strategies" and "reference materials" declined progressively with age; "repetition" was most frequently cited by Group B (25.3%), but became less important for Group D (4.5%). "Classifying" and "copying strategies" presented quite distinct patterns from those observed at T1, as the former appeared to decrease with age, while the latter did just the opposite.

At T3, after subjects have received 726 hours of instruction, an increase from Group A to Group B can be noted in the use of "classifying" (8.8% vs. 15%) and "analysing" (5.8% vs. 9.3%) strategies, as well as a decrease in the use of "mnemotechniques", "reference materials", "copying" and "repetition" with increasing age. It is also worth noting, that at this data collection time no mention was made of "social strategies' by either of the two groups.

Pronunciation strategies

At T1, we note (Table 9.5) that in the case of two of the strategies, namely, "exposure to input" and "noting down", the percentages reported by Group A (15.7%; 5.2%) are slightly lower than those in Group B (17.1%; 8.5%), which in turn are markedly lower than those observed in Group D, whose subjects reported using these strategies more frequently (24.4%; 18.3%). Similarly, the "use of reference materials" appears to be more popular with the oldest learners (14.2%) as are "practice strategies" (8.1%), the latter being barely mentioned by either of the two younger groups at this time. By contrast, "social strategies" were much more frequent among the younger students, while they were barely mentioned by the group of oldest learners. Likewise, "repetition strategies" were more frequently

Table 9.5 Pronunciation strategies

Strategy types	Time 1			Time 2			Time 3	
	GA	GB	GD	GA	GB	GC	GA	GB
Practice	1 (2.6%)	0	4 (8.1%)	1 (1.2%)	1 (1.2%)	2 (10.5%)	3 (8.8%)	2 (10.5%)
Exposure to input	6 (15.7%)	6 (17.1%)	12 (24.4%)	10 (13%)	12 (14.6%)	10 (66.5%)	15 (44.1%)	10 (66.5%)
Reference materials	2 (5.2%)	1 (2.8%)	7 (14.2%)	4 (5.1%)	3 (3.65%)	2 (10.5%)	1 (2.9%)	2 (10.5%)
Social	11 (30%)	7 (20%)	1 (2%)	19 (24.6%)	15 (18.2%)	0	3 (8.8%)	0
Noting down	2 (5.2%)	3 (8.5%)	9 (18.3%)	2 (2.5%)	10 (12.1%)	3 (15.7%)	3 (8.8%)	3 (15.7%)
Repetition	11 (30%)	15 (42.8%)	8 (16.3%)	33 (42.8%)	33 (40.2%)	2 (10.5%)	5 (14.7%)	2 (10.5%)
Other strategies	5 (13.1%)	3 (8.5%)	9 (18.3%)	8 (10.3%)	8 (9.7%)	0	4 (11.7%)	0
Total counts	38	35	50	77	82	19	34	19

reported by the two younger groups, among whose subjects high proportions reported their use (30 and 42.8%, respectively).

At T2,"repetition strategies" still feature as being quite important among members of the two younger groups, with proportions ranging from 40 to 42%, whereas they were mentioned less frequently by the oldest group (10%). In contrast, this latter group has a clear preference for strategies that involve "exposing oneself to input", as observed by the markedly higher figure reported (66%) compared to those reported by Groups A and B (13% and 14%, respectively). Similarly, Group D also scored higher in the reported use of "practice strategies" – barely mentioned by the other two groups – and in the use of strategies that involve the use of "reference materials". Finally, whereas the use of "social strategies" fell with age, "noting down" followed a reverse pattern.

At T3, an increase in the reported use of "practice", "the use of reference materials", "noting down" and "exposure to input", and a decrease in the frequencies obtained for "social strategies" and "repetition", were observed with age.

Spelling strategies

As shown in Table 9.6, at T1, a steady increase was recorded in the use of strategies that involve "exposure to input" as students grow older (4.5%; 7.5%; 10.3%); "analysis strategies" are also most frequently cited by the group of oldest learners (31%), being barely mentioned by the two younger groups. In contrast, the "use of reference materials" appeared to

Table 9.6 Spelling strategies

Strategy type	Time 1			Time 2			Time 3	
	GA	GB	GD	GA	GB	GD	GA	GB
Analysis	1 (2.2%)	0	9 (31%)	0	0	0	1 (3.7%)	2 (6.8%)
Practice	2 (4.5%)	0	1 (3.4%)	7 (8.3%)	5 (8.7%)	2 (11.7%)	2 (7.4%)	4 (13.7%)
Exposure to input	2 (4.5%)	3 (7.5%)	3 (10.3%)	2 (2.3%)	7 (12.2%)	0	1 (3.7%)	0
Reference materials	12 (27.2%)	7 (17.5%)	2 (6.8%)	26 (30.9%)	12 (21%)	3 (17.5%)	0	2 (6.8%)
Social	3 (6.8%)	6 (15%)	0	6 (7.1%)	3 (5.2%)	0	0	0
Copying	15 (34%)	13 (32.5%)	9 (31%)	26 (31%)	18 (31.5%)	9 (52.9%)	12 (44.4%)	11 (37.9%)
Repetition	7 (16%)	10 (25%)	3 (10.3%)	14 (16.6%)	11 (19.2%)	1 (5.8%)	4 (14.8%)	3 (10.3%)
Other strategies	2 (4.5%)	1 (2.5%)	2 (6.8%)	2 (3.5%)	5 (8.7%)	2 (11.7%)	7 (26%)	7 (4.1%)
Total counts	44	40	29	83	61	17	27	29

lose popularity with increasing age (27%; 17.5%; 6.8%), while "social strategies" were not even reported by the oldest students. The proportions of "copying strategies" remained constant across the three groups (ranging from 31 to 34%) and "repetition strategies" were, once again, reported as being most frequently used by Group B members (25%).

At T2, "copying strategies" were the most frequently reported across the three age groups, but they were considerably more popular among Group D members (53%) than among those in the other two groups (31 and 31.5%, respectively). Reports of the use of strategies that involve the "use of reference materials" and "social strategies" became less frequent with increasing age. The reported use of strategies of "repetition" and "exposure to input" peaked among the students in Group B, while reports of "practice strategies" were highest among the oldest group of learners (Group D).

At T3, "copying" was still a very important strategy for both Group A (44%) and B (38%) students, while a slight decrease was recorded in their use of "repetition" and "exposure to input". By contrast, "analysis", "practice" and the "use of reference materials" underwent a slight increase from Group A to B.

Sentence writing strategies

Strategies that involve "using a model" to write sentences feature as the most frequently cited strategy by all three groups at T1 (see Table 9.7), particularly among the youngest learners (52%), who reported using them in higher proportions than those in Group B (26%) and Group D (27%). In contrast, the "use of studying" appears to increase progressively with age (9%; 18.5%; 37.8%). Finally, a non-linear pattern of development was recorded across the three age groups in their use of "social", "exposure to input" and

Table 9.7 Sentence writing strategies

Strategy type	Time 1			Time 2			Time 3	
	GA	GB	GD	GA	GB	GD	GA	GB
Studying	4 (9%)	5 (18.5%)	14 (37.8%)	11 (19.2%)	8 (14.5%)	6 (42.8%)	2 (6.8%)	6 (28.5%)
Practice	5 (11.3%)	2 (5.4%)	5 (13.5%)	4 (7%)	2 (3.6%)	5 (35.7%)	0	6 (28.5%)
Exposure to input	3 (6.8%)	3 (11%)	2 (5.4%)	2 (3.5%)	3 (5.4%)	0	1 (3.4%)	1 (4.7%)
Use of a model	23 (52.2%)	7 (26%)	10 (27%)	24 (42.1%)	24 (49%)	0	19 (65.5%)	5 (23.8%)
Social	1 (2.2%)	5 (18.5%)	1 (2.7%)	4 (7%)	4 (7.2%)	0	0	0
Other strategies	8 (18.1%)	5 (18.5%)	5 (13.5%)	12 (8.7%)	11 (20%)	3 (21.4%)	7 (24.1%)	3 (14.2%)
Total counts	44	27	37	57	52	14	29	21

"practice" strategies, since the reported frequencies of use by Group B members clearly deviated from those observed in the other two groups.

At T2, there was a marked contrast in the strategies reported by the oldest learners (Group D), on the one hand, and those described by members of the other two groups (Groups A and B), on the other. Thus, while the "use of a model" for sentence writing was the most popular strategy reported by Group A (42%) and, even more markedly so, by Group B (49%), this was not the case for Group D. Likewise the oldest students did not report using "social strategies" or "exposure to input", while the other two groups did. Indeed, Group D members predominantly reported the use of two strategies – "studying" (43%) and "practicing" (37%), which were used in much lower proportions by members of the two younger groups.

At T3, the "use of models" was reported as being used considerably more frequently by Group A (65%) than by Group B (24%). In contrast, Group B shows higher percentages in the use of "studying" (28.5%) and "practicing" strategies (28.5%), which were barely mentioned by Group A.

Discussion of the Cross-sectional Results

An analysis of the data reveals a complex scenario of strategy use, in which some strategies clearly follow a developmental pattern across the three age groups, others point to similarities between the two oldest or the two youngest groups, while for others we discern a fairly irregular pattern across the three groups. Furthermore, these patterns are not always systematic across the three time points, which shows that as students advance from one learning stage to another, some of the differences that were apparent at an earlier time may disappear, and their reported strategic behaviours become more similar to those observed in the older or younger group. Thus, this section presents the various patterns that can be identified after comparing the frequencies of strategy uses mentioned by each of the groups at the different data collection times.

Strategies that show a linear pattern across the three groups[7]

Some of our findings suggest a linear association between strategy use and age, with six strategies becoming more predominant with age and two becoming less so. Hence, after receiving the same number of hours of instruction, the older the students, the higher were the reported frequencies of "analysis" (T1 and T2), "mnemotechniques" (T1) and "classifying" (T1) strategies for recording vocabulary; "noting down" for pronunciation (T1 and T2), "exposure to input" for learning spelling (T1), and "studying grammar" for sentence writing (T1). Among the strategies that showed a fall in use with age were the use of "social strategies" for vocabulary learning (T1 and T2), pronunciation (T1 and T2) and spelling (T2), and those that involve the use of "reference materials" for learning vocabulary (T2) and spelling (T1, T2).

Taken together, these results show, in line with those observed elsewhere (Kojic-sabo & Lightbown, 1999; Oxford, 1989), that with increasing age, students make greater use of more cognitively demanding strategies, such as analysing, classifying, studying and using mnemotechniques, all of which require a higher degree of elaboration on the part of the learner than simple memorisation strategies. The increased use of these strategies would seem to be indicative, following Brown and Palincsar (1982), of a growth in cognitive maturation and natural development. Likewise, as the subjects in our study became older, they also seemed to become more aware of the need to expose themselves to different types of input, as a means of improving their pronunciation and word spelling. On the other hand, younger learners seem to be more dependent on the use of external sources, such as reference materials and friends or relatives who can provide clarification, or on working together, a finding further supported by Zimmerman and Martinez-Pons (1990) who observed a significant decline in students' reliance on adult assistance between the 8th and 11th grades. Overall, these findings seem to parallel those observed in our previous study (Victori & Tragant, 2003), in which similar differences were identified with 11, 14 and 18-year-olds. Yet, whereas in the former study these differences could not be attributed exclusively to age variation, here, the number of hours of instruction was constant across the groups, which serves as a stronger indication that strategic variation may be attributed to differences in the subjects' age.

Strategies that show variation in one of the groups

For some of the strategies reported, differences only appear to exist in the reported uses of one of the groups of learners with the other two presenting similar results. Three different patterns can be identified here. First, the frequencies reported by the youngest learners (Group A) clearly differ from those reported by members of the two older groups (Groups B and D). Thus, greater proportions of younger learners report using "copying" and "social" strategies (at T1) for vocabulary learning. A more frequent pattern is that in which the frequencies reported by learners in Groups A and B are higher than the frequency reported by Group D members. This was the case of the use of "reference materials" (T1) for improving vocabulary and "repetition" for improving pronunciation (T2), both of which are not very commonly reported strategies in the oldest group. Finally, the reverse is observed for several strategies, whereby Group D members report much higher frequencies than those reported by Groups A and B. This was the case of the use of "mnemotechniques" (T2), "practice strategies" (T1 and T2), "exposure to input" (T1 and T2), and the use of "reference materials" (T1 and T2) for improving pronunciation;

"studying" (T2) for improving grammar; and "analysing" (T1) and "copying" (T2) for improving spelling.

These three patterns would seem to suggest that certain strategies may not develop progressively with age, but rather they start being used, or fall into disuse, at a specific age. Indeed, certain strategies are reported as being used in high percentages by Group D as early as T1, a phenomenon that is not observed with the two younger groups, which do not start using these strategies until a later time and then increase their use progressively. This is the case of "mnemotechniques" and "analysing" for learning vocabulary and spelling; "noting down" for improving pronunciation; and "studying" and "practicing" for learning grammar. This shows, that for these strategies, at least, age is a markedly more important factor than the amount of instruction received. Finally, the fact that more similarities are observed between the reported strategy use of Groups A and B at T2 (up to 20 instances of similar percentages obtained by the two groups) than at T1 (just 11 instances) seems to suggest that between the ages of 11 and 13 (corresponding to T1) more differences can be expected in the reported strategies of these groups of learners than between the ages of 13 and 15 (corresponding to T2), when strategic behaviours seem to become more similar.

Strategies that show other patterns of development

A final, albeit smaller, group of strategies was identified here that do not seem to follow any logical pattern of development – oral repetition strategies being the most obvious example. Thus, when comparing strategies across the three groups and times of data collection, the reported percentage proportions of this strategy use in Group A and Group D were lower than the corresponding percentage reported by Group B; a similar pattern was observed for learning vocabulary (T1, T2), pronunciation (T1) and spelling (T1, T2). Similarly, we observed that "practice" strategies for improving sentence writing (T1, T2) and strategies that involve "exposure to input" (T1) were reported in lower proportions in Group B. The fact that these patterns were observed at more than one data collection time raises many questions concerning the resulting curvilinear relationship between these particular strategies and the age factor: why do certain strategies become more prominent particularly with the learners of Group B? and why do other strategies become less prominent? The fact that such irregular patterns have been noted elsewhere (Ehrman & Oxford, 1995; Gardner *et al.*, 1997; Green & Oxford, 1995; Philips, 1990, cited in Lan & Oxford, 2003; Yamamori *et al.*, 2003) suggests that more research should be undertaken into this area.

Longitudinal Results

In our longitudinal study, a quantitative analysis of the data will first be presented, followed by a qualitative analysis. The former involves quantifying the extent to which students actually answered the questions posed at each time of data collection. This analysis should show whether these longitudinal subjects are better able to describe their learning processes as they grow older. The qualitative analysis, on the other hand, seeks to describe changes in the nature of the strategies that students mentioned over time. Data for this longitudinal analysis are drawn from learners from Group A, who were aged 10;9, 12;9 and 16;9 at T1, T2 and T3 of the data collection respectively, and Group B learners, who were aged 12;9 and 14;9 at T1 and T2 respectively. The quantitative analysis for Group A includes the subjects for whom information was gathered at the three times of data collection ($n = 44$),[8] whereas the qualitative analysis is based on the whole subsample ($n = 48$). Both the quantitative and qualitative analyses for Group B are based on a subsample of 38 learners.

Quantitative results

In our quantitative analysis of the four questions posed to Group A, five patterns have been identified according to whether students answered these questions at the three data collection points. In Table 9.8, Patterns B and C represent those students who showed some progression in their answers: these include students who did not answer at T1 and T2 but did so at T3 (Pattern B), as well as students who did not answer at T1 but did so at T2 and T3 (Pattern C). Pattern A represents students who failed to respond at any of the three times and Pattern D those who answered on each occasion. Pattern E, under the heading of "other patterns", represents those students who showed some type of regression or an irregular evolution in their answers over time. Examples of these patterns are: providing an answer at T1 and not at T2 and T3 or providing an answer at T2 but not at T1 and T3.

If the responses across the four questions included in Table 9.8 (Group A) are totalled, it can be observed (see last column) that in more than 60% of the cases analysed students either answered at the three times of data collection (Pattern D, 12.5%) or answered progressively more questions over time (Patterns B and C, 19.9% and 25% respectively). About 40% of the remaining cases correspond to students who did not answer at any of the three times of data collection (Pattern A, 17%) as well as to cases showing a regressive pattern (Pattern E, 25.6%). The frequencies for Pattern A are comparatively high in respect to the question concerning sentence writing and distinctively low in the case of vocabulary, while the frequencies for Pattern E are lowest in respect to the questions concerning spelling and pronunciation.

Similar conclusions can be drawn from the analysis of the answers given by Group B students as shown in Table 9.9, where almost 60% either answered at both data collection times (Pattern D, 32.9%) or answered progressively more (Pattern B, 27%), although there was a considerably

Table 9.8 Patterns of questions answered at T1, T2 and T3 by Group A

	Voc. (n = 44) F (%)	Pron. (n = 44) F (%)	Spelling (n = 44) F (%)	Sentence writing (n = 44) F (%)	Total (n = 176) F (%)
A. Students who never answer	2 (4.5%)	7 (15.9%)	6 (13.6%)	15 (34.1%)	30 (17%)
B. Students who answer at T3	7 (15.9%)	10 (22.7%)	8 (18.2%)	10 (22.7%)	35 (19.9%)
C. Students who answer at T2 and T3	13 (29.6%)	11 (25%)	15 (34.1%)	5 (11.4%)	44 (25%)
D. Students who answer at T1, T2 and T3	6 (13.6%)	7 (15.9%)	6 (13.6%)	3 (6.8%)	22 (12.5%)
E. Other patterns	16 (36.4%)	9 (20.5%)	9 (20.5%)	11 (25%)	45 (25.6%)

higher proportion of students (Pattern A, 40%) who failed to answer the questions both at T1 and T2. As in Group A, these non-responses were found mainly in the question concerning sentence writing and, to a lesser extent, in the question about vocabulary learning.

In sum, whereas there is a considerable proportion of students, regardless of their age, in both Groups A and B who were either unable to report any strategies or who failed to demonstrate any changes in this ability over time, a large proportion of our longitudinal subjects were able to report the strategies they use from as early as T1 (ages 10;9 and 12;9 for Groups A and B respectively) or were able to report more strategies as they grew older and received more hours of instruction. These results show that in most cases the metacognitive skills that enable students to explain how they go about learning English develop continuously throughout their secondary

Table 9.9 Patterns of questions answered at T1 and T2 by Group B[a]

	Voc. (n = 38) F (%)	Pron. (n = 38) F (%)	Spelling (n = 38) F (%)	Sentence writing (n = 38) F (%)	Total (n = 152) F (%)
A. Students who never answer	6 (15.8%)	9 (23.7%)	9 (23.7%)	16 (42.2%)	40 (26.3%)
B. Students who answer at T2	15 (39.5%)	11 (28.8%)	7 (18.5%)	8 (21%)	41 (27%)
D. Students who answer at T1 and T2	14 (36.8%)	11 (28.9%)	14 (36.8%)	11 (28.9%)	50 (32.9%)
E. Other patterns (students who answer at T1 but not at T2)	3 (7.9%)	7 (18.5%)	8 (21%)	3 (7.9%)	21 (13.8%)

Note: [a] Unlike Table 9.1, there is no Pattern C in this table because there is not a T3 of data collection for this group education, although we found considerable variability in metacognitive awareness among students of the same age.

Qualitative results

The qualitative analysis was carried out by comparing individual students' answers at T1 and T2 in Groups A and B, as well as those at T2 and T3 in Group A. Answers at T1 and T3 were only compared in the case of those students who did not provide an answer at T2. Because some students did not answer all the questions, the total number of pairs of strategies under study will vary depending on the particular area of language learning or skill.

In our analysis of the question concerning vocabulary learning, in which the number of pairs of strategies analysed was 45, there were 18 cases where the same, or a similar strategy, was mentioned at two data collection times. Of the remaining 27 cases, a change in strategy towards a qualitatively different way of learning was recorded in 18 instances. In all these cases, students first mentioned specific observable actions for dealing with vocabulary (that is, "the use of the dictionary", "asking another person", "copying" and "repeating words") and at a later stage referred to less overt or more creative ways of dealing with vocabulary ("revising word lists", "memorization", "studying", "word association", "comparison with the L1" and "sentence writing"). Two representative illustrations of this type of change are provided by Examples 9.1 and 9.2 (note that translations of students' answers into English are provided within brackets and in italics). Of the remaining nine cases, in seven there was a change either from "the use of dictionaries and class notes" to "copying" or "repeating words" or vice versa.

In our analysis of the question concerning pronunciation, from a total of 38 pairs of strategies mentioned, we recorded 11 instances in which the same, or a very similar, strategy was mentioned at two data collection times. There were a further 18 instances in which we recorded a change

Example 9.1 Student 21 (Group A)

T1	T2	T3
	Diccionari. (*The dictionary*)	Les memoritzo unes quantes vegades. (*I memorise them several times*)

Example 9.2 Student 12 (Group B)

T1	T2	T3
Busco al diccionari. (*I use the dictionary*)	Intento former frases (*I try to make sentences*)	

towards a qualitatively different type of strategy. In half of these cases, the move was from strategies involving "self-repetition" and "asking for repetition" to strategies focusing on listening (to music, to others, to cassettes, or a general reference to "repeated listening" in class or outside class) (see Example 9.3, T1→T2). The other nine cases involved either a move towards a more systematic or analytical type of pronunciation strategy ("the use of the annotation of pronunciation" or "the looking for features in common with the students' L1") (see Example 9.3, T2→T3), or a move towards largely metacognitive types of resource ("the use of intuition", "trying to remember if you've heard the word in the past", "self-correction") (see Example 9.4). In the remaining 9 pairs of strategies from the total of 38, no pattern of change could be discerned.

Example 9.3 Student 30 (Group A)

T1	T2	T3
Pronunciant-les sense parar. *(Pronouncing them non-stop)*	Escoltar música *(Listening to music)*	Miro les últimes planes del llibre. *(I look up the last pages in the textbook)*

Example 9.4 Student 43 (Group A)

T1	T2	T3
	Preguntar-ho al professor. *(I ask the teacher)*	Recordar si la paraula ja l'he sentit pronunciada. *(Thinking about whether I have heard the word being pronounced before)*

In our analysis of the question concerning the learning of spelling, in which 41 pairs of references to strategies were analysed, 13 instances were identified where the same, or a very similar strategy, was mentioned at two data collection times. Ten of these involved the strategy of "copying the word" or a more general reference to "studying" or "memorization". There were another 13 instances in which there was a change towards a qualitatively different type of strategy. This change tended to involve a move from a less sophisticated strategy involving "memorization" or the use of an outside resource ("dictionary" or "asking someone") towards strategies that require the learner to adopt a more active role ("practice with dictations", "comparison with other words", "spelling of words out loud") (see Example 9.5), an explicit focus on form ("trying to remember spelling", "paying attention to words") (see Example 9.6) and a more advanced-level learner strategy ("learning by reading"). Of the remaining 15 instances, 10 of them involved a move from the use of an outside resource ("dictionaries", "asking the teacher") and "the study of spelling" to the "copying of words".

Example 9.5 Student 31 (Group A)

T1	T2	T3
	Escriure-les uns quants cops *(Writing them several times)*	Comparar amb altres paraules angleses que s'escriguin semblant *(Comparing with other English words that are written in a similar way)*

Example 9.6 Student 27 (Group B)

T1	T2
Me les llegeixo i les escric en un full a part quan me les sé. *(I read them and when I know them I write them on a separate sheet of paper)*	Fixar-me en com s'escriuen i escric alguna redacció. *(I pay attention to how to write them and I write some compositions)*

In our analysis of the 27 pairs of references to strategies concerning sentence writing, there were 6 instances in which the same, or a similar type of, strategy was mentioned (see Example 9.7, T2→T3). Of the remaining 21 cases, a move towards a different, more sophisticated type of strategy was observed in 15 cases. These included a move from "repetition", "studying" or "asking someone" to the use of strategies that help simplify the task of writing, such as "the use of translation", "the application of grammar rules" and "the use of short sentences and example sentences" (see Example 9.7, T1→T2). There were also instances of moves towards "the use of memorization" and "the studying of grammar". Two qualitative changes were found: the first involved a move from a strategy at the sentence level to one at the textual level, while the second involved a move from "the use of dictionaries" to "the use of revising" when writing. In the remaining six cases, no clear pattern of change was identified (see Example 9.8).

By way of summarising the findings reported in this section, the above analysis presented in terms of frequencies is reported in percentages in Table 9.10. Here, the results from the four questions under study have been totalled in a separate column. In this column (labelled "total questions"), it

Example 9.7 Student 45 (Group A)

T1	T2	T3
Copiant-les i repetint-les. *(I copy them and repeat them)*	Primer la dic en castellà i després la repeteixo en anglès. *(First I say them in Spanish and then I repeat them in English)*	Primer ho escric o penso en català i després ho escric. *(First I write it or think in Catalan and then I write it)*

Example 9.8 Student 28 (Group B)

T1	T2
Dir-les a una germana. *(I say them to a sister)*	Aprendre-les de memòria. *(To learn them by heart)*

can be seen that, out of a total of 151 pairs of strategies under comparison, in 31.8% a repetition of strategy type occurred from an earlier stage to a later one; moves without any pattern account for 25.8% of the pairs; and, most importantly, in 42.4% of the pairs under analysis a patterned move – one that shows a developmental change – was detected from one data collection time to another. In many cases, such patterned moves tend to involve a shift from a limited range of strategy types that are similar in all four areas (typically involving "repetition" or "copying", "the use of the dictionary" and "asking others") to a wider range of strategies (involving mostly cognitive strategies such as "analysis", "practice", "exposure to the L2" but also some metacognitive strategies such as "revision"). These strategies tend to be more sophisticated in terms of their cognitive demands, requiring students to take a more active part and to call on their creative and analytical skills, most of which are not amenable to observation.

Table 9.10 Qualitative analysis of pairs of strategies

	Voc. F (%)	Pron. F (%)	Spelling F (%)	Sentence writing F (%)	Total questions F (%)
Same or similar strategy	18 (40%)	11 (28.9%)	13 (31.7%)	6 (22.2%)	48 (31.8%)
Patterned moves	18 (40%)	18 (47.4%)	13 (31.7%)	15 (55.6%)	64 (44.4%)
Unpatterned moves	9 (20%)	9 (23.7%)	15 (36.6%)	6 (22.2%)	39 (25.8%)
Pairs of strategies compared: total	45 (100%)	38 (100%)	41 (100%)	27 (100%)	151 (100%)

Discussion of the Longitudinal Results

The present study has allowed us to confirm aspects of strategy use that have been described in the few previous longitudinal studies to have been carried out to date. For example, stability in strategy use was noted in Chamot et al.'s four-semester study (1988), a trait that was also evident in our data both in students who reported the same number of strategies at T1, T2 and T3, as well as in those who reported using similar strategies over time. Exceptions to this more common trend of change were also present in our results, particularly if we take into consideration those students reporting fewer strategies over time and others that mentioned using less mature strategies as they grew older. This is another common finding that has been pointed out in earlier studies involving university students (Chamot et al., 1988), high-school learners (Yamamori et al., 2003) and children (Chesterfield & Chesterfield, 1985).

Nevertheless, what comes out most clearly from the present analysis is the fact that for a considerable number of learners there was an observable progress in their reported strategy use, either in the number, or in the nature, of strategies reported or both. As these learners grew older they were able to report more strategies, showing therefore, at the same time, an increase in metacognitive awareness. Similarly, a good proportion of the learners reported a wider range of behaviours over time, including more sophisticated strategies. An increase in strategy use or a progression in the range of strategies has been previously reported in case studies (Carson & Longhini, 2002) and studies involving small samples (Chamot et al., 1988; Chesterfield & Chesterfield, 1985). However, taking into account the larger sample size used in the present study, as well as the variety of age groups involved, it seems fair to conclude that the growth in strategic use portrayed in the data can be considered a fairly common trait for a reasonable proportion of the population.

Conclusions

This study was set up to investigate two main questions: first, whether any differences could be identified in the strategies reported by EFL learners of different ages but who had received the same number of hours of instruction; and, second, whether any developmental changes in strategy use could be traced in a group of learners over an extended period of time. Our cross-sectional and longitudinal data provide evidence in support of both questions, since the learners in different age groups presented a variation in their strategy use within and across the different data collection times. Our study suggests, therefore, that learners tend to undergo developmental changes in strategy use as they increase in age, regardless of their level of proficiency or learning stage. These changes, however, are not systematic for all learning strategy types, nor do they always show a linear association with age. Thus, we should be cautious when generalising or making claims about strategy variation and age beyond the findings presented in this section.

Based on our results, at early ages there seems to be a marked tendency to use learner strategies that depend on external sources, such as the "use of reference materials" and "social" strategies (mainly, asking, or studying with, friends or relatives), This tendency becomes less marked as learners get older and more autonomous in their learning approach. Similarly, at early ages, there seems to be a strong dependence on the use of "repetition" and other "memorization" strategies that involve a simple rehearsal of the words to be learnt. Whereas these strategies remain important for all age groups and at different stages of learning, our cross-sectional data suggest that older students exhibit a wider repertoire of strategies from the very beginning of their learning and make use of more complex and elaborated strategies that involve "mental associations", "inferencing", "classifying", "analysis" as well as a wider "exposure to input" in the L2. These results find further support in our longitudinal data in which we noted a clear move from a more limited range of strategies at an early stage to a wider and more sophisticated range at a later stage.

The fact that more complex strategies are rarely observed in the group of younger learners during their early stages of learning suggests that strategy variation might be directly associated with the learners' age, regardless of their proficiency level or the number of hours of instruction received. This being the case, we could then speculate that strategic development may be governed by a natural order of acquisition, as has been pointed out elsewhere (Chesterfeld & Chesterfeld, 1985). While extensive research is needed in order to analyse this question more rigorously, the following additional findings, derived from our study, show how complex this question is.

First, while developmental changes in strategy use can be identified in learners from different age groups, these changes do not always seem to follow a linear association with age. Our cross-sectional data showed different patterns of development, so that while for some strategies only the frequencies reported for the youngest or the eldest group differed markedly from those observed in the other two groups, for others, a curvilinear pattern was sometimes observed for some strategies, albeit less frequently. On the whole, our data seem to indicate that more changes in strategic use are to be expected in learners aged 11 to 13 than in learners aged from 13 to 15. This may suggest that the aforementioned progress, or shift towards more complex strategies, precedes the onset of adolescence, an important finding that would also require further investigation.

Furthermore, our cross-sectional and longitudinal findings also suggest that students' reported use of strategies varies depending on the skill under investigation. Hence, learners appear to be more aware of the strategies they use when recalling the meaning, pronunciation and spelling of vocabulary and less so when being asked about their writing strategies, a finding that has been described elsewhere (Kellerman, 1991). While this differing degree of awareness may be due to the learners' familiarity with specific skills, as well as to the types of classroom practices to which they have been exposed (De Prada, 1993), it is also an indication that the learners' domains of perceived strategic knowledge that they develop when learning a language may not develop homogenously for all skills. This is certainly another important aspect that should be borne in mind in future studies that seek to analyse the developmental changes in strategic use among learners of different ages.

Bearing in mind the aforementioned aspects, we would like to conclude by suggesting some of the directions in which future research should be conducted. First, we feel it is essential that future studies should strive to combine cross-sectional and longitudinal data so as to provide a wider picture of strategic behaviour over time. Likewise, drawing on large samples of data, as we have done here, is another element that we would like to recommend to make findings more robust. Finally, the use of either structured instruments of data collection or qualitative techniques to elicit strategy use, such as interviews, think-aloud protocols or diaries, are needed to further validate the present findings.

Acknowledgements

The study was funded by grants from the Spanish Ministerio de Educación y Cultura (grant no. PB94-0944, grant no. PB97-0901 and grant no. BFF2001-3384). We would also like to express our appreciation to Sara Feijoo and M. del Mar Suárez for their help with the preparation of this chapter.

Notes

1. These results may have been influenced by the methodological caveats encountered in the study as the interviews with the beginner groups were conducted in the students' first language, while those with the intermediate group were conducted in English.
2. According to Chaudron (2003), in order to be able to establish causality, statistical techniques other than those used previously are required.
3. Students from Group C (AoO = 14) were not included in the sample as the number of valid students (that is, only school exposure students) was too low for this type of study.
4. The youngest group of students started learning English at an earlier age than the students in the other two groups because the former studied under a new education system (LOGSE) in which FL instruction was introduced at an earlier age than in the previous system (EGB); see Chapter 1.
5. A subsample of 38 longitudinal students from Group B (T1 and T2) was analysed in Victori and Tragant (2003). No longitudinal students were available at T3 in this subsample. Note, an insufficient number of subjects were available in Groups C and D.

6. Inter-rater reliability was calculated using simple percentage agreement.
7. As the objective in this discussion is to compare the three groups' reported strategies, only the frequencies obtained at T1 and T2 will be considered, given that at T3 data was only gathered from Groups A and B, though not D. Results obtained at this time are reported in section 4.1.
8. For three of four students, data was only available at T1 and T2 and for the other student, data was only available from T2 and T3.

References

Bremner, S. (1999) Language learning strategies and language proficiency: Investigating the relationship in Hong Kong. *The Canadian Modern Language Review*, 55 (4), 490–514.

Brown, A.L. and Palincsar, A.S. (1982) Inducing strategic learning from texts by means of informed, self-control training. In D.K. Reig and W.P. Hresko (eds) *TL & LD: Metacognition and Learning Disabilities* 2 (1), 1–18. Rockville: Aspen Publications.

Carson, J.G. and Longhini, A. (2002) Focusing on learning styles and strategies: A diary study in an immersion setting. *Language Learning* 52 (2), 401–438.

Chamot, A.U. and El-Dinary, P.B. (1999) Children's learning strategies in language immersion classrooms. *The Modern Language Journal* 83 (3), 319–338.

Chamot, A.U., Küpper, L. and Impink-Hernández, M.V. (1988) *A Study of Language Learning Strategies in Foreign Language Instruction: Findings from the Longitudinal Study*. McLean, VA: Interstate Research Associates.

Chamot, A.U., O'Malley, J.M., Küpper, L. and Impink-Hernández, M.V. (1987) *A Study of Learning Strategies in Foreign Language Instruction: First Year Report*. Rosslyn, VA: Interstate Research Associates.

Chaudron, C. (2003) *Learner Strategies*. Review paper commissioned by the Diagnostic Assessment Procedure Project, the Center for Advanced Language Studies, University of Hawai'i.

Chesterfield, R. and Chesterfield, K.B. (1985) Natural order in children's use of second language learning strategies. *Applied Linguistics* 6 (1), 45–59.

De Prada, E. (1993) La adquisición de la autonomía en contextos académicos: Introducción a la problemática en el caso de la enseñanza secundaria. In J.L. Otal and M.L. Villanueva (eds) *Primeres Jornades sobre Autoaprenentatge de Llengües* (pp. 125–131). Publicacions de la Universitat Jaume I.

Ehrman, M.E. and Oxford, R.L. (1995) Cognition plus: Correlates of language learning success. *The Modern Language Journal* 79 (1), 67–89.

Gan, Z., Humphreys, G. and Hamp-Lyons, L. (2004) Understanding successful and unsuccessful EFL students in Chinese Universities. *Modern Language Journal* 88 (2), 229–244.

García López, M. (2000) Estrategias de aprendizaje de vocabulario de inglés utilizadas por los estudiantes de secundaria. *Lenguaje y Textos* 15, 61–69.

Gardner, R.C., Tremblay, P.F. and Masgoret, A.M. (1997) Towards a full model of second language learning: An empirical investigation. *The Modern Language Journal* 81 (3), 344–362.

Green, J.M. and Oxford, R.L. (1995) A closer look at learning strategies, L2 proficiency, and gender. *TESOL Quarterly* 29 (2), 261–297.

Grenfell, M. and Harris, V. (1999) *Modern Languages and Learning Strategies. In Theory and Practice*. London: Routledge.

Griffiths, C. (2003) Patterns of language learning strategy use. *System* 31, 367–383.

Gu, Y. (2003) Fine brush and freehand: The vocabulary-learning art of two successful Chinese EFL learners. *TESOL Quarterly* 37 (1), 73–104.

Gu, Y. and Johnson, R.K. (1996) Vocabulary learning strategies and language learning outcomes. *Language Learning* 46 (4), 643–679.
Kellerman, E. (1991) Compensatory strategies in second language research. A critique, a revision, and some (non-)implications for the classroom. In R. Phillipson, E. Kellerman, L. Selinker, M. Sharwood Smith and M. Swain (eds) *Foreign/Second Language Pedagogy*. Clevedon: Multilingual Matters.
Kojic-sabo, I. and Lightbown, P. (1999) Students' approaches to vocabulary learning and their relationship to success. *The Modern Language Journal* 83 (2), 176–192.
Lan, R. and Oxford, R.L. (2003) Language learning strategy profiles of elementary school students in Taiwan. *IRAL* 41, 339–379.
Leeke, P. and Shaw, P. (2000) Learners' independent records of vocabulary. *System* 28, 271–289.
Naiman, M., Fröhlich, M., Stern, H.H. and Todesco, A. (1978) *The Good Language Learner*. Ontario: Institute for Studies in Education.
O'Malley, J.M. and Chamot, A.U. (1990) *Learning Strategies in Second Language Acquisition*. New York: Cambridge University Press.
O'Malley, J.M., Chamot, A.U., Stewner-Manzanares, G., Küpper, L. and Russo, R. (1985) Learning strategies used by beginning and intermediate ESL students. *Language Learning* 35 (1), 21–46.
Oxford, R.L. (1989) Use of language learning strategies: A synthesis of studies with implications for strategy training. *System* 17 (2), 235–247.
Oxford, R.L. (1990) *Language Learning Strategies: What Every Teacher Should Know*. Rowley, MA: Newbury House.
Oxford, R.L. and Burry-Stock, J.A. (1995) Assessing the use of language learning strategies worldwide with the ESL/EFL version of the Strategy Inventory for Language Learning (SILL). *System* 23 (2), 1–23.
Oxford, R.L. and Crookall, D. (1989) Research on language learning strategies: Methods, findings, and instructional issues. *The Modern Language Journal* 73 (4), 404–419.
Politzer, L.R. (1983) An exploratory study of self reported language learning behaviours and their relation to achievement. *Studies in Second Language Acquisition* 6, 54–65.
Purdie, N. and Oliver, R. (1999) Language learning strategies used by bilingual school-aged children. *System* 27, 375–388.
Rubin, J. (1975) What the good language learner can teach us. *TESOL Quarterly* 9 (1), 41–51.
Schoonen, R., Hulstijn, J. and Bossers, B. (1998) Metacognitive and language-specific knowledge in native and foreign language reading comprehension: An empirical study among Dutch students in grades 6, 8 and 10. *Language Learning* 48 (1), 71–106.
Stern, H.H. (1975) What can we learn from the good language learner? *The Canadian Modern Language Review* 31 (3), 304–318.
Takeuchi, O. (2003) What can we learn from good foreign language learners? A qualitative study in the Japanese foreign language context. *System* 31, 385–392.
Vandergrift, L. (2003) Orchestrating stretegy use: Toward a model of the skilled second language listener. *Language Learning* 53 (3), 463–496.
Victori, M. and Tragant, E. (2003) Learner strategies: A cross-sectional and longitudinal study of primary and high-school EFL learners. In M.P. García Mayo and M.L. García Lecumberri (eds) *Age and the Acquisition of English as a Foreign Language* (pp. 182–209). Clevedon: Multilingual Matters.
Wharton, G. (2000) Language learning strategy use of bilingual foreign language learners in Singapore. *Language Learning* 50 (2), 203–243.

Yamamori, K., Takamichi, I., Tomohito, H. and Oxford, R.L. (2003) Using cluster analysis to uncover L2 learner differences in strategy use, will to learn and achievement over time. *IRAL* 41, 381–409.

Zimmerman, B.J. and Martinez-Pons, M. (1990) Student differences in self-regulated learning: Relating grade, sex, and giftedness to self-efficacy and strategy use. *Journal of Educational Psychology* 82 (1), 51–59.

Chapter 10
Language Learning Motivation and Age

ELSA TRAGANT

In many countries around the world, both parents and educational institutions have shown an interest in initiating foreign language (FL) instruction in primary school or before. These early experiences seem to have a positive effect on the attitudes and motivation of the children, even if the benefits in terms of their linguistic achievement are not always evident. This is made clear in a report published by CILTR (the Centre for Information on Language Teaching and Research) about reforms and pilot experiences in England (Hawkins, 1996; Satchwell, 1996) and Scotland (Johnstone, 1996) in the last 30 years. Blondin *et al.*'s work (1998) within the framework of the European Union about the learning of languages in kindergarten and primary school in the 1990s confirms this trend. Nevertheless, the real challenge in contexts where foreign languages are introduced early in the life of the primary schoolchild is to be able to sustain the initial positive attitudes that the new language tends to raise in students. Given that most European students learn a foreign language for as long as six to ten years, the question of sustainability is obviously important – as it is in contexts where FL instruction is restricted to one or two sessions a week, with the serious risk that students will have difficulty in seeing any progress over time. In Spain, an educational reform was introduced in the 1990s that brought forward the age at which students began FL instruction by three years, which meant that for a period of time there co-existed in the school system students who had started learning English at the ages of 8 and 11. This unique situation opened up the possibility of a systematic study of the dynamics of language learning motivation over time, a relatively unexplored area of research in second language acquisition (SLA) (Dörnyei, 2001). The present study examines the interplay of motivation and age of onset as well as the development of motivation and motivational orientations as students progress through the educational system. Data from a group of students who started learning English at the age of 18 or later were also included in order to extend the analysis into adulthood.

Motivation and Second Language (L2) Learning
Liking to learn English: change or stability

It has been shown in students from different countries and cultural backgrounds that attitudes towards modern languages in primary school are largely positive (see for example Alabau, 2002; Donato *et al.*, 2000). Nevertheless, the picture becomes more complex as students grow up. Attitudes towards the learning of a foreign language seem to be sensitive to the language that is being learned, and specifically to students' awareness of it as an important life skill. This became evident in Chambers' work (2000) where British students learning German were compared with German students learning English. While at the age of 13 more than three-quarters of the former group (77.3%) said they would not bother learning German if it was not taught at school, the proportion was much lower (33.3%) in the latter group when asked the same question with reference to English. Lamb (2004) also attributes Indonesian students' extremely positive impressions towards learning English in their first year at high school (age 11–12) to their perception of English as a means of acquiring a global identity, though they did not report that learning English in school classrooms was a source of pleasure.

Attitudes also seem to be affected by the age of the learners. As early as 1975, Burstall reported that positive attitudes to French as a school subject tended to decrease after the age of 10/11. A decrease in enthusiasm towards the foreign language at age 11 was also found in an eight-year study conducted in Hungary (Nikolov, 1999) with students who had started learning English at the age of 6. More positive attitudes on the part of the younger learners emerge from a comparison of two national surveys in Spain, one focusing on primary schoolers (Alabau, 2002) and the other on secondary schoolers (González García, 2004). The proportion of the latter who said they "liked learning English" or "liked it a lot" was only 50% in the second year of secondary education (age 13) and remained the same two years later (age 15), compared with a figure of 74% in the last year of primary school. A decrease in motivation with age among Spanish students aged between 10 and 15 was also found in a study conducted in a summer language programme (Masgoret *et al.*, 2001). In Britain, Chambers (2000) reported early enthusiasm for FL instruction when introduced at the age of 11 in secondary school but within two years the interest had waned. In French late immersion programmes in Canada, a similar phenomenon was reported in junior high students who were highly motivated on entering the programme at the age of 12 (MacIntyre *et al.*, 2002) but lost motivation between the ages of 12 and 13 – though not between the ages of 13 and 14. This latter phenomenon had already been observed in previous research on long-term immersion programmes (see for example, Gardner & Smythe, 1975), who found a rebounding of attitudes later in the learning process. Indeed, the pattern may not be limited to immersion programmes since a rebounding of attitudes towards the learning of English is also patent from the comparison of a number of official surveys of students in Spain as a whole and in Catalonia (Bonnet, 2004; Departament d'Ensenyament,

2003; Gil & Alabau, 1997; González García, 2004), where proportions were higher in upper than in lower secondary education.[1]

Conflicting evidence from other studies presents an even more complex picture. Williams *et al.* (2002) found no significant differences concerning "liking" and "desire" between 12- and 14-year-old learners of French and German in England, even though significant differences were found in other subscales. Mixed results were also found by Julkunen and Borzova (1996) who compared students from Russia and Finland aged 12, 14 and 17. Whereas they found practically no age-related differences in motivation in the Russian sample, the 14-year-old Finnish students were clearer less motivated than other age groups. No major variation was identified either by Massey (1986) in a study where the AMTB (Attitude Motivation Test Battery) was administered twice to students aged 11 and 12, first at the end of the school year and then after four weeks of the following school year. However, in this case, the short interval between the first and second measurements may have been the explanation for the lack of variation. In any case, the decline in attitudes towards learning English seems to stop at some point in upper secondary education and stabilises later on: no age-related differences were found by Lasagabaster (2003) in a study involving university students aged 17–50 in the Basque Country.

In spite of the above evidence, it seems that some general patterns can be traced regarding the relationship between "liking" FL learning and age. When FL instruction starts early in primary school there seems to be a decline in the learners' attitudes around the age of 10/11; when most students start a foreign language or enter immersion programmes in secondary school, their initial attitudes are positive but their interest soon wanes. A number of reasons have been proposed to explain these variations over time. One is that there may be a general trend among adolescents in secondary school to view all school subjects negatively. Another explanation is the novelty of the experience, which inflates motivation in the first year of FL instruction or in the first year of an immersion programme. A third explanation is that educational practices become less motivating (i.e. feedback becomes more negative, the teaching approaches are less dynamic) as students progress through school.

The interaction between language learning attitudes and age can also be studied in educational contexts that allow for a systematic comparison of students who started learning a second or foreign language at different ages. Experiences with different models of immersion programmes in Canada have made a great contribution to this area, where the higher motivation among students who began the programme earlier seems to be the cause for lower drop out rates (Reid & Fouillard, 1982). In Spain, a change in the age of introduction of English in the educational reform of 1993 (from the age of 11 to the age of 8) offered another chance to analyse the interplay between language learning attitudes and age. To date, two studies of the issue have been carried out in two bilingual regions in Spain. In Catalonia, Tragant and Muñoz (2000; Muñoz & Tragant, 2001) compared two groups of students who had started English at the age of 8 (after 200 and 416 hours of instruction) with three groups of students who had been introduced into English at the age of 11 (after 200, 416 and 726 hours of instruction respectively). Based on a single question that asked students whether they liked learning/studying English, the answers showed that the introduction of English at the age of 8 or 11 did not have a significant influence on motivation.

In the Basque Country, the progressive introduction of English as a third language at an even earlier age (4) in many Basque schools has offered an equally interesting setting for the analysis of the effect of age on language learning attitudes. In Cenoz's work (2004), a school where Basque is used as the language of instruction provided the setting for a comparison of groups of primary and secondary school students who had started their English classes at three different ages (4, 8 and 11) after 500, 600 and 700 hours of instruction inside the same bilingual programme. In contrast to the study conducted in Catalonia (Muñoz & Tragant, 2001; Tragant & Muñoz, 2000), the author found a trend towards more positive attitudes in students who had started learning English at the age of 4. The difference was not so marked when comparing the levels of motivation in students who had started at the age of 8 with those who had started at the age of 11. These findings were based on students' answers to 13 Likert-format items to measure motivation and to eight Osgood-format prompts to measure attitudes towards English.

The study of the interaction between age and different types of orientation offers further insights into this area. In Nikolov's longitudinal study (1999), 6–8-year-old children in Hungary who were asked about their experience of learning English often mentioned teacher-related aspects. In contrast, from the age of 8 on these children tended to look ahead to the future and, therefore, their answers were of an utilitarian type, especially in the group of 11–14-year-olds. A deterioration with age of the evaluation of the instruction was also observed among students in Catalonia in three large-scale surveys involving students aged 11, 13, 15 and 17 (Departament d'Ensenyament, 2003), as well as in Julkunen's work (1989) involving 12- and 14-year-old Finnish students. In the context of Catalonia, whereas, at the age of 10, 74.2% of students valued the learning situation favourably, the percentage gradually fell (to 58% at the age of 13 and to 50.1% at the age of 15) reaching low percentages among the oldest learners (34.1%). As in Nikolov's work, utilitarian motives (learning English to meet people, to travel, for future study) also obtained very high scores at the age of 11 (ranging from 89.4% to 92.2%) and remained high in the other age groups. In contrast, the students' response to the statement "Learning English is easy" got the lowest scores in all age groups. Positive responses decreased with age: while, at the age of 11, 50% of students agreed with the statement, the percentage gradually fell, reaching its lowest figure at the age of 17 (34.1%). The interaction between age and type of orientation was also analysed in another major study involving adult English as a second language (ESL) learners in Egypt (Schmidt *et al.*, 1996), where a significant relationship was found with a factor called "expectancy". This factor, which at the positive end of the dimension included statements of success, determination, confidence and positive thinking, increased with age. However, no significant main effects were found for the other two factors in the study, "enjoyment of learning English" and "goal orientation".

Motivation and L2 achievement

Compelling as the interaction between motivation and age seems to be, it has not been researched in as much depth as the interplay between motivation and achievement, which was in fact one of Gardner and Lambert's main interests in their 1959 study. Work in the 1970s, basically involving bivariate relationships, led Gardner and his colleagues to propose a strong relationship between motivation and achievement (Gardner & Smythe, 1975) and in subsequent research (Gardner, 1979) he showed empirically that the other two components of integrative motivation (that is, integrativeness and attitudes towards the learning situation) had an indirect effect on achievement via the motivation component. Many other studies have obtained significant correlations between motivation and a measure of achievement both when motivation was measured with Gardner's AMTB (1985) and also using other instruments. In the context of Spain, the relationship of motivation and achievement in English has been consistently found with language learners of all age groups, from children as young as 4 (Bernaus *et al.*, 1994) to primary and secondary schoolers (Alabau, 2002; González García, 2004) and university students (Lasagabaster, 2003). Positive relationships have also been obtained in studies involving students from different Spanish autonomous regions, both monolingual (Madrid, 1999) and bilingual (de Prada, 1990; Masgoret *et al.*, 2001; Sans, 2000).

Research carried out in the 1980s and 1990s showed that the relationship between these two variables is a complex one since it has been found to be sensitive to the type of measure used to assess achievement. Students' self-perceptions of achievement in the FL seem to obtain the strongest correlations (Masgoret *et al.*, 2001). Moreover, course grades obtain stronger correlations than objective measures of achievement in the FL/L2 (Gardner *et al.*, 1997), even though these differences are at times only slight. The relationship with motivation is also sensitive to the nature of the test employed to obtain objective measures of achievement, as is evidenced in both Lasagabaster (2003) and Tragant and Muñoz (2000), who found a tendency towards significant correlations in integrative tests but not in discrete-point tests.

In this complex interplay between motivation and outcomes, the role of the learner's age and of the learning experience has been the focus of interest for some researchers. On the one hand, the components of motivation that most influence achievement seem to change as a result of these two factors and, on the other hand, the strength of the relationship seems to change with the passage of time. For example, in younger students in Grades 7 to 9 in Canada the evaluation of the learning situation was the factor that most influenced the decision to stay in or give up a French programme, whereas for older students in Grades 10 and 11 the attitude towards learning other languages was the best predictor of perseverance (Gardner & Smythe, 1975; Gardner et al., 1976). The influence of the learning experience was also analysed by Smit (2002) in university students in Vienna. The study, which explored the relationship between six motivation-related factors at the beginning and end of a pronunciation course, showed that the factors that correlated with the final grades were not the same at the two times of data collection. The strength of the relationship between motivation and achievement as a function of age was the focus of study in Tragant and Muñoz (2000), where four age groups were involved. In their work, a tendency for the interaction with achievement was found to be stronger among the younger learners. A stronger correlation with younger students was also found by Graham (2004), where effort obtained the highest correlations with achievement in the group aged 16 but did not obtain any significant correlations with the groups aged 17 and 18. This decrease in the correlation with age was not identified earlier by Jones (1949) but has been recently confirmed by Masgoret and Gardner (2003) in their meta-analysis of studies conducted by Gardner and associates. Nevertheless, in this major review involving as many as 75 independent samples and 10,489 individuals the authors conclude that even though correlations with elementary students tend to be higher, there is "strong support for the idea that the correlations will largely be positive regardless of age" (2003: 200). This meta-analysis has also produced evidence that the nature of the influence between achievement and motivation is similar in L2 and FL contexts. In addition, it reached the firm conclusion that motivation is more closely related to second language achievement than either attitudes towards the learning situation, integrativeness or integrative and instrumental orientations, even though all five classes of variables related positively to achievement.

Progress in the study of motivation has also been made in the area of its relationship with learning outcomes. By using causal modelling techniques, Gardner et al. (1997) determined how an array of affective variables, including motivation, relates to L2 achievement. This analysis found strong evidence that motivation is the cause of achievement together with language aptitude and language learning strategies, a relationship that had already been found by Gardner in 1985 with the use of a different modelling technique and fewer variables. Results from studies using powerful statistical procedures provide further support to Skehan's tentative conclusion in 1989 that motivation is the cause of achievement. The results also weaken Hermann's (1980) resultative hypothesis according to which it is the degree of success within instruction that determines different degrees of motivational intensity. Skehan's evaluation of the methodological shortcomings of studies such as Burstall (1975), Savignon (1972) and Hermann (1980) further weakens the interpretation of motivation as the result of achievement rather than its cause, even though his perception is that more research, of a longitudinal and ethnographic type, is needed to make a final judgement.

Reasons for L2 learning

As evidenced in the previous section, one of the major contributions of Gardner's concept of "integrative motivation" has been to show its relationship with achievement. Partially because of this leading role of integrative motivation, the concept of "orientation", which refers to reasons for studying a second language, has at the same time become a line of research of its own. Several studies have followed up Gardner's original distinction in the AMTB between integrative and instrumental orientations, with the primary interest of looking into language learning orientations. As a result, an array of other types of orientation has been identified in factor analytical studies. For example, Clément and Kruidener (1983) proposed two additional motives, "travel" and "knowledge", in a study involving a variety of contexts in England and Canada. Julkunen and Borzova's factor analysis (1996), based on teenagers in Finland and Russia, yielded three other factors ("challenge motive", "anxiety factor" and "teacher/method") besides an instrumental and an integrative orientation. Cid *et al.* (2002) made a distinction between two factors that are instrumental in nature, "functional" and "career-oriented", the first one covering the use of English for personal purposes (everyday language, songs, media, tourism, movies) and the latter covering the use of English for future studies and work.

The most important contribution of this focus on orientation lies in the fact that it has helped redefine the concept of integrativeness, which was originally said to involve "emotional identification with another cultural group" (Gardner, 2001: 5). As early as 1983, Clément and Kruidener identified a "friendship" orientation and added that this factor did not refer to an eventual identification with members of the L2 community. A decade later, two other factors ("cultural" and "identification" plus "friendship") were found to be related to an integrative orientation in a study of Hungarian secondary school learners (Clément *et al.*, 1994). But whereas both "cultural" and "identification" factors refer to aspects of the world of English and its speakers, the "friendship" orientation concerns foreigners in general. Today, it seems clear that in contexts where the L2 is basically learned as a school subject, it is more realistic to think of integrativeness within a broader frame of reference. Dörnyei has advocated this wider conception: "we suspect that the motivation dimension captured by the term is not so much related to any actual, or metaphorical, integration into an L2 community as to some more basic identification process within the individual's self-concept" (Dörnyei & Csizér, 2002: 453). According to these authors, such a conception does not conflict with Gardner's original notion but provides a more flexible framework to be applied to a variety of learning contexts. At the same time, it reflects learners' reactions to a world in which English plays a predominant role. Besides, the fact that there are some factorial studies where the distinction between an integrative and an instrumental orientation is not confirmed gives further impetus for a redefinition of the term. Of special interest here are two such studies based on an adaptation of a short version of Gardner's AMTB (the mini-AMTB) involving school-aged students in Catalonia: one in the context of an English summer camp (Masgoret *et al.*, 2001), the other in the context of Spanish/Catalan as a second language (Bernaus *et al.*, 2004). In spite of the different student profiles in the two studies, a single orientation emerged from the factor analysis performed on the two occasions.

In addition, a number of qualitative studies offer data that challenge the existence of an integrative orientation in the context of FL learning. These studies compile data using instruments such as open questions, focus group discussions, essays or semi-structured interviews, sometimes in combination with questionnaires, sometimes not. In two studies carried out in Asian countries, LoCastro (2001) and Lamb (2004) agree that their learners' concerns were predominantly instrumental and derived from a concern for international communication, which grew independently of their national identities and caused no interference. Thus, the students' comments in Lamb were in reference to foreigners and foreign countries in general rather than to a specific English-speaking community. In the same way, LoCastro's students did not feel that their Japanese identities were threatened by English language proficiency. Lamb further noted that motives appeared to be mixed together in the children's answers, which made it very difficult to distinguish the two traditionally distinct constructs of integrative and instrumental orientations. Data from Europe with young learners point in the same direction. Nikolov (1999) notes that attitudes towards speakers of English did not emerge in the data (including students as old as 14) and thus concludes that "no trace of integrative motivation was found in the answers to the open-ended question" (1999: 47), even though the students are reported to have had direct experience with the L2. These results are similar to those obtained in Nikolov's previous work (1996 cited in Nikolov, 1999) involving 13- and 14-year-olds: out of 147 reasons obtained in response to the question of why they studied English, there was only one comment about another culture, while most of the comments referred to intrinsic reasons ("liking the language", "finding it easy"), pragmatic reasons ("English being useful and necessary") as well as to the role of English for international communication. Nor was any trace of an integrative type of orientation present in Chambers' study (2000) of 11-year-old British students of German: most answers can be traced back to intrinsic reasons ("liking or not liking the language", "not being good at languages", "having always wanted to learn languages") as well as to an interest in communication ("ability to talk to other people", "holidays").

There are several possible explanations for the absence of an integrative type of orientation in these studies performed using a bottom-up research methodology. It has often been argued that an integrative orientation may only be characteristic of learners who have experienced prolonged contact with the target culture (Dörnyei, 1990; Oxford & Shearin, 1994). An additional factor might come from the types of instruments that are used in eliciting orientations from students. By using Likert scales, one may be inducing learners to provide responses that they would be unlikely to produce spontaneously in answer to an open question. The result of using structured procedures like this may be that different contexts have been made to appear similar (Lamb, 2004). However, the use of less structured procedures in English as a foreign language (EFL) contexts, as in the studies mentioned above, shows that sometimes the learners' notions of why they are learning a language may not match the categories included in questionnaires originally developed in ESL contexts.

The following sections of this chapter deal with a study of motivation for learning English involving students from primary and secondary education as well as adults in Catalonia, an autonomous region of Spain. The study pays special attention to the possible changes in motivation as a function of age and learning experience.

The Study

The present study, which is part of a larger project about the effects of age in an EFL context, was motivated by a change in the educational system (LOGSE, 1990) which brought forward the age at which pupils started to learn a foreign language in Spain (see Chapter 1). The General Education Act of 1970 had stipulated that a foreign language should be introduced in Grade 6 of primary education (age 11), but according to the new Act foreign language was to begin three years earlier, in the Grade 3 of Primary Education (age 8). So as the new Act was brought in, there coexisted for some time students who had started learning English at the age of 8 alongside others who had started at the age of 11, a situation that allowed us to collect data from students of different ages but the same hours of formal instruction. To be able to further analyse the effects of age in FL learning, data were also collected from students who had started learning English after secondary education (at the age of 18 or later).

The purpose of the study

The first part of the study analyses three types of relationships related to motivation. First, we examine its relation with the hours of instruction received in order to investigate the impact of the learning experience on motivation. We are particularly interested in determining whether the initial motivation that students show in primary education diminishes, increases, or is sustained throughout secondary education. Second, we analyse its relation with the age of onset to establish whether students who started learning English at the age of 8 show higher levels of motivation than those who started at the age of 11. It is also interesting to compare these data with those from students who started learning English at a much later stage (age 18). Finally, we will focus on the interaction of motivation and achievement to determine whether the strength of this interaction is sensitive to the age of the learners or the learning experience. The second part of the study describes the types of orientations as a function of the age of the students and their school grade. Though language learning orientations and attitudes have been studied in some depth in the literature, the interaction with these two factors, age and grade, has not been dealt with systematically.

Subjects

Data were collected from a total number of 2010 students who had started learning English at the ages of 8 (Group A, $N = 1,055$), 11 (Group B, $N = 821$) and 18 or later (Group D, $N = 134$). Out of this total, there were 759 students whose exposure to English had been limited to the classroom at school and who were considered as "valid" for the first part of the study, where it was important to keep the variable "hours of instruction received" constant. The students who were repeaters were excluded for the same reason. The school-aged sample includes 48.8% male and 51.2% female learners, a proportion that remains constant in the subsample of "valid" subjects (47.7% vs. 52.3%). The sample of adults as well as the subsample of "valid" subjects include a higher proportion of female learners (72%). The data from primary and secondary school students come from 27 publicly funded schools located in the city of Barcelona. The pupils present a wide socio-economic and cultural diversity. The data from the older group were gathered from four language schools in Catalonia, three of which are managed by universities and the other one by the regional Department of Education.

Data were collected from subjects after different amounts of classroom instruction (see Table 10.1). For the sample of students who had started learning English at the age of 8 (Group A) data were collected after 200

(Group A1), 416 (Group A2), 726 (Group A3) and 800 (Group A4) hours of instruction. Students' ages at testing for this group were 10;9, 12;9, 16;9 and 17;9 respectively. For the sample of students who had started learning English at the age of 11 (Group B), data were collected after 200 (Group B1), 416 (Group B2) and 726 (Group B3) hours of instruction. Time 3 for this group of students coincided with their last year of high school before they entered university, which is why no data were collected at Time 4. Students' ages at testing for Group B were 12;9, 14;9 and 17;9 for Times 1, 2 and 3 of data collection. Finally, the sample of students who had started learning English at the age of 18 or later (Group D) were assessed after 200 (Group D1) and 416 (Group D2) hours of instruction. Data from this group were also collected at Time 3 within the larger project but will not be analysed in the present study because of the small size of the sample. The same applies for data collected from a group of students who had started learning English at the age of 14 (Group C in the larger project). Students' ages in Group D1 ranged from 19;3 to 49;2, the mean age being 28;9; 75% of the sample were 33 or younger. Students in Group D2 were a little older and their ages ranged from 21;8 to 48;3, the mean age being 31;4; 75% of the sample were 36 or younger. Because of the complexity of the design of the project as well as the fact that some students were followed up longitudinally, it took several years to gather all the data starting in the academic year of 1995–1996 until 2003–2004.

As mentioned above, when comparisons between groups are made to examine the results of the tests as a function of the age of onset or hours of instruction received, subjects who had some exposure outside English class at school were excluded. So the subsample constitutes 37.76% of the total. However, when the objective is to describe the types of orientations, all subjects who completed the questionnaire were included, no matter the

Table 10.1 Design of the study

		Group A AoO = 8		Group B AoO = 11		Group D AoO = 18+
Time 1 200 h	A1	AT = 10;9 N = 284 OSE = 164	B1	AT = 12;9 N = 286 OSE = 107	D1	AT = 28;9 N = 91 OSE = 67
Time 2 416 h	A2	AT = 12;9 N = 278 OSE = 140	B2	AT = 14;9 N = 240 OSE = 105	D2	AT = 31;4 N = 44 OSE = 21
Time 3 726 h.	A3	AT = 16;9 N = 338 OSE = 71	B3	AT = 17;9 N = 296 OSE = 58		
Time 4 800 h	A4	AT = 17;9 N = 155 OSE = 32				

Notes: AoO = age of onset; AT = age at testing; OSE = Only schoool exposure.

amount of exposure received. This procedure was deemed valid after checking that the results were not affected. In addition, the wide range of categories obtained made it necessary to be able to deal with as many subjects per category as possible.

Instruments and method

A questionnaire was completed by all subjects during class time, together with a battery of language tests to measure their competence in English: a dictation (50 words), a cloze (30 gaps), a multiple choice grammar test (25 items with three responses each) and an oral comprehension test (30 stimuli and sets of 3 pictures). In addition to the questions on students' motivation, the questionnaire included a number of biographical questions about their parents' jobs, their use of Catalan and Spanish (the two official languages in Catalonia), and exposure to English and learning strategies (see Tragant & Victori, this volume).

The present study focuses on the analysis of the two questions in the questionnaire about motivation. The first one was a yes/no question about whether students liked learning/studying English. The second was an open-ended question where students were asked to explain why they liked or disliked learning/studying English. The objective was to obtain information about types of motivation.

Analysis

In the first part of the study, Chi-square tests were performed to assess the statistical relationships between amount of instruction and the age of onset. When relationships were sought with biological age and achievement tests, independent-sample t-tests were run. The second part of the study was descriptive, since it involved the analysis of the open-ended question. The last section presents a description of the procedure followed to classify students' answers and of the resulting categories.

The taxonomy used to classify students' answers to the question was developed in Tragant and Muñoz (2000) and it was informed by factors resulting from previous studies, especially Clément *et al.* (1994) and Gardner (1985), in which both attitudes and types of orientations are present. The resulting classification is an eight-category taxonomy, each category including positive and negative arguments on the same topic area (see Appendix 10.1). Among the eight categories, the taxonomy includes four types of orientations ("Instrumental/career orientation", "Knowledge orientation" "Communication/travel orientation" and "Receptive orientation") and four components of motivation.

The positive arguments classified as "Instrumental/career orientation" refer to the importance of English as a lingua franca or to how useful this language is or may be for one's career or studies, at present or in the future. The negative arguments denote a lack of appreciation of an immediate need to know English or the fact that English is not necessary for the kind of job that the student would like later on in life.

The positive arguments under "Knowledge orientation" include relatively vague statements such as "It's always good to speak other languages" or "The more I know the better", in which the emphasis seems to be on the outcome of the learning process, that is, on knowing a "new" language other than their first language or on acquiring a higher level of education, rather than on the process of learning itself. No negative arguments were identified under this category.

The "Communication/travel orientation" is probably the broadest category and it refers to contexts in which English is used for interaction. It includes both statements that denote a practical interest in travelling as well as those that denote a more genuine interest in using English to meet people from other countries or to spend some time living in an English-speaking country. In any case, in an overwhelming number of the answers under this category there are no explicit references to communicating with native speakers but with speakers from "other countries" around the world. The negative arguments under this category refer to a lack of opportunity to travel or to rather ethnocentric attitudes, that is, a lack of interest in using languages other than Spanish or Catalan.

The fourth type of orientation, "Receptive orientation" (positive statements) refers to the use of English in non-interactive contexts such as reading books, magazines and newspapers, listening to songs, watching movies, using the Internet, and so on. The category also includes explicit cultural/intellectual motives ("I like learning about other cultures"), although these are marginal in our data and scarce among school-aged learners and are not usually country-specific. No negative arguments were identified under this category.

Some answers in the data do not correspond to any type of orientation but to components of motivation. These are "Attitudes towards L2 instruction", "Interest in L2", "Determination to learn English" and "Self-confidence in L2". The first of these components includes general evaluations (both positive and negative) about the subject of English at school as well as more specific references to the teacher or the methodology used as well as to comparisons between how English is taught at school and at private language schools students are attending. The second component is "Interest in L2" and its positive statements denote an intrinsic attraction to the English language or foreign languages in general. "Lack of interest in L2", on the contrary, includes statements about not liking English or foreign languages or statements of a preference for studying a different foreign language. The next component, "Determination to learn English" refers to personal objectives. Many of the positive statements are not very specific ("I want to learn languages", "I'd like to improve"), while others are more concrete ("I would like to be able to speak it the way I speak Catalan"). The negative statements under this category show the opposite attitude: a lack of predisposition to spend time or devote effort to studying the language. The last component of motivation, "Self-confidence in L2" includes references that may influence students' expectations of success or failure as language learners. The positive statements under this category refer to an aptitude or a lack of aptitude for L2 learning as well as to perceptions of English being an easy or difficult language.

The need to classify students' answers into broad categories for later quantification and comparison across age groups did not allow us to obtain categories that are usually present in other studies but were only rarely recorded in this study. This was the case of a statement such as "I'd like to learn about other cultures", which commonly comes under the category "Integrative orientation" in most studies, while in this study this statement is found under the more general category of "Receptive orientation" since it was rarely mentioned even by upper secondary school students. Other examples are statements such as "It's very important for my parents" or "Because the English language is an imposition", which have been classified as "others" because we do not have a specific category for parental encouragement or reactions to the domination of English as a result of economic factors. Because statements such as these did not occur frequently enough in our data, no such categories could be specifically created. Another feature of the raw data that is lost once students' answers are classified is a number of statements that were made only by students who have been studying English for several years ("At the beginning I did not make any effort to learn it and now I am lost", "Because as time goes by everything gets more complicated"), or from students who started learning English as adults ("I have always wanted to do it").

Results

Out of the total number of students who answered the question "Do you like learning/studying English?" most of them (78.5%) answered positively. This proportion varies across the different ages and hours of instruction received but, in general terms, the highest percentages of students who say they are interested in learning English were found in the older age groups, regardless of the age of onset, and the lowest percentages in the younger groups.

Four sections are used to present the results. The first section presents a detailed account of the interaction between hours of instruction and motivation for the three groups: those students who started learning English at school at the age of 8 (Group A), at the age of 11 (Group B) and those who started at the age of 18 or later (Group D). The second section will present an account of the interaction between motivation and age of onset in students after 200, 416 and 726 hours of instruction (Times 1, 2 and

3 respectively). In the third section, the results from the study of the relationship between motivation and a number of measures of linguistic achievement are reported. Finally, in the final section, students' answers are analysed on the basis of the reasons they gave for liking or disliking English.

Motivation and hours of instruction

An analysis of students' positive answers in Group A (see Figure 10.1) shows that motivation fluctuates across the first three times of data collection (Time 1, age 10;9 = 69.5%; Time 2, age 12;9 = 80.4%; and Time 3, age 16;9 = 71.2%) and is highest at T4 (age 17;9 (91.3%)), the last school grade before students enter university. Nevertheless, the differences are only significant between T1 and 2 ($n = 297$, Chi-square = 4.14, $p < 0.05$).

A similar pattern is found in students' answers in Group B (see Figure 10.2), where the subjects that obtain a highest proportion of positive answers are those in their last year of high school (Time 3, age 17;9 = 89.7%), followed by those at Time 2 (age 14;9 = 85.8%)). The youngest group of students, aged 12;9, is also the one with a lowest proportion of positive answers (64.4%). As with Group A, the difference between the frequencies obtained between Times 1 and 2 is significant ($n = 203$, Chi-square = 10.99, $p \leq 0.001$) but not between Times 2 and 3.

In Group D, both at Times 1 (age 28;9) and 2 (age 31;4), very high frequencies are obtained for students who say they are motivated (94% and 90.55% respectively), with a slight tendency to decrease at Times 2^2 (see Figure 10.3). An additional test (a t-test for independent measures) was run with students in this group given that, in contrast to students in Groups A and B, the range of students' ages within each time of data collection varied considerably. Results show that there is a significant difference between students who say they like learning English ($M = 356.55$, $SD = 96.26$) and those who say they don't ($M = 286.17$, $SD = 20.07$; $t(30.6) =$

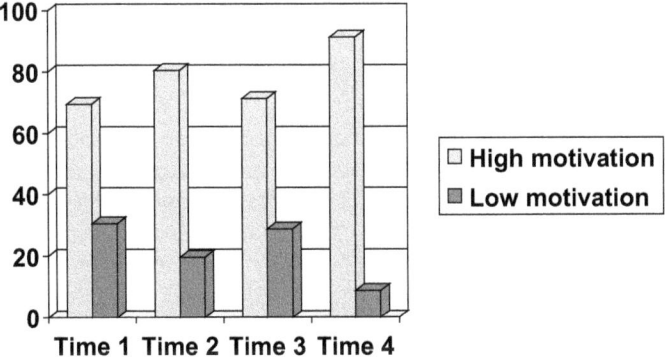

Figure 10.1 Motivation in Group A according to hours of instruction

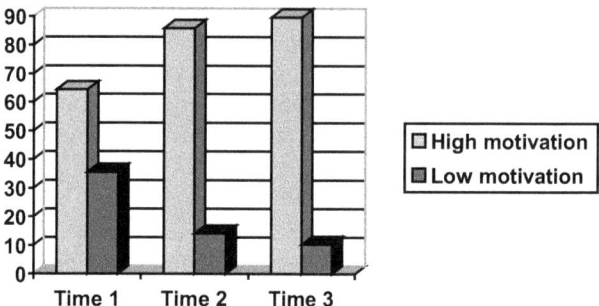

Figure 10.2 Motivation in Group B according to hours of instruction

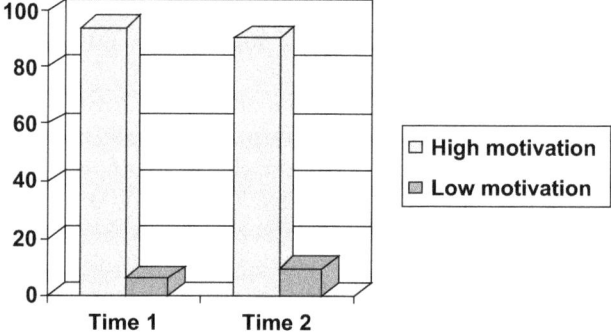

Figure 10.3 Motivation in Group D according to hours of instruction

5.24, $p = 0.00$) according to their age, with older students showing a more positive motivation than younger ones.

Motivation and age of onset

After 200 hours of instruction (Time 1), the distribution of students who say they like or dislike learning English is very similar (and non-significant) in Groups A1 (69.5%) and B1 (64.4%), the two school-aged groups. The results are different for Group D1 (94%), the group of adults who started learning English at the age of 18 or later (see Figure 10.4). More students in this group like learning English than in the other two groups; the difference is significant both between Groups A1 and D1 ($n = 221$, Chi-square = 14.49, $p < 0.001$) and between Groups B1 and D1 ($n = 171$, Chi-square = 18.00, $p < 0.001$).

After 416 hours of instruction (Time 2), the distribution of students' responses across the three groups (80.4%, 85.9% and 90.5% for Groups A2, B2 and D2) shows a tendency for growth as age of onset increases (see Figure 10.5). However, no significant differences are found between the two school-aged groups.[3]

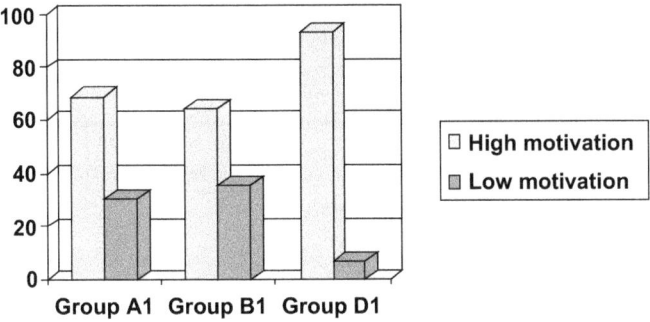

Figure 10.4 Motivation at Time 1 according to age of onset

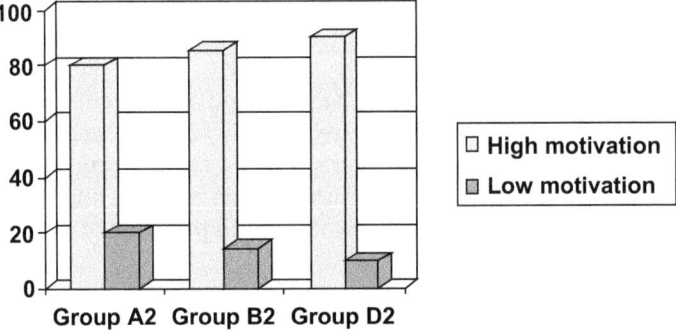

Figure 10.5 Motivation at Time 2 according to age of onset

After 726 hours of instruction (Time 3), a significant difference is found between Groups A3 and B3 ($n = 99$, Chi-square = 5.43, $p < 0.05$). More students have a positive attitudes towards learning English among those who started at the age of 11 (89.7%) than among those who started at the age of 8 (71.2%) (see Figure 10.6).

Motivation and achievement

When students say they are interested in learning English, there is a tendency towards better results in most tests and age groups. The tests where this tendency is clearest are the cloze test and the dictation. In the cloze test, significant levels are reached at the three times of data collection in Group A (A1, A2 and A3) and at two times in Group B (B1 and B3),[4] as measured by a t-test for independent measures (see Tables 10.2 and 10.3). Results from the dictation test show that significant levels are reached in the younger groups (A1, A2 and B1). As for the other two tests, the grammar test and the oral comprehension test, significant levels are only reached by the older groups and never in both tests simultaneously (A3

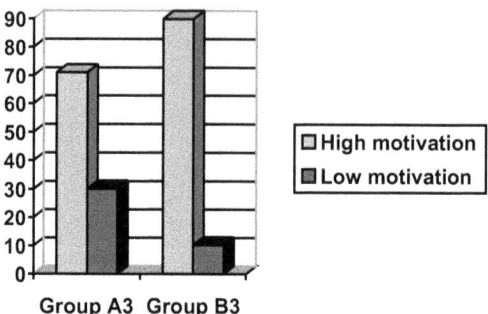

Figure 10.6 Motivation at Time 3 according to the age of onset

oral comprehension test and B3 grammar test). In sum, not all the tests used in this study are equally successful in showing a relationship between motivation and achievement. In particular, the cloze test, an integrative measure of proficiency, consistently showed a significant relationship across students at different stages of learning and at different ages of onset. On the other hand, the other integrative test, dictation, is a successful predictor of motivation with the younger students. The grammar test and the oral comprehension test, which measure specific abilities, are less effective tools when seeking to correlate motivation with proficiency.

Types of motivation

In this section, students' answers to the open-ended question about why they liked or disliked learning/studying English are analysed and their answers classified according to the taxonomy presented previously (see Appendix 10.1) and their school year. The data come from a larger population ($n = 2010$) than in the previous sections, given that students with exposure to English outside school are not excluded from the analysis. As the age of the learners in Groups A and B is controlled, we can perform a descriptive analysis of the nature of motivation in relation to the biological age of the learners. For Group D the level of proficiency is the independent variable, since students are assigned to a grade level based on their results on an assessment (most commonly, an exam or a placement test).

Table 10.2 Motivation and achievement in Group A

	n	df	Cloze test t-value	Dictation t-value	Grammar test t-value	Oral comprehension t-value
Time 1	141	139	−3.562***	−3.262***	n.s.	n.s.
Time 2	128	126	−5.590***	−3.076**	n.s.	n.s.
Time 3	65	63	−3.151**	n.s.	n.s.	−2.472*

Notes: *$p < 0.05$; **$p < 0.01$; *** $p < 0.001$; n.s. = non-significant.

Table 10.3 Motivation and achievement in Group B

	n	df	Cloze test t-value	Dictation t-value	Grammar test t-value	Oral comprehension t-value
Time 1	93	91	−2.06*	−2.883**	n.s.	n.s.
Time 2	81	79	n.s.	n.s.	n.s.	n.s.
Time 3	53	51	−2.834**	n.s.	−2.307*	n.s.

Notes: *$p < 0.05$; **$p < 0.01$; ***$p < 0.01$; n.s. = non-significant.

A total of 1729 reasons were identified from students in Groups A (Times 1–4), B (Times 1–3) and D (Times 1–2), 1391 of these (80.4%) being positive arguments and 338 (19.6%) being negative ones. The proportion of students who provided more than one answer is higher as students grow older as well as in students who report disliking English. This latter group often accompany negative statements with a positive one, most commonly an acknowledgement of the usefulness of learning English for work or communication as in "I think it is useful but it is very difficult for me". In some of these statements (for instance, "I don't like languages but they have to be learned"), students' mixed feelings towards language learning come to light. This may explain the mismatch that LoCastro (2001: 69–70) mentions between "professed positive attitudes towards learning English and their language-related behaviours" or the struggle with the "ought self" (people's sense of duty, obligations and responsibilities), a concept introduced by Dörnyei and Csizer (2002) that comes from an important line of research in social psychology.

Tables 10.4, 10.5 and 10.6 show the results for Groups A, B and D respectively. A double line is used to visually separate the positive arguments from the negative ones. In the following description of results as well as in the tables, only those factors that have obtained a percentage of at least 5% in one of the age groups under analysis have been taken into account. As a consequence, some categories will not be dealt with here: "Determination to learn" and "Self-confidence in the L2" as regards the positive arguments, and "Instrumental/career orientation", "Communication/travel orientation" and "Determination to learn" as regards negative arguments.

In Table 10.4, where students from Group A are compared, one can see similar proportions of answers in students from the age of 12;9 on (Times 2, 3 and 4). The proportions for "Instrumental/career orientation", the most frequently mentioned reason, range from 24.45% to 33.1% and those for "Communication/travel orientation" range from 18.2% to 20.1%). Similar proportions among these three age groups are obtained from less frequently mentioned categories: "Interest in the L2" with proportions ranging from 11.7% to 8.6%, and "Positive attitudes towards L2 instruction" with proportions ranging from 0.6 % to 4.9%. For these three groups

Table 10.4 Type of motivation in Group A: the most frequent arguments

	Instrumental/ career orientation	Communication/ travel orientation	Interest in L2	Receptive orientation	Knowledge orientation	Pos. attitudes towards L2 instruction	Neg. attitudes towards L2 instruction	Lack of interest in L2	Low linguistic self-confidence
Time 1 (AT = 10;9) (n = 140)	10%	22.4%	16.8%	0.7%	9.3%	14.9%	10.6%	1.2%	3.7%
Time 2 (AT = 12;9) (n = 252)	24.4%	19.2%	8.6%	4%	11.3%	4.9%	6.4%	2.6%	9.4%
Time 3 (AT = 16;9) (n = 394)	31%	20.1%	10.1%	4.3%	4.8%	1.01%	3.8%	4.3%	11.95%
Time 4 (AT = 17;9) (n = 154)	33.1%	18.2%	11.7%	5.8%	1.9%	0.6%	5.8%	6.5%	6.5%

Notes: AT = age at testing; n = total number of positive and negative arguments.

of students, "Low self-confidence in the L2" is the negative reason that obtains the highest percentages (ranging from 6.5% to 11.95%). In contrast to the commonalities in these students, the youngest group (aged 10;9) stands apart in that students' positive reasons are less frequently attributed to an "Instrumental/career orientation" (10%) but to two factors where the other three groups scored lower, that is, "Interest in the L2" (16.8%) and "Positive attitudes towards L2 instruction" (14.9%). Another difference is that these learners report "Negative attitudes towards L2 instruction" (10.6%) more than the older learners. This young group, together with those aged 12;9, also mention "Knowledge orientation" more often (9.3% at T1 and 11.3% at T2) than the two older groups. Finally, in spite of these differences, the proportion of mentions of a "Communication/travel orientation" remains stable across the four age groups, being the most frequent answer in students aged 10;9 and the second most frequent one in students aged 12;9, 16;9 and 17;9. Similar scores are also obtained for "Receptive orientation", which is among the least frequently mentioned reasons in all four groups.

Table 10.5 shows percentages from Group B students aged 12;9 (T1), 14;9 (T2), 17;9 (T3). In many respects, the figures confirm the observations made in the paragraph above when comparing students from Groups A2 aged 12;9, A3 aged 16;9 and A4 aged 17;9. On the one hand, "Instrumental/career" and "Communication/travel orientations" are the two most frequently mentioned reasons in both Groups A and B. In both groups too there is an increase in "Instrumental orientation" as students grow older, whereas the percentages of "Communication/career orientation" remain stable. The proportions obtained for "Interest in L2" are similar to those obtained in Group A, this factor being the third most frequently mentioned in the three age groups (ranging from 8% to 15.7%). Another parallelism is that "Low self-confidence in the L2" is the negative reason that obtains the highest scores in both groups of students. A similar pattern in the percentages of Group B1 (age 12;9) and Group A2 (age 12;9) is found in "Knowledge orientation", with a reasonable percentage (12% and 11.3% respectively) in both groups of learners at this age, though it falls at the ages of 14;9 (Group B2) and 16;9 (Group A3). In addition, the same two factors, that is, "Receptive orientation" and "Positive attitudes towards L2 instruction", receive low percentages in both groups.

Of special interest in the analysis of Tables 10.4 and 10.5 is the comparison between students from Group A2 and Group B1, and between those from Group A4 and Group B3. This is so because these two pairs of groups include learners of the same age (12;9 in the first case and 17;9 in the second) who have received different hours of instruction (200 and 416 in the first case and 726 and 800 in the second). The similarities of the percentages obtained in most of the variables at these two ages show that biological age is a more determinant factor than hours of instruction received.

Table 10.5 Type of motivation in Group B: the most frequent arguments

	Instrumental/ career orientation	Communication/ travel orientation	Interest in L2	Receptive orientation	Knowledge orientation	Pos. attitudes towards L2 instruction	Neg. attitudes towards L2 instruction	Lack of interest in L2	Low linguistic self-confidence
Time 1 (AT = 12;9) (n = 190)	22%	13.5%	8%	0.5%	12%	3.5%	12%	4%	6.5%
Time 2 (AT = 14;9) (n = 175)	41.9%	19.9%	8.9%	3.4%	5.2%	3.1%	1.1%	2.1%	6.3%
Time 3 (AT = 17;9) (n = 206)	37.3%	18.4%	15.7%	3.4%	2.8%	3.7%	2.3%	3.7%	4.1%

Notes: AT = age at testing; n = total number of positive and negative arguments.

Table 10.6 shows data from adult students (Group D) after 200 (Time 1) and 416 hours of instruction (T2). A comparison of the percentages obtained both from the positive and the negative statements indicates that these are quite similar for the two times of data collection. This observation further confirms the findings reported in the previous paragraph, i.e. that hours of instruction received do not translate into differences in the types of reasons students use to explain why they like or dislike learning English. This would be so except for "Instrumental/career orientation" and "Positive attitude towards L2 instruction", where the age of the learners might have also exerted an influence. Most students in Group D2 were older, which may explain the higher proportion obtained in the former work-related category, probably to the detriment of the low proportions obtained in the latter, an intrinsic type of motive.

The data from Table 10.6 also allow us to compare these two groups of adult students with the older learners in Groups A and B (A4 aged 17;8 and B3 aged 17;8). As far as positive reasons are concerned, the proportions per factor in Group D are similar to those in Groups A4 and B3, except for "Receptive orientation" which is a more frequent answer in adults at both times of data collection. In the two adult groups we find more references to learning the language in order to understand other cultures and for intellectual enrichment. For instance, if we take students aged 17;8 (Group A4), there was not even one reference of this kind out of a total of 121 positive responses, whereas there were 3 out of 54 in one of the adult groups (Group D1). As for negative reasons, "Low self-confidence in the L2", the most frequent negative reason provided by students in Groups A4 and B3, also obtains the highest scores in Groups D1 and D2.

Discussion

The analysis above of the interaction between motivation and hours of instruction shows that, in both Groups A and B, primary school students (A1 and B1), who had been learning English for three and two years respectively, are the least likely to report that they like learning English. In both groups, these proportions rise once students move on to secondary education and they remain quite stable until the last year of high school. So the present data do not confirm the drop in motivation that is often reported in the literature among teenage students who have been studying the foreign language for several years (MacIntyre et al., 2002; Massey, 1986; Williams et al., 2002). But the comparison of students' reasons for liking or not liking English in primary and secondary school learners suggests that the two groups may have interpreted the question of whether they liked learning English or not in different ways: for older students the importance of English might have been more salient than the teaching approach (as was the case with the German students of English in

Table 10.6 Type of motivation in Group D: the most frequent arguments

	Instrumental/ career orientation	Communication/ travel orientation	Interest in L2	Receptive orientation	Knowledge orientation	Pos. attitudes towards L2 instruction	Neg. attitudes towards L2 instruction	Lack of interest in L2	Low linguistic self-confidence
Time 1 (AT = 28;9) (n = 129)	28.7%	20.2%	10.1%	10.9%	4.6%	6.2%	12%	1.6%	5.4%
Time 2 (AT = 31;4) (n = 64)	35.9%	17.2%	12.5%	10.9%	0%	1.6%	1.1%	3.1%	7.8%

Notes: AT = age at testing; n = total number of positive and negative arguments.

Chambers, 2000) and the opposite might have been the case for younger learners. The predominance of answers among secondary school learners mentioning extrinsic types of orientation would explain the higher levels of motivation observed among these students as well as the fact that these levels remain constant. In contrast, the higher proportion of references to attitudes towards the learning situation that students in primary school report may explain the lower levels of motivation these students show. As regards the data from the group of adult students (Group D), the results obtained do not corroborate those found by Lasagabaster (2003), who detected no significant age-related differences in attitudes towards English learning. This apparent contradiction could be explained by the different nature of the samples in the two studies. In Lasagabaster's study, the sample included a younger population (92.5% of the sample were between the ages of 17 and 23 and they were all studying a university degree). In the present study, the sample included an older population whose ages were more widely spread (see second section of "Results"), and there were both learners who were studying a university degree and learners who were not.

When examining the relationship between motivation towards language learning and age of onset, one predictable finding was corroborated: that students who started learning English at the age of 18 or older report being more motivated than those starting at the age of 8 or 11. This observation is not surprising given that these adult learners were studying English on their own initiative, unlike the school-aged students in this study. A less predictable result comes from comparing students who started learning English at the age of 8 and 11, for whom no significant differences are found either after 200 or after 416 hours of instruction. Significant differences are found later, however, after 726 hours of instruction: students who started later, and who had been studying the language for seven years, showed higher levels of motivation than those who started at the age of 8 and had been studying the language for nine years. These results are not in overt contradiction with Cenoz (2004), who did not always find significant differences when comparing students who had started learning English at the ages of 4, 8 and 11. So evidence from this and Cenoz's study (2004) lead us to think that having students start learning English earlier, while keeping the number of hours of instruction constant, does not significantly alter the level of motivation in students. One may hypothesise that more drastic changes in the educational system (like, for example, accompanying an earlier introduction of the foreign language with more hours of instruction per week) would be required for there to be more systematic differences in school-aged learners' levels of motivation towards language learning.

Findings from the data on motivation and achievement in the third section of "Results" are in line with findings from recent investigations.

Both in this study and in Masgoret and Gardner's review (2003), correlations were higher with younger learners. Similarly, both in this study and in Lasagabaster's (2003) the strength of the relationship with motivation was sensitive to the type of test used.

Finally, the general picture that emerges is that it is the biological age of the language learners rather than the hours of instruction received that, to a large extent, determines the type of orientations observed, both positive and negative. This becomes most evident by looking at learners aged 12;9 from Groups A and B, who in spite of having received different hours of instruction, have very similar types of reasons for learning English. This same observation is also applicable to learners aged 17;9 from Groups A and B after different hours of instruction.

Regarding positive arguments, students at the age of 10;9, seem to distribute their reasons for learning English more evenly than older learners between intrinsic motives, on the one hand, such as the learning situation and a liking for English or foreign languages in general, and, on the other hand, more practical motives, such as its usefulness for travel and work. At this age, as well as at the age of 12;9, learners also seem to be less precise than older groups in articulating the practical advantages of learning English, as can be observed in the higher percentages obtained in these groups of students under the category "Knowledge orientation" where students produce vague, general statements such as "One never knows enough" and "In this way I will know another language". This type of orientation was also found to be most prominent at the age of 10 in the Zagreb Project 1991 (Mihaljevic Djigunovic, 1993 cited in Nikolov, 1999).

From the age of 12;9 onwards (including the two adult groups), the learning situation is no longer a frequent answer among students. Instead, the extrinsic gains of learning English ("Instrumental/career" and "Communication/travel orientations") account for the majority of the answers, followed by "An interest in English or foreign languages" as the third most frequently mentioned motive. Lamb (2004), in his study of Indonesian learners of English in their first year of high school, also found that the majority of the comments obtained directly related to a pragmatic orientation, a strong general need for English, even though for most of those students the process that learning English entailed (the lessons) may not be particularly motivating (English was not a favourite subject).

The only difference between teenage groups (aged 14;9, 16;9 and 17;9) and adult groups (aged 28;9 and 31;4) is that the latter mentioned English as a useful tool for dealing with books, songs, the media (including the Internet) and movies ("Receptive orientation") as frequently as "An interest in the L2". In contrast, this factor obtained much lower percentages in all school-aged groups (from 10;9- to 17;9-year-olds) even in those that had received many more hours of instruction (Group A4). This observation further confirms the idea that the types of orientation that have been obtained in this study are more dependent on the age of the learners than on the amount of instruction received or the age of onset. It also confirms the findings in a study involving eight European countries (Bonnet, 2004), where 15-year-old students in Spain were found to be the ones who practiced English least outside the classroom (i.e. by means of trips, television, films, books, magazines, newspapers).[5]

In spite of the differences between the groups mentioned above, there is one type of orientation (the "Communication/travel orientation") that remains stable across all age groups from the age of 10;9 until adulthood. A similar finding was reported in a longitudinal study with younger learners of English (aged 7 and 10) in Croatia (Mihaljevic Djigunovic, 1993 cited in Nikolov, 1999), where a substantial majority at both times of data collection referred to "communication" and "travel" when asked about the benefits of learning a foreign language.

As for the negative reasons put forward to explain a dislike of learning English, the main difference is found between the group aged 10;9 and older learners including adults. Whereas the former attribute this dislike predominantly to the learning experience, the classroom seems to be far less important for the older groups who most often attribute a negative attitude towards the learning of English to the difficulty of the task, either because they feel they are not good at languages or because they find this particular language too complex to learn or difficult to understand orally.[6] In fact, in a comparative study of France, Sweden and Spain in students aged 16;5 (Gil & Alabau, 1997), the number of Spanish students who thought language aptitude was important to get good grades in English was considerably higher than that of Swedish students. This perception of English being difficult to learn also came up in a national survey (González García, 2004) of over 8000 Spanish students (aged 13 and 15). Only 29% and 22% respectively thought learning English as "easy" or "quite easy", while 41% and 47% thought it was "not quite easy" or "not easy at all".

In any case, it can be observed that statements expressing negative orientations such as "I don't think I will use it [English]", "I would like everyone to speak the same language" or "I'm not especially interested in English culture, not to mention American culture' are scarce in all age groups. This shows that an overwhelming majority of students in this analysis are most aware of the role English plays as a global language and rarely show ethnocentric attitudes, which is something that LoCastro (2001) also observed in her study of Japanese EFL university students.

Conclusion

Evidence from this study suggests that the relation between motivation and age varies depending on whether we look at the age of onset or the hours of instruction received. As regards the age of onset, it can be concluded that, in the short term, having students start learning English earlier (in the second instead of the third cycle of primary education), does not significantly alter the level of motivation in students. One may hypothesise that more drastic changes in the educational system (like, for example, accompanying an earlier introduction to the foreign language with more hours of instruction per week) would be needed for more systematic differences to emerge in school-aged learners' levels of motivation towards language learning. Hours of instruction received and the biological age of the learners were important factors in language learning motivation. Motivation seems to be stronger in secondary than in primary education, probably due to a greater awareness of the role of English worldwide as students grow older. Similarly, in the context of language learning among adults, the motivation is stronger among older students. This is probably because older students are more likely to be working instead of studying for a degree and, consequently, they may perceive a more immediate need for having a good command of English. Moreover, the types of orientations identified in this study coincide for the most part with the types obtained in similar studies and are clearly sensitive to the range of ages under study. It is precisely by looking at the reasons students give to explain their motivation for learning English and by analysing how these reasons remain constant or undergo changes as students receive more hours of instruction that we can gain more of an insider's view of what learning English at different ages is like.

Acknowledgements

The study was funded by grants from the Spanish Ministerio de Educación y Cultura (grant. no. PB94-0944, grant no. PB97-0901 and grant no. BFF2001-3384). I would also like to express my appreciation to Cristina Aliaga for her help with the preparation of this chapter.

Notes

1. Lower secondary education is compulsory for all students in Spain, but upper secondary education is only for those who intend to go to university.
2. We could not calculate whether this decrease is significant because, when running the Chi-square test, some cells had expected frequencies lower than five.
3. The Chi-square test could not be run to compare Groups A2 and B2's responses with Group D2 because, when the tests were run, one expected cell size was lower than five.
4. Statistical tests were not run for Group A4 and Groups D1 and D2 because of the low number of students who showed negative motivation towards the learning of English.
5. The case for songs is different: Spanish students reported listening to music in English as much as students from other European countries.
6. The frequencies corresponding to "Low self-confidence in L2" were always at least twice as high as those corresponding to "Self-confidence in the L2" (a positive orientation). That is, the number of students who thought they were not good at English or found learning this language too difficult was not counter-

balanced by a similar group of students who thought they did have an aptitude for language learning and found the task easy.

References

Alabau, I. (2002) *Evaluación de la Enseñanza y el Aprendizaje de la Lengua Inglesa: Educación Primaria 1999.* Madrid: Ministerio de Educación, Cultura y Deporte, Instituto Nacional de Calidad y Evaluación (INCE).
Bernaus, M., Cenoz, J., Espí, M.J. and Lindsay, D. (1994) Evaluación del aprendizaje del inglés en niños de cuatro años: Influencias de las actitudes de los padres, profesores y tutores. *APAC of News* 20, 6–9.
Bernaus, M., Masgoret, A.-M., Gardner, R.C. and Reyes, E. (2004) Motivation and attitudes towards learning languages in multicultural classrooms. *The International Journal of Multiculturalism* 1 (2), 75–89.
Blondin, C., Candelier, M., Edelenbos, P., Johnstone, R., Kubanek-German, A. *et al.* (1998) *Foreign Languages in Primary and Pre-school Education.* London: CILT.
Bonnet, G. (2004) *The Assessment of Pupils' Skills in English in Eight European Countries 2002.* The European network of policy makers for the evaluation of educational systems. On www at http://www.utdanningsdirektoratet.no/upload/Rapporter/Assessment_of_English_BED.pdf.Accessed 21.2.2006.
Burstall, C. (1975) Primary French in the balance. *Foreign Language Annals* 10 (3), 245–252.
Cenoz, J. (2004) Teaching English as a third language: The effect of attitudes and motivation. In C. Hoffman and S. Ytsme (eds) *Trilingualism in Family, School and Community* (pp. 202–218). Clevedon: Multilingual Matters.
Chambers, G. (2000) Motivation and the learners of modern languages. In S. Green (ed.) *New Perspectives on Teaching and Learning Modern Languages* (pp. 46–76). Clevedon: Multilingual Matters.
Cid, E., Grañena, G. and Tragant, E. (2002) On the development of a data-based questionnaire on motivation. *Proceedings of the XXVI Congreso de AEDEAN*, 349–354.
Clément, R. and Kruidenier, B.G. (1983) Orientations in second language acquisition: The effects of ethnicity, milieu, and target language on their emergence. *Language Learning* 33, 273–291.
Clément, R., Dörnyei, Z. and Noels, K.A. (1994) Motivation, self-confidence and group cohesion in the foreign language. *Language Learning* 44 (3), 417–448.
Departament d'Ensenyament (2003) *La Situació de la Llengua Anglesa a l'Ensenyament no Universitari de Catalunya* (No. Informes d'Avaluació 6). Catalunga Consell Superior d'Avaluació del Sistema Educatiu.
de Prada, E. (1990) La incidencia de la motivación y actitud hacia la L2 en el proceso de aprendizaje. *Actas del VIII Congreso Nacional de Lingüística Aplicada (AESLA)*, 609–618, Vigo.
Donato, R., Tucker, G.R., Wudthayagorn, J. and Igarashi, K. (2000) Converging evidence: Attitudes, achievements and instruction in the later years of FLES. *Foreign Language Annals* 33 (4), 377–393.
Dörnyei, Z. (1990) Conceptualizing motivation in foreign language learning. *Language Learning* 40 (1), 45–78.
Dörnyei, Z. (2001) New themes and approaches in second language motivation research. *Annual Review of Applied Linguistics* 21, 23–59.
Dörnyei, Z. and Csizér, K. (2002) Some dynamics of language attitudes and motivation: Results of a longitudinal nationwide survey. *Applied Linguistics* 23 (4), 421–462.
Gardner, R.C. (1979) Social psychological aspects of second language acquisition. In H. Giles and S. Clair (eds) *Language and Social Psychology* (pp. 193–220). Oxford: Basil Blackwell.

Gardner, R.C. (1985) *Social Psychology and Second Language Learning: The Role of Attitudes and Motivation*. London: Edward Arnold.

Gardner, R.C. (2001) Integrative motivation and second language acquisition. In Z. Dörnyei and R. Schmidt (eds) *Motivation and Second Language Acquisition* (Vol. 23), pp. 1–20). Manoa: Second Language Teaching and Curriculum Center, University of Hawai'i.

Gardner, R.C. and Smythe, P.C. (1975) *Second Language Acquisition: A Social Psychological Approach* (Research Bulletin No. 332). London: Department of Psychology, University of Western Ontario.

Gardner, R.C., Tremblay, P.F. and Masgoret, A.-M. (1997) Towards a full model of second language learning: An empirical investigation. *Modern Language Journal* 81, 344–362.

Gardner, R.C., Smythe, P.C., Clément, R. and Gliksman, L. (1976) Second language learning: A social psychological perspective. *Canadian Modern Language Review* 32, 198–213.

Gil, G. and Alabau, I. (1997) *Evaluación Comparada de la Enseñanza y el Aprendizaje de la Lengua Inglesa: España, Francia y Suecia*. Madrid: Ministerio de Educación, Cultura y Deporte, Instituto Nacional de Calidad y Evaluación (INCE).

González García, M.M. (2004) *Evaluación de la Enseñanza y el Aprendizaje de la Lengua Inglesa: Educación Secundaria Obligatoria 2001*. Madrid: Ministerio de Educación, Cultura y Deporte, Instituto de Evaluación y Calidad del Sistema Educativo (INECSE).

Graham, S. (2004) Giving up on modern foreign languages? Students' perceptions of learning French. *The Modern Language Journal* 88 (ii), 171–191.

Hawkins, E. (1996) The early teaching of modern languages. A pilot scheme. In E. Hawkins (ed.) *Thirty Years of Language Teaching* (pp. 155–164). London: CILT.

Hermann, G. (1980) Attitudes and success in children's learning of English as a second language: The motivational vs. resultative hypothesis. *English Language Teaching Journal* 34, 247–254.

Johnstone, R. (1996) The Scottish initiatives. In E. Hawkins (ed.) *Thirty Years of Language Teaching* (pp. 171–175). London: CILT.

Jones, W.R. (1949) Attitudes towards Welsh as a second language: A preliminary investigation. *British Journal of Educational Psychology* 19, 44–52.

Julkunen, K. (1989) *Situation- and Task-specific Motivation in Foreign-language Learning and Teaching*. Joensuu: University of Joensuu, Publications in Education.

Julkunen, K. and Borzova, H. (1996) *English Language Learning Motivation in Joensuu and Petrozavodsk*. Joensuu: University of Joensuu, Research Reports of Faculty of Education (No. 64).

Lamb, M. (2004) Integrative motivation in a globalizing world. *System* 32, 3–19.

Lasagabaster, D. (2003) *Trilingüismo en la Enseñanza: Actitudes hacia la Lengua Minoritaria, la Mayoritaria y la Extranjera*. Lleida: Milenio.

LoCastro, V. (2001) Individual differences in second language acquisition: Attitudes, learner subjectivity, and L2 pragmatic norms. *System* 29, 69–89.

MacIntyre, P.D., Baker, S.C., Clément, R. and Donovan, L.A. (2002) Sex and age effects on willingness to communicate, anxiety, perceived competence, and L2 motivation among junior high school French immersion students. *Language Learning* 52 (3), 537–564.

Madrid, D. (1999) *La Investigación de los Factores Motivacionales en el Aula de Idiomas*. Granada: Universidad de Granada, Grupo Editorial Universitario.

Masgoret, A.-M. and Gardner, R.C. (2003) Attitudes, motivation, and second language learning: A meta-analysis of studies conducted by Gardner and associates. *Language Learning* 53 (1), 167–210.

Masgoret, A.-M., Bernaus, M. and Gardner, R.C. (2001) Examining the role of attitudes and motivation outside of the formal classroom: A test of the mini-AMTB with children. In Z. Dörnyei and R. Schmidt (eds) *Motivation and Second Language Acquisition* (Vol. 23). Manoa: Second Language Teaching and Curriculum Center, University of Hawai'i.

Massey, D.A. (1986) Variations in attitudes and motivation of adolescent learners of French as a second language. *The Canadian Modern Language Review* 42 (3), 607–618.

Muñoz, C. and Tragant, E. (2001) Motivation and attitudes towards L2: Some effects of age and instruction. In S. Forster-Cohen and A. Nizegorodcew (eds) *EUROSLA Yearbook* (Vol. 1, pp. 211–224). Amsterdam: John Benjamins Publishing Company.

Nikolov, M. (1999) "Why do you learn English?" "Because the teacher is short." A study of Hungarian children's foreign language learning motivation. *Language Teaching Research* 3 (1), 33–56.

Oxford, R. and Shearin, J. (1994) Language learning motivation: Expanding the theoretical framework. *The Modern Language Journal* 78 (1), 12–28.

Reid, M. and Fouillard, C. (1982) *High School French Enrollment in Newfoundland and Labrador*. Newfoundland/Labrador: St John's Canadian Parents for French.

Sans, C. (2000) Bilingual education enhances third language acquisition: Evidence from Catalonia. *Applied Psycholinguistics* 21, 23–44.

Satchwell, P. (1996) The present position in England. In E. Hawkins (ed.) *Thirty Years of Language Teaching* (pp. 165–170). London: CILT.

Savignon, S. (1972) *Communicative Competence: An Experiment in Foreign Language Teaching*. Philadelphia: Center for Curriculum Development.

Schmidt, R., Boraie, D. and Kassabgy, O. (1996) Foreign language motivation: Internal structure and external connections. *University of Hawai'i, Working Papers in ESL* 14 (2), 1–72.

Skehan, P. (1989) Motivation. In *Individual Differences in Second Language Learning* (pp. 49–72). London: Arnold.

Smit, U. (2002) The interaction of motivation and achievement in advanced EFL pronunciation learners. *IRAL* XL (2), 89–116.

Tragant, E. and Muñoz, C. (2000) La motivación y su relación con la edad en un contexto escolar de aprendizaje de una lengua extranjera. In C. Muñoz (ed.) *Segundas Lenguas. Adquisición en el Aula* (pp. 81–105). Barcelona: Ariel.

Williams, M., Burden, R. and Lanvers, U. (2002) "French is the language of love and stuff": Student perceptions of issues related to motivation in learning a foreign language. *British Educational Research Journal* 28 (4), 504–528.

Appendix 10.1 Types of orientations

Positive statements	Negative statements
Instrumental/career orientation	
"It may be of some use later on"	"It is not useful for me now"
"It is the language of the future"	"I don't think I will ever use it"
"When I grow up, I want to work in computers and I'll need English"	
Knowledge orientation	
"One never knows enough"	—
"It is always good to master several languages"	
Communication/travel orientation	
"To travel"	"I never travel"
"If you go to other countries and you can speak English, people will understand you better"	"I'd like everybody to speak the same language"
"To meet more people"	"I already have one language"
Receptive orientation	
"To understand the songs that I like"	—
"To read books"	
"In order to learn about other cultures"	
Attitudes towards L2 instruction at school	
"Fun subject"	"Boring"
"I like the teacher"	"The method they (teachers) use is not good"
Interest in L2	
"Beautiful"	"I'd rather study French"
"I like languages"	"I don't like English"
"I like the way it sounds"	"I don't like foreign languages"
Determination to learn English	
"I'd like to be able to speak it well"	"I don't like studying"
"I'd like to improve"	"I'd have to make an effort to study"
"I had always wanted to learn it"	
Self-confidence in L2	
"I'm good at it"	"I can't understand it"
"English is easy"	"It is quite difficult for me"
"I like it because I can understand it"	"I never feel I am making any progress"

Appendix 1

Cloze Test

Now you'll read a story where some words are missing. You will know when a word is missing because there appears a line in its place. On each line you can ONLY write ONE word, and contractions (e.g. "isn't") count as a single word.

La Caputxeta Vermella

(LITTLE RED RIDING HOOD)

A

Hello. I am "La Caputxeta Vermella".
My favourite colour is (1) _____
I am ten years old.
I live with my parents.
I have got no (2) _____ or sisters.
I have got a grandmother.
She is (3) _____ years old.

B

There was a little girl. She was a very good girl. Her grandmother loved the girl (4) _____ lot and she often gave her presents. One day Little Red Riding Hood's (5)_____made her a beautiful red cape and hood. The little (6) _____ liked it a lot and she always wore (7) _____ cape and hood.

Little Red Riding Hood lived with her mother and father (8) _____ a village near a large forest. Her mother worked at home and her (9) __ _____ worked in the forest. He was a woodcutter.

Little Red Riding Hood's grandmother (10) _____ a kilometre away. She lived alone in a little (11) _____ inside the forest. Little Red Riding Hood loved her grandmother and every (12) _____ she went to visit her.

C

One day her mother called her (13) _____ said, "Little Red Riding Hood, There (14) _____ a cake and a bottle of milk in this basket. I (15) _____ like you to take it to your grandmother. She (16) _____ ill this morning and she needs to eat."

Before the (17) _____ left, her mother told her "Be careful and (18) _____ stop to play in the forest. And walk carefully. Don't run or you (19) _____ break the bottle. Then you will have no milk for your (20) _____ ." Little Red Riding Hood took the basket. Then she (21) _____ goodbye to her mother and started to walk to her grandmother's (22)_____ .

Ten minutes later, Little Red Riding Hood (23) _____ a wolf. She had never seen a wolf before and she (24) _____ not know he was a bad creature. She thought he (25) _____ a large dog and she was not afraid of (26) _____ .

"Good morning, Little Red Riding Hood. Where are you going so early (27) _____ the morning?" asked the wolf. "To my grandmother's house," she answered.

Then the wolf asked her, "And what have (28) _____ got in your basket?". Little Red Riding Hood said, "A cake and some (29) _____ . My grandmother is ill and this basket is (30) _____ her."

Appendix 2

Listening Comprehension Test

Instructions: You will now hear some words and sentences in English. Mark with a cross the drawing that corresponds to each word or sentence. You will only hear it once.

Three illustrative examples of the Listening Comprehension Test:

(3) The boy is wearing black shoes.
(4) There are three children in the garden.
(5) The bird is under the chair.

Appendix 3

Semi-guided Oral Interview

(1) What is your name?
(2) How old are you?
(3) Do you like this school?
(4) What time did you arrive this morning?
(5) When will you leave?
(6) What will you do when you finish today?
(7) What do you like to do in your free time?
(8) What did you do last weekend?
(9) Let's talk about your family now. How many brothers and sisters have you got? (*Talk about them*)
(10) Which language do you speak with your parents/with your mother/father?
(11) Where do you live?
(12) How many people live in your house?
(13) How many rooms are there?
(14) Tell me about your room. How many (beds, etc.) are there?
(15) Now, would you like to ask me any questions (about me or my family, etc.)?
(16) I am going to show you a little story. Can you tell me the story? It begins here …
(17) Yes, very good. And what are they going to do now? What do you think? (*If he/she needs some help*:)
    (a) Where are they going here? (*n 3*)
    (b) Why is the basket empty? (*n 6*)
    (c) Who has eaten their food? (*n.6*)
    (d) Yes, very good. And what are they going to do now?
    (e) What do you think?
(18) Have you ever had a dog (or a cat)? (*If too difficult*: Do you have a dog (or a cat)?)
(19) Did he ever eat your food? (*If too difficult*: Does he eat your food?)

(20) Now I am going to play a tape with some pairs of words. I'd like you to tell me, after you hear each pair, if they are/sound the same or different.
(21) Now repeat the words you hear on the tape.
(22) Now you are going to do something with another student from your class, so let's move to .../let's see/let's wait ... Let's pretend A is a mother and B is a boy/girl who wants to have a party on Friday after school. Decide on:
   – where to have the party;
   – who to invite;
   – what to buy to eat and drink;
   – time to start and finish;
   – activities/games to play.

Appendix 4

Students' Questionnaire

GRADE:
SCHOOL:

(1) Name:
(2) Last name:
(3) Age: _____ years
(4) Date of birth (dd/mm/yy):
(5) Place of birth:
(6) Sex: ☐ Female ☐ Male
(7) Home address:
(8) Phone number:
(9) Languages you speak at home:
with your mother_____ with your father_____
with your siblings_____ with other people (specify)_____
(10) Which language do you feel more comfortable with?
☐ Catalan   ☐ Spanish   ☐ Both of them
(11) (a) Mother's job:
(b) Father's job:
(12) At which age did you start learning English?
In which grade?
PRIMARIA ☐1 ☐2 ☐3 ☐4 ☐5 ☐6
EGB   ☐1 ☐2 ☐3 ☐4 ☐5 ☐6
In which type of school? ☐ State ☐ Private
How many hours of English per week did you take in Primaria or EGB?
(13) Did you repeat any grades? Which (ones)?
(14) Have you ever or are you currently learning extracurricular English?
In which language school?
At which age did you start?
For how long?
How many hours approximately per week?
☐ more than 4h per week ☐ 4h per week ☐ 3h per week ☐ 2h per week ☐ 1h per week

(15) Have you ever been to an English-speaking country?
YES ☐ ☐ NO
How many times?
Where?
How old were you?   For how long?
With whom?
Did you take an English course?

(16) Which mark did you get in English last year?

(17) Have you ever studied any other foreign languages?
Which (ones)?
Where?
For how long?
Grades awarded:

(18) Do you like learning English?
☐ Yes ☐ No
Why?

(19) When you learn English in class or you study it at home, do you use any tricks or tips that help you in the process? That is to say, what do you do in order to (answer the following questions)?

   (a) to remember the *meaning* of English words?
   (b) to learn English *pronunciation*?
   (c) to remember the *spelling* of new English words?

(20) And in order to *understand* what you read in English, do you use any tips?

(21) Finally, do you use any tricks or tips in order to *write* English sentences correctly?

(22) Have you ever read books in English? YES ☐   NO ☐
If your answer is YES, specify what kind of readings and the amount:
Readers
☐ Less than 5   ☐ Between 5 and 10   ☐ More than 10
Unabridged stories
☐ Less than 5   ☐ Between 5 and 10   ☐ More than 10
Unabridged comic books
☐ Less than 5   ☐ Between 5 and 10   ☐ More than 10
Unabridged books
☐ Less than 5   ☐ Between 5 and 10   ☐ More than 10
Others (specify) _____
☐ Less than 5   ☐ Between 5 and 10   ☐ More than 10

(23) Have you ever listened to English outside school?
　　　☐ Never ☐ Sometimes ☐ Very often
　　If your answer is YES, specify through which means:
　　TV programmes ☐ Never ☐ Sometimes ☐ Very often
　　Radio programmes ☐ Never ☐ Sometimes ☐ Very often
　　Movies (with or without subtitles) ☐ Never ☐ Sometimes
　　☐ Very often
　　Songs ☐ Never ☐ Sometimes ☐ Very often
　　Others (specify) _____ ☐ Never ☐ Sometimes
　　☐ Very often

(24) Have you ever spoken English outside school?
　　　☐ Never ☐ Sometimes ☐ Very often
　　If your answer is YES, with whom?
　　With friends ☐ Never ☐ Sometimes ☐ Very often
　　With acquaintances ☐ Never ☐ Sometimes ☐ Very often
　　With foreigners ☐ Never ☐ Sometimes ☐ Very often

(25) Do you participate in the English class?
　　　☐ Never ☐ Sometimes ☐ Very often
　　Do you participate in English?
　　　☐ Never ☐ Sometimes ☐ Very often

(26) When you do not understand or you do not know how to say something in English, what do you do?
　　Keep silent ☐ Rarely ☐ Often
　　I search for other words ☐ Rarely ☐ Often
　　I ask for help ☐ Rarely ☐ Often
　　I shift into Catalan or Spanish ☐ Rarely ☐ Often
　　Other _____ ☐ Rarely ☐ Often

(27) When you speak in English and they do not understand you, what do you do?
　　Do you correct what you said? ☐ Rarely ☐ Often
　　Do you repeat what you said? ☐ Rarely ☐ Often

Index

Authors

Abrahamsson, N. 3, 38, 129, 155
Abutalebi, J. 5
Alabau, I. 238, 239, 261, 263, 265
Altman, R. 89, 103
Álvarez, E. 21, 32, 35, 130, 134, 150, 153, 189, 206
Andersen, R.W. 108, 109, 112, 123, 124
Archibald, A. 156, 158, 179
Arnaud, P.J.L. 158, 179
Asher, J.J. 9, 35, 41, 61, 91, 103

Bacha, N. 157, 179
Bailey, N. 108, 112, 124, 155
Basturkmen, H. 203, 206
Bates, E. 37, 104
Bazergui, N. 88
Beddor, P.S. 45, 61
Bell, H. 102, 105
Beneke, J. 190, 206
Berman, R.A. 151, 153
Bernaus, M. 241, 244, 265
Best, C.T. 41, 47, 61
Bialystok, E. 3, 5, 11-13, 36, 129, 153
Birdsong, D. 3, 7, 36, 60, 61
Bley-Vroman, R. 5, 36, 129, 148, 154
Blondin, C. 237, 265
Bohn, O.-S. 62
Bongaerts, T. 3, 36, 41-43, 60-61, 129, 154
Bonnet, G. 238, 261, 265
Boraie, D. 267
Borzova, H. 239, 243, 266
Bossers, B. 235
Boustagui, E. 38, 63, 155
Brambati, S. 39
Bremner, S. 208, 209, 212, 234
Broeder, P. 21, 36, 88, 94, 103
Browman, C.P. 76, 86
Brown, A.L. 223, 234
Brown, J.D. 109, 124
Brown, R. 108-110, 116, 123, 124
Brumfit, C. 65, 86
Burden, R. 267
Burry-Stock, J.A. 208, 235
Burstall, C. 9, 36, 90-91, 99, 103, 130, 154, 238, 243, 265
Burt, M.K. 108-109, 112-113, 116, 123, 124, 127, 154

Calvo, V. 103
Candelier, M. 265
Cappa, S. 35
Carson, J.G. 231, 234
Carubbi, S. 103
Cebrián, J. 42-43, 46, 54, 56-59, 61, 62
Celaya, M.L. 20, 32, 36, 105, 155, 156, 158-160, 163, 168, 179, 181, 182
Cenoz, J. 9, 36, 130, 153-155, 159, 180, 240, 261, 265
Chafe, W. 66, 86
Chambers, F. 66, 68, 86
Chambers, G. 238, 245, 261, 265
Chamot, A.U. 208, 210, 212, 215, 231, 234
Chapelle, C.A. 91, 103
Chaudron, D. 17, 21, 36, 181, 209, 233, 234
Chen, S.Q. 188, 206
Chenoweth, N.A. 156, 180
Chesterfield, K.B. 212, 231-232, 234
Chesterfield, R. 212, 231-232, 234
Chipere, N. 104
Chomsky, N. 2, 5
Cid, E. 243, 265
Clément, R. 243, 248, 265
Coe, N. 46, 48, 51, 62
Cohen, A.D. 157, 180, 185, 206
Cohen, S. 103
Colombo, J. 6, 7, 36
Connor, U. 156, 180
Connor-Linton, J. 157, 180
Cook, V. 108, 124, 127, 154, 157, 180
Coppieters, R. 3, 36
Cortés, S.M. 42, 62
Craik, F.I.M. 89, 105
Crerand, M. 158, 180
Crookall, D. 212, 235
Cuenca, M.H. 61, 62
Cumming, A. 156-157, 180
Cummins, J. 8, 11-12, 36, 37, 90, 103
Curtiss, S. 1, 37

D'Odorico, L. 89, 103
Daller, H. 92, 102, 103
de Bot, K. 66, 82, 86
de Groot, M.D.B. 39, 154
De Pew, K.E.D. 156, 181
De Prada, E. 209, 233, 234, 241, 265

277

de Villiers, J. 108, 124
de Villiers, P. 108, 124
DeKeyser, R. 3-6, 10, 33, 37, 109-112, 122-123, 124, 128, 129, 150, 154
Dénes, M. 65-67, 69, 76, 78, 87
Dennis-Rounds, J. 89, 105
Departament d'Ensenyament 238, 240, 265
Derwing, T.M. 70, 88
Deschamps, A. 69, 87
Dewaele, J.-M. 70, 87
Dewey, D.P. 87
Dietrich, R. 155
Diller, K. 5, 37
Doiz, A. 100, 104, 158, 159, 180
Donato, R. 206, 238, 265
Dörnyei, Z. 22, 37, 237, 244, 245, 255, 265
Doughty, C. 6, 37, 125, 186, 206, 207
Dulay, H.C. 108, 109, 112, 113, 116, 123, 124, 127, 154
Dunn, L. 90, 103
Dupoux, S. 39
Durán, P. 104

Ehrman, M.E. 209, 224, 234
Ejzenberg, R. 66-67, 87
Ekstrand, L.H. 8, 9, 37, 107, 124, 130, 154
El Tigi, M. 38, 63, 155
El-Dinari, P.B. 208, 210, 234
Elliott, A.R. 42, 62
Ellis, N. 33, 36, 37, 39, 89, 103, 105
Ellis, R. 37, 108, 124, 127, 148, 154, 186, 190, 191, 202, 203, 206
Elman, J.L. 2, 37
Engel, D. 89, 103
Ervin-Tripp, S. 107, 124
Espí, M. J. 265
Extra, G. 36, 103

Fabbro, F. 33, 37, 90, 103
Faerch, C. 92, 104, 185, 189, 194, 195, 206
Fathman, A. 109, 112, 113, 124, 125, 201, 204, 206
Feldman, L. 125
Felix, S. 5, 37, 111, 124, 127, 154
Ferreiro, E. 157, 180
Fillmore, C. J. 65, 87
Flege, J. E. 41-42, 44, 46, 53-54, 56-60, 62, 63, 64, 87
Foster, P. 69, 88, 150, 155
Foster-Cohen, S. 157, 180
Fouillard, D. 239, 267
Franceschini, R. 40
Freed, B. F. 67-71, 74-75, 81, 87
Fröhlich M. 235
Frota, S. 186, 207
Fullana, N. 21, 41, 45, 60-62, 150

Gallardo, F. 42-44, 55, 57-59, 63
Galles, N.S. 39

Gálvez, L. 15, 37
Gan, Z. 208, 210, 234
Ganschow, L. 40
García López, M. 211, 234
García, R. 41, 61, 63,
García-Lecumberri, M.L. 39, 41-44, 50, 55, 57-59, 63, 155, 180, 235
García-Mayo, P. 39, 63, 155, 180, 235
Gardner, R.C. 150, 155, 209, 233, 234, 238, 241-243, 248, 261, 265, 266
Gass, S. 109, 124, 186, 206, 207
Genessee, F. 3, 40
Gil, G. 239, 261, 266
Goldschneider, J. 109-112, 122-123, 124, 128, 154
Goldstein, L.M. 76, 86
González García, M.M. 238-239, 261, 266
Gost, C. 123, 124
Gottfried, T.L. 45, 61
Graham, S. 242, 266
Grañena, G. 151
Green, J.M. 208, 209, 224, 234
Green, S. 33, 37, 181
Greenbaum, S. 155
Grenfell, M. 211, 234
Griffiths, C. 208, 209
Griffiths, R. 66, 68, 72, 77-78, 80, 82, 87
Grinder, R. 9, 37
Grosjean, F. 69, 78, 87
Gu, Y. 208, 234
Guion, S.G. 70, 87
Gutiérrez-Clellen, V. 104

Haastrup, K. 104
Hahn, A. 127, 154
Hakuta, K. 3, 5, 35
Hamilton, A. 89, 104
Hamp-Lyons, L. 157, 180, 234
Han, Z. 178, 180
Hanna, G. 38
Hargreaves, M. 103
Harley, B.K. 3, 8, 37, 91, 104, 107, 114, 124, 129, 154, 156, 180
Harris, V. 211, 234
Hart, D. 40, 126, 129, 154
Hatch, E. 108-109, 124
Hawkins, E. 66, 88, 237, 266, 267
Hayes, J. R. 156, 180
Heaton, J. B. 21, 37
Hermann, G. 243, 266
Hernández, E. 15, 37
Hickmann, M. 133, 154
Hidalgo, L. 181
Hieke, A.E. 68, 82, 87
Higa, C. 151, 155, 183. 186, 207
Hirose, M. 181
Hirsch, J. 38
Hoefnagel-Höhle, M. 3, 4, 8, 10-12, 16, 32, 40, 43, 56-60, 63, 106, 129, 155
Holmstrand, L.S.E. 9, 38

Hopper, P. 133, 154
Hudson, J. 152, 154
Hughes, A. 19, 38
Hughey, J.B. 104
Hulstijn, J. 89, 104, 235
Humphreys, G. 234
Hyde, J. 188, 206
Hyltenstam, K. 3, 38, 90, 92, 104, 129, 155

Idar, I. 113, 125
Igarashi, K. 201, 206
Impink-Hernández, M.V. 234
Inagaki, S. 182
Ioup, G. 3, 38, 41, 63, 129, 155
Ishikawa, S. 156, 158, 180

Jackson-Maldonado, D. 89, 104
Jacobs, H.L. 100, 104
Jamieson, M. 103
Jang, S. 62
Jarvis, S. 92, 93, 102, 104
Jeffery, G.C. 156, 179
Johnson, J. 3, 4, 38, 40
Johnson, R.K. 208, 235
Johnston, M. 110, 125
Johnstone, R. 237, 265, 266
Jones, P.E. 1, 38
Jones, W.R. 242, 266
Julkunen, K. 239, 240, 243, 266

Kamin, J. 38
Kantor, R. 180
Kasper, G. 185, 189, 194-195, 206
Kellerman, E. 3, 38, 185, 206, 233, 235
Kenworthy, J. 46, 63
Kessler, C. 113, 125
Kim, H.Y. 5, 38, 182
King, M.L. 156, 180
Klein, W. 128, 154, 155
Kojic-Sabo, I. 223, 235
Kormos, J. 65-67, 69, 76, 78, 87
Kotake, N. 106
Kowal, S.H. 82, 87
Krashen, S.D. 2, 10-12, 38, 61, 63, 107-113, 120-123, 124, 125, 127, 155, 207
Kroll, B. 39, 154, 157, 180
Kuhl, P.K. 41, 63
Küpper, L. 234
Kurusu, J. 106
Kyoung-Min, L. 38

Labov, W. 132-133, 146, 151, 155
Lamb, M. 238, 244, 245, 261, 266
Lan, R. 208-210, 224, 235
Lanvers, U. 267
Lapkin, S. 8, 32, 38, 40, 126, 180
Lardière, D. 153, 155
Larsen-Freeman, D.E. 108-111, 113, 122, 125, 127, 155, 183, 206

Larson-Hall, J. 6, 10, 33, 37, 129, 150, 154
Lasagabaster, D. 100, 104, 158-159, 180, 239, 241, 261, 262, 266
Laufer, B. 102, 104, 158, 180
Lavin, E. 158, 180
Lawson, D.S. 90, 105
Lázaro, A. 10, 31, 38
Leech, G. 155
Leeke, P. 208, 235
Leki, I. 156, 180, 181
Lengyel, Z. 39, 63
Lenko-Szymanska, A. 101, 104
Lenneberg, E. H. 1, 5, 6, 38, 41, 63, 129, 155
Lennon, P. 65, 67-69, 75, 87
Levin, J. R. 105
Liceras, J. 109, 126
Lightbown, P. 109-112, 120-122, 125, 156, 181, 223, 235
Liu, E.T.K. 156, 181
Liu, S.H. 87
Lo Castro, V. 244, 255, 261, 266
Loewen, S. 191, 202-204, 206
Loewenthal, K. 64
Long, M.H. 3, 5-7, 16, 38, 41, 61, 63, 108-110, 122, 124, 125, 154, 155, 183, 188, 192, 206, 207
Longhini, A. 231, 234
Lorenzo-Dus, N. 102, 104
Lüdi, G. 40
Lumley, T. 157, 181
Lyster, R. 190, 202, 203, 207

MacIntyre, P.D. 238, 259, 266
MacKay, I.R.A. 45, 59, 60, 62, 63
Mackey, A. 202, 207
MacNamara, T. 17, 19, 38
Madden, C. 124
Madrid, D. 241, 266
Mägiste, E. 90, 104
Malvern, D. 92-95, 101, 103, 104, 105
Manchón, R.M. 156, 181
Marchman, V. 104
Martínez-Pons, M. 211, 223, 235
Martín-Uriz, A. 156, 181
Masgoret, A.-M. 150, 155, 234, 238, 241, 244, 261, 266
Massey, D.A. 239, 259, 267
Matsuda, P. K. 156, 181
Mbaye, A. 156, 180
McCormick, C.B. 105
McDonough, K. 207
Meara, P. 95, 102, 104
Meyer, A. 62
Miralpeix, I. 95, 101-102, 105
Molfese, D. 5, 38
Molis, M. 3, 36
Morales-López, E. 74, 88
Moselle, M. 38, 63, 155
Moyer, A. 41-42, 60, 63

Munro, M.J. 58, 62, 63, 70, 88
Muñoz, C. 14, 15, 21, 31, 32, 35, 38, 39, 40,
    61, 63, 72, 73, 105, 107, 123, 124, 125, 130,
    149-151, 153, 155, 181, 183-185, 205,
    240-242, 248, 267
Murphy, L. 181

Nagato, N. 9, 39, 91, 99, 105
Naiman, M. 208, 235
Nation, P. 158, 180
Navés, T. 61, 63, 101, 105, 158, 160, 162, 168, 181
Neville, H.J. 90, 105
Newport, E. 1, 3, 38, 39
Nikolov, M. 238, 240, 244, 261, 267
Noyau, C. 154, 155
Nystrand, M. 156, 181

O'Malley, J.M. 209, 212, 235
Oliver, R. 183, 199, 202, 207, 210, 235
Oller, J.W. 9, 16, 19, 38
Oppenheim, N. 66-67, 88
Ortega, L. 158, 162, 181
Otomo, A. 37
Oxford, R.L. 208, 209, 210, 212, 223, 235, 245, 267
Oyama, S. 41, 63

Palincsar, A.S. 223, 234
Palmberg, R. 190, 207
Papalia, A. 89, 105
Paradis, M. 33, 39, 90, 105
Patkowski, M. 3, 7, 39, 63
Patton, L. 40
Paulesu, E. 39
Pawley, A. 66-67, 79-81, 88
Peck, S. 124, 155, 206
Penfield, W. 1, 5, 39
Perani, D. 5, 33, 35, 39
Pérez-Vidal, C. 36, 130, 155, 159-160, 179,
    180, 181, 182
Perkins, K. 111, 125
Phillipson, R. 104, 235
Pica, T. 111, 114, 116, 119, 120, 122, 125
Pienemann, M. 110, 125
Piske, T. 41, 59, 60, 63
Planken, B. 36, 61, 154
Plunkett, K. 89, 104
Polio, C. 157, 181
Politzer, L.R. 209, 235
Pontecorvo, C. 157, 180
Powers, D. 180
Precup, L. 201, 204, 206
Pressley, M. 89, 105
Price, B. 9, 35, 91, 103
Pulvermüller, F. 3, 5, 39
Purdie, N. 210, 235

Qi, D.S. 156, 181
Quirk, R. 153, 155

Rallo, L. 42-43, 56-57, 59, 63
Ranta, L. 190, 202-203, 207
Raupach, M. 66, 68-69, 80, 87, 88
Recasens, D. 46, 62, 63
Rehbein, J. 66-67, 88
Reichelt, M. 156, 181
Reid, M. 239, 267
Relkin, N.R. 38
Riazantseva, A. 66, 68-69, 72, 88
Richards, B. 92-95, 101, 103, 105
Richards, J.C. 88, 124, 154
Riggenbach, H. 65-69, 74-76, 88
Ringböm, H. 89, 105
Roberts, L. 1, 5, 38
Roca. de Larios, J. 156, 181
Rosansky, E. 108, 125
Rubin, J. 208, 235
Russo, R. 235
Ryan, L. 4, 12, 40, 107, 114, 125, 184, 207

Salerni, N. 103
Samuel, A.G. 89, 105
Sánchez, L. 123, 125
Sans, C. 241, 267
Sasaki, M. 156, 181
Satchwell, P. 237, 267
Sato, C. 108-110, 122, 125
Savignon, S. J. 17, 39, 243, 267
Scarcella, R. 37, 61, 63, 151, 154, 155,
    183-186, 207
Schachter, J. 3, 39
Schils, E. 36, 61, 154
Schmidt, R. 66, 88, 186, 191, 207, 241, 267
Schoonen, R. 89, 106, 211, 235
Schumann, J.H. 3, 5, 39
Scifo, P. 39
Scovel, T. 7, 39, 41, 63
Segalowitz, N. 66, 70, 74, 87, 88
Seliger, H. 5, 6, 16, 40, 125
Selinker, L. 109, 124, 235
Sengupta, S. 156, 181
Service, E. 89, 105
Sferlazza, V. 125
Shapiro, L. 152, 154
Shaw, P. 156, 181, 208, 235
Shearin, J. 245, 267
Silverberg, S. 89, 105
Singleton, D. 4, 11, 12, 34, 40, 43, 58, 59, 63,
    105, 107, 114, 125, 129, 155, 184, 207
Skehan, P. 17, 40, 65, 69, 88, 150, 155, 243,
    267
Skelton, L. 62
Slavoff, G.R. 4, 40
Slobin, D.I. 151, 153
Smit, U. 242, 267
Smith, V. 60, 62, 63
Smythe, P.C. 238, 241-242, 266
Snow, C. 3, 4, 8, 10-12, 16, 32, 40, 43, 56, 57,
    59, 60, 63, 90, 105, 106, 129, 150, 155

Sökmen, A.J. 89, 106
Southwood, M.H. 60, 64
Spada, N. 125, 156, 181
Sparks, R. 32, 40
Spreen, O. 89, 106
Stankowski Gratton, R. 91, 106
Stern, H. H. 208, 235
Stewner-Manzanares, G. 235
Strömqvist, S. 103
Svartvik, J. 155
Swain, M. 7, 8, 11, 38, 40, 107, 126, 186, 207, 235
Swan, M. 62
Sweedler-Brown, C.O. 157, 181
Syder, F.H. 66. 67, 79-81, 88

Tahta, S. 41, 64
Takatsuka, S. 106
Takeuchi, O. 208, 212, 235
Thal, D. 104
Thompson, I. 129, 155
Thompson, S.A. 151, 155
Todesco, A. 235
Tomasello, T. 2, 40
Tomohito, H. 236
Torras, M.R. 14, 20, 31, 32, 36, 40, 150, 155, 157-158, 160, 168, 179, 180, 181, 182
Towell, R. 66-70, 75, 88
Toyota, W. 37
Tragant, E. 22, 32, 40, 150, 156, 179, 213, 214, 223, 233, 235, 240-242, 248, 267
Treffers-Daller, J. 103
Tremblay, P.F. 234, 266
Tucker, G.R. 206, 265
Turnbull, M. 8, 32, 40, 107, 126
Turner, G. 89, 106, 269

Ure, J. 92, 106

van Hout, R. 36, 103

van Summeren, C. 61, 154
van Wuijtswinkel , K. 3, 40
Vandergift, L. 211, 235
Verhallen, M. 89, 106
Vermeer, A. 92, 101, 102, 106
Victori, M. 22, 32, 156, 182, 213, 214, 223, 233, 235
Vihman, M. 89, 106
Voinmaa, K. 103

Wachal, R.S. 89, 106
Wallace, R. 125
Wang, W. 3, 37, 89, 104
Wattendorf, E. 5, 40
Wennerstorm, A. 68, 88
Wesche, M. 65, 88
Westermann, B. 40
Wharton, G. 209, 210, 235
White, L. 3, 40
Whitehead, M.R. 89, 103
Whittaker, R. 181
Wiemelt, J. 181
Willey, B. 185, 207
Williams, J. 186, 206, 207
Williams, M. 239, 259, 267
Wolfe-Quintero, K. 158, 162, 172, 182
Wood, M. 64
Woodall, B.R. 156, 182
Wormuth, D.R. 104
Wudthayagorn, J. 206, 265

Yamada, J. 91, 106
Yamamori, K. 209, 210, 212, 224, 231, 235
Yeni-Komshian, G.H. 87
Yoshida, M. 89, 106

Zappatore, D. 40
Zimmerman, B.J. 211, 223, 235
Zinkgraf, S.A. 104
Zobl, H. 109, 126

Subjects

Academic/cognitive L2 skills 11
Accent ratings 48, 51 57, 58, 61,
Accented L2 Input Hypothesis 44
Accommodation 184
Accuracy 20, 21, 30, 65, 67, 69, 71, 75, 107-123, 130, 137, 152, 153, 156, 158, 159, 160-167, 176, 209
Accuracy measures 30, 69
Accuracy, phonetic 71
Accuracy orders 107, 108, 109, 110, 111, 112, 114, 119, 123, 153
Age at learning 34
Age of onset 4, 7, 14, 15, 24, 39, 42, 43, 52, 54, 59, 131, 159, 160, 161, 163-165, 167, 214, 237, 246-248, 250, 252-254, 261, 263

Amount of exposure 7, 9, 32, 43, 56, 58, 60, 73, 93, 102, 107, 122, 123, 129, 153, 248
Appeals for assistance 185-187, 189, 190, 192-198, 200, 201, 204
– explicit indirect appeals 90, 94-96, 98, 201, 202, 204
– implicit indirect appeals 190, 192, 194-199, 201-205
Articulation rate 68, 76, 79
Attention 5, 16, 17, 33, 51, 68, 70, 88, 89, 128, 158, 185, 186, 189, 191, 200, 204, 207, 216, 228, 229, 245
Auditory discrimination task 45
Automaticity 33, 67, 69, 71, 75, 88
Average order 109, 119, 120, 121, 122, 123

BAF project 1, 13, 14, 16, 23, 30, 31, 32, 44, 60, 72, 91, 93, 94, 101, 102, 115, 123, 130, 157, 158, 159, 160, 161, 162, 168, 187, 205
Basic variety 128
Bilinguals 9, 13, 14, 23, 45, 55, 89, 93, 99, 103, 153, 187, 212, 240
Breakdown 183, 184, 185, 186, 189, 201

Clause-level syntax 141, 143, 144
Cloze 8, 10, 16, 17, 18, 19, 22, 23, 24, 25, 26, 27, 28, 30, 31, 32, 33, 35, 39, 91, 92, 94, 97, 99, 100, 139, 205, 248, 253, 254, 255, 269
Cognitive development 4, 32, 33, 34, 121
Cognitive maturity 8, 11, 151, 178, 213
Competition hypothesis 5

Critical period 1, 2, 5-7, 41, 89, 104, 105
Critical period hypothesis/CPH 1, 2, 3, 4, 6, 7, 10, 41, 113, 129, 155

D 92, 93, 95, 96, 97, 98, 99, 101, 102, 103, 104
Discourse component 132, 134-139, 148

Early starters/ES 1, 3, 9, 10, 13, 24, 25, 31, 32, 55, 70, 71, 83-86, 90, 91, 93-97, 99, 100-102, 130, 131, 139, 140, 150, 159, 187
English as a foreign language/EFL 127, 131, 132, 150, 153, 155
Exceptional late learners 3, 6, 10, 33, 34, 36, 37, 39, 89, 103, 105, 129, 150
Explicit learning 6, 10, 33, 89, 103, 105, 129, 150

Feedback 186, 189, 190-191, 192, 197, 198, 200, 201, 202, 204, 205
Filled pause 75, 81, 83
Fluency 65, 66, 71, 75, 86-88, 158-172, 176, 177
Focus on Form 186, 190, 201-203, 228
Foreground 133, 138, 149, 154
Foreign Accent 43, 51, 52, 58, 60, 61
Formal context/setting/instruction 9, 11, 12, 31, 32, 34, 42-44, 49, 50, 51, 54-9, 70, 71, 73, 83, 85, 90, 91, 99, 107, 111, 113, 122, 128, 130, 148, 157, 214, 246
Frequency 54, 66-69, 75-81, 83, 86, 110, 112, 122, 194, 198
Functors 108-111, 114, 118, 121, 123
Fundamental Difference Hypothesis 5

Grammatical complexity 75, 158-161, 163-168, 170, 172, 174, 176, 177

Imitation task 45-47, 51
Immersion 4, 7, 8, 12-13, 32, 33, 90, 107, 114, 203, 238, 239
Implicit learning 5, 6, 10, 33, 34, 89, 129, 150, 153

Initial exposure 129, 150, 152
Integrative tests 16, 17, 19, 22, 162, 241, 254
Integrative orientation/motivation 241-245, 250
Instrumental orientation/motivation 150, 242-244, 248, 255-260, 262, 268
Interactional processes 183
Interactional skills/strategies 183, 185, 186
Interview 92, 94-96, 99, 100, 104
Intrinsic motives/reasons 245, 249, 259, 262

L1 Phonological system 41
Late starters/LS 9, 10, 13, 25, 83-85, 90, 91, 93-102, 131, 140
Learning situation 4, 6, 9, 11, 107, 240-242, 261, 262
Lexical acquisition 89
Lexical complexity 158-160, 164, 168, 170, 176
Lexical Density/LD 90, 92, 101, 106, 153, 159, 163
Lexical richness 21, 92, 93, 95, 99, 102, 158
Lexicon 67, 78, 82, 90
Long-term advantage 3, 7
Longitudinal data/study 23, 24, 26, 108, 160, 211-214, 224-225, 231, 232

Maturational constraints 3, 7, 36, 38, 39, 63, 89, 104, 155
Mnemonic strategies 89
Morphemes 107-110, 112-114, 116-118, 122-125, 127, 149, 155
Morphosyntax 3, 6, 7, 89, 90, 136
Motivational orientations 237, 242-248, 257, 262-265, 268

Native language effects 3
Natural order/sequence 107, 108, 110-112, 124, 125, 127, 128, 154, 212, 232, 234
Negotiation for meaning 183
New introduction 133
NLM 41
Noticing 186, 191, 203

Obligatory context 108, 109, 114, 116, 118, 121, 123

Patterns of written development 170-174, 177
Pause frequency 67, 69, 72, 75-77, 79-84, 86
Pause length 66
Perception 6, 31, 41-45, 54, 55, 57-59, 61-63, 66, 67, 87, 88, 180, 184, 207, 238, 241, 243, 250, 263, 266, 267
Perceptual Assimilation Model/PAM 41, 42
Phonology 6, 7, 41, 45, 57, 89
Phrase-level syntax 141, 143
Productive vocabulary 91, 94, 97, 99-102

Pronunciation 3, 4, 8, 10-12, 32, 41, 42, 53, 71, 76, 78, 90, 112, 113, 121, 215-217, 219, 222, 223-225, 227, 228, 233, 242, 275

Questionnaire 16, 22, 93, 94, 215, 248

Rank orders 107, 117, 119, 120
Rate 2, 4, 9, 10-12, 25, 30, 34, 35, 48-49, 50, 51, 68-71, 74, 75, 78-80, 82-86, 89, 92, 112-114, 118, 121, 127-130, 150, 153, 157, 159, 160, 170, 177, 202
Repetitions 66, 68, 71, 77, 79, 84, 86, 94, 184, 203
Role-play 16-18, 21-23, 92, 94, 95, 97, 99, 100
Route 127, 128, 130, 144, 148, 150, 152

Saliency (perceptual) 110, 122
Sensitive periods 16
Short-term/run advantage 3, 90, 91
SOC 108, 109, 111, 114, 116-119
Speech Learning Model/SLM 41
Speech rate 66, 68-71, 75, 77-80, 82-87
Speech run 68, 74, 75, 78, 79, 82-85
Stage 127, 128, 130, 132-153
Storytelling 4, 11, 21, 70-72, 74, 75, 77, 82, 84, 92, 94-96, 98-101, 132, 133
Strategies, analysis 218, 220
Strategies, pronunciation 219
Strategies, repetition 218-221, 224
Strategies, sentence writing 221

Strategies, social 218-223, 232
Strategies, spelling 220
Strategies, vocabulary learning 208

Temporal discourse markers 133, 137
Test reliability 17
Test validity 17
Textual cohesion 21, 23, 24, 26, 27, 132-133
Transfer 89, 105
Type token ratio/TTR 92, 95-103

Ultimate attainment 2-4, 6, 10, 12, 16, 42, 127, 129, 150, 177
Uptake 190-192, 198-200, 202-205

Vocabulary acquisition/development 89, 91, 93
Vowel contrasts 48, 49, 51, 56, 57
Vowel identification task 47, 48, 52, 54, 57, 58, 60

Word-families 95, 97-100
Word-level syntax 141, 143, 144

Young learners, 5 14, 33, 71, 183, 244
Younger learners (comparison with older learners) 2, 3, 5, 10-12, 30-34, 55, 57, 89-91, 114, 121, 123, 130, 150, 151, 171, 183-185, 202, 205, 223, 232, 238, 242, 261-263

For Product Safety Concerns and Information please contact our EU Authorised Representative:

Easy Access System Europe

Mustamäe tee 50

10621 Tallinn

Estonia

gpsr.requests@easproject.com

www.ingramcontent.com/pod-product-compliance
Ingram Content Group UK Ltd.
Pitfield, Milton Keynes, MK11 3LW, UK
UKHW022218250326
4937IPUK00005B/43